Inside
The Family-Held
Business:
A Practical Guide for
Entrepreneurs and Their Advisors

Inside
The Family-Held
Business:
A Practical Guide for
Entrepreneurs and Their Advisors

—— Milton H. Stern ——

Law & Business, Inc.
Harcourt Brace Jovanovich, Inc.
New York   Washington, D.C.

Printed in the United States of America

Library of Congress Cataloging-in-Publication Data

Stern, Milton H.
   Inside the family business.

   Includes index.

   1. Family corporations—United States. I. Title.
KF1466.S74   1985   346.73'0668   85-23853
ISBN 0-15-004402-X   347.306668

To my wife, Joan,
and my children,
Andy, Ken, Tom, Tricia and Ellen,
whose love and support
enabled me to complete this project;
and to my editor,
Dan Mangan,
who converted a bunch of ideas into a book.

CONTENTS

5 BASIC INCOME TAX STRATEGIES   79

8 PROVIDING FOR A SURVIVING SPOUSE 161

9 MANAGING A SURVIVING SPOUSE'S PROPERTY— ADVANTAGES OF A TRUST 177

10 HOW TO HANDLE THE CHILDREN WHO ARE NOT IN THE BUSINESS   211

13 THE IMPORTANCE OF LIFE INSURANCE 279

16 | SALE OF THE BUSINESS   357

17 **TECHNIQUES OF COUNSELLING THE CLOSE CORPORATION** 383

PREFACE

I have been practicing law for over 36 years. My specialty would be labeled as taxation and estate planning. Yet that classification doesn't begin to identify the engrossing and fascinating nature of what I do. In fact, it usually conjures up visions of a highbrow lawyer burning the midnight oil in quest of tax loopholes for a complex will or trust. What I really have been is a counsellor to a host of remarkable businessmen including close corporation entrepreneurs, heads of family businesses, the principals of publicly held companies where ownership and management still go hand and hand, and individuals who own corporations which they operate essentially as partnerships.

I have become intimate with these hard-driving individuals, who have steered companies with limited resources successfully through difficult challenges, precarious developments, and rapidly changing technology. They have shared their hopes with me and told me about their disappointments, including their problems with children and in-laws. I have become a convenient sounding board because of the knowledge of their affairs and their families that I absorbed while serving their interests over the course of many years. What I've found is that no two family-run businesses or incorporated partnerships are identical in all respects. This is what makes the job of counselling them so stimulating. One never gets bored.

For some time, I have wanted to record my thoughts about these businesses. In particular, I hoped to identify significant personal concerns that can be so damaging, to point out recurring problems and offer some solutions, and to share with the entrepreneurs of these businesses, as well as their lawyers, a number of good management and planning concepts that I have learned from my association with many clients. Thus, with the encouragement of my publisher, Stephen Glasser, and the partners in my firm, I have written this book.

Actually, my partners did far more than give me time to write. Several of them devoted a lot of time and effort to the issues and subjects discussed in this book. They offered me suggestions, know-how, and the benefit of their experience. In truth, my text is an expression of the beliefs and feelings of our entire firm.

Lest any client or acquaintance fear a loss of anonymity, I should mention that the names used to describe the individuals mentioned in this book have been "picked out of the air." They bear no relationship to the actual names of the persons depicted. And, as a further protection, I have modified fact patterns whenever I felt that an accurate reproduction might disclose the true identity of the persons involved.

Milton H. Stern

INTRODUCTION

CLOSE CORPORATIONS GENERALLY

The term "close corporation" can mean many things. In this book it is used to mean a corporate business organization which has one distinguishing feature: ownership and management of the company are in the hands of the same people. Several entities are included in my classification of a close corporation. The most common are family businesses that are owned and run by members of one or two families. Then there are what I call "incorporated partnerships," that is, corporations whose stock is held by two, perhaps three, unrelated individuals, who run the business as partners. A family business can come to resemble an incorporated partnership when all of the interests are held by members of one generation. For example, a company with a father in control and two sons active in the business, is clearly a family business. But after the father's death, the two sons will probably relate to each other more as partners than brothers once they become equal owners of the business. Although a family relationship will continue, it is a far cry from the one that existed between the sons and their father. The sons may begin to act like two unrelated parties in business together.

Finally, there is the publicly held corporation where control is held by one or two families, or a few individuals, who manage the business. At first blush, it may seem contradictory to include an entity in which a lot of people hold stock in a discussion of close corporations. A semanticist could properly cringe. My justification for including this kind of public company is that it has many of the same characteristics, human relations factors, and management, tax and estate planning problems that traditional close corporations do.

The fact that the public has an investment in the enterprise makes very little difference with respect to the issues this book is concerned about.

The clearest contrast to the close corporation is the industrial corporation which is managed by a crew of professional executives who own only a nominal part of the equity. The stock of this kind of company is owned by institutional investors and individuals, no one of whom may hold a meaningful interest. In other words, it is the linkage of ownership and management that is the key to the character of the close corporation. To owners who give their all to this kind of a business, the close corporation becomes an expression of themselves. "It is mine—or ours," they often say. Indeed, much of their sense of accomplishment in life is tied to what the business does. If it grows and is successful, the owner feels gratified and proud. Each milestone—the new plant, hitting the million dollar net profit level, opening a branch, the commercial on television—brings a feeling of satisfaction. The converse is also true. If the business of a close corporation declines, the proprietor's sense of personal failure is extreme. The loss is his.

Many American close corporations conduct very large businesses. The first 100-200 of these companies have annual sales ranging from 400 million up to 30 billion dollars. Here is a list of twenty of the better known privately held enterprises, from various industries, with their ranking in size and their yearly volume:

Company	Rank	Annual Sales
Cargill, Inc.	1	30 billion
Continental Grain Co.	2	16 billion
Bechtel Group	4	11 billion
United Parcel Service	5	5.2 billion
Hughes Aircraft Co.	6	4.9 billion
Mars, Inc.	11	2.5 billion
Publix Super Markets	13	2.45 billion
Best Western International	20	1.9 billion
Hallmark Cards, Inc.	31	1.37 billion
Congoleum Corp.	40	1.1 billion
Allen-Bradley Co.	65	880 million
Amway Corp.	75	800 million
Timex Corp.	113	594 million

U.S. Lines, Inc.	119	567 million
Helena Rubenstein, Inc.	146	500 million
Field Enterprises, Inc.	158	484 million
Stroh Brewery Co.	178	440 million
Perdue Farms, Inc.	243	330 million
Hartz Mountain Corp.	265	310 million
Encyclopedia Brittanica	286	286 million

FAMILY BUSINESSES

A businessman friend of mine, who has traveled and done business throughout the world, once commented that the most unique aspect of American business is the preponderance of family-owned enterprises. Indeed, the New Jersey Society of Certified Public Accountants recently found that there are more than 12 million family-held companies in our country and that these family companies represent 95% of all American businesses. Moreover, they account for nearly half the gross national product and employ half the private-sector work force. These are very impressive statistics. They bear out what most business lawyers and accountants have always felt, namely that the family business is truly the role model in the United States.

Despite its popularity, however, the American family business venture is short on staying power. Recent statistics indicate that the average life span of a family business is 24 years. Only 30% of these entities survive into the second generation and fewer than 15% make it through the third generation. The figures bear out the old adage: "Shirt sleeves to shirt sleeves in three generations."

This limited life span is only one of the problems that beset the family business. Many family businesses that do endure are often full of personal tensions that cause the participants much unhappiness and bring about bitterness, alienation, and discontent. All kinds of human relations and psychological factors are involved. There are the complex relationships between fathers and sons, or husbands and wives, who work together. Nepotism in hiring and promotion practices, sibling rivalry among children who are active in the enterprise, and a discrimination against daughters coming into the business are issues that arise frequently. And, of course, the son-in-law who joins the family company faces many particular difficulties.

Despite the problems it causes, family businesses undoubtedly will continue to hire family members for key positions. It is the assumed course of events. I have felt aspects of this tradition myself. Two of my three sons are practicing lawyers. They are extremely capable and would be a welcome addition to the law firm in which I am the oldest active partner. Our relationship is and always has been close and warm. Nonetheless, for a number of reasons, we mutually agreed that it would be better for them to pursue their legal careers elsewhere. When people ask me what my sons are doing, I respond that two of them are lawyers, practicing apart from my firm. At that point, some interesting vibrations usually occur and I end up having to explain that this arrangement is not indicative of bad family relationships.

Needless to say, the family head should be careful about bringing everybody into the family business. There may be too many mouths for the business to feed. When a single child starts to work, his initial salary may not be hard to handle. But when he marries and has his own family, the amount of dollars he will need grows by large multiples. Furthermore, there can be serious financial problems when a number of children are looking to the business to provide them with a good way of life. If the family business does not grow, there will be trouble. Achieving harmony among siblings in a family business—a difficult task in any case, as we will observe later in Chapter 1—becomes virtually impossible when each of them is fighting for a larger share of profits that do not grow.

What counselors of family businesses should strive for is an understanding of the special problems that these businesses must deal with and some practical ways to solve them—all in the interest of establishing and preserving a successful, harmonious, and enduring enterprise.

MANAGEMENT

The owners of close corporations are generally hands-on executives. They are immersed in and knowledgeable about all facets of the business. Many of them have confided in me that this involvement in all areas, initially a must, later becomes a management weakness. As time goes on, the owner finds it hard to delegate responsibility to others and rely on their judgement. All of us experience difficulty in relinquishing control as we shift from being doers to supervisors. New skills and attitudes must be learned. Unfortunately, all too often, close corporation entrepreneurs ignore this need to change their style. They criticize a plan of action worked on for hours by a subordinate and jump in to show him how it should have been done. This kind of thing is a real turn-off and sometimes pushes executives out of the company.

These prevalent weaknesses in the management structure of entrepreneurial businesses are described in Chapter 2 and suggestions for correcting them are given. What should be done to deal more effectively with key employees who have no relationship to the owners, by blood or marriage, is considered in Chapter 4.

CONTROL

Another characteristic of close corporations is the lack of formality regarding governance and decision-making. The directors do not hold regular meetings and the minute book usually contains little information, despite the fact that the corporation has been in existence for a long time. Since the directors are generally the people who are running the business, and sometimes their spouses as well, there is no reason to hold formal meetings, for the participants would only be accounting to themselves.

Young lawyers are often shocked by the close corporation owner's lack of attention to formalities. A typical example is the opening of a new bank account for the company. Someone goes over to the bank and gets the forms and signature cards. Everybody is clear about the identity of the officers who can sign checks on behalf of the company. But no one pays any heed to the fact that the form is really a certificate, stating that the resolutions set out in it were duly adopted at a meeting of the directors. Of course, one would search in vain for the minutes of such a meeting.

The worst example of this informality that I ever saw related to a series of real estate development corporations. For tax reasons, the developers had organized a separate corporation for each street in a very large tract on which several hundred homes were being built. I was called in to do some tax planning at a time when most of the houses had been sold. In my fact-gathering meeting with the three principals, I inquired about the stockholdings of the various corporations. After hedging their responses for some time, one of the owners directed my attention to a large bookcase. On the shelves of this bookcase there were corporate outfits (minute and stock certificate books and a seal). "Look at any of them," I was told. I reached back, and pulled one out, and opened it. I heard the cracking sound one hears when a new binding is opened for the first time. Not a single entry had been made! The same was true of the next few that I sampled. I couldn't believe it. These corporations owned land. They executed mortgages and delivered deeds, and did a lot of other things—without a single entry in the corporate outfits.

Older lawyers have seen so many examples of this kind that they are no longer surprised. In fact, this way of operating has come to be accepted as the norm for the close corporation. Some help has been provided through corporate laws which now permit directors to evidence their determinations by executing a certificate, signed by all of the directors. These laws make meetings unnecessary. Fortunately, many close corporations use a more formal style of operation. Those with public stockholders for example, have regular meetings of directors, keep detailed minutes and adhere to many other protocols.

Whatever the style of governance, informal or "by the book," the crucial issue is who runs the show. Control of the corporation is the key to power. He who has the majority vote ultimately decides what course the business will take, who has what role, and how much each participant will be paid for his efforts. The patriarch usually clings to this power throughout his lifetime, even though others in his family are actually more active in the company, have greater responsibilities, and are more knowledgeable. The transfer of control to the next generation is hard to accomplish. This can cause very serious problems, particularly in the case of the senior stockholder's disability or mental impairment. Some ideas about how a transition in control can be achieved are discussed in Chapter 3.

STOCK AND DIVIDENDS

One of the most shocking aspects of close corporation ownership is the realization that unless the business is sold, or the company goes public, the stock itself is worth nothing. I have greatly upset many entrepreneurs when I said that to them. Their reaction was understandable. How can their stock which represents their owner-ship of a sizeable, successful business have no value? What we have here is a play on words. Certainly the stock has value. But there is no yield on it; and the owner can't convert it into money unless he sells all of his stockholdings or the entire business. In some instances, a market for the stock can be established by going public.

The return on stock is dividends. The typical close corporation avoids the declaration of dividends like a plague because of the double tax consequences. That is, the profits of the business are first taxed to the corporation; and then, when the corporation distributes the after-tax dollars as dividends to the stockholders, they are taxed a second time. Consider, for example, a close corporation in the maximum tax brackets that has $100,000 of taxable income. Using a rounded percentage of state and federal taxes, the corporation will have to pay about 50% of this amount, or $50,000, in corporate taxes. If the $50,000 that is left in the hands of the corporation is then distributed to the stockholders as dividends, they will keep only $25,000 after taxes, for they too will be in the 50% tax bracket. What all this means is that $75,000 of the $100,000 will be eaten up by taxes.

For this reason, the corporation may decide to pay out profits as additional compensation and fringe benefits to the owners. So long as the amounts paid out are deductible by the corporation, it pays no tax on what is distributed. The stockholders now pay only tax on the monies that the corporation pays out to them as compensation, which means a lot more in-pocket. Fringe benefits that are deductible by the corporation and non-taxable to the owners are even better than compensation. The point to keep in mind is this: it is better for a close corporation to pay deductible compensation and fringe benefits than dividends. Indeed, it is commonplace to find successful close corporations that have paid little or no dividends during their entire history.

The Internal Revenue Service is well aware of the tax advantages of compensation and the tax disadvantages of dividends for the proprietors of close corporations. Indeed, it is widely recognized that deciding whether to tag a distribution to an owner as compensation or as a dividend is entirely a matter of whim. There are no "arms-length" aspects to this issue, since the controlling stockholder, or the incorporated partners, can do whatever they please. Consequently, the government takes the position that compensation paid by a company to a stockholder-employee must be reasonable in amount in order to be deductible. The IRS polices the reasonable compensation area with great care. It is a "hot issue" on audits and one of the most commonly litigated tax controversies. How close corporations can effectively contend with this reasonable compensation limitation is discussed in Chapter 5. In that same chapter, the plusses and minuses of a Subchapter S election by a close corporation are considered. With the maximum individual income tax rate—very little more than the top corporate rate—many profitable companies have elected to be taxed under Subchapter S. This means there is no Federal income tax at the corporate level, and all income is taxed directly to the stockholders.

PERQUISITES

Close corporation owners also commonly benefit from a number of non-taxable perquisites. Automobiles used to be the number one fringe benefit, but the 1984 Tax Reform Act changed that. There are still available, however, medical insurance, life insurance, and pension and profit-sharing plans. Attendance at conventions and travel and entertainment are also very popular. A fuller description of these benefits can be found in Chapter 4, and the legal and tax implications of perquisites for the stockholders are reviewed in Chapter 5.

FINANCES

Another significant facet of close corporations is that they are usually undercapitalized, despite the fact that most of their net-after-tax earnings have been plowed back into the business. Although publicly held companies can obtain more capital by selling securities to investors, that avenue is not open to close corporations. Instead, they have to rely heavily on bank credit. Consequently, one of the most valuable intangibles a close corporation can have is a good relationship with a bank. The bank may end up advancing a very large part of the company's working capital. Indeed, a bank's willingness to provide funds may be the key to making certain deals. For example, a major stockholder in the close corporation might want to sell his interest, or the corporation might want to buy a new plant or a very expensive piece of machinery or equipment. The "doability" of these transactions often depends on how much the company's banker is willing to advance.

In my view, the weakest link in the management skills of most close corporation owners is their financial know-how. Some of them have recognized this problem and hired capable financial executives. But it is not easy for close corporations to find such help. Most of the good financial and accounting people are attracted by large publicly held companies. For close corporations who cannot hire a top-notch financial executive, the corporation's accounting firm usually fills the void. It counsels the company on a potpourri of financial issues, including such things as budgeting and planning, cost controls, management systems, financing capital improvements, and computer technology.

The largest accounting firms in the country have begun to actively solicit the business of the more substantial close corporations. Since they have been relegated to a very limited audit roll by their biggest clients, who have their own accounting and tax departments, these accounting giants see a much better chance to utilize their talents on behalf of smaller businesses. Nevertheless, many close corporation owners shy away from the big accounting firms. They are used to dealing with the top people in smaller accounting firms, and are afraid of becoming a very small frog in a big pond if they shift. The "big eight" accountants understand this problem. Some of them have acquired, by merger, middle-sized accounting firms who are very experienced in dealing with close corporations.

DEATH OF THE OWNER

The death of the owner of a major interest in a family business poses many special problems. How will the surviving spouse and children be able to maintain the standard of living they enjoyed when the proprietor was alive? What is the best way to manage a widow's property? Should children who are not involved in the business nonetheless be given stock, since they too are offspring entitled to equality of treatment? Then there are the death taxes on the value of the stock that must be faced and the question of where the money for the payment of those taxes will come from. Faced with these serious concerns, it is imperative that the senior member in the business get his estate plan in shape and review it regularly. Yet so many entrepreneurs keep putting it off.

These estate planning considerations are examined in detail in Chapters 6 through 10. In Chapter 6 there is a hopefully easily understood explanation of the significant estate and gift tax concepts that are involved in doing estate planning for the close corporation owner. The reasons why businessmen procrastinate about doing estate planning are examined in Chapter 7 and some ideas on how to counteract the delaying tactics are proposed. Ways and means of providing income for a spouse while avoiding negative tax consequences are outlined in Chapter 8. In Chapter 9, the advantages of a trust for a surviving spouse are explained. And finally, in Chapter 10, there is an examination of methods of maintaining financial equality among children, while keeping out of the corporation those children who are not involved in the business.

THE INCORPORATED PARTNERSHIP

The unrelated individuals who are the stockholder-managers of an incorporated partnership often develop a remarkable kinship as a result of working side by side in a business venture. They are frequently best friends. In many respects their relationship is akin to a marriage. And like so many marriages, the union can sometimes terminate in divorce.

What should be done to avoid incompatibility among the partners in this kind of enterprise and to prevent disagreements and personal difficulties from interfering with the successful operation of the business? How should the business prepare for potentially devastating contingencies such as the death or permanent disability of a partner? These and other issues are examined in detail in Chapters 11 and 12.

LIFE INSURANCE

Life insurance plays a vital role in enabling an incorporated partnership to buy the stock of a deceased partner. In fact, the purchase price may be pegged to the amount of insurance the corporation can afford to carry on each of the principals. Life insurance is perhaps even more important for the resolution of many problems that the family business faces. It has many uses which should be known by close corporation owners and those lawyers who counsel them. The different kinds of insurance, how premiums can be funded, and the most advantageous ways to structure the insurance for tax purposes are covered in Chapter 13.

DIVORCE

Some readers may initially feel that Chapter 14 is out-of-place. Why include a chapter dealing with the effects of divorce in a book about close corporations? The answer is simple. Divorce has become a very commonplace event. In many jurisdictions, property acquired by either spouse during marriage can be divided or "distributed" between both spouses upon divorce. Therefore, the handling of a divorced spouse's interest in a close corporation is bound to present some very difficult issues. The divorce can have very damaging effects on the stability of the company. It may severely impair or destroy the relationship between partners in an incorporated partnership. Close corporation owners and their advisors need to appreciate more than they presently do the severity of what can happen when a stockholder gets divorced. Some ideas on how this problem can be handled are discussed in Chapter 14.

GOING PUBLIC AND SALE OF THE BUSINESS

Some close corporations do "go public." As used in this book, "going public" means offering shares of the close corporation's stock to outsiders. By my definition, so long as the identity between major stock ownership and management remains intact after the sale of shares to the public, the entity still is a close corporation. Notwithstanding the presence of outside stockholders, the nature of the enterprise and the concerns of those in control are essentially unchanged. Why, when, and how a close corporation goes public are discussed in Chapter 15.

More close corporations sell out than go public. But selling out is a very emotional experience. It causes tremendous changes in the owners' way of life. What makes the proprietors of a successful enterprise decide to get rid of it? The common reasons for selling are reviewed in Chapter 16, together with an explanation of the procedures and the legal and tax considerations involved in a sale of the business.

COUNSELLING TECHNIQUES

The final chapter in the book is my attempt to share with other çounsellors of close corporations the things I have learned about relating to entrepreneurs. While entrepreneurs are generally hard-driving, aggressive clients, often impatient, they are also special human beings, capable, courageous and colorful. I have had the good fortune to establish close ties with many entrepreneurs, which have existed for decades. In Chapter 17, I have tried to record the things that I believe contributed to the solidity of these relationships.

THE FAMILY BUSINESS $\boxed{1}$

The family business has all the characteristics of the typical close corporation, with one further ingredient: the owners and top executives are all from one family—or sometimes two, in the case where each family holds a 50% interest. What this means is that interpersonal attitudes that have been developed in the home are carried over to the office, leading to some obvious problems. In the area of the father-son relationships, for example, the sons are put at a decided disadvantage.

FATHERS AND SONS

During a son's rearing, his father was the boss, or at least shared that authoritative position with the mother. Dad doled out the dollars and felt free to criticize and make demands regarding his children's behavior, hopefully fairly, but in accordance with his standards and principles. Even on subjects where they have little or no background, many fathers do not hesitate to issue pronouncements, believing they are better equipped to make decisions. A typical example concerns the choice of college that their children will attend. Dad may not have gone to college, or he may have graduated 25 years ago. Even though the children have the benefit of guidance counsellors and the experience of peers, the father may still try to choose a college for them. This kind of thing carries over from the home to the family business. The father continues to feel that he is the dominant force and that his judgment is much better than his children's. During the time when the sons are growing up, this evaluation is probably correct. Problems occur, however, when a

1

father is unwilling to recognize and appreciate that his 35 or 40 year old son is a very different individual.

A longstanding client once made me aware of how difficult this change in attitude may be for a father. He was then 69 years of age, and he had two sons, Bob and John, who were not only in the business, they really were running it. The sons were very able, motivated and conscientious managers. After many months of thoughtful study, Bob and John had concluded that their manufacturing company had to move to a larger, more modern plant and automate to remain competitive. This would involve a very large capital outlay and some extensive financial commitments by the company, as well as some personal guarantees by my client and his sons. The sons submitted a detailed plan of action which outlined business and tax benefits, cost projections, and sources of money and explained how repayment was to be made. It was an impressive job. When I commented to the client about the thoroughness and logic of the presentation by his sons, he startled me with his response: "Milt, with so much at stake, I somehow can't help but get a flashback to the time when a motor the kids were developing short circuited all the electricity in the house, while Stella and I were on a European trip." It all comes down to this: some fathers find it extremely hard to see their children as adults. They cannot shake the memory of bad judgments that an immature son may have made while he was growing up.

It is important for fathers in family businesses to recognize this mind set and combat it. Many of my clients have been able to accomplish this. They realize that sons should be evaluated on the basis of what they are now—not tarred for a lifetime because of foolish things they may have done when they were kids. People grow and mature.

Confrontations

Open and frank communications between executives can be particularly difficult in the family business. Taking a position that varies substantially from the one espoused by a fellow executive is hard, even where the differing parties have no contact outside the business. Strong words can be exchanged. Someone can feel betrayed. But these differences between unrelated parties do not begin to have the same emotional content and long range effects as a comparable disagreement between two generations in a family business.

The difference, of course, is the presence of family ties. Applying the Freudian theory that sons both love and hate their fathers, the resolution of a dispute between them regarding a business matter can bring to the surface a myriad of emotional responses. Every part of the son, who believes he is 100% correct, may want to cry out: "Dad, you're nuts!" But he represses that exclamation because of fear, guilt, love—who knows what—and may even back down on a particular issue, because the stakes of defying his father are too high.

Often the grown children contending with the dominating, unyielding father throw in the sponge and stop fighting. The most independent of them will leave the family business. Others will decide that the best path to follow is to accept Dad's rules, limit involvement, and accept the economic benefit of participation in the business. There is a great loss to the family business if it cannot get the benefit of the perspectives and creativity of the younger generation. It will undoubtedly go down-hill when Dad can no longer effectively make all the judgment calls.

Image and self respect

Some of the personal problems in the family business stem from the tough time that sons have in achieving a sense of accomplishment for their efforts, even in instances where they enter a modestly successful business and develop it into a colossus. Let me share with you some of the "peeves" that I have heard from sons on this subject:

> **1.** *A son calls on a customer having prepared carefully the presentation he is going to make. When he is announced, before he can get started, the buyer virtually knocks him over with an outburst like this: "So, you're Jeff! You look a lot like your dad. Great guy, your dad. Been doing business with him for years. If you do half as well as he does, you'll be great. Now, what do you have on your mind?"*

This is not what the son was looking for. He wants the buyer to treat him like any other salesman. Then, if he gets the order, he feels he has done something. When the buyer in my example gives Jeff an order, undoubtedly he will have the feeling that his father—rather than he—made the sale.

2. Sons often feel that the community will judge them harshly. They do not expect to receive plaudits for building up the enterprise. A typical attitude is this: - " No matter how much more successful we are, people will say that with a start like that, how could they miss? On the other hand, if the business goes bad when we take command, people will undoubtedly lay the blame on our less capable management."

Early in my practice, I thought these impressions of the public's attitudes bordered on paranoia. I have now listened to this complaint from so many different second and third generation individuals—and I have heard these smears by envious peers so many times—that I realize how tough it is for sons to feel a sense of achievement in their own community.

3. In many instances that I know of, sons have been criticized because they outspokenly pointed out—in response to innuendos to the contrary—that it was their efforts which built the enterprise into what it is today. For some reason the attitude persists that such talk amounts to self-aggrandizement and is in bad taste, since it can be construed as denigration of the owner-father.

A number of the heads of family businesses that I represent understand their sons' need for recognition and do something about it. What do they do? Simple! They continually downplay their role in the recent successes of the enterprise and highlight what the sons have done. One of them, for instance, tells anyone who asks him about the business: "Oh, yes, it was a good little business for a long time. But the boys—not I—have built it into what it is today, a major force in our industry." Sometimes he says this in the presence of his sons. Other times he does it when they were not there, but it gets back to them. This is a very easy script to follow. Every father must understand that it is a bad thing to ignore the ego-needs of sons working in the family business or to interfere with their ability to achieve a sense of accomplishment.

4. Father, for his own ego building, repeatedly reminisces about the serious obstacles he had to overcome to make the business successful. With each repetition of the story, there is an enlargement of the difficulties that were faced. The effect is a put down of the sons because they have had it so much easier.

I recall one son who was so vexed by his father's often told story of having to sell newspapers as a young man to keep going, that he finally blurted out: "Dad, it's true you made it possible for me to get ahead without having to sell newspapers. But I must tell you, if I had to sell them, I would have sold them better than you did." Fathers should guard against this kind of thing.

> **5.** *A father heaps guilt on the next generation family members in the business: "I could have sold the company for $2 million and gotten a juicy employment contract from the purchaser. This would have made mother and me very comfortable for the rest of our lives. But I didn't want to jeopardize your future."*
>
> *Equally thoughtless is the scene with dad talking to his cronies about his last trip to the west coast to meet with a very upset and irate customer. In the earshot of his sons, he proclaims: "If it weren't for Dick and David and their future, I would never have taken that guff from this customer. I would have told him to go to the Devil. But even though I had acute indigestion for two days after, I stuck it out so that the boys would not lose this important customer."*

There are many versions of this scenario. They all add up to the father's making some ostensible sacrifice for the good of his children. However honest the father's comments may be, these are difficult sentiments for the children in the business to handle. They also make it much harder for sons to relate to their father on an executive-to-executive basis. After all, how can a son speak his mind openly and directly to an ancestor concerned for the younger man's good?

Cycles of shifting relationships

The relationships between a father and his sons in the family business seem to go through stages. In the first period, when it is clear to all concerned that the father is the key person, the father usually exaggerates the talents and achievements of the sons. The "chip off the old block" attitude pervades. During this period, sons can easily get an unrealistic evaluation of how well they are doing as businessmen. After all, the "teacher" in this institution is constantly praising their efforts.

The next phase, which I think is the most difficult one, is when the sons have about 10-15 years of activity in the enterprise. By this time, dad is usually going through the mid-life crisis stage. He has fewer years ahead of him than behind him. His drives are on a downturn. Ailments start plaguing him and he is tired of the pressures. The sons, on the other hand, are now coming into their own as managers. They have meaningful roles and responsibilities. Plans for changing and revitalizing the business start to emerge and the father's status quo is under attack.

This is the confrontational decade. The head of the family is concerned about business shifting away from "his-way". He needs to justify his decision-making and to demonstrate that he is not losing his touch. But the sons have now started to move into middle age. They have families and significant financial obligations. They want to control their own destinies. That means being a real force in the management of the family business.

I have found this stage of father-son business relationships to be the most complex because it involves a period of transition. There is a shift from autocratic rule to a partnership between fathers and sons. Contrary to what many fathers have confided in me, at this point the sons generally do not want to kick dad out and take over. What they do want is to have their opinions and ideas heard. Understandly, they feel that management issues should be resolved by the management team jointly, after thoughtful consideration. They don't want these decisions to be at father's whim.

The final stage occurs when father is in his late 70's or early 80's. Now the tables are turned. The sons look at their father as a loadstone. If he still has the lion's share of the equity in the enterprise, the sons may complain: "Look how much Dad receives for doing nothing." They may bitterly resent his continuing need to retain control of the corporation and, consequently, over them as well. Of course, the father himself is beset with the insecurities that trouble most older people. He feels threatened by his sons and clings to control of the business because he views it as an economic insurance policy.

While the relationships between a parent and children, working in a family business, keep changing, it is the sons who invariably must adjust to the new circumstances. The father, the patriarch, has control and he generally exercises it in whatever manner he sees fit. The unexpressed, but underlying concept is that father can do no wrong. In fact, it is extremely difficult for the sons even to air their complaints about dad's attitudes or conduct.

SIBLING RIVALRY

Whenever there are two or more principals in a closely held business, a certain amount of competition for position and recognition is to be expected. The ego of each of the principals requires him to feel that his contributions to the business are critical to its success. I remember a life insurance seminar I participated in many years ago. One of the members of the panel was a very well known and successful life insurance man, whose forte was selling insurance to solve certain business problems. During the question and answer period someone made this inquiry: "I have been told that the key to making a sale of life insurance to a company that has a few partners, is to find out which of them is the dominant person—so that you can relate to him. Do you find that to be the case?" The very knowledgeable underwriter responded that this was not his experience. Said he, "Down deep, each of the owners is convinced that without him the business would not be successful. If he initially had any doubts on that score, his wife has convinced him."

When the partners are unrelated, these problems are easier to work out. The prognosis is not as optimistic when the principals are brothers working in a family business. The difference is the greater intensity of the rivalry between siblings. Indeed, most parents are familiar with the existence and ramifications of sibling conflicts. At social gatherings, P.T.A. meetings, coffee clutches—at almost any get-together where people are talking about their children—the effects of sibling rivalry are noted. For some reason, however, the phenomenon is very often overlooked by the head of the family business, despite the fact that this omission can be costly. The antagonisms that can develop between children who are principals in a company can have serious adverse consequences for the enterprise. For example, one child can be forced out, litigation can erupt between them, or the business may be sold.

Without advance planning, the first child in the business has a big advantage. He backstops the father and often acts as something akin to "assistant to the president." By the time the next family member joins the firm, the son who got there first takes advantage of the savvy he has developed, and sometimes relegates the new arrival to a subordinate role. Unless something is done to rectify this situation before too much time passes, the older son can legitimately argue against equality of compensation and position for his younger brother. If that happens, the difficulties of a third sibling, the kid brother, coming on board will be even worse.

Reducing the friction

What actions can be taken by the head of the family to reduce the friction among children who are working in a family business? I can only describe what I have observed being done by fathers who have successfully contended with the issue. The first step is to acquire a real understanding of what sibling rivalry is all about, and how it can affect the behavior of children in the business. The fathers who took meaningful steps to contend with the problem exhibited an appreciation of its significance and manifestations. Some, I know, consulted with experts. Others apparently garnered their knowledge of the subject on their own.

Next, they developed a plan of action. Different roles in the company were allocated to the sons, so that each could find an important niche and feel that he played a substantial part in the company's operations and success. The capabilities and personalities of the siblings were considered in this assignment of areas of responsibility. In one instance, the more outgoing, aggressive son moved into marketing and sales; while the other, more practical, detailed, and introspective, found his place in production. In another instance, where three sons were involved, they were assigned, respectively, to marketing, production and finance.

Finally, there were frank discussions between the father and the children, from time to time, about the implications to all concerned of a deep seated competitiveness. The way in which such competitiveness could harm the business was outlined clearly. Each of the sons participated in the decision concerning the area of management he would ultimately handle. Each received proper training and adequate preparation for that position.

Drawbacks of the "one boss" approach

A serious obstacle to the achievement of harmonious relationships among siblings is the concept that in any business, there must be one boss. I have heard this theorem announced by several fathers. It presents no difficulties when dad is the one boss. But the principle serves to heighten the competition among brothers who are fighting for the one top job. Of course, there are many viable exceptions to this one boss idea. For example, there are incorporated partnerships (discussed later on in this book), where two or three principals operate as equals in the business. There is also a growing practice in large, publicly held corporations of having a committee that shares the duties and responsibilities of the chief executive office. I suspect that the father who urges the one boss idea may be reflecting his own need to be the kingpin. Foisting this doctrine on the sons can be damaging.

Some advisors claim that sibling rivalry can best be handled by mandating equality of interest and compensation, and by requiring unanimity in action. For example, three brothers who are equal stockholders in a manufacturing business enter into an arrangement making them the directors and officers of the corporation, declaring that their compensation and perquisites shall always be equal, and stating that no action may be taken by the directors or stockholders unless all three of them agree. In this way, no two of the brothers can "gang up" on the third. If there are only modest differences in talent, responsibilities and commitment to the business, this is a feasible arrangement. I believe, and I have said this to many siblings, that the strongest child in the family business must be prepared to overlook modest differences in value to the enterprise, and accept equality of economic return and status. It would be a rare situation where three brothers were all of identical value to the company. Thus, without this compromise, there will always be a battle royal among siblings. In short, this is the price that must be paid for family peace.

But mandating equality irrespective of performance can encourage the weakling to take it easy. So long as he is entitled to the same return and so long as nothing can be done unless he approves, what incentive is there for him to put in long hours and suffer anxieties? I have seen a few situations where this arrangement has resulted in terrible injustice. The resulting anger and frustration on the part of the capable, hardworking stockholders ultimately resulted in litigation or a sale of the business. For this reason, I think it is better for sibling-managers to act by majority voice. A minority stockholder who is taken advantage of has available rights and remedies. For example, he can go to court demanding that his brothers repay excessive compensation or perquisites to the company, or seek the appointment of a receiver for the corporation, or its dissolution.

A case study

One of my partners, Stephen Lichtstein, once developed a "group dynamics" technique to deal with a serious sibling rivalry situation. The critical issue that created the need for this remedy was a battle among the three children in a business over their levels of compensation. They were all equal stockholders. But the oldest child was by far the most able and valuable. The second son, while a far cry from his older brother, was more effective than the youngest son—who complained bitterly that no one would give him a chance to demonstrate his capabilities. The oldest son felt entitled to more compensation than his brothers. They did not dispute that. The bone of contention was his position that he, and he alone, should decide the amount that he should be paid, as well as what his younger brothers should receive. All three sons constantly badgered the father to step in and resolve the matter. The father was semi-retired, but still in control of the corporation. He confided to Steve that he did not know what to do. He recognized that unless something was done to ameliorate the situation, the family would be split apart and the business, severely damaged.

Steve first interviewed each of the four principals, getting their viewpoints and attitudes and an understanding of their duties and responsibilities. He had a review made of compensation publications to get some guidelines on levels of pay for persons with comparable roles in the industry. A committee was established to set compensation for the forthcoming fiscal year. The committee consisted of the father, the three sons, and Steve. Steve presented suggested base salaries for the three sons, which were accepted. A bonus potential of 50% of the base pay was also established for each of them. The guidelines that would be used in evaluating individual performances were discussed in detail and specific objectives were established for each brother to achieve. All of these agreements were reduced to writing.

About seven months later, half-way through the fiscal year, the committee met. Each of the sons evaluated his performance against the criteria and objectives that had been recorded. He graded himself on each item, from A to F, and then set down an overall performance grade. Others made observations about the individual's performance. At the end of the year, the group met again. They went through a similar evaluation process. Bonuses for the year were fixed. The base pay for the following year was set. Personal goals and objectives for the three sons for the next year were established and recorded. This procedure has continued successfully. There is now a remarkable cohesiveness among the siblings. They feel that the process is fair. They are becoming better managers since they are thoughtfully criticizing their performance, identifying weaknesses, setting forth objectives they want to attain, and analyzing why some of them were not achieved.

Perhaps the most telling consequence was one self-appraisal by the oldest son. The company had somewhat of a flat year from an earnings standpoint. Because he was the senior executive, this son gave himself a very low grade on his profit objective. He also admitted a major error of judgment in connection with two projects where a significant, probably non-recoverable loss was suffered. He gave himself a reduced over-all grade because of these factors. Nevertheless, his two younger brothers felt that he was too hard on himself. They raised his bonus from the 65% level which he had suggested for himself to the 75% range, an increase of over $5,000. What a change in the sibling environment!

HUSBAND AND WIFE AS BUSINESS PARTNERS

I have been associated with a number of close corporations where both husband and wife were active employees. In most of these situations the husband was the boss, and the wife played a supporting role. She ran the office, kept the books or sometimes was in charge of personnel. Once in a great while the spouses had the equivalent of an incorporated partnership. The two of them had an equal say in decision-making, and each considered the other to be at the same level in the governance of the corporation's business and affairs. I have even seen some cases where the wife was the powerhouse and worked hard to disguise that fact, in the interest of preserving a happy marriage.

We all recognize that today it is commonplace for married women to have careers. There are many instances where a wife earns more than her husband and would be objectively described as more successful. Husbands have adjusted to the domestic demands occasioned by working wives, by doing such things as cooking, shopping, setting the table, taking care of the kids and transporting them to doctors, dentists, etc.

But the marital stresses are much greater when a husband and wife are working together in a business—their family business. The time that the two of them spend together is greatly enlarged. This can produce problems between them. A wife who quit a business that she had built up with her husband, a very capable executive, put it very simply: "I'm with Brooke all day long, every day. We have no separate space. As a result we're getting on each other's nerves. Before it breaks up our marriage, I'm getting out."

When a husband and wife are in business together, marital disputes arising in the home spill over into the company. Virtually all married couples have fights. Marriage counsellors say fighting is healthy. If a couple has a fight at home, and they don't work in the same place, the separation produces a "cooling-off" period. But when they go to the same office and have to relate to one another intimately, the chances are good that an issue in the business will become a spark that rekindles the argument. The intensity of the battle in the place of business will now be far greater, because it builds on the antagonisms that were created in the home.

Effect on children in the business

The tension between spouses increases even more when children come into the business. Differences between father and mother as to how best to raise their children, reduced by the kids' absence at college and graduate school, are revived. For example, a son who believes he has been treated unfairly by dad, complains to mom. His rendition of what happened triggers the accusation in mother's mind: "Emil never had enough patience with Richard. He always was too hard on him." The chances are very good that mother will present the complaint to her husband in that context—his repeated failures to relate to Richard properly—instead of dealing with the specifics, as she would do if an unrelated employee were involved.

Put to him in this fashion, it is hard for dad to say: "I'm sorry. A customer had just balled me out about a delivery, and I took out my anger on Richard. I'll apologize to him. But you have to encourage Richard to come directly to me with his complaints. Being able to deal with me, face-to-face, is an important part of his management maturation." Now, instead, dad must defend his entire relationship with Richard. With his competence as a father at stake, dad will probably counterattack. The incident has been blown out of proportion.

Effects on subordinates

These disagreements between spouses in the office create a lot of uneasiness for subordinates. Partners in an incorporated partnership try very hard not to air their interpersonal problems in front of employees. They appreciate the importance of maintaining a solid leadership front. Employees are upset by the scene of an angry open exchange between their bosses. They tend to exaggerate the implications. But unrelated executives find it easier to control their hostilities than do a married couple. The needs of a husband and wife to preserve their status and position, are so great, that it is much harder to keep emotions under wraps.

Separate careers usually work better

In my opinion, an exceptional marital relationship is needed when a husband and wife join together in the operation of a business. Even in the best of circumstances these arrangements involve serious risks both for the marriage and the business. When the husband is the boss and his wife plays a much less significant role, she is bound to have resentments. A wife in those circumstances has to question whether her being held down is not just one more expression of male chauvinism. Acceptance of lesser capability than her husband also creates ego problems for her. Where the married couple have equal status in the company, competitiveness between husband and wife can develop, and difficult decisions will arise regarding the allocation of responsibilities and authority between them. In every instance, there are the concerns about too much togetherness and the carryover of marital difficulties into the business environment. On balance, I think it is more sensible for spouses to pursue separate business careers. This approach usually proves less of a strain on their marriage.

When a widow takes the helm

Mothers sometimes find themselves in charge of a business. This usually happens after the husband's death. Mom may be put in the position of leadership as a compromise, to avoid the consequences of dad's having picked one of the children in the business to be the head. In other situations where the mother has played an important part in the operations of the enterprise, she may be the best choice. In either case, whether mom is inexperienced or a very effective and knowledgeable manager, this is a terrible spot for her to be in. With her husband gone, she has a need for close ties with her children, in-laws and most importantly her grandchildren. Those relationships will not be helped if she has to decide the role each family member working for the company should play, and how much compensation and what fringe benefits each should receive, and if she has to direct, evaluate and criticize the performance of her children. There is no way she can please everyone with her actions and judgments.

A widow in this position quickly figures out a way to get out from under. She does what her husband should have done. The widow arranges for a shift in the leadership of the enterprise from her to the children. In my experience this is most effectively accomplished with a group dynamics technique—the offspring in the business, in a setting that fosters dialogue, themselves spell out the chain of command and assign areas of responsibility. Sometimes professionals, the corporation's lawyer and accountant, or a management consultant, are involved in the process. In a few situations, where the choice of the president was obvious, the mother made that decision, and then helped to define the roles of the other offspring, making sure their status and income were safeguarded.

Some observers believe that a widow, particularly one over 60, should never run a family business for a quite different reason. They feel that she won't be able to cope with the pressures and the problems. A typical comment is: "Milt, at Melanie's age—she's 70, you know—it's not right for her to have such burdens. She has the right to take it easy and not have such worries." Hogwash! These same wise men would react completely differently if a widower were involved. They are acting out their own images of what widows can and should do. Actually, keeping active in a business may be the best antidote a widow has for the emptiness in her life that she feels, resulting from her husband's death.

We represent a widow who in her mid-seventies took over the management of a very large apartment complex. Her deceased husband and she were extremely close, and his death devastated her. She had learned a great deal about running apartment projects from her husband, who was recognized as the best in the business. With fervor and commitment, this widow took charge of the real estate development. She revitalized the property with substantial capital improvements. Now, five years later, the complex has been sold for an enormous profit. She did a whale of a job. I repeat, the widows whom I have seen renounce the top position in a business have done so because of the difficulties in remaining on good terms with their children who would be subordinates, and their families. They were well able to cope otherwise.

SEXISM AND THE EXCLUSION OF DAUGHTERS

Another ingredient of the family business should be noted, namely a stereotyped approach toward the role of women, especially daughters, in the workplace. I realize that many readers probably feel that male chauvinism exists in virtually all American businesses. I am not suggesting otherwise. My contention is that the situation for females is even worse in family businesses. The irony is that these businesses can ill afford such prejudice. Generally speaking, it is harder for family enterprises to attract unrelated top level executives.

Instead, they need to look to family members for management succession. Thus, by excluding daughters, the family business is losing an important reservoir of needed talent.

Another serious consequence of a father's discouraging his daughters from active participation in the family business concerns their inheritance. Chapter 10 of this book describes some methods of providing for children who are not in the business. These methods can be burdensome and, in many instances, only go part way in achieving equality. The worst answer to this quandry is for the father to give stock of the corporation to a daughter who is not in the business. All that does is to create serious frictions and antagonism within the family. It would be much easier for a father in this situation, if his daughter were involved in the business. Then she could be treated just like a son.

This practice of excluding daughters from the family business continues to mystify me. Over the years I have discussed it with many clients, in the hope of having some light shed on the reasons for it. What I am left with are some probable contributing factors, which I will share with you. The first startling revelation is the honest belief of parents that the daughters were not kept out. The typical response is: "My daughter never showed any interest in working in the company." But when these parents were pushed to compare the attitudes they manifested with their sons, all those queried acknowledged the extent of the difference. Early in the game, the sons were talked to about the business. The hope that they would join the company was expressed often. In some instances, fathers even acknowledged the use of some coercion to get a son into the business. Of course, no similar suggestion or encouragement was directed to the daughters. The simple truth is that the parents did not look forward to a daughter's participation in the business. This attitude seems to prevail even where the nature of the business is peculiarly suited to females. For example, I know of two daughters, one of whom is a lawyer and the other a business executive, who were never considered for roles in a family company that made fasteners for ladies' lingerie and sportswear.

The disinclination to have daughters in the family business is usually not an expression of father's lesser opinion of their capability. I know many parents who have gloried in the achievements of a daughter—excellent student, good athlete, and leader in community affairs. I know fathers who were most impressed by the maturity of their daughters and their ability to relate to people. Some even outspokenly acknowledged that their daughters were the most able of all their children. Nonetheless, there was not even a suggestion of the daughters having a role in the management of the business.

Stereotyped attitudes

Why do daughters wind up on the outside of the family business? Let me offer some speculations. It might have to do with a father's mental image of what a woman's role in life should be. The picture of his daughter, as a good wife and mother, running the home, caring for her husband, playing the major part in raising the children can be captivating. By the same token, a mother may want her daughter to have a life akin to that which she has enjoyed.

Another possibility is that dad, desirous of grandchildren, does not want to push his daughter into the stress and strain of being a career woman as well as a mother. He might be anticipating the difficulties he will experience when his executive-daughter is caught in the working mother's squeeze. As the head of the family business, he will not want his daughter to ignore her business responsibilities because of family needs. On the other hand, he'll probably be even more upset, as a grandfather, if his daughter's commitment to the business causes her to ignore her children. Still another explanation commonly given by fathers goes like this: "It will be bad for my daughter's marriage if she makes more money and is more successful than her husband." That attitude does not make much sense to me.

Even in those unusual instances where a daughter does come into the family business, she is generally given a position of lesser significance than her brothers. Typically, daughter will be assigned to an accounting, administrative, or service function, since the males often refuse to believe that a woman can be successful in marketing or production. Perhaps this is their means of making sure that their sister will never be a threat to their power.

We had one situation where a sister, Emily, was in business with her father and two brothers. Emily was clearly more competent than either of the sons. She had remarkable marketing skills, was organized, and could motivate and direct subordinates very effectively. The time came for father to step down as the head of the company.

He decided that Emily was the best choice as his successor, and he so informed his children. One of Emily's brothers, Scott, could not accept this result. He did not dispute his father's evaluation. But his macho needs would not permit him to accept a position subservient to Emily. "The guys at the country club will needle me unmercifully."

To avoid what would have been a bitter battle, a segment of the business was spun off and given to Scott. His company stagnated, while the family enterprise he left prospered and grew dramatically under Emily's leadership. Scott paid a big price for his prejudice.

Regardless of its source, male chauvinism in the family enterprise must be recognized and dealt with because it denies daughters the opportunity for equal treatment and career achievement. The real loser may be the business.

PLIGHT OF SONS-IN-LAW

It is customary for the head of a family business to push his daughter's husband to come into the company. Why is this so often done? Very little thought and attention have been given to this issue. That is unfortunate, because the probabilities are that the son-in-law who succumbs to the patriarch's pressures will have serious regrets years later. By that time, however, he will be trapped. There is nothing malicious in the father's attempt to have a son-in-law join the business. The head of the family believes he is serving the economic interest of his son-in-law and daughter. My gut feeling is that the major concern of the father is for his daughter and her offspring, his grandchildren—a very understandable attitude—and the son-in-law becomes the vehicle through which the daughter and grandchildren will be well taken care of.

The involvement of the son-in-law in the enterprise does permit the daughter to be an equal stockholder with her brothers, without running into the usual problems that accompany the presence of an inactive stockholder in a close corporation. He gets the compensation and the benefits. These are used, however, for the betterment of the daughter and the children of the marriage. Daughter is thus the indirect beneficiary of these distributions from the corporation. With this scenario, there is peace, comfort and pride for dad. He has treated all of his children equally. The next generation are all participants in the family venture. The "It" will now take care of all of them, as well as their offspring, and hopefully in grand style. What a nice neat package!

There is often a plus for the business too. The son-in-law may be talented and fill a need. Family companies have trouble attracting good management people from the outside. Many of these businesses pick up very able executives through marriage. In some instances, the son-in-law is more capable than one or more of the sons in the business.

The pressure on a son-in-law to become active in the family corporation does not always emanate from father. The daughter herself is often the instigator or a strong second force. She looks upon her successful father as the tower of strength. It is he, in daughter's mind, who has developed the enterprise and keeps enlarging the business. Why shouldn't she and her husband share the spoils of dad's productivity with the families of her brothers? That is her birthright, as well. A daughter's pressure on her husband, to become a part of the business, is very much the result of her instinct of self-preservation. Her spouse will make more money and she and their children will live better. Also, the daughter expects to benefit from a better marriage relationship because her husband will not have to work so hard, travel so often and suffer as much anxiety, if he works in the family corporation.

When is this decision regarding entry into the company made by the son-in-law? Normally, when he is at the beginning of the career path he prepared for—or today, very commonly, when the son-in-law is trying to find his place in the business or professional world. For his young wife, with one or more children, the contrast is striking. At one end of the spectrum she sees the struggle of her husband to get ahead in a hard, competitive, dog-eat-dog arena. On the other side, she pictures a comfortable niche in the close corporation, where you usually get paid what you need to live on comfortably, have fringe benefits, own an interest and have as a boss the loving head of the family who is committed to watch over you.

The father-in-law's perspective

In this consideration of whether or not a son-in-law should come into the family enterprise, very little heed is paid to the son-in-law's identity needs and his probable second-class status. I raised these matters with a number of patriarchs who had one or more sons-in-law in the corporation. They looked at me askance. Some had very angry reactions. Each of them felt he had done a good deed for his son-in-law; and here I was, they felt, suggesting that the son-in-law had been imposed upon. A typical response was: "The kid is making a lot more money working for me than he could have earned outside. He has a good life and his family lives a lot better than mine did when I was his age. He is treated the same way as my son."

I soon realized that my inquiries were getting me into hot water and I backed off. From a materialistic standpoint, the sons-in-law were doing very well. The head of the family was correct in his assessment of their economic status. They were living "high off the hog," and were not entitled to any sympathy on that score. What I was searching for was a sensitivity to the particular psychological problems that a son-in-law experiences as a member of the family business. These were difficulties that sons-in-law confided in me. Unfortunately, it is a rarity for a businessman father-in-law to appreciate how hard it is for a son-in-law to get gratification from his career in the typical family business.

Common sources of discontent

Why is it difficult for the son-in-law to be content? Chiefly because the son-in-law is different. In the expression, "blood is thicker than water," he is the water and the children in the business are the blood. There are ties that exist among his brothers-in-law—despite the sibling rivalry—that do not run to him. He is not a direct descendant of the fountainhead. Another hurdle for the son-in-law is the negative connotation associated with going to work in your father-in-law's business. He has to overcome the belief that he came into the company because he couldn't otherwise adequately support his wife and family. Admittedly, some of this feeling may result from hostile reactions of envious peers. My hunch is, however, that most often it represents a personal hang-up of the son-in-law. It may well be an unconscious reaction to the well-publicized doctrine of marrying a woman for her money. The son who is lacking in capability and seeks refuge under the umbrella of the family enterprise, has a quite different point of view. He does not feel beholden or sensitive about this course of action. Neither do his friends. This only highlights the distinction between a son and a son-in-law.

The most prevalent example of the son-in-law's different status is the way in which his family's stock is owned. It is almost an automatic to have the stock owned by the daughter, his wife, or a trust for her primary benefit. It is unusual for the son-in-law himself to be the stockholder. In fact, the exclusion of the son-in-law as the equity owner is so commonplace that it is assumed to be right and proper, without thoughtful evaluation of the reasons or consequences.

The story of Louis and Richard

I remember one situation very vividly. It was a very prosperous service corporation, headed by a father, Louis. Son, Morton, and son-in-law, Richard (who was married to Louis' daughter, Carol), had been actively engaged in the business for many years. Dad considered Richard to be the most competent person in the company—with the exception of himself, of course. He relied heavily on Richard's judgment. The relationship between Louis and his son-in-law, outside the company, was very close. Richard was the most responsible, considerate and understanding individual in the whole family. Louis found it easier to relate to his son-in-law than either of his children, Morton or Carol. He repeatedly declared to friends that his son-in-law was just like a son to him.

Louis came in to do some estate planning. We decided that he should make some gifts of the equity in the business to the next generation. This brought us to the issue of the identity of the persons to whom a gift of the non-voting common—the growth stock— should be made. For tax reasons, it was advantageous to split the 50% stock interest between daughter, Carol, and her husband, Richard, since this would produce additional $10,000 gift tax exclusions. I raised with Louis the idea of giving some stock to Richard, his son-in-law. He flatly rejected it. Knowing of his affection and regard for Richard, I asked him, "Why not?" His response was one that I have heard so many times: "What happens if Richard and Carol get divorced or Carol predeceases him. He will undoubtedly remarry. I don't want him as a stockholder in the corporation if he is married to someone other than my daughter." In truth, Louis' commitment to Richard was premised on his being Carol's husband. It did not run to Richard, individually. This is the reality that most sons-in-law must face.

Vesting stock ownership in the daughter's name

The vesting of stock ownership in the name of the inactive daughter means that the son-in-law is working for his wife. As the years go by, he starts to resent this position. The son-in-law may feel that his masculinity is at stake. He suffers when he socializes with fellow entrepreneurs who own their business interests outright. I have seen instances where this arrangement has adversely affected the marriage. The son-in-law feels that his wife is demeaning him by hanging on to the stock. His frustration may be aimed at his father-in-law, who created the situation, but it is his wife who catches it. He may become more susceptible to an affair with a woman who sees him only as a strong, successful businessman, rather than as daddy's son-in-law.

In a few cases that I was involved in, a father treated his son-in-law as an individual, deserving of recognition in his own right, not merely as his daughter's husband. All or most of the stock interest was held by the working son-in-law, individually, rather than by his wife. But these are very much the exceptions.

How to handle the situation

What can be done to improve the status of the son-in-law? The easiest first step is to implement the principle that those who are active in the business should hold the voting rights. Here we fall back on the creation of two classes of common stock, voting and non-voting. The great bulk of the equity value is in the non-voting common. The son-in-law gets the voting common of lesser value and his wife keeps the valuable non-voting common. In my last example, after Louis' death, there would be issued 100 shares of voting common and 10,000 shares of non-voting common. Son, Morton, would own 50% of both the voting and non-voting common stocks, which means he would receive 50 shares of voting common and 5,000 shares of non-voting common. Richard, the son-in-law, would own the other 50 shares of the voting common. Daughter, Carol, would be the owner of the other half of the valuable non-voting common, 5,000 shares. This is a good compromise. Richard, as the member of his family who is knowledgeable about the business and affairs of the corporation, is the proper individual to have the vote. He can best relate to son, Morton, regarding the governance of the entity. The 50% voting position also assures Richard of an equal position of power in the corporation. Carol, however, continues to own the lion's share of the equity—5,000 of her family's total of 5,050 shares.

A better solution is a 50-50 overall stock division between daughter and son-in-law. This is reflective of the equal partnership between husband and wife. To accomplish this, Carol would give Richard a gift of 2,475 shares of her non-voting common stock, leaving her with 2,525 shares. Richard would hold an equivalent number of shares (50 shares of voting common, plus 2,475 non-voting common shares that he received from his wife). However sound and equitable this 50-50 division may be, Carol may be hesitant to give up something that came to her from her father—particularly if she has held the stock for a long time. This reluctance to part with a sizeable chunk of her stockholdings was more easily defended by a spouse on tax grounds before the unlimited marital deduction was established. Only 50% of the value of the stock passing from wife to husband used to be covered by the marital deduction. Thus a gift from one spouse to the other could mean a sizeable gift tax liability. Today any amount of property can pass between spouses without any gift tax implications. This makes equalization easy to accomplish; and the wife cannot point to a tax problem as an excuse for not giving up stock.

The family counsellor can find himself in a ticklish situation when the issue of stock ownership arises between the daughter, who is the descendant of the owner of the business, and her husband who is a major executive in the company. The marital relationship is severely tested by this encounter between spouses. Feelings can run high and tempers can flare. There are many Solomon-like determinations that the counsellor often must make. I have had one exceptional experience in that regard. The founder of the business had three daughters. They married very unusually capable men, who went to work in the family business. The sons-in-law built the enterprise into a colossus, the largest of its kind in the area. With understanding, open and honest communication, the father, three daughters and their husbands worked out a format of equal stock ownership between each daughter and her husband. The three sons-in-law took voting control, but the overall equity was divided equally between each pair of spouses.

The son-in-law may even be victimized by the actions of his parents. This may seem bizarre but it has happened. Frictions develop between a son-in-law's mother and father and his wife's parents. It can start with arguments over how many guests each side can invite to the wedding. As a result of these disagreements, the wife's father, the boss of the son-in-law, may attribute to the son-in-law traits of his parents that have offended the father. This is a specially conceived heredity theory. It produces comments such as: "He has to be over-aggressive having been raised by parents like that!"

In sum, the lot of the son-in-law in the business is often an unhappy one. He is placed in the position of accepting many belittlements of his self-esteem as a means of obtaining substantial material benefits for his family and himself. He is often placed in a secondary status in the company, limited forever, despite his capabilities, because he is not of the blood. With greater awareness of his son-in-law's plight, the head of the family business can greatly improve the son-in-law's standing in the close corporation. I truly hope that this problem gets the attention it deserves.

MANAGEMENT OF THE CLOSE CORPORATION

2

Experts in the field of appraising companies invariably tell you that the key to the success of any business is the capability of its management. In the case of most close corporations, "management" means the owners, because they are the people who run the business. Since many of these close corporations are successful, logic leads to the conclusion that the companies are well managed. Somehow the evaluation of the management of close corporations is not as simple as that.

I think it is fair to say that the owners of the close corporation, who build up the business against great odds, are capable. They have to be, to overcome all the obstacles and problems they encounter in developing the enterprise. From my standpoint, a lot of them are remarkable managers. But the owners' managerial abilities often take a downturn when the business grows to a point where their unilateral control of it can no longer be maintained. Other people must then be given significant positions and responsibilities in the company and the owners must be able to motivate and direct these employees effectively. Their management competence is sorely tested when the next generation of the family joins the company. Contending with nepotism and providing for an orderly transition of authority usually prove to be tough challenges.

In this chapter, I'm going to discuss management weaknesses that I have observed and suggest some workable solutions. As I see it, the four principal problems with the management of close corporations are:

1. Management methods, principles and training are not given enough attention.

25

2. The owners find it difficult to relate to other executives.

3. Very few heads of close corporation pay much attention to the difficulties and resentments that nepotism can produce.

4. The transfer of management leadership to the next generation is done badly.

LACK OF SOPHISTICATION

The management of many close corporations is too informal, undirected and inconsistent. Decisions of consequence are often made with little in-depth fact-gathering or thoughtful consideration. I find it disturbing when a commitment involving tremendous amounts of money and great economic risks to the corporation is resolved at a luncheon meeting, on an "off the top of the head" basis. The owner's "instinct" usually plays a significant role. "Look how well it worked," he'll say later on. But times have changed. Businesses are becoming more complicated and the entrepreneur no longer has all of the applicable facts and circumstances at his fingertips. A mistake by top management can be much more costly.

It makes sense for the management of close corporations to slow down the decision-making process and reduce hip-shooting to a minimum. All those in management who can add something of value to corporate deliberations should have some input in major decisions. More often than not, the process of putting a group together and brainstorming leads to more creative solutions. A good way to make sure this combined input on a subject is obtained, is to hold regular management meetings, preferably weekly. The owners should encourage subordinate executives, including family members, to voice their opinions, and even disagree with suggestions offered by the proprietors. If the owners evidence an attitude of autocracy at these sessions, the result will be censorship of the views of others. No one will dare take them on.

Widely accepted management principles are ignored in many close corporations. For example, well run companies in this country adhere to the principle of "management by objective." Under this procedure specific goals are thoughtfully set and it is the obligation of the executive to achieve them. As an illustration, the head of personnel of a large company, having been told that the annual 40% employee turn-over rate is too high, does not respond, "Next year you can count on that percentage being lower." Instead, applying management by objective, he states: "During our next fiscal year that turn-over rate will be reduced to 20%." The concept is that by fixing a definite objective, however hard it is to do, and notwithstanding the external factors over which no one in the corporation has control, a manager will put in more time and effort in order not to fail. It works. Yet most close corporations pay little or no heed to this procedure.

Perhaps the top management people, the owners, do not want to go out on a limb and make projections that they have to meet. It's easier for them to formulate the goals for everyone else and then chastize subordinates who don't measure up to the demands. A senior executive in a close corporation that operates in this fashion was asked whether or not "management by objective" was practiced in his company. His answer was very revealing: "Our guiding management principle is management by apology."

Long range planning is usually scoffed at. "Why waste time worrying about where we'll be in five years? I can't predict where we'll wind up at the end of this fiscal year." You often hear this kind of comment. Marketing plans generally receive the same brush-off from the owner-executives. In fact, many of them do not distinguish between marketing and sales.

Management training

I sometimes suspect that standard management methods are ignored in close corporations because top management does not really comprehend them. This is understandable. A good number, perhaps the majority, of close corporation owners have not been trained for their roles. Some have had a very limited education. Others are college graduates who majored in liberal arts subjects. Even those who pursued a business curriculum may have only scratched the surface of effective management. The answer to this problem is for more close corporation owners to get involved in continuing management training. A good way to start is by attending courses and seminars at business schools in the area. Another possibility is to attend the Small Business Management Program given by the Harvard Business School. For three weeks in each of three years, attendees get helpful instruction on important facets of management. The education and training programs put on by the Young Presidents

Organization (YPO) are terrific. They are open only to younger top executives of close corporations (in by 40 and out by 50). A consulting firm can be brought in to train the leaders of the company in specific management areas.

HOW OWNERS DEAL WITH MANAGERS
AND EMPLOYEES

Dealing with the close corporation proprietor in his capacity as chief executive officer is very difficult. He has not come up the ranks, moving step-by-step to the top spot, because of demonstrated competence. The entrepreneur is the president of the corporation because he owns the company. If he learns how to conduct himself properly as the management leader, that's great. But there is no requirement that he do so. And nobody can do anything about his weaknesses as a manager.

Many owners conduct themselves like kings or dictators. They will often say something like: "This is my business and I can run it the way I see fit." Consistent with this outlook, they glory in the attitude that anyone but them is replaceable. They consider ownership to be a justification for venting their spleens when an employee fails to perform as the stockholder-president thinks he should. Regular and objective evaluations of subordinates are seldom held. Instead, they give performance appraisals to executives only when compensation is being discussed—which experts will tell you is the wrong time to do it. As a result, many key employees are fired without ever having been told that they were performing badly.

Owners of sizeable close corporations have to become more aware of the dichotomy between their position as owners and their role as leaders of the management team. Because they are the owners, they can manage in any way that they choose. But if they want the business to grow and prosper, they need effective executives. Consequently, they must be patient, and learn how best to direct, supervise, and motivate their executives. The entrepreneur who ignores his responsibilities as a manager, and browbeats his subordinates, often winds up surrounded by very submissive people who no longer propose their own ideas and are only willing to say what they think the boss wants to hear. Fear becomes their dominant emotion and their creativity is stifled. Their dependence on the owner's sole judgment keeps increasing. Finally, the business itself suffers, for there are limitations on how long a one-man business can remain prosperous and grow. And the situation is even worse when the subordinate executives are family members, especially sons. In such cases, the submissiveness is even more pronounced because the father expects to call the shots in any relationship between him and his sons.

Employees of incorporated partnerships

Employees of incorporated partnerships probably have the most trouble trying to figure out how to relate to the owners. Here we have not one boss, but two kings or dictators. They are peers, each having the same power and authority as the other, irrespective of corporate titles. Rarely are there carefully delineated areas where one of them has complete jurisdiction. Either principal feels privileged to jump in on any issue, even one where the other 50% stockholder has more competence. The need for the partners to communicate a unified point of view is frequently overlooked. It is common for the two partners to take contrary positions regarding the same business matter.

I remember one incorporated partnership where the differences in management attitudes between two partners drove their number one marketing person out of the company. "Gene insists that I submit detailed marketing plans, with back-up market research, strategies— the works. He is constantly nagging me about the sufficiency of my proposals. The other partner, Harry, is always taking me aside and telling me that I'm putting in too much time preparing these 'fancy-dancy' marketing plans. Harry scoffs at their usefulness. He feels I should spend more time improving the sales force and pushing the advertising agency to come up with more effective copy. How can I possibly satisfy both of them!"

It is imperative that the co-owners in an incorporated partnership avoid these conflicting communications. A table of organization must be prepared and distributed, identifying the areas in which each partner is in charge. Executives will then know to whom they are accountable. No longer will they be put in the middle when the two bosses articulate different points of view. If Gene had been given the exclusive responsibility of overseeing the marketing program, the head of marketing would have been spared the anguish of coping with Harry's criticisms. Harry would not get involved with subordinates in that area. If he believed the corporation's marketing was not as effective as it should be, he should discuss it with his partner, Gene. Face-to-face is the proper forum for the partners to air differences of opinion. They can fight about them, compromise, adjust, review or what-have-you, and then ultimately communicate a policy that they both stand behind.

Assistance from consultants

How much help in improving management procedures can close corporations get from consultants? I think that a lot of assistance can be obtained from them. But the close corporation has to pick a consultant who understands and appreciates the special management problems of corporations where the top executives are also the owners. The consultant needs to have a great deal of psychological awareness, particularly when dealing with a family business. I have seen some very good work done by consultants who understood close corporations. Let me give you two illustrations.

A corporation I once advised used to be dominated by one person, the top man. He had a brother in the company as well as his two sons. A good number of unrelated executives also held very important positions. It was the largest company of its kind in the area. The top man was a brilliant, creative, efficient individual who somehow kept abreast of every aspect of the enterprise. He recognized the ability of others and rewarded them very handsomely for their efforts. But he was such a force that all major decisions were essentially made by him. There did not seem to be any future for the company without him. A management consultant was eventually retained. He concluded that it would be impossible for the president to take a back seat on any issue, if he were around. So he recommended that the top man take six weeks off in the winter and vacation a long distance away from the plant. During this period, other executives would have to take command.

The idea worked so well that the vacation period was extended to two months after a few years. Moreover, the confidence of the other senior managers in their own judgments increased remarkably. Even more important, the major domo now found it easier to have others make decisions—just as they did when he was away.

The other example involves a company that was run by three brothers. Their father still had voting control, but he was not active in the business. The brothers had no defined management procedures nor were their respective duties delineated. Their relations with each other and with subordinates were strained. A management consultant was brought in and he turned things around. The company now has an effective table of organization. Regular management meetings are held with agendas and reports. The brothers are involved in strategic planning and outlining objectives. Spirit is high and profits have soared.

Use of outside directors

Another positive force in improving the management of a close corporation is the involvement of outside unrelated directors. Regular meetings of directors are then held, usually on a quarterly basis. The discipline of having to report at a regular meeting of the corporation's directors serves to make the management more effective. Matters are given more time and thought, because executives must make a presentation to a group, including respected outsiders. No one ever wants to make a fool of himself before his peers. This system also helps the executives. Accounting to a board of directors including respected outsiders is more objective and impersonal than the exchange that takes place when an executive goes one to one with the owner of the enterprise, who is also the chief executive.

The presence of these outside directors is also a great help in dealing with emotion-laden issues. They serve as intermediaries. Sons can communicate their needs and problems regarding the owner-father much easier to these people. And because they are usually his appointees, the father will probably pay much more attention to a suggestion, or even a criticism, from the outside directors, relating to the way in which he conducts himself with family members who are in the business. These directors can assist in the transition in management control from fathers to sons.

Outside directors can also step into sibling rivalry situations, cool the hostility, and work out solutions based on objective criteria such as the childrens' respective abilities, experience and commitment to the business. In many such cases their involvement will make the offspring in the business a lot more effective as executives. They will have the benefit of guidelines worked out with the assistance of experienced managers. When the partners in an incorporated partnership reach an impasse on a major issue, these outside directors become a force for compromise without either principal losing face. They can play a vital role in making a partner, who has started to give less attention to the business, understand the serious consequences that his lesser commitment can cause, and essentially pressure him to get back to work.

Is it difficult to find qualified people to serve as directors of the close corporation? Not at all. There are entrepreneurs who have sold their businesses and are looking for something to keep them involved in business matters. Retired executives of large companies are also available. Even some active businessmen can be tapped for these jobs. A good source are close corporation owners who endorse this board of directors concept. A number of bank officers and other executives can be found. It is not important for the selected individuals to have a first hand knowledge of the close corporation's business or industry. I have heard a highly regarded management consultant to close corporations state his belief that it is better if an individual is not intimately familiar with the company's type of business. It avoids preconceived opinions.

Hiring outside directors is not a costly affair. Many of them, good people, will serve for $1,000 to $1,500 a meeting. This is a bargain when one considers the great benefits to the close corporation that their involvement can produce.

Nepotism

A son coming into a business owned by his father has a number of prejudices to contend with. The rank and file resent him from the day he starts. From their vantage point, they have to fight for everything they get in the company. They are always being tested and judged. "Then in comes this kid, who in a short while is going to have an important job and make a lot of money. Just because his old man owns the company." The son's difficulty in obtaining a sense of achievement goes unnoticed by his fellow employees. All they see is his "easy street."

A lot of the top executives hate the son because his father, who is so tough and hard-nosed with them, is so generous with his child. A typical observation is: "I had to fight with the old man for almost ten

TRANSITION

Not only must management of the close corporation be improved, transition must be provided for. This is a complex matter in the close corporation, where there is no mandatory retirement age and continuing participation in the enterprise is an important part of the owner's *raison d'etre*. Nevertheless, owners often fail to bring others into key relationships because they do not recognize how important that is to the future of the corporation.

I served as a consultant to a very large life insurance agency for many years. One of my tasks was to assist agents in developing a fact-finding form for estate planning clients. One of the crucial questions, if the agent learned that the client owned a close corporation business, was: "Are you a key man?" Most of the agents, even those who were very experienced, felt this was a sound inquiry. After many years of playing the role of a doubting Thomas, I convinced them that the term, "key man," was much too vague. First of all, it is hard, even for the most conceited individual, to blurt out: "Certainly I am the key man. Without me the business would never be successful." This is not considered to be in good taste.

The real problem with the term, however, is that it does not focus attention on the truly unique aspects of the owner's role in the company. "Key man" conjures up visions of hard work in the plant, supervising production, running around the country calling on customers. The father-owner may no longer do that at all. In his mind, he is less involved in the business now, and his sons are more active. Thus he concludes that he is not a key man. Of course, his assessment may be totally wrong.

Let me offer some examples of the difference between the key man mind-set and the reality:

1. The close corporation has borrowed a substantial amount every year from the same bank. All loans have been repaid. Who deals with the bank? Dad. He tells everyone that the current president of the bank was the company's loan officer for many years. Dad and this bank officer have the closest ties. Is dad a key man in this financing area? Of course. But unless there is a shift to the sons in the dealings with the bank, there is a great risk that dad's death will precipitate a reduction in the line of credit.

2. The major customer of the close corporation is a large chain. Dad captured the account many years ago. A senior executive of the customer is dad's good friend. One of dad's remaining areas of active involvement in the business is entertaining the "right" people in the customer organization. Dad is surely a key person in the relationship with this customer.

3. The close corporation is a sales agent for a manufacturer of ladies wear. The president of the manufacturing concern and father (Harry) have been friends for years. Harry's son, Robert, is now the force in the sales corporation. He is an excellent salesman and business man. But nothing has been done to cement a relationship between Robert and the head of the manufacturing company. There can be no effective management transition in these circumstances, unless Harry gets Robert the recognition he needs with the manufacturer. Absent that, the future of the corporation's business is in jeopardy.

I know of many examples like these. They all add up to a failure of the present top management to arrange for an effective management transition to the next generation. Done gradually, with thought and the cooperation of the senior management person, the transition can be accomplished.

Holding unrelated executives

A very important part of this management transition is developing a program to hold unrelated executives when the head of the business dies, or ceases to run the enterprise because of incapacity or choice. This can be a critical concern for the family. The sons need the support of these experienced people when they take over after dad's death or retirement. Absent a program developed with some involvement of these key employees, the chief executive's death can signal a lot of trouble. This is the time when these executives may band together, show their muscle and make tough demands. If nothing has been discussed with them during the top man's lifetime, they have a rationalization when he dies. "No one worried what would happen to us after the boss died. He left us at the mercy of the kids. We better make sure that they don't trample on us."

One of my clients recognized the need to have the commitment of the heads of marketing, production and finance after his death. He designed and discussed with these individuals an incentive compensation plan, to take effect at that time. It would yield them a good deal of money, if the earnings of the corporation remained strong. At the death of this owner, there should be no mutiny or conflicts. The importance of these unrelated executives has been acknowledged. They have financial security and growth opportunity. More close corporations should follow this example.

CONTROL OF THE CLOSE CORPORATION | 3

What does control of a close corporation mean? Generally it means holding more than 50% of the outstanding voting stock.* Stock with voting power is the only stock that counts in this regard. Consequently, someone who owns much less than a majority of the close corporation's stock can still have voting control. The majority voting stockholder has the right to elect directors. It is the directors who make major policy and operating decisions for the close corporation. The directors are also the people, generally, who elect and compensate the officers of the company. If it is not the directors who select certain officers, then it is the stockholders—which gives the person in control the same right of governance.

The controlling stockholder, for his best protection, should have a majority of the board of directors made up of his designees. This gives him control of the corporation at all times. It is sometimes difficult for a father who has two sons actively engaged in the corporation to achieve this goal. The board of directors can be made up of the father and his two sons, but this arrangement puts the father in a minority position if the sons choose to defy him. For this reason, many family businesses wind up having four directors: the father, the mother and the two children-executives. Although the alliance between husband and wife means that the controlling stock-

---

* Nevertheless, the certificate of incorporation or by-laws of some older corporations may require more than a majority vote of stockholders before certain kinds of actions can be taken. For example, the concurrence of two-thirds of the stockholders entitled to vote may be needed for a sale or exchange of substantially all the assets of the enterprise, or a merger or reorganization. Sometimes this two-thirds approval of stockholders for these major steps is mandated by state law.

holder and his spouse cannot be outvoted, there can still be a stalemate.

The controlling stockholder's safeguard against insurrection, and his method of ending a stalemate, is the annual meeting of the corporation. Let us imagine that sons, who represent a majority of the board of directors, do certain things in defiance of their father, the controlling stockholder. At the next annual meeting of the shareholders, the majority voting stockholder can kick out the sons as directors and pick his own people. Because the stockholder with voting control wields this ultimate power, it is rare for others to challenge him.

I adhere to the principle that there should always be a majority of the directors who are loyal to the owner who has voting control. This strategy eliminates the risk that control will be lost until the annual meeting is held. Outside directors selected by the person in control can help to assure this majority voice.

SIGNIFICANCE OF MAINTAINING CONTROL

Control of close corporations is not exhibited frequently. Since these entities are governed informally, very few votes are ever taken. Nevertheless, maintaining control of the close corporation is of major significance for three reasons:

1. It guarantees the controlling stockholder the right to direct the business and affairs of the corporation. He decides on the identity of the executives and the roles they will play. This makes him the dominant force in the company.

2. The person in control can derive whatever economic return from the close corporation that he wants. He determines how much compensation and benefits he gets. This is most important, since the close corporation is usually the major source of his income and support. The controlling stockholder also fixes the salary and perquisites of everyone else. He can make sure that nobody makes more than he does—irrespective of their worth as employees. This total power over the amounts paid out to executives, is very important to the owner in later years. At that juncture, he can work much less and still earn a great deal.

3. No major change in the character of the close corporation can take place unless it is consistent with the goals and desires of the individual who has voting contol. He decides whether the business should be sold or merged, whether it should be recapitalized, or whether another company should be acquired.

Self-image: the truth about Tom

Maintaining control of the close corporation is also a way of securing prestige. The controlling stockholder can maintain his image, and gratify his ego, by preserving the identity between himself and the business. Keeping the title of chief executive officer, and referring to the close corporation as "my company," gives him status with his peers.

I recall one instance where a woman named Mary, the wife of an 80 year old businessman, came to see me, very troubled. Her middle-aged sons were active in the family business. As a matter of fact, they were running the company. Mary complained to me that her husband, Tom, was working much too hard. She feared that such a pace would seriously reduce his life span.

I knew that Tom's pattern was to come into the office for a few hours in the morning, have a long lunch with his cronies, and spend almost every weekday afternoon at his country club, golfing or playing cards. In the winter Tom and Mary spent several months in a warm climate. I was very confused by the contradiction between my understanding of Tom's way of life—which was easygoing and virtually devoid of pressures—and his wife's concern that he was doing much more than a man of his age should. Seeking some explanation, I questioned Mary about the basis for her conclusion that Tom was so deeply involved in the business.

Her answer was revealing. "Milt, every time we are with other people, at dinner or at a party, Tom tells everyone that even though the company is now much larger, and he has a lot of good executives, including his sons, he never had as many pressures and responsibilities. His standard line is that he's fortunate to be blessed with the energy to cope with the problems he faces every day." I explained to Mary that Tom was using this technique to "blow his own horn," and build himself up. It was his way of combatting the image of the former business giant who has now taken a back seat.

SETTLING DISPUTES

Control is often used by the head of the family as a means of serving as a referee for his children who are in the business. The idea is that dad, with this power, can move in and keep peace when the siblings start battling among themselves. I have never thought much of this approach. If the combat between the children is really intense, the father will find it hard to maintain harmony. In any event, getting in the middle of such battles will become less and less inviting for dad as time goes on.

A STRATEGY FOR SHIFTING CONTROL

At some point in time, the control of a close corporation shifts from the controlling stockholder to others. This usually occurs on the death of the controlling stockholder, but it can also take place during his lifetime if he decides to give up that power. Nevertheless, a father's transfer of control over his business during his lifetime usually requires some assurances. He must be convinced that: (1) his financial well-being will be preserved; (2) his wife will be adequately taken care of after his death; and (3) his image will be preserved.

Sons who want to take over control of a family business have to recognize these needs and satisfy them. If the sons resist, gripe about the amount that dad is taking out of the company, and question the level of support their mother will require when she is a widow, then the father will become insecure and anxious. He won't risk the loss of control. Instead, the sons should strive to assure the father that they want him to receive enough from the business so that he can live comfortably for the rest of his life and that after his death, the business will take care of their mother.

Here is an arrangement that can be used to shift control and future equity growth to the sons from the older father, while protecting the security and position of both parents:

1. The father exchanges his common stock for non-cumulative, non-voting preferred stock. This means his equity in the enterprise is frozen. The preferred stock cannot be worth more than its par or liquidation value. On the other hand, in case the business is

sold or the corporation is liquidated, dad gets his money first. The sons get nothing until dad receives the full value of his preferred stock.

2. The father gets a contract for life, assuring him of the level of compensation and the perquisites that he needs to live on.

3. A provision is included in the father's agreement obligating the business to pay his wife a stated amount of post death compensation for as long as she should survive him. In addition, the agreement can require the corporation to purchase the father's preferred stock from the mother, after his death, upon terms.

4. All the status symbols that are important to the father are preserved for him. He can continue to hold a significant corporate title such as Chairman of the Board.

5. The father's office remains his, and there are no announcements whatsoever to banks, customers or the outside world of the change in his position.

This plan has many variations. The crucial factors in each instance, however, are a binding commitment for the economic security of the controlling stockholder and his spouse and a preservation of the stockholder's image.

Sometimes a "sweetener" can be given in connection with the shift of control to the next generation. The sons purchase the father's voting stock, with payments made over a period of years, together with interest. This gives the father capital gain on the installments of the purchase price that he receives. Of course, the voting stock may be too expensive for the boys to buy. In that case, the value of the voting stock can be watered down by creating two classes of common stock, voting and non-voting. A much smaller portion of the equity is then attributed to the voting stock by issuing many more shares of non-voting than voting.

DE FACTO CONTROL

It often happens in family companies that the person who is legally in control of the enterprise is not actually in charge. I have seen a number of situations where the father was the owner of a majority of the voting stock, but his sons made all the decisions and managed the business completely. The father spent only a modest amount of time at the office, basically for the sake of having some-thing to do. The patriarch hung on to the controlling stock position as his "security blanket," unwilling to put his complete trust in his children. In fact, the retention of voting control by an inactive family head, notwithstanding the fact that his sons are truly running the show, is the rule; turning over the voting stock to the next generation during the father's lifetime is the exception.

What do most children do under these circumstances? They grin and bear it, although they may greatly resent the father's role. A very common observation by a hardworking son, on the eve of his father's return from a winter's stay in a warm climate, goes something like this: "It is so peaceful when dad is away. We really get things done so much more effectively when he is not around. As soon as dad comes back, he drifts in and out of the plant, bugging us with questions and constantly criticizing and disagreeing with us. He drives us up a wall. Milt, no matter how experienced you may be, if you're not on top of things, you can't make sound judgments. Frankly, my brother and I have learned to let dad's suggestions and comments go in one ear and out the other." Humoring the "old man," because he still holds the legal power, is the way in which his offspring paint the picture of their business relationship.

The father, of course, sees it very differently. "If I hadn't gotten involved when I got back from Florida, the boys would have put in a new assembly line and killed our profits for the year." The persistent reference to his children in the business as "boys," irrespective of their ages, is a tip-off concerning the father's basic attitude. He views himself as a senior statesman, with greater maturity and wis-dom. His role in the business is to use his many more years of involvement as a restraint against the foolhardiness that he believes is exhibited, from time to time, by all aggressive younger individuals "who have not lived through the tough and lean years." Invariably, the older father is much more conservative and negative than his sons. Risk taking and change are not what he is looking for. At his stage of life, preserving the status quo and maintaining peace of mind are more important than striving to double the sales of the company.

A trained observer recognizes that each side in this struggle over-states the case. But the merit of each point of view is not the issue. These deeply felt, antagonistic attitudes lead to a format of governance that is clearly not in the best interests of an enterprise fighting to make it in a highly competitive business world. As I indicated in Chapter 2, outside directors or a management consultant may be able to step in and work out a transition in control or some other arrangement that effectively solves the problems. The corporation's lawyer or accountant, even though he has a close relationship with the combatants, is usually not too effective because he has allegiances to both father and sons. More often than not, despite all efforts to work out a satisfactory compromise, the conflicts continue until the death or incapacity of the father brings about the transfer of total control to the sons.

There have been a few instances during my practice where sons refused to accept *de facto* control, unless the father relinquished the majority vote as well. This approach stripped the father of his power and his right to second guess and veto.

I remember one confrontation very well. The oldest son, acting as spokesman for the others of his generation, who accompanied him, confronted his father with an ultimatum. Either turn over the voting stock to them or they were going to walk out of the company. They quickly reassured the father about his economic security by offering him a lifetime consultation employment contract, with continuing fringe benefits, and a lesser amount of deferred compensation for their mother following his death. But they would brook no compromises or alternatives. It was a "take it or leave it" proposal—which the father quickly accepted. The probability is that this kind of family unpleasantness will continue, and will increase, unless more fathers, who have really abdicated the leadership role, turn over complete control of the business to their children.

EFFECT OF OWNER'S DEATH

Control generally passes at death to family members who are active in the business. That makes sense. They are the individuals who are best qualified to run the show. If the mother knows nothing about the business she is a bad choice. Sometimes a father thinks of giving his wife voting control, to avoid controversies between the children who are active in the company. This is a very difficult and distasteful position for the wife, who has to resolve conflicts between knowledgeable children with little business experience of her own. It is unpleasant for the children, because they have to go to mother, hat in hand, for approval of many actions. All in all, the arrangement is bad.

When the father decides he will hold on to voting control of the corporation until his death, the children in the business have legitimate worries. Until his death, the father can change his will and leave the voting control to anyone he sees fit. What if he has a change of heart, or undergoes a change of personality, and bequeaths the voting stock to his wife or someone other than the children working in the business? This could put those offspring in a terrible position. A simple cure for this anxiety is an agreement obligating father's estate, shortly after his death, to sell his voting stock to those children who are then active participants in the business. The price and terms should be spelled out as well.

When there are two or more offspring working in the corporation, an equal disposition of voting stock to them results in no one person any longer having control. For example, if a father owning 100% of the voting stock, leaves it equally, by will, to his two sons, each of the sons will then have only a 50% interest. Each son has a veto, but affirmative action will require their joint approval.

I have been involved with a number of fathers who concluded that one child working in the business was much more capable than the others. As a result, voting control was bequeathed to that son. Nevertheless, the father did not want this decision to cause a significant difference in the equity that each child received. How do you get the voting control into the hands of one child without causing that descendant to have a much more valuable stock interest than his siblings?

Here again, the creation of two classes of common stock is the answer. To illustrate: dad's 100 shares of the single class of common stock is converted into 100 shares of voting common and 10,000 of non-voting common. The rights and benefits of the two classes of stock are identical, with a single exception. Only the holders of the voting common can vote. Son number 1 gets 51 shares of the voting common and 5,000 shares of the non-voting common. Son number 2 gets 49 shares of voting common and the same 5,000 shares of non-voting common. The equity advantage of son number 1 is 2 shares of voting common. This is 2 shares out of the 10,100 shares that are outstanding—or about 2/10 of 1% of the equity.

TRUST HOLDING CONTROL

What is to be done if no family members are active in the business—or they are not competent to exercise control? A trust of the controlling stock interest is usually the answer. The father selects one person (or perhaps more) that he feels is qualified to make decisions about the business and would be able to relate to the management effectively. That person is the trustee, who votes the stock and exercises the control. The beneficiaries, who receive any income produced by the trust fund and ultimately receive the property, are members of the father's family.

When there is a minority non-family stockholder, a trust can also safeguard the control position of the family. Take the case where an elderly stockholder owns two-thirds of the voting stock and another individual, very active in the business, owns the other one-third. Suppose the holder of the 66-2/3% interest has three children. In the event that he transfers his stockholdings to the children equally, each of them will receive a little more than 22%. If one child holding 22% joins forces with the stockholder owning the one-third interest, they will represent a majority vote—about 55.5%. To guard against this possibility, the two-thirds stock interest should be put in trust. The trust instrument should specify that the trustees must vote the shares as a block. This way, the risk of splintering is avoided.

Bank as trustee

When a trust holds control of a close corporation, the identity of the trustee becomes a serious issue. If no family members are qualified to exercise control, entrepreneurs often choose their bank to serve as trustee. The bank is chosen because it has substance, people who understand business, responsibility, and continuity. Nevertheless, banks are generally reluctant to undertake this responsibility. The role of trustee is risky, calling for a significant level of involvement. In most states, there is no compensation arrangement which entitles a bank to receive the much larger commissions that it justifiably should receive for overseeing the activities of a business.

Compare the situation of a bank serving as a trustee of two trusts, each with principal of $1,000,000. The first trust fund is made up of marketable securities. The second consists of a controlling stock interest in a close corporation that manufactures widgets. The portfolio of securities can be handled by people trained in the investment field. When they decide on a good investment in certain stocks, for example, they buy for a host of trusts they are managing.

The problems of the bank are more complex with respect to the business interest. It has to make sure the company has good management and figure out ways to keep those executives happy. It must make difficult decisions about major capital expenditures, new product development, research, acquisitions and many other significant matters. The bank may receive more commissions for its services as trustee of the trust owning the close corporation stock. But the additional amount will not come close to compensating the bank for its much greater efforts and risks.

As a consequence, the bank that is appointed as a trustee of the stock of a close corporation, very soon starts thinking about selling that stock. If a meaningful price can be obtained, the beneficiaries of the trust will receive a good income. The principal will be in a form that can be invaded more quickly and easily to meet emergent substantial needs. The bank is relieved of the risks and pressures that go with overseeing the operations of a business.

I have worked out special compensation arrangements with a bank, in a few instances, when the client felt that the institution was clearly the best choice as trustee of his controlling stock interest. First, the bank was entitled to receive all of its regular commissions. In addition, the will directed that a representative of the bank, selected by the institution, would be elected as an officer and director of the corporation. This individual would participate in the management of the business, usually in a capacity such as "Financial Vice President." The compensation that he would receive was also spelled out. This combination of the commissions and compensation made it economically worthwhile for the bank to take on the responsibilites. I think that we will see more of this kind of arrangement in the future.

Individuals as trustees

There are many owners who prefer to select individuals as trustees of their controlling interest. Some entrepreneurs don't think that bank personnel can do the job. Others are bothered about who will be acting for the bank in the future. They want to have complete control over the identity of the people who will serve. In those cases where the close corporation has outside directors, those individuals become good choices for the job. Interestingly, when a bank officer who has been serving as a director of a corporation is tapped to served as a trustee—in his individual capacity—the head of the bank's trust department will undoubtedly fume. The trust man feels that the officer should have declined to serve, in which event the bank would have been named. That is sheer petulance. The bank was never in the running.

A mix, with some outsiders and some family members acting as trustees, is a good idea. In one situation that we worked on, one of the two sons who was involved in the business was picked to be a co-trustee; the other son was to be elected a director of the corporation. Neither son will be in a controlling position, for there will always be at least three trustees and directors serving. But their appointment will assure that the family members remain informed and involved.

Special problems can arise where unrelated individuals who are active in the management of the business serve as trustees of a trust that holds stock of the close corporation. These executives have a conflict of interest. In their individual capacity, they are seeking the most money, the greatest benefits and the best way of life that they can obtain from the corporation. But when they act as trustees on behalf of the owners of the equity, their job is to make sure that those in management are highly productive and receive as compensation and perquisites only what is fair and reasonable.

On any issue where there is a clash between the executive's personal ambitions and his trustee obligation, the doubts are resolved against him. Consequently, in case of a challenge to the amount that he is paid, or a benefit that was given to him, the executive serving as a trustee will be at a distinct personal disadvantage. The dual role is also a source of concern to the beneficiaries of the trust. It will be hard for them to believe that the trustee-executive is really looking out for their interests. These beneficiaries will undoubtedly feel that the trustee who works for the enterprise is primarily motivated in all decisions by a "what's in it for me?" attitude.

A very desirable choice as a trustee of a trust having control of a close corporation is a member of its accounting firm. Very often this professional is fully familiar with the business and the key employees. He is respected by them, which is a very important advantage. If the accountant serves as trustee, his firm cannot certify the corporation's financial statements. This prohibition applies to any company in which a partner in the accounting firm holds stock, individually or as trustee.

I know of two instances where the majority stockholder decided to name his accountant as trustee notwithstanding this rule. He felt the accountant was by far the best person to be in control of the enterprise. The result of this decision is that another firm of accountants will be called in to conduct the audit and provide the needed certification.

Thought must be given to the method of compensating individual trustees. The stock that they hold may receive no income. How then will these people be paid for their services? This situation can be handled in the same way as that involving a bank. Direct that these trustees shall be elected as officers and directors of the corporation and fix the income they will receive for their services. To provide greater incentive some of the compensation can be tied to increases in the corporation's net income.

EFFECT OF OWNER'S PHYSICAL OR MENTAL IMPAIRMENT

A father's continued control of the family corporation at an advanced age is fraught with peril. What would happen, for example, if he suffered a stroke or underwent a significant change in competence or personality? Appointing a guardian or conservator is traumatic, expensive, cumbersome and time-consuming. Furthermore, the most probable appointee as guardian or conservator, his wife, is usually a poor choice. If she has not been active in the business, all of the problems associated with an inexperienced mother directing a family business, that were discussed earlier in this chapter, will arise once she steps into her husband's shoes.

Power of attorney

A power of attorney is a much simpler technique for dealing with the physical or mental impairment of the senior who is in control of the entity. This is an instrument which empowers one or more individuals to act on behalf of the person who executes the power. In this instance, the father can execute a power of attorney in favor of his sons or other persons, authorizing them to take over if he becomes incapacitated. The disadvantage of a power of attorney, if is it unconditional, is that the holder of the power can do what he wants with the father's property before the father is unable to fend for himself. This can be very threatening to the father.

One way to protect the father is to provide in the power of attorney that it is not operative unless and until he is unable to manage his own affairs with reason and judgment. How is that to be determined? A commonly employed method is to require a certificate to that effect from two qualified physicians. Unfortunately, there is a question in some jurisdictions as to the validity of this kind of "springing power of attorney"—one that only becomes effective upon the happening of an event. This has caused many attorneys not to use it.

Advisors kept searching for some other way to use the much simpler power of attorney, and yet eliminate the client's concerns about granting his children, or anyone else, rights to deal with his property holdings while he was healthy. They finally hit upon a procedure that is gaining popularity. Father executes the general power of attorney designating the individuals he wants to take control of the company if he were to become disabled. But he does not deliver the instrument to them. Instead, it is deposited with the father's attorney, to be released only if, and when, the father's capacity to act is impaired.

While this is an ingenious concept, I have found that it creates some problems. There are a lot of close corporation owners who do not have sufficient trust and confidence in their attorney to put this kind of power in his hands. The older family head may worry that the lawyer now has closer ties with his sons who deal with him more. This arrangement is a difficult one for the lawyer too. How does he suggest the idea to his client without seeming to be presumptuous or power hungry, and in a manner that enables the client to reject the idea without impairing the relationship? If that hurdle is overcome, and the attorney becomes the sole arbiter of whether the father is or is not incapacitated, anything less than an obvious conclusion can cause him serious embarrassment. A situation where there are some doubts about the level of the father's reason and judgment could put the lawyer in the middle of a serious family dispute:- the wife contending that her husband is still able and the sons, who are the people who take control if the power is released, urging that he is not.

Revocable trust

Our office has recently tried another idea, the revocable trust, to accomplish a shift of control of the close corporation in the event of the senior's physical or mental impairment. The father puts his voting stock of the corporation in the trust, designating himself as the sole trustee. The instrument provides that he will cease to serve as a trustee and will be succeeded by those family members who are active in the business, in the event he is found to be incompetent. To avoid a court proceeding over the issue of the father's competence, the trust instrument should set forth a definition of the term which refers to the father's inability to make sound judgments regarding the company. A unanimous decision that the father is incompetent, made by a group of individuals named in the trust agreement, would then be determinative.

Obviously, the father will be very concerned about the identity of the people who will be empowered to decide conclusively that he is incompetent. For his protection, at least one of the group should be an individual who will be reluctant to make that finding. His wife, personal attorney, or close friend may be selected for that reason. The procedure for succession should be spelled out as well, to make sure that the father will not be taken advantage of.

The fact that the father can revoke the trust and end the arrangement, whenever he chooses to do so, is reassuring to him. It is also easier for the revocable trust to be accepted, because it relates only to the controlling stockholder's interest in the family business. His other assets are free and clear of the trust. The mother will like that better too, because in case of her husband's incapacity she will be able to serve as guardian or conservator of the cash and other liquid assets.

EQUAL PARTNERSHIPS

When there are two individuals or families, each holding a 50% interest in the close corporation, no one is in control. These are truly equal partnerships. Neither 50% stockholder can control the other.

The two factions must agree before anything can be done. Sharing and compromise are the essence of the relationships between 50-50 stockholders. The assumption is that all financial benefits will be shared equally.

One of the touchy issues that comes up in these incorporated partnerships is who shall be the president of the company. One solution is to have one of the partners, perhaps Dan, serve as president and the other partner, Dave, as chairman of the board. If the chairman of the board office is not desired, then perhaps the older of Dan and Dave will be elected president. In some instances the solution is to have Dan and Dave take turns. Each one serves as president for a few years. Once in a while the title of president is given to the "outside man" who deals more with customers, suppliers and banks.

When one of the equal stockholders transfers the stock to more than one family member, either by testamentary bequest or by a lifetime transfer, thought must be given to protecting the 50% voting status. Here again, dividing up the stock between offspring creates the risk that a son or daughter will join forces with the other 50% interest. The trust talked about earlier in this chapter can be used here. But there is another format that is tailored to this situation which is easier to administer. I'll explain it using an example.

The Stanley family, with three sons in the business, holds 50% of the outstanding stock. The Rogers family, with a son and son-in-law active in the company, owns the other 50% of the stock. Mr. Stanley and Mr. Rogers are about to give their stockholdings to their children. They want the 50-50 voting relationship to be maintained between the families. All concerned want the five children (three Stanleys and three Rogers) to enter into a buy-sell agreement, so that at the death of any child—or the son-in-law's death in the case of the Rogers daughter—the child's stock will be bought back by the corporation. The families are willing to have a child's death reduce that family's equity in the enterprise. But they still want the equal voting rights to be maintained.

The close corporation is recapitalized. Two classes of common stock, Class A and Class B, are created. The Stanley family gets the A stock; the Rogers family gets the B. No matter how many shares of a class of stock are outstanding at any time, the holders of each class, by majority vote, are entitled to elect one-half the directors of the corporation and cast a 50% vote on any issue which calls for action by the stockholders. Each of the three Stanley sons gets 100 shares of Class A stock. The Rogers son and daughter each receive 150 shares of the Class B stock.

What happens upon the death of a Stanley son? His stock is sold to the corporation. That means that there are now only 500 shares of stock outstanding. Two hundred shares of A are held by the remaining Stanleys; and 300 shares are still owned by the Rogers family. The equity of the Rogers family has increased to 60% (300/500). But the two Stanley sons will still hold a 50% vote.

MINORITY STOCKHOLDERS

How does a minority stockholder protect himself against a controlling stockholder? This can be the problem of any stockholder in a close corporation where another person holds more than 50% of the voting power. It also applies to one of a group of stockholders in the event that others, who own more than 50%, get together and treat him as a minority stockholder. The majority can elect their slate of directors and do terrible things to the minority stockholder: fire him, reduce his compensation substantially, or greatly increase theirs.

At the outset of this kind of relationship, a minority stockholder can try to obtain an agreement that essentially upgrades him to a 50% position. For instance, the agreement can state that he must be elected a director, and that nothing can be done by the directors or stockholders unless he agrees. But chances are he will not be given this status. The next step is to get protection for his economic position in the corporation and require his concurrence as a stockholder on major actions. Thus, the minority stockholder is given an employment contract and the relationship between his compensation and benefits level and that of the other stockholders is fixed. His consent must be obtained for: a sale of the business, the issuance of stock to others, a merger with another entity, borrowing money in excess of a certain amount, or a major capital expenditure. Whether these conditions are obtainable is a matter of negotiation. It depends, of course, on how important the controlling stockholder feels the anticipated contributions of the minority stockholder will be to the success of the business.

A minority stockholder does have some redress in any event. If he is forced out of the corporation, then he picks up the rights of any inactive stockholder who holds an equity interest in the close corporation. He screams for dividends. He charges those owners who are still working in the company with taking more compensation than they are worth and using corporate dollars for personal benefits. In New Jersey, we have created a special remedy for an "oppressed" minority stockholder. He can sue for the appointment of a receiver or custodial director of the corporation, or seek the liquidation of the company. This is part of the so-called deadlock statute* which is discussed in Chapter 12, "Incompatability in the Business Marriage."

The statute is so new that the factors necessary to establish the "oppression" which triggers the statutory remedy are not yet clear. If the minority stockholder's salary is cut without justification, and he argues that he acquired the stock with the expectation of a lifelong job at that level, that may be a sufficient showing of oppression. No one is sure. Despite the lack of interpretation to date, it is a valuable additional protection for a minority stockholder.

---

* N.J.S.A. 14A:12-7.

HOW TO RETAIN
UNRELATED EXECUTIVES

4

When the business of the close corporation grows beyond a certain point, it can no longer be run effectively only by family members. There may not be enough of them available, or the children may not be ready to assume the responsibilities of management leadership. The company must now hire outsiders, described in this book as unrelated executives, for key positions in the organization. Finding competent people, integrating them into the management of the family business or incorporated partnership, and keeping them happy, pose serious challenges for the close corporation owners.

GENERAL ATTITUDES TOWARD
WORKING FOR A CLOSE CORPORATION

Owners of close corporations should work hard to hold on to good unrelated executives. They are not easy to find. Aggressive, capable people are not attracted to close corporations. They prefer a career with companies where ownership and management are separated. Here are some of the advantages they see in those entities, and a look at the disadvantages they see in a close corporation:

1. The top officers of the large corporation with widely diffused stockholdings have usually come up the management ranks. This gives rise to a legitimate hope: "If I work hard and do a very good job, some day I can be the president of this company."

In the close corporation the owners are the top executives. This is more an expression of their prerogatives than the result of an objective determination that they are best suited for these positions.

2. The competition among executives for promotion is much fairer. Sure there are politics and in-fighting. But that is much less troublesome than contending with the owner's sons, sons-in-law, nephews and daughters.

3. The company is owned by the public, pension funds and institutions. These stockholders are much more dependent on the competence of management. The increased earnings that bring about an appreciation in the value of the stock will be produced through the efforts and talents of these managers. Holding on to these key executives and keeping them happy is of major importance to the stockholders.

The owners of close corporations generally have a very different outlook. They believe that the success of the enterprise depends on them. Other management people are cast in the mold of helpful, but always replaceable, subordinates.

4. The big, broad based companies have mandatory retirement for executives. This means that openings will develop for those who are below them on the management ladder.

Owners of close corporations often die with their boots on. Even those who retire do it at the point in time that they choose. There is no predictable retirement age.

5. The people running the enterprise, where ownership and management are separated, become rich through rewards for doing their job well. The stockholders, who look to the managers for the protection and growth of their investment, are very willing to compensate them handsomely for a job well done. No one stockholder usually owns a sufficient percentage of the stock that he really feels the impact of a large bonus.

The people in control of the management of close corporations are primarily capitalists—not workers. They may receive most of their income in the form of compensation and benefits, but this is only for tax reasons. An owner-executive measures his riches by how valuable his interest in the corporation is. While the close corporation is a separate entity, the stockholders feel that every raise or perquisite is coming out of their pockets. Part of this reaction stems from the reality that an owner usually holds a significant portion of the corportation's equity. Another reason for this point of view is the "this is mine" concept that so many close corporation proprietors feel down deep.

Professionals who serve those corporations are well aware of this feeling on the part of the principals that they, and not the corporation, are paying. Lawyers and accountants must do more than demonstrate that the bill is a fair reflection of the time that was spent on the matter. The close corporation owner insists that he receive his money's worth. In our firm we have adopted the term, "cost effective," to describe the kind of services that are demanded.

ADVANTAGES CLOSE CORPORATIONS CAN OFFER

Despite the general conception that it is better to be employed as an executive by large companies where ownership and management are separated, the reality may be otherwise. What the big, widely owned corporations have going for them is the fact that men and women who choose career paths are very much influenced by status and outward appearances, and there these corporations are in a far better position. Those entities and their leaders have much greater visibility. Virtually every one of the companies has a highly paid public relations firm building image. The desirability of working for them is promoted by their recruiters at colleges and business schools. "Head Hunters" plug these entities probably because they get much more placement business from them. On the other hand, who is out there promoting to talented young people the virtues of close corporations and the desirability of working for them? Essentially there are no organized efforts to point out the plusses of working for owner-operated companies.

I have had the pleasure of working with a client who expends a lot of time and effort trying to communicate to top candidates some reasons why the role of an executive in the close corporation is better than that of his peer in IBM, DuPont, Exxon, Citicorp and the like. He has made a believer out of me. Rudy Schmidt, Jr., at the age of 32, heads a successful electronics business, of which he is the president and owner of 100% of the common stock. His father, a very wise and wonderful man, converted his stockholdings into preferred stock, relinquished control to Rudy, Jr., and while the father still works for the company, he has taken a back seat to his son.

Rudy, Jr. has attracted to the company a number of very capable unrelated executives, and he attributes a great part of the organization's success to their performance. This unusual young businessman is so committed to the concept that there is a great opportunity for non-owners and non-family members in close corporations, that he regularly attends career days at colleges, advocating coming to work for companies like his. On most occasions, he is the only representative of the enterprises where the owners are the top management. Every once in a while, he tells me, there is someone else.

Let us examine some of these little publicized advantages of working for family businesses and incorporated partnerships:

1. The executive enjoys a much closer relationship with the people who control his career. There are frequent and intimate contacts with the heads of the business. The top brass get to know a lot about the executive and his family, and they often involve themselves in his problems. The converse is usually true as well. The executive becomes privy to a lot of information about the personal life of the owners and their family. For example, the top financial person in many of these companies knows all about the owner's property holdings and sources of income, his obligations, and may play a significant role in the entrepreneur's estate planning. This creates a sense of belonging, an attachment to the enterprise and its stockholders. It is a far cry from the impersonality of the very big corporation led by an ever changing corps of professional managers, who generally try to separate their business and personal lives.

2. There is greater job security for the executive in the close corporation. I recognize that the general feeling is the opposite. But think of the things that happen regularly in the widely-owned public company:

(a) Mass lay-offs resulting from cost trimming programs, designed to make sure that the level of overall company profitability is maintained;

(b) The discharge of even senior executives, because the newly appointed top man wants his own team;

(c) Replacement of the executive whose annual compensation and benefits have reached too high a level, by a much "lower cost" younger man; and (**d**) The termination of an executive who is satisfactory at his current job, but does not have the potential to move up higher on the management ladder, especially where the company has an"up or out" policy.

In entrepreneurial companies, it is rare to see an important executive terminated because the corporation's return on invested capital is insufficient. Changes in the top management do not happen, since the owners fill that role, so that the "new broom sweeps clean" doctrine does not apply. The detached (some call them cold-blooded) personnel practices and performance standards usually do not exist. Perhaps most important, the close corporation owners do not have "hatchet men" who do the discharging. They have to deliver the bad news personally to a subordinate with whom they have had a close relationship, and feel the accompanying guilt. It is my observation that it is extremely difficult for an owner of a business to fire an unrelated executive who has been around for a number of years, and as a consequence many employees of questionable competence stay on.

3. The individual holding an important position in the close corporation gets much more responsibility and action. These entities can't carry the very large cadre of executives that one finds in the giant company. Consequently, the employee who is hired for a significant marketing, production or financial role in the family business or incorporated partnership is given much more generalized assignments, and is expected to handle a very broad range of activities. It is unusual to find a detailed job profile or an articulated table of organization. The owners expect him to be able to take "the heat in the kitchen." As a result, the executive in the close corporation gets invaluable experience in a hurry, and his know-how and confidence grow rapidly.

The individual who joins a company, whose top management is made up of the owners and members of his family, is correct in his appraisal that it is unlikely that he ever will be the number one or two person in the organization—no matter how competent he is or how hard and well he works. When he takes a job with a General Motors, he at least has a shot at reaching one of the very highest positions in the organization. But young men and women making the choice have to weigh this very slim chance of getting to the head of this enormous pack, against the much greater probability that they will find themselves in a very circumscribed and limited role, closely superintended by superiors. In the close corporation, with the same talents and hard work, they can enjoy much more authority, recognition and gratification. As someone said to me recently: "The alternatives are somewhat like playing in the major leagues and sitting on the bench a good part of the time, or being an important player on a team in the minor leagues, but not the top star."

4. The probability of being shifted from place to place, like a nomad, is much less in the typical close corporation. This moving around is a very upsetting and common experience for executives in the large publicly owned corporations and their families. A significant reason for the lesser frequency of these transfers in owner-operated companies, is the fact that the heads of the business did not go through this kind of management development. Even in third generation family business, with world-wide locations, the sons generally are not assigned to distant places for training. A father running a business doesn't like to send his children and grandchildren away. And he would have to face the wrath of his wife, if he did so.

Whatever the reasons and motivations, and despite the perceived disadvantages, many close corporations are able to hire good non-family executives. In this chapter we are going to look at the kinds of arrangements that should be provided for such people, so that they will stay on for many years and have the incentive to give their best efforts to the enterprise.

COMPENSATION

The starting point is adequate compensation. In these times of high costs, it takes a lot of dollars to maintain a good standard of living. Unless the unrelated executive has enough income to provide that for himself and his family, he will be looking to move on. Moveover, a good salary for a top level non-stockholder employee is helpful taxwise to the owner-managers. For instance, if the highest paid unrelated executive is getting paid $125,000 a year, rather than only $75,000, it is easier to justify the reasonableness of $250,000 of annual compensation for the owner who serves as the chief executive of the corporation.

Incentives

Somewhere along the line, usually after a meaningful period of years with the company, the important unrelated executive starts to think about "getting a piece of the action." He wants to share in the company's prosperity, because he feels strongly that he is making a significant contribution to this success. Contingent incentive compensation is one of the answers to this desire. The key executive shares in the profits after some figure is reached, or pursuant to a formula that first gives the owners a return on their capital. A typical format is X% of net profits, before taxes, in excess of 15% of the net worth of the corporation at the beginning of the year. The definition of net profits should exclude unusual items such as gains realized from the sale of assets.

The measure should be net profits, not sales or gross income. We have done some work for a corporation that agreed many years ago to pay the head of marketing and sales a sizeable percentage of sales. This format has been disastrous. The employee pushes to make sales, regardless of whether or not they are profitable and the company has trouble keeping its prices competitive, because it has to absorb a sizeable commission which its competitors do not.

If there are several executives who are to receive incentive compensation, it is common to fix a formula for computing the total bonus amount. That amount is then apportioned among them. I have seen some companies that have made the division on the basis of the respective salaries of the participants. This benefits the people in marketing and sales, because they are usually more highly paid than the executives in production or finance.

Every one of the corporations that used this allocation approach dropped it after a while. The owners realized that in years where the increased profits were much more attributable to greatly improved production controls or cost reduction, the marketing head—who may have had a flat year—still received the greatest share. This resulted in serious discontent, which the heads of the business realized was justified.

Another approach to "splitting the pie" is to have the shares fixed by the president or a committee of the board of directors, all of whom are ineligible to receive anything. This system permits special recognition to be given to an executive whose efforts were outstanding in a particular year. If no one stood out, then all executives receive an equal share. But this procedure also has some drawbacks. It fosters competition among the top executives. There must be very clearly delineated criteria to convince those who receive less, that they are being treated fairly. From my observations, for the close corporation that is usually dealing with a limited number of key people, an equal division among the group seems to work best. It fosters cooperation and mutual assistance. Competition is downplayed.

There can be situations where the executives who will share the incentive compensation have a different influence on the company's profits. A personnel (now human resources) director can be very valuable. But his effect on the success of the company can be much less than the head of sales. Some proprietors still cling to the equality concept in this situation, feeling that differentiations in salary and benefits are a better way to reflect the difference in importance. Others provide a somewhat larger share of the pool—but still equally divided—to the top executives, and a smaller per capita segment to the others.

Many owners hesitate to have incentive compensation for unrelated executives because of their concern about charges that net income has been understated arbitrarily. What they picture is the executives screaming about unreasonably high salaries paid to stockholders and the fact that essentially personal items have been charged against income. I think this is an unrealistic fear. A properly drawn incentive compensation plan makes the determination of net income by the corporation's accountants binding and conclusive on all concerned. A good standard is the net income of the corporation that is reported by the accountants for federal income tax purposes, without any adjustments resulting from audit. Those who are sharing incentive compensation are less likely to complain when tax figures are used.

An even more important reason why an executive doesn't make a serious issue about the propriety of certain corporation expenses, which reduce his incentive bonus, is the fact that there is little economic advantage for him to do so. Obviously, the minute he takes a hostile position and threatens the owners with law suits or what-have-you, he risks his future with the company. Putting his good job in jeopardy is not warranted by the amounts involved. To illustrate, Russell is one of four unrelated executives who are entitled to share, equally, 10% of the net profits of the corporation, before taxes. In a particular year, there are $200,000 of company expenses that seem to be more for the benefit of the owners than the business (I have deliberately picked a much higher number than the usual). If all these items are improper deductions from the income of the corporation, the pool that Russell and the three other participants will divide has been understated by $20,000 (10% of $200,000). Russell is maximally out-of-pocket $5,000, before the offset for his income taxes on that amount. It would be foolhardy for Russell to jeopardize his position with the corporation for that amount.

STOCK OWNERSHIP

While sharing in income gives the executive a proprietary feeling, the ultimate goal is equity participation. This elevates the unrelated employee to a new plateau. He becomes an owner. Stock ownership arrangements are also beneficial to the stockholders of the close corporation. They are assured that if the executive grows wealthy, they will be many times richer.

Let me give an example of what I mean. As an additional means of tying him to the business, Russell was given a 5% interest in the equity of the close corporation. The arrangement is that when he leaves the company, dies or is disabled, he (or his estate) will receive 5% of the book value or net worth of the corporation at that time. When the stock came into Russell's hands, the corporation had a total book value of $1,000,000, making the value of Russell's stockholdings $50,000. The business of the company enjoys spectacular success, so that after five years, the overall book value has jumped from $1,000,000 to $10,000,000. Russell's equity has increased tenfold from $50,000 to $500,000. While Russell may have gotten a much greater benefit than was anticipated, the stockholder-owners have nothing to complain about. The book value of their holdings has risen a lot more, from $950,000 to $9,500,000.

The close corporation that has public stockholders can readily use the qualified stock option route to give the key people a stake in the stock's projected growth in value. There is no income tax when the option is granted or exercised. Properly timed, employees only pay tax, as capital gains, when they dispose of the stock. The mean between the bid and asked price, or Stock Exchange quotations, can be used to fix the value at the time the option is given. This is a key requirement for the grant of a qualified stock option. Bank financing is available for the purchase of the shares, when the option is exercised. The public market permits the executive to convert the appreciation in value into money.

The situation with the non-public close corporation is quite different. It is a burdensome and costly task to arrive at a price per share for the shares that are subject to the option, which can be relied upon for tax purposes. There are many who believe that it is impossible to determine with exactitude the value of the untraded stock of a close corporation at any point in time.

Then the executive has to worry about where he gets the money to pay for the stock when he exercises the option. Financing is much harder to get, because the stock, if pledged as security, is essentially unsaleable. And, unless the corporation itself agrees to purchase his shares, the employee cannot sell his holdings. Furthermore, the stock that the unrelated executive buys pursuant to the option may decline in value, in which case he has to worry about paying off the loan incurred to finance the purchase of the stock.

Close corporations with few stockholders rarely use the stock option method. The owners of these entities generally issue stock directly to the executive. In many instances they do this without fully appreciating what a Pandora's box they have opened. Merely giving shares of stock to an executive does nothing for him. When and how does he convert the stock into money? Since meaningful dividends are generally not paid on the stock, what benefits does he derive from his ownership of the pieces of paper? In many instances, after the stock has been issued to the key person, the initial glow changes to bitterness. This is particularly true when the recipient has tax problems in connection with the transfer of the shares to him.

The difference between the value of the stock that is issued to the executive and what he pays for it is taxable to him as additional compensation. Thus, if he buys stock with a value of $100 a share for $2 a share, he has $98 per share of taxable ordinary income. This also applies if the controlling stockholders sell him the stock for a price below market value. In fact, the tax situation is worse when the stockholders, individually, make the sale. When the corporation gives the executive a bargain, the benefit that is taxable to him is also deductible by the corporation. A bargain sale by the stockholders gives nobody a deduction. The generous sellers are treated as having made a contribution of the excess value to the capital of the corporation. Because of these differing tax consequences, it is better for the corporation to transfer shares to the executive. An Internal Revenue Service examining officer will have less incentive to push for a higher value of the stock, if the corporation will be able to deduct the value in excess of the price.

The immediate tax to the executive on the purchase can be prevented by imposing restrictions on his right to sell or deal with the stock. For example, he may be required to offer the shares back to the corporation, at the same price that he paid, if he leaves the employ within some stated period of years. The employee may be nervous about those conditions from a financial point of view. In addition, if the stock value goes up, his tax problem will be worse. When the restrictions lapse, he is taxed on the spread between the value then and what he paid.

Some owners find it simpler to give the shares to the key man as a bonus. The obligation of the recipient is then limited to paying the income tax on the value of the shares that are distributed to him. Here again, there is the problem of the employee's finding the money to pay the tax on the bonus.

All of these issue problems can be helped by watering down the value of the stock that is transferred to the unrelated executive. The following example shows how this works. Let us assume that the close corporation has a worth of $1,000,000. If the executive obtains a 5% stock interest, he receives something worth about $50,000.* This value is a measure of past successes. What the non-owner really wants is participation in the future. As a means of reducing the executive's cost or tax problems, prior to his getting any stock, a dividend is declared of $950,000 of non-cumulative preferred stock. This stock will never grow in value. There is no intention to pay dividends on it. The 5% common stock interest now acquired by the executive is worth much less. But he keeps the same interest in the corporation's appreciation.

---

* I am ignoring discounts for a minority stock interest and the fact that the stock is not marketable.

Another step that is usually taken before implementing a stock ownership program is the authorization of non-voting common stock. This is the class of stock that will be issued to the executive. Through the use of non-voting stock, the employee can be left out of routine stockholder actions and there is no disturbance in any voting relationships. This is particularly important in an incorporated partnership where the voting rights are held equally by two individuals.

Terms and conditions

At the time of the issuance of stock to a key employee, a number of important items must be spelled out. Both sides will then have a clear understanding of the economics and mechanics of the arrangements. The stockholder status must end when the executive is no longer employed by the corporation. This means he must sell his stock to the corporation if he leaves, is discharged or dies. Close corporations do not want inactive stockholders. Even less would they desire a stockholder who may be working for a competitor.

Vesting requirements must also be considered. It is very common to impose a length of service requirement before the executive gets the full amount of the growth in value of his stockholdings. If his employment ends before he has been employed for that number of years, he only gets a part of the appreciation—except in case of death, when he usually gets 100% irrespective of the duration of his employment.

The price to be paid for the executive's stock has to be fixed. In most instances the measure is book value per share. This means the net worth of the corporation (the excess of its assets over its liabilities), less the par or liquidation value of any preferred stock, divided by the number of outstanding shares of common stock. To avoid interim accounting adjustments, the book value is generally based on the figures for the last fiscal year end of the corporation prior to the termination of employment. Thus, in the case of a calendar year corporation, if an executive leaves on June 15, 1986, the book value as of December 31, 1985 is used.

There can be recourse to other standards in determining value. Multiples of earnings can be utilized. There can be combinations of book value and capitalization of earnings. An appraisal can be made by a selected independent valuation expert. Most parties shy away from the appraisal method because no one knows, in advance, what the price will be. Also, it is cumbersome and costly.

The terms of payment must be articulated. To protect the company's financial position, the purchase price is usually payable in installments over a period of years, together with interest. This spreadout of the payments also prevents the terminated executive from using the purchase price of his stock as a stake for organizing or buying an interest in a competing business.

Phantom stock plan

We have used, in many instances, an alternative to stock ownership which has the same goal—to give the executive an equity interest in the entity. This is generally described as a "phantom stock plan." This plan is a deferred compensation arrangement. It measures the benefit of the key individual by the appreciation in value of a percentage of the common stock of the corporation.

The "phantom" tag is used because no stock is actually issued. The employee is given a certificate that states that he owns a certain number of stock units, which is the equivalent of owning the same number of shares of common stock. However, it only applies to future growth in value of those stockholdings. Sometimes the document recites that the employee is being treated as the owner of the appreciation in value of a stated percentage of the outstanding stock of the corporation.

Let me illustrate how this phantom stock concept works. Jack, a very important executive, is given 100 units. This is the equivalent of 100 shares of common stock of the corporation. At the time that these units are issued to him, the value per share of common stock is $500. When Jack retires, each share is worth $1500. He is entitled to receive the increase of $1,000 per unit, on his 100 units, or a total of $100,000.

The key to the phantom stock plan is that the employee does not receive any share of the corporation's present value. This means there is nothing to pay for or to be taxed on. He participates only in future growth, which is what he is looking for. He risks no money and his investment can only go up. He cannot lose. With phantom stock, all concerns about having to deal with a new stockholder are eliminated. No stock is issued.

How does the phantom stock format otherwise compare with actual stock ownership? They are identical in one very significant respect. If the executive's stock equivalent becomes very valuable, the stockholders will have prospered much more. In the example, when Jack retired, his 100 units, representing 5% of the common stock, appreciated by $100,000. The stockholders' equity would have grown almost $2,000,000.

One big advantage of phantom stock to the close corporation is the fact that what is paid out to the executive is income tax deductible. The actual net-after-tax cost of Jack's $100,000 could be only about one-half that amount. In the case of the purchase of stock from an employee who has left the company, there is no tax deduction.

The key employee has a worse tax position with phantom stock. Anything that is paid out to him, or to his beneficiary in case of his death, is taxable as ordinary income. The appreciation in case of the purchase of stock is capital gain. This disadvantage can be ameliorated through more generous awards. The close corporation owners can give away more because what is distributed to the participant produces a tax deduction.

PERSONAL LOANS

A common problem with either the stock ownership or phantom stock is the fact that generally nothing is distributable until the executive ceases to be an employee. It is an excellent way to build up a retirement nest egg. But what does the executive do if he needs money while he is still an employee for his childrens' education costs, a vacation home or a much more sumptuous residence?

To cope with this, a number of these programs give the executive the right to borrow from the company, using his accumulated benefits as security. There are a number of tricky matters that must be taken into account in designing a right to borrow. Only what is vested can be treated as security. There will be a tax liability for the employee when his debt is satisfied by applying appreciated stock or phantom units. Since the top income tax rate is 50%, the maximum loan can be limited to one-half of the vested benefit. The possibility of a downturn in the value of his stock or units must be considered—or the aspect of future reduction in value must be eliminated from the arrangement.

As an added benefit, when there are only a few people involved, the corporation may charge a lower than prevailing rate of interest on these loans, or no interest at all. The Tax Reform Act of 1984 dealt harshly with gift loans or loans by corporations to shareholders, where no interest, or a lesser than market rate of interest, is charged. In the case of loans to employees, there is effectively no adverse income tax result.

The law gets to this result in a complex fashion. Let us look at what the tax consequences would be if the close corporation loans $50,000 to Jack, without interest, secured by his $100,000 of phantom stock appreciation. I am assuming that the imputed interest rate at that time is 12%. In the first year of the loan, the close corporation will be deemed to have paid to Jack, as additional compensation, $6,000 (12% of $50,000). Jack will be treated as having paid that same amount of interest to the corporation. This means the corporation has $6,000 of interest income and a like amount of deduction for compensation. Jack picks up $6,000 as additional compensation, but he gets a $6,000 deduction for interest. Both the corporation and Jack have a balance of income and deduction. There is a "wash."

MEDICAL EXPENSE REIMBURSEMENT

The next very important concern for the executive are his medical expenses and those of his dependents. Medical care costs keep escalating. A severe illness, without adequate insurance coverage, can be financially demoralizing. A good start in meeting this problem is participation in a company-wide medical expense reimbursement plan, covering employees, their spouses and dependents. This type of plan usually will not provide full reimbursement because of the deductibles, co-insurance features and some exclusions (e.g., dental and psychiatric expenses). This means that the employee may have to pay significant amounts of medical expenses himself.

The unrelated executive will generally not get any tax benefit from out-of-pocket medical expenses. These costs can only be deducted, for Federal income tax purposes, to the extent that they exceed 5% of his adjusted gross income. By reason of his higher rate of compensation, this 5% figure can be sizeable. The unrelated manager can participate in an insurance program that provides payment for those expenses that are not covered by the basic medical expense reimbursement plan. This kind of insured excess medical coverage can be discriminatory. For instance, only the owners, their family members in the business and these executives can be included.

Sometimes the close corporation uses a simpler technique to provide the non-owner employees whom the company is anxious to please more complete medical expense coverage. They have the executives take out their own supplemental medical insurance coverage. The corporation will then increase their salaries so that, net-after-tax, they will have enough dollars to pay the premiums.

DISABILITY AND LIFE INSURANCE

Disability and early death are also serious economic concerns of the unrelated executive. He may have purchased an expensive house. He wants his children to be well educated and the family to enjoy vacations together. If this high level employee becomes disabled or dies, his family will face tough sledding. But it is hard for him to find the dollars to provide adequate insurance to cope with these risks.

Disability insurance coverage for the unrelated executive is a much appreciated fringe benefit which is not very expensive. The key to keeping the cost down is to have a longer period before payments begin. For example, it will be far less expensive if the initial payment is made after thirty days of disability, rather than seven days. The corporation should certainly be willing to pay the disabled individual for the first thirty or sixty days that he is unable to work. For the best income tax result, the executive should carry the insurance himself. In this way all disability payments will be tax free. An increase in salary is the medium for providing the employee with the wherewithal to pay the premiums.

Group life insurance is the best way for the close corporation to provide life insurance protection for the owners and this limited number of important people. There are ways in which the categories of coverage are fixed so that the higher paid personnel receive the bulk of the insurance. Group insurance is less expensive and the premiums are tax deductible by the corporation. The first $50,000 of insurance is free of income tax to the individual in the group. The one year term cost of the insurance in excess of $50,000 is taxed to the employee. It is still far cheaper for the executive to pay the tax on the cost of this excess insurance than to buy the insurance himself.

Sometimes a death benefit program is coupled with a deferred compensation or retirement plan. If the executive dies before he reaches retirement age, his family receives a substantial sum, most often payable in installments. Should he work until his retirement date, he starts receiving distributions thereafter. For example, a close corporation wants to provide this kind of program for Al, a very valuable executive. The corporation takes out a $300,000 ordinary or whole life policy of insurance on Al's life, making it the owner and beneficiary of the insurance.

The arrangement is that if Al dies before reaching age 65, while he is still employed by the company, $50,000 a year, for 10 years, will be paid to the beneficiaries selected by Al. These payments will be taxable as ordinary income to the recipients. They will be deductible by the corporation. The tax impact for Al's beneficiaries can be reduced by designating a sprinkle trust as the beneficiary. This is a trust which permits the trustee to make distributions to Al's wife and children, or to accumulate monies, thereby creating the possibility of a multiplicity of taxpayers paying tax on each $50,000 payment by the close corporation. Another means of reducing the income taxes is for Al himself to name his wife and children as the recipients.

Why does the corporation agree to pay out $500,000 when the insurance is only $300,000? The first reason is that the $300,000 comes to the corporation free of income tax. Life insurance proceeds are non-taxable. Moreover, the payments that the corporation makes to Al are tax deductible. If the tax benefit of this deduction were 50% (46% top federal income tax bracket plus 4% of net state tax cost), the corporation could actually fund $600,000 of payments to Al's beneficiaries. In addition, the corporation is getting the after tax yield on the portion of the $300,000 that will not be paid until many years after the death of Al.

What happens when Al reaches age 65? The company can then take down, and pay to Al, the cash surrender value of the policy in guaranteed installments over Al's lifetime. These payments constitute taxable income to Al. But he may then be in lower tax brackets. By receiving somewhat lesser amounts while he is living, Al can be assured that at least ten years of payments are made. Under this option, if Al dies before reaching age 75, the company will continue the distributions to his chosen beneficiaries for the balance of the ten years following the retirement date.

Here again the corporation can increase the amounts going to Al, because what the insurance company distributes to the corporation is non-taxable to the greatest extent. On the other hand, everything that is paid by the company to Al, or his beneficiaries, is deductible. Working with a competent life underwriter and with Al, the corporation can design postretirement payment terms that protect the company and satisfy Al's desires.

The corporation's benefit from this plan is that it ties the key man to the company. Payments are only made if he is an employee at the time of his death or he stays with the corporation until age 65. Sometimes there is an amelioration of the forfeiture, if the employee is fired by the corporation without cause. This seemingly fair provision may be a problem to the company. Many owners feel that an executive who wants to get himself fired can do so, without his actions constituting justifiable cause for the termination.

PERQUISITES

Special perquisites are another method of giving special recognition to the limited number of important unrelated executives. The top of the list in this area, for many years, was a company car. The 1984 Tax Reform Act put a large income tax dent in this benefit, at least for so-called luxury cars—those that cost more than $16,000. Depreciation is restricted in the first three years and the investment tax credit is limited to $1,000. Where the car is used 50% or less for business, there are more stringent restrictions.

Attendance at industry conventions and meetings, at the corporation's expense, is another nice gesture. This is particularly so when the gathering is held at a lovely vacation spot, and the spouse accompanies the executive.

Payment for an annual head to toe physical for a key employee is also popular. This is a concrete expression of the corporation's belief that he is vital to the well being of the business. It is also a very sensible thing for the company to do.

A key unrelated executive should be given an office that befits his status. Let him pick out certain things, like his desk, chair, some artwork or plants. So many close corporation owners have offices that are magnificent and all other executives are in cramped and unattractive quarters.

The key unrelated executive should be allowed, at the company's expense, to make use of an eating club or good restaurant for lunches with other top employees, or people with whom he is dealing on behalf of the corporation. It pumps up his ego when he is greeted by name and fawned over by the maitre d' because he is a regular patron.

Moreover, the key unrelated executive should be provided, without cost, tax, estate or financial planning services. I have learned from experience that senior people, non-owners, are very flattered when the head of the corporation urges them to do this kind of planning with the same professional that the boss uses. To prevent the employee from being taxed on their value, by reason of the 1984 Tax Reform Act changes, these services should be of the type that would be deductible if the employee paid them.

These suggestions are not very expensive for the close corporation. But they go a very long way in saying: "You are important to the company and me. We appreciate and need you." There are also non-material things that can be done to convey these sentiments. Give the executive a good sounding title. Make him a member of the board of directors, even if the owner has to enlarge the board to maintain control. Create top level committees that elevate these people in the eyes of other employees. A management or executives committee is a good example.

Many owners of close corporations scoff at the importance of these status symbols. That's because they have them all. All lawyers who have witnessed the quest to make partner, to have your name in the firm name, to get a better located office, or be listed higher on the letterhead, appreciate their significance.

AVOIDING CONFLICTS WITH MEMBERS
OF THE OWNER'S FAMILY

It may not be enough to provide an important unrelated executive with economic security, good benefits and even an interest in the equity of the family business. All too often, notwithstanding the costs in money, valuable, long-standing employees have left family enterprises, including incorporated partnerships where different generations are involved in the business, because they can't get along with one or more family members. I remember vividly the comment of one such individual, when I met with him at the direction of the head of the business, to try and convince him to change his mind about leaving: "Milt, I just can't stand it anymore. All those needles and crazy demands from Sam and Frank (the sons). I don't care about how much more they make than I do. Their family are the owners and they can take what they want. But how could their dad move them above me in the organization and make me report to them? Because they are kids with very little experience, I wind up taking all the responsibilities and making all the real decisions. But that doesn't stop Sam and Frank from bugging me with their hare-brained ideas, expecting me to perform miracles and in general making my life miserable."

This experience is common. While the conflict can be between the unrelated executive and the father, generally it is not. The unrelated executive is junior in age to the head of the family, appreciates the father's position and the role he played in building the business, and is more willing to accept his impatience and idiosyncrasies. When you get to the younger generation, sons and sons-in-law, the attitude changes. The employee is the senior in all respects and cannot understand why these "kids" fail to show him respect. Their disregard of his sensitivities angers him, gnaws constantly at his pride, until at last he may leave. Even if he stays, the commitment and drive of an important employee are greatly reduced, a result that the family business can ill afford.

How to handle the problem

In Chapter 2, these conflicts between offspring and unrelated executives in the family business were discussed, but primarily from the standpoint of dealing with nepotism. Here we are looking at the issue as one of the major factors adversely affecting the relationships between close corporations and management talent that can be vital to the success of the business. Things can be done to improve the situation, but first the leaders of family companies must have real awareness of the potential for trouble when a son comes into the business. There must be foresight in planning and a game plan that will prepare children properly for their role in management—and eventually to take control of the corporation's affairs—without alienating the unrelated executives who can be invaluable in assisting the next generation. Let me offer some suggestions, using a son whom I will call Dick, as an example:

1. The son, hopefully properly educated and prepared, should initially be subordinate to the experienced unrelated executives, who hold significant management positions in the company. Specifically, if Dick is assigned to work in the area of production, he must be made to understand that the head of production is his boss. Efforts must be made to try and forget what Dick's last name is and the fact that his father is the owner. An unrelated executive (or a group of them, in the case of a large company) is probably the best choice to train a son and develop him into a competent manager. In a recent very provocative article,* Doctor Srully Blotnick, a research psychologist and author, reached this conclusion based on a study of 73 firms over two decades. Here is the procedure that Dr. Blotnick suggests. The father selects a top executive to whom ' ? can give a lot of authority. This person should not only be co..1petent and experienced, but have the ability to inspire young workers to do their best. Son Dick is assigned to work with him.

This preceptor will help Dick relate more effectively to his own father. He can serve as a buffer between father and son, protecting Dick from the destructive ego battering that children in the family business often experience at the hands of the patriarch, and preventing dad from spoiling Dick or excusing his poor performance. The chances are that Dick will work hard in order to get his boss's approval, because of his admiration for the superior's know-how and his appreciation of the genuine and objective nature of the executive's comments and criticisms.

2. In the next stage, Dick and the top unrelated executives become peers. The son is now in his late 30's or early 40's. He has become very knowledgeable about the conduct of the business, production, sales, finance and administration. Now seasoned and more mature, Dick is easily accepted as an equal by the other

---

* "A Gift to Your Children," *Forbes Magazine*, July 30, 1984.

key management personnel. He may hold a title such as vice president and serve as a member of the corporation's board of directors. He joins with the others in formulating strategies and recommendations that are presented to the father and directors. The only distinctions that exist between Dick and the other senior second-level officers are his higher level of compensation, which everyone expects, and his access, through the father, to confidential information and long-range plans for the company and the family.

3. Finally, Dick moves to the position of president or executive vice-president of the corporation. Now he is the boss of the unrelated executives, although once in a great while, there is one of them who is at his level. This transition is easy to achieve. Many of the unrelated executives who were working in the business when Dick joined the company have retired or left. Those who remain are close to retirement. A large segment of the executive corps can be made up of individuals who are younger and less experienced than Dick, some of whom he may have hired or supervised along the way.

# BASIC INCOME TAX STRATEGIES	# 5

In this chapter, I am going explain the significant income tax provisions that affect the close corporation and its stockholders. The aim is not to make the reader a tax expert, but to create a better understanding of the impact of these tax considerations on the family business and incorporated partnership. The key word is "understanding." I feel that a real contribution could be made to close corporation entrepreneurs and their advisors, if tax terms that are often bandied about, with so little grasp of their implications, could be expressed in plain, easy to understand language. This chapter represents my best effort in that regard.

SOME FACTS ABOUT SAMUELS-RITTER COMPANY

To illustrate the basic tax strategies for close corporations more effectively, I am going to begin by describing a hypothetical business, the Samuels-Ritter Company. Samuels-Ritter manufactures gift novelties. The head of the family, 64 years of age, is A. J. Samuels, whose first name is "Albert," but everyone in business calls him "A. J.," and I will too. The enterprise was started by A. J. and a partner named "Ritter" many years ago. The partner, who put in most of the start-up capital—A. J. only put in $10,000 when the corporation was organized—was bought out about 10 years ago, after serious inter-personal difficulties developed between the two "partners." A. J., at this juncture, owns 100 shares of the single class of common stock of Samuels-Ritter Company, which represents 100% of the stock that is now outstanding.

A. J. Samuels has been married to his wife, Bernice, for almost 40 years. It has been a very close and loving relationship, with Bernice serving as A. J.'s best friend and confidante. The couple have two children, Sarah age 35, and David, 32. Sarah, after graduation from college, got her Master's degree in speech therapy. Since her marriage to Jason Maloney, a psychiatrist, and the birth of her two children, Sarah combines a part-time speech therapy profession with a full time job as a homemaker.

Son, David, after he finished college and had a stint working elsewhere, came to work for Samuels-Ritter. The father will admit that one of the reasons he decided to get rid of Ritter, his former partner, who was childless, was the anticipated disinclination of Ritter to have David join the business. David is married to Arlene, and they very recently had a son, a third generation candidate for entry into the family business.

Samuels-Ritter Company is going great guns. The profits have grown considerably, and there is a sizeable throw-off of cash, each year, which is not needed for current operations. The last payment due to Ritter for his stock will be paid at the end of the year, so that this drain on the corporation's finances will be over. A. J. Samuels is a typical close corporation owner. Outside of A. J.'s very valuable stockholdings in Samuels-Ritter, he and Sarah have a lovely home, beautifully furnished, and about $75,000 of liquid assets.

The problem

Samuels-Ritter Company, like many close corporations, is prosperous and has cash that could be handed over to A. J. Samuels. What, then, is the problem? Why doesn't the corporation, at the end of the year, finding it has an extra $50,000, just draw a check payable to A. J. and hand it over to him? There is no difficulty in accomplishing that. Since A. J. is the sole stockholder of the company, and the chief executive officer, he has every legal right to move dollars out of the corporate stream and into his pocket. The problem is income tax. The proper classification of Samuels-Ritter's distribution, as a dividend, bonus, reimbursement of business expenses, or purchase price of stock will produce substantially different income tax consequences, for both the business and the stockholder-employee.

WHY DIVIDENDS SHOULD BE AVOIDED

As I mentioned in the introduction, profits of a close corporation that are distributed as dividends can result in an almost 75% tax erosion, leaving the proprietors with only a quarter of what the company earned. That is because they are taxed first to the corporation and then to the recipient stockholders. To get the $50,000 into the corporate treasury, Samuels-Ritter had to make almost $100,000, since there is a corporate federal income tax of 46% and some state tax liability. If this $50,000 is paid out to A. J. as a dividend, he will have to pay another 50% tax on that distribution. Only about $25,000, or 25% of the $100,000 of profit realized by the corporation, is left to be spent or invested by A. J. Because of this onerous tax cost, tax advisors shun the dividend route, and look to other means of getting dollars out of the close corporation and into the pockets of the shareholders.

If lower tax rates come to fruition, the tax bite on corporate profits distributed as dividends will still be significant. What is contemplated is a corporate tax rate of 33%, and a top tax of 35% on individuals' income. These rates will produce only about $43,500, in-pocket, on $100,000 of Samuels-Ritter profits paid out as dividends.

SALE OF STOCK TO AN OUTSIDER

The stockholder in a large public company, which has stock that is regularly traded on the stock exchange, or over-the-counter, has the opportunity to get a return on his investment, in the form of long term capital gain. A long term capital gain results from the profitable sale of property which has been owned for more than six months. Ordinary income, on the other hand, consists of such items as dividends on stock, interest, compensation for services, rents, royalties, etc. What is the advantage of long term capital gain over ordinary income? Only part of the profit on the sale, 40%, is subject to income tax. This makes the maximum federal income tax rate on such a capital gain equal to 20% (50% maximum income tax rate) on the 40% of the profit which is subject to tax.

When a stockholder holds shares of a corporation which has regularly traded stock, the prosperity of the company, reflected in its higher earnings, can push the price of the stock up. The increase is attributable to the fact that the market price is usually based on a multiple of the per share earnings of the corporation. A. J. Samuels appreciates the benefits of the public markets for stocks. A few years ago, he got a tip from his stock broker that All-American Oil was a good buy. A. J. purchased 1,000 shares at $20 a share, for a total cost of $20,000. After eight months, All-American Oil announced the discovery of new oil fields, with very extensive reserves. The price of the stock shot up to just over $100 a share. Delighted by his good fortune, A. J. decided to cash in on half his investment. He sold 500 of his 1,000 shares. After paying all commissions and costs, the sale of 500 shares netted A. J. $50,000, giving him a profit of $40,000 ($50,000 less the cost of $10,000 for the 500 shares).

A. J.'s income tax on the long term capital gain was $8,000, since only $16,000 of the $40,000 gain was reportable (40% of $40,000), and the maximum tax rate on the $16,000 of gain was 50%. If this $40,000 gain had been considered ordinary income, A. J.'s income tax on it would have been $20,000. A. J. pocketed $42,000, after paying his tax on the sale of one-half of his All-American Oil stockholdings, more than twice what he paid for all of the stock of that corporation. He used his money to help finance a swimming pool in the back of his home. He still holds another 500 shares of All-American Oil, selling now at $110 per share, with the potential to grow even more.

A. J. would like to do the same thing with some of his stock of Samuels-Ritter Company. Actually, bearing in mind that he originally paid only $10,000 for all 100 shares of the stock of the corporation that he owns, the profit on the sale of some of his stockholdings of his corporation would be tremendous. The problem is that there is no available buyer for part of A. J.'s stockholdings. He cannot call up his broker and instruct him to sell ten shares of Samuels-Ritter at the market. There is no market. Even if there were, nobody, certainly not A. J., wants to have an unknown minority stockholder in the close corporation.

SALE OF STOCK TO THE CLOSE CORPORATION

Why can't A. J. sell some of his shares of Samuels-Ritter stock to the corporation itself? This transaction, in which a corporation buys its own stock from a shareholder, is called a redemption. The business has plenty of extra cash to pay for A. J.'s stock. Furthermore, there is an advantage for A. J. in the case of a stock transaction with his corporation. No matter what number of shares A. J. sells, he winds up in the same stockholder status, after the sale is made, that he had before. Shares purchased by a corporation are held in its treasury, and whether or not they are retired, the shares cannot be voted and do not participate in the equity. Consequently, if A. J. were to sell 10 of his 100 shares to the corporation, and would then hold 90 shares, which were still the only outstanding shares, he would continue to have 100% voting control and own all of the equity.

The hitch is that any and all sales to the corporation, which leave A. J.'s position relatively unchanged, will not produce a capital gain, with a 20% maximum tax, but ordinary income with a tax cost of 50%. Let me explain the reasons for this adverse tax result. When a stockholder sells stock to his close corporation, the purchase price paid is always treated as the equivalent of a dividend, unless there is a substantial change in the stockholder's position after the redemption of stock. Without this rule, no close corporation would ever pay dividends. Instead, it would distribute its accumulated profits by buying back shares of stock, giving the stockholders capital gain instead of ordinary income.

Reduction of stockholder's status

What is a sufficient change in a stockholder's status to qualify a purchase of stock for capital gain treatment? There are two kinds of stock purchases that meet this standard. The first is a redemption which is considered to be substantially disproportionate (which I will call the "substantially disproportionate exception"). To meet this exception:

1. After the transaction, the stockholder must have less than 80% of the interest in the corporation that he had before; and

2. The selling stockholder, after the redemption, must own less than 50% of the voting stock of the corporation.

The substantially disproportionate exception is not a commonly utilized path to capital gain for close corporation owners. Very few of them are willing to give up a good deal of their stock and become minority stockholders in a family business or incorporated partnership.

Complete termination of stockholder's interest

The other kind of sale that qualifies as a capital gain, and the one that is availed of most often, is a complete termination of the stockholder's interest in the corporation (the "complete termination exception"). This is how Ritter got favorable tax treatment when he left the business and sold all of his shares back to the entity.

But let's go back to Samuels-Ritter. A. J., having been told by his tax counsel that the only way a stockholder can get capital gain treatment on his sale of stock to the corporation, is by accomplishing a complete termination of his or her stock interest in the corporation, comes forward with an idea: "Why don't I give 30 of my 100 shares to my wife, Bernice. Then, a few months later, the corporation can acquire all of her 30 shares of stock. We will then meet the complete termination test and Bernice will get money out of Samuels-Ritter taxed at the maximum capital gain rate of 20%." This is good thinking but the plan won't work. Here's why:

1. In applying the exceptions that yield capital gain, rather than ordinary income, the shares held by the selling stockholder are lumped together with the stockholdings of his spouse, parent, child or grandchild. When Bernice's 30 shares are bought back by Samuels-Ritter Company, she will be deemed to hold 100% of the outstanding stock both before and after the sale. Before, she held 100 shares, her 30 directly and A. J.'s 70 constructively. After the sale of her 30 shares to the company, she is deemed to own A.J.'s 70 shares, which are the only shares still outstanding. The same result would follow if A. J. gave shares to his children, which were redeemed.

2. For A. J.'s 70 shares *not* to be considered as owned by Bernice, either before or after the redemption of her 30 shares, Bernice would have to file a specified form with the Internal Revenue Service and have no relationship whatsoever with Samuels-Ritter for 10 years after the sale of stock. For a decade, she could not be a stockholder, director, officer or employee. So far so good. Neither of these restrictions bothers either A. J. or Bernice.

3. But there is another obstacle. The person whose stock is redeemed, in this case, Bernice, cannot have given stock to, or received stock from, another family member within 10 years prior to the redemption of her shares—if the reason for the shift of shares is income tax avoidance. In this case, it certainly would be. Thus, Bernice would have to wait 10 years before her stock could be acquired by the corporation, with the capital gain result assured.

It is crucial to keep in mind that the only intra-family transfers that cause trouble, if they occur within 10 years prior to a complete termination of a shareholder's interest, are those motivated by income tax avoidance. Gifts made to reduce estate taxes are all right. If stock were to pass from A. J. to his children, as a part of his estate planning, that would not run afoul of his stock transfer limitation. Consequently, stock can be redeemed from a child, who is inactive in the family business, to produce capital gain, even though the seller received the stock, by gift from the father, within the last 10 years.

GIFTS OF STOCK TO CHARITY

A stockholder in a close corporation can obtain cash by giving shares of stock to his favorite charity. For instance, A.J. Samuels might contribute three of his 100 shares of Samuels-Ritter to the local hospital, to be used for new microsurgery equipment. The three shares given to the hospital have a value of $60,000. When A. J. takes a charitable deduction in that amount on his income tax return, it reduces his tax liability by $30,000, which means he is able to retain an additional $30,000 in cash.

A. J. does not want the hospital to own stock in his close corporation. The hospital feels the same way, since it certainly cannot buy the needed microsurgery items with pieces of paper. Both parties are relieved of any concern in that regard, because the expectation is that after A. J.'s gift of the stock to the hospital, the institution will want to sell the three shares, and Samuels-Ritter will be happy to accommodate the hospital. The corporation uses $60,000 of its dollars to assist A. J. in obtaining a sizeable tax benefit, while at the same time giving A. J. recognition for a substantial contribution to a very worthy cause. When the dust settles, A. J. still owns 100% of the stock of Samuels-Ritter.

For a long time the Internal Revenue Service was not happy about this type of arrangement in which a stockholder gives shares of his business corporation to charity, followed, in a very short time, by a redemption of the charity's stock by the company itself. If, as was usually the case, the transfer of the shares to the charity and their subsequent redemption from the charity were part of a prearranged plan, the Government sought to treat the transactions differently by reclassifying them as first a redemption by the corporation of the shares given away, and then as a gift of the proceeds by the stockholder to the charity. While this characterization produced the same charitable contribution deduction, the IRS sought to collect the tax, at ordinary income rates, on the imputed sale by the stockholder to his corporation.

As it turned out, the Government was unsuccessful in its attempt to redefine the nature of the arrangement. So, the IRS capitulated. Today, so long as the charitable organization is not *required* to sell the shares given to it by the generous entrepreneur, the donor gets the charitable deduction for the value of the contributed stock, and escapes any tax involvement in connection with his corporation's later purchase of the shares from the charity.

WHAT "BASIS" MEANS IN STOCK SALES

An important term in tax parlance is "basis." It is the amount that is subtracted from the proceeds received on a sale, in order to determine the gain that is realized. Normally, the basis of stock is its cost, the amount that was paid for it, including in the case of traded securities, brokerage commissions and stock or local taxes. Since all that A. J. paid in for his Samuels-Ritter stock was $10,000, that is the cost of his 100 shares, or $100 per share. No matter how much the corporation's net worth goes up, and what the amount of the capital account is on the company's balance sheet, A. J.'s basis remains the same. A sale of the company for $3,000,000 net, and its liquidation, or a sale by A. J. of all of his stock at that price, would mean an enormous gain ($3,000,000 less $10,000 basis). This is the typical situation of the very successful close corporation owner.

Right now Samuels-Ritter Company has only one class of common stock outstanding. For many tax reasons, some of which are discussed in various parts of this book, the corporation may eventually be recapitalized by distributing shares of preferred stock and/or splitting the common stock into two classes, voting and non-voting. To illustrate, let us assume that A. J. surrenders his 100 shares of common stock, and receives in exchange, as part of a recapitalization of the company, 20,000 shares of preferred stock, with a par value of $100 per share, or an aggregate par value of $2,000,000, 100 shares of voting common stock and 10,000 shares of non-voting common. What happens to A. J.'s $10,000 basis in the stock he gave up? It is divided among the three new classes of stock in proportion to their respective values. But there is no overall increase in basis. The total basis of all the newly acquired shares is still $10,000.

What if A. J. gives some stock of Samuels-Ritter Company to his children, which is worth much more than his original cost? Do the donees get a higher basis—commonly referred to as a "stepped-up basis"—reflecting the enhanced value of the transferred shares? No! Their basis would be the same as A.J.'s, plus the amount of any gift tax paid by him, in cash, on the appreciation in value of the stock given away.

By contrast, there is a step-up in the basis of those shares that pass to heirs and beneficiaries, at the death of the close corporation owner. The beneficiary who inherits the stock gets a new basis, which is the fair market value of the shares on the date of death of the stockholder—or the alternate valuation date, which is six months after the decedent's death. Subject to some limitations, the executor of the estate can choose which of the two dates to use in valuing stockholdings for Federal estate tax purposes.

This increase in the basis of stock, at death, is a key factor, in shaping many estate planning strategies. It is particularly true now that the combination of the unlimited marital deduction, and estate tax credit, which will be discussed in detail in the next chapter, enables the stock of a deceased head of a family business to pass to a surviving spouse or child, free of estate tax. For example, A. J. would like to pull some money out of the business, right after his death, in order to give his wife, Bernice, more to live on when she is widowed. He bequeaths some stock to her. No Federal estate tax will be payable when A. J. dies, because of the marital deduction. Nontheless, the shares inherited by Bernice will get a new basis equal to their value when A. J. dies. When Samuels-Ritter then buys Bernice's stockholdings, for the date-of-death value, there will be no gain subject to income tax. Bernice's basis and what she receives for the stock will be equal.

The fact that a new basis is acquired at death can also have an effect on the decision to sell a family business during the lifetime of the now aged father. Picture A. J. having reached his 75th birthday. For one of a number of reasons, he decides that it makes sense to sell the company. A very good price, $3,000,000, can be realized. Since. A. J.'s basis for his stockholdings is $10,000, a sale can mean a capital gain tax of almost $600,000—20% of the excess of $3,000,000 over the basis of $10,000. If the sale of the enterprise is postponed until after the death of A. J., that substantial income tax can be avoided.

COMPENSATION

We have seen that the dividend route, as a means of getting cash out of the close corporation, into the hands of the stockholders, is much too costly taxwise. If some of the owner's shares of stock are sold to the company, the proceeds of the sale are treated as though they were dividends. Nothing is gained by that method. A disposition of a limited number of shares to a third party is unavailable and would be undesired in any event. What, then, is the tax strategy that is most commonly employed, to get dollars into the pockets of the entrepreneurs, so that they can enjoy life a little more? The answer is compensation and perquisites. The difference between compensation and dividends is that compensation is deductible by the corporation, while dividends are not. This means that there is only one tax on amounts that are treated as compensation to the owners—the tax paid by the recipients. With the top tax brackets of both the corporation and the individual being approximately the same, 46% corporate and 50% individual, it is better for the dollars to move out of the corporate stream into the pockets of the owners. This will remain the same if the top corporate bracket is reduced to 33%, and the maximum rate for individuals is lowered to 35%. Should the business need an infusion of capital at some future time, the principals can always loan money back to the corporation. Fringe benefits are an even better medium for shifting dollars to the stockholders, because the corporation still gets the deduction, while the individuals pay little or no tax on the benefits.

Of course, as I pointed out in the introduction, a stockholder can call a distribution of cash whatever he pleases. For example, there is nothing to prevent A. J. Samuels from increasing his compensation by $50,000 as a way of getting his hands on some of the liquid funds sitting in Samuels-Ritter. All he has to do is direct that result. While technically the corporation is making the payment, the owners are the people who make all the decisions for the corporation. Nevertheless, the law is that compensation must be reasonable in amount to be deductible by the corporation. Any portion of the compensation that is deemed excessive is disallowed and treated as the equivalent of a dividend, meaning that it is non-deductible to the corporation but taxable to the recipient.

Because of the high tax stakes, the reasonableness of compensation is very carefully considered by Internal Revenue Service agents when they audit the income tax returns of close corporations. They appreciate the advantages to the stockholders of compensation versus dividends, and the agents are well aware of the complete control that the owners have over the classification and amounts of the payments. The issue is complicated by the fact that there are no precise guidelines for the determination of what is a reasonable amount of compensation. Disagreements between taxpayers' representatives and the Internal Revenue Service are commonplace. The courts which resolve these disputes over what is reasonable compensation to a stockholder of a close corporation make *ad hoc* determinations listing a host of factors that must be taken into account, and declaring that each case must be decided on its own set of circumstances. As you might suspect, there is a tendency to compromise somewhere between the low figure that the Government feels is reasonable and the higher figure that has been paid by the close corporation.

One very frustrating aspect of the reasonable compensation issue is the Service's reliance on what is paid to others in the industry, doing the same job, as a general standard. Getting that information from competitors and other close corporations is virtually impossible. Even a good friend will hesitate to give it out, knowing that it will be used to justify a level of compensation and fearing that the Government may allege that he too is being overpaid. Besides, no two jobs are totally identical. There are always variations.

Establishing reasonableness

To contend with the reasonable compensation problem, stockholder-executives can take a number of steps, including:

1. Draw an employment agreement. A formal document that spells out the details of the owner's compensation package adds substance to the owner's claim of reasonableness. It also evidences the fact that the terms were fixed prior to the performance of the services.

2. There should be an automatic cost-of-living adjustment to the base compensation. The position can then be taken that the adjustment is not an increase. All it does is to keep the purchasing power of the salary at a constant level.

3. Do not pay discretionary year end bonuses. Certainly, everyone would like to see what the profits are going to be for the year, and then determine the size of the bonus. Everyone wants to pay more in a year of high earnings; and less when profits are small. The trouble with this format is that it has all the earmarks of a dividend. The owner-employee has the unrestricted choice either to give himself a bonus or pay a dividend on his stock. Calling it a bonus, in order to get a tax deduction, is suspect when the decision of what to pay is made after the results are in.

4. The best incentive compensation arrangement for the stockholder-senior executive is one that is formulated in advance, and is tied to what he achieves. For example, a five year contract can be entered into which calls for annual additional compensation equal to a percentage of net profits, before taxes, in excess of a 15% return on capital. This is modeled after the compensation arrangements that many very large publicly held corporations have with their top officers. Setting the terms of the contingent compensation in advance represents the incentive for the executive to use his best efforts to enlarge the company's earnings.

There is, of course, a significant difference between a close corporation proprietor who works for his company and even the president of a very large corporation, who owns only a nominal amount of the entity's equity. The enhanced profits of the close corporation make the very substantial investment of the owner of the corporation more valuable. That is incentive enough for his efforts, the Internal Revenue Service argues. Why does he have to be offered another form of motivation in his capacity as an employee?

The response to this query is that in resolving the reasonable compensation issue, the stockholder status of the close corporation employee should be ignored. He is entitled to receive fair remuneration for the value of the services he performs for the company. If it is customary to provide incentive compensation for executives who have a role and responsibilities akin to those of the owner-executive, then he is entitled to have the same program.

5. Have a tax lawyer do a compensation study. We have followed this practice for many years and it has been a great help. The stockholder's background and those capabilities and attributes that make him a very desirable person for the corporation to have as a top manager are recorded. Unique qualities are highlighted. The stockholder's duties, obligations and efforts on behalf of the corporation are set forth in detail. Available compensation comparisons are also noted. The end result is to recommend a compensation plan that is deemed to be fair and reasonable.

FRINGE BENEFITS

The fringe benefits that stockholder-owners can take from a close corporation include medical expense reimbursement, insurance coverages, convention expenses, travel and entertainment, luncheon clubs and, of course, luxurious autos. The life insurance benefits provided for the entrepreneurs are usually quite extensive because of the estate planning importance of the proceeds, a subject discussed later on in this book. Furthermore, the new emphasis on making sure company cars are used for business, has curtailed the choice of **cars** as tax perqs. Business usage, other than commuting to and from work, must now be proven. In a number of instances, the stockholders of close corporations have decided to purchase the company cars, at a favorable price, pay the expenses for those autos, and seek reimbursement from the company to the extent that there is a clear business connected use. Cars for wives and children are disappearing as a fringe benefit.

Overreaching in the fringe benefit area can be costly, taxwise, for the close corporation owner. If an expense paid for by the company is held to be solely for the personal benefit of the stockholder, the corporation loses its deduction for that amount and the individual has to pick up the item as ordinary income. Once again, just as in the instance of excessive compensation, the amount is treated as though it were a dividend to the stockholder. With a corporation in the 46% bracket and a stockholder at the maximum 50% rate, virtually the entire disallowed amount has to be paid in taxes. Even the proposed reduced maximum income tax rates—33% corporate and 35% individual—produce 68% of tax on what is disallowed. I have seen very hefty sums paid out, particularly when there are several tax years under audit and there is significant interest on the deficiency. In a few instances, the personal and non-business nature of very substantial outlays by the corporation were so clear that it led to tax fraud investigations.

PENSION AND PROFIT SHARING PLANS

Probably the most effective and substantial fringe benefit for the corporate stockholder-employee is participation in a pension or profit-sharing plan. Our firm has made extensive use of this tax planning tool in counselling close corporations. The main advantages of the pension or profit-sharing plan are the tax deductibility of the contributions made by the corporation to the plan and the tax-free build-up of the benefits. In many instances, it is far better for corporate profits to be invested in such a plan rather than being held in the corporate treasury or paid out to the stockholders as deductible compensation.

The key to evaluating the advantages of a pension or profit-sharing plan is to determine how much of the corporation's contribution is for the benefit of the principals of the business. Even though these plans must be non-discriminatory, there are many techniques that can be used to augment the share of the company's contribution that is attributable to the owners. Benefits can be keyed to age and length of service. Plans may be integrated with social security. Vesting requirements can be imposed so that those who leave the company—and they are rarely the stockholders—forfeit all or a part of their benefits. There are a number of ways in which experts in this area can maximize the participation of the proprietors.

To appreciate the advantages of a pension or profit-sharing plan, let us go back to A. J. and his corporation, Samuels-Ritter Company. A. J. still wants to get some of the cash out of the company and into his hands. He has decided to raise his salary $50,000 and take his chances on the deductibility of this sizeable increase. Our entrepreneur wants to start building up liquidity outside the company, and the $25,000 a year he will keep, after taxes, on the $50,000, will be a good start. The corporation's lawyer and accountant, while appreciating A. J.'s desires, are very worried about the reasonable compensation issue, and suggest consideration of a pension plan as an alternative.

An employee benefits consulting firm is retained which designs a pension plan, integrated with social security, that will cost Samuels-Ritter $100,000 per year. But now the entire amount will be tax-deductible by the company. Sixty percent of the company's contribution, or $60,000, will fund the retirement benefits of A. J. and his son, David, $50,000 for the father and $10,000 for the son. A. J. is getting the same increase in compensation. However, unlike the raise in pay, no tax is payable by him on the $50,000 that Samuels-Ritter is contributing on his behalf. Thus, A. J. is putting away twice as much, per year, than the $25,000 that would remain after paying a 50% tax on the $50,000 additional salary. In addition, the earnings on the pension plan contributions are not taxable. The $50,000 will be growing at the full prevailing rate of return on high yield investments, whereas A. J. would have to invest the $25,000 in much lower yield tax exempts, in order to cope with the 50% federal income tax on all other investments. Because of this tax-free compounding, the stockholder-employee will still have more money in-pocket upon distribution of the pension funds, despite the fact that the funds themselves are taxable upon distribution. A big boon in that regard is the special 10-year averaging tax relief provision, if the plan proceeds are taken down as a lump sum upon termination of employment. Under the proposed tax reform proposals, this averaging advantage would be eliminated, ostensibly because the top individual rate would be lowered to 35%.

In our example, Samuels-Ritter Company has to put $100,000 a year into the pension plan to provide A. J. with a $50,000 share of its contributions. That is a break-even. If the $100,000 were retained by the corporation, it would be taxed at about $50,000, leaving the company with $50,000. But those dollars would still be locked up in the close corporation. Now they are in A. J.'s account, able to earn a greater after-tax yield for his personal benefit.

UNREASONABLE ACCUMULATION OF EARNINGS

The close corporation does not have complete discretion in deciding how much of its profits should be shifted to the stockholders, and what portion should be retained in the corporate treasury. Notwithstanding the desirability, from an income tax standpoint, of avoiding dividends like a plague, the income tax collector has a weapon that can be used against close corporations who are trying to avoid paying dividends because of the double tax. There is a penalty tax payable by any corporation that unreasonably accumulates earnings by not paying dividends. The rate is 27½% on the first $100,000 of the year's undistributed income (essentially net income after taxes, with some adjustments). Over $100,000, the rate is 38½%. This, of course, is in addition to the regular corporate income tax.

There are a number of ways this tax can be avoided. First, a corporation, other than a personal service company, can accumulate $250,000 of net-after-tax earnings without worrying about the penalty tax at all. Then there are a goodly number of justifications for a business' hanging on to its profits. A very important one is providing enough liquidity to finance a manufacturing cycle (the *Bardahl* formula). This permits a corporation to retain sufficient capital to fund costs starting with the purchase of raw materials, moving through the manufacture of the products, their sale, and the collection of the accounts receivable from customers. Even though the company may have a sizeable line of credit from a bank, which has been used regularly, the availability of those loans does not have to be taken into account. Another good reason for holding on to money is funding for anticipated capital needs such as a new plant, major items of equipment, or financing customers. Opening new markets, new product development and research needs are commonly employed explanations for hanging on to earnings, instead of distributing them as dividends.

Proprietors facing possible imposition of the penalty tax for unreasonable accumulation of earnings have to avoid certain actions. They cannot borrow money from the corporation. There is no persuasive response that I know of to an Internal Revenue Service agent's query: "If the company can't afford to pay dividends, why can it afford to loan money to a stockholder." Expenditures by the corporation for the personal benefit of the stockholders and investments that are unrelated to the business are also hard to explain. A close corporation that has to contend with this penalty tax should not play the market or make long term investments. Surplus funds are best held in easily liquidated, non-risk holdings, communicating the idea that they are only being invested to produce a return until the time comes when they must be utilized in the company's business. A justifiable and often very profitable investment is the acquisition of a goodly amount of acreage adjacent to a plant, obstensibly to permit an expansion of facilities when the need arises.

SUBCHAPTER S STATUS

The simplest way to get money out of a close corporation, without double tax, and with fewer tax risks, is the election of Subchapter S tax status. The term "Subchapter S corporation" describes a corporation that decides to be taxed like a partnership. What this means is that there is no federal income tax on profits at the corporation level. No matter how much Samuels-Ritter makes in any year, it pays no income tax, except in certain states which tax Subchapter S corporations in the same ways as other corporations. The entire tax on the business' net income is paid by the stockholders, individually. In our case, A. J., the sole stockholder, would pick up all the corporate income when he files his own income tax return. Where there is more than one stockholder, each of them must report his proportionate share of the corporation's taxable income. If A. J. gave 10 of his

100 shares of stock to his son, David, and a like number to his daughter, Sarah, leaving him with 80 shares, 10% of the Samuels-Ritter profits would be taxed to each of David and Sarah, and A. J. would report 80%.

This Subchapter S status frees the stockholder from the reasonable compensation limitations. It eliminates the double tax (first to the corporation and then to the stockholders) if profits are paid out as dividends—or if there is a holding that what was called compensation or a fringe benefit was really a dividend. Moreover, there are no more worries about the penalty tax for unreasonably accumulating income. The use of Subchapter S as a vehicle was fostered by the virtual equivalency between the top tax rate of the close corporation and the owners of its stock. A 50% maximum federal income tax rate for individuals is not very much more than the 46% tax rate on corporate taxable income in excess of $100,000. This will continue if the corporate tax rate is fixed at 33% and the maxmium individual tax is set at 35%. In fact, if one factors in the capital gain on retained earnings that is payable when the stock is disposed of, there is a lesser tax cost with Subchapter S.

Let me explain. Samuels-Ritter, a regularly taxed corporation in the top federal income tax bracket, has an additional $100,000 of taxable income. It will pay $46,000 in federal income tax on the $100,000, leaving the corporation with $54,000. If the business is sold and the corporation liquidates, when A. J. Samuels receives the $54,000, he will have to pay a capital gain tax on it. At a capital gain tax rate of 20%, A.J. will pay almost $11,000 on the $54,000 he receives. He will have in-pocket approximately $45,000 of the original $100,000. About 55% will have been paid out in taxes. What would have been the result if Samuels-Ritter had elected Subchapter S and the $100,000 was distributed to A. J.? Assuming it were taxable to him at the maximum 50% rate, he would have kept $50,000. This is 11% more.

The use of Subchapter S has also been stimulated by some recent statutory liberalizations. A close corporation can now have two classes of common stock, one voting and the other non-voting, and still qualify for Subchapter S tax treatment. This would permit A. J. Samuels to shift business income to his son, daughter or spouse, without affecting his complete control of the enterprise. All he would have to do is convert the single class of common stock into two classes, only one of which would have the right to vote, and give away only the shares without voting power. The voting control also enables the controlling stockholder in the Subchapter S family business, who feels he may have been too generous in the number of shares he gave to members of his family, to enlarge his portion of the profits simply by raising his salary, or working out a percentage-of-net income bonus arrangement. He is not hampered by any reasonable compensation limitations in doing this.

Another relatively new provision permits stock of a Subchapter S corporation to be held in trust. For many years only outright ownership was permitted. This prevented the giving of stock to descendants who had not reached the age of financial maturity, were incompetent to handle large sums of money, or where there were other fears about outright ownership, legitimate or not. A. J. Samuels, for instance, might worry a good deal about giving stock outright to his daughter, Sarah, because of his concern that his psychiatrist son-in-law, Jason Maloney, "will probably blow all of Sarah's income from the business in some crazy investment, like most doctors do."

Disadvantages

One disadvantage of Subchapter S can be the loss of the lower taxes on the first $100,000 of corporate taxable income. The first $25,000 of taxable income is taxed at 15%. From $25,000 to $50,000, the rate is 18%. Between $50,000 and $75,000, 30%, and from $75,000 to $100,000, 40%. The total federal income tax on the first $100,000 of corporate earnings is $25,750. This has to be compared with what the stockholders would pay in tax on this first $100,000, if the corporation changed to Subchapter S. Under President Reagan's tax proposal this disadvantage would be eliminated, since there would be a single corporate tax bracket of 33%, only slightly less than the maximum rate of 35% payable by the stockholders.

There is another problem with Subchapter S classification, in the area of estate planning. Redemption of preferred stock at a proprietor's death provides a tax advantageous way of getting money out of the company, to care for the surviving spouse and children. Shares of preferred stock may be bought back by the corporation to help finance the payment of death taxes and estate administration expenses. Through the creation of preferred stock, the value of the corporation's common stock can be greatly reduced, "watered down," so that common stock, representing a very large proportion of the future growth potential of the entity, can be given away, with much reduced gift tax exposure. Unfortunately, a corporation with preferred stock cannot qualify for Subchapter S status. Because of the significance of the preferred stock in much of an entrepreneur's post-death planning, it is common to see the income tax advantages of Subchapter S given up, in order to deal more effectively with estate planning concerns.

LIFE INSURANCE

Without exception, there is a profit on an insurance policy when the insured dies. That is, if one measures what the beneficiary receives against the total premiums paid from the inception of the policy until death, the proceeds exceed the premium outlays. This gain is not subject to income tax, no matter how large it is. For example, if Samuels-Ritter took out a $1,000,000 policy of insurance on A. J.'s life, paid one premium of $40,000, and A. J. died two months later, the corporation would not have to pay income tax on the $960,000 gain. This makes life insurance a great medium for handling problems which require a certain sum at death. The fund springs into existence at the very moment it is required, without any diminution for taxes.

Because of the income tax exempt nature of life insurance proceeds, the premiums are not deductible. Consequently, if Samuels-Ritter is considering a $1,000,000 policy on the life of A. J., with a $40,000 premium, it is going to take $80,000 of pre-tax profits, each year that A. J. is alive, to carry the policy. One way to cut the premium cost is to buy term insurance, which stays in effect only for a stated period of time. But the close corporation problems that generate the need for life insurance generally call for insurance that stays in force during the entire lifetime of a close corporation owner like A. J. Samuels. So, term insurance does not fit the bill.

Minimum deposit funding

What close corporation owners really need is permanent insurance with a cost closer to term. The creative life underwriters in the field have come up with the solution. Minimum deposit funding was the method they developed. To understand how this works, the reader must keep in mind that when a premium is paid on a permanent life insurance policy, ordinary or whole life, the cash surrender value automatically increases, and this increase can be utilized to pay that premium. Going back to the $1,000,000 policy on A. J. Samuels' life, with a $40,000 annual premium, let us assume that in a particular policy year, a $40,000 premium payment resulted in a $20,000 increase in the cash surrender value. It would not be necessary for Samuels-Ritter Company to pay the $40,000 premium in full and thereafter borrow the $20,000 of additional cash surrender value. The two steps can be joined together. The $40,000 premium can be paid by borrowing $20,000 against the new cash surrender value and paying only the balance, $20,000, in cash.

With this background, let us examine how Samuels-Ritter would use the minimum deposit method to pay the premiums on this $1,000,000 on A. J.'s life, of which the corporation is the beneficiary. Each year, with the exception of any four of the first seven years of the policy's existence, the corporation will borrow the increase in the cash surrender value, apply that against the premium, and pay the balance of the premium. These policy loans are not the same as bank loans. They do not have to be repaid. So long as Samuels-Ritter, the owner of the policy, pays the premiums, when due, together with interest on the policy loans, the insurance remains in force. When A. J. dies, the insurance company will first repay the policy loans to itself, and remit the balance of the proceeds to the designated beneficiary, Samuels-Ritter Company. If the premiums or the interest on the policy loans are not paid up, no liability will be asserted against Samuels-Ritter. The policy will simply be cancelled.

This format of borrowing the increase in the cash surrender value greatly reduces the amount that the owner of the insurance pays on account of premiums. In the year that the $40,000 premium was paid by first borrowing $20,000, the owner of the insurance, Samuels-Ritter, only outlayed half the premium in cash. Since the cash surrender value increases go up as the policy ages, the borrowing percentage increases and the cash payment towards the premium keeps going down. Of course, Samuels-Ritter also has to pay the interest on the loans. The interest increases annually as the policy loans keep enlarging. The benefit here is that the interest is tax deductible, whereas the steadily declining premium payments are not. The net-after-tax cost to the close corporation owner, in a 50% combined federal and state tax bracket, is only one-half of the interest it pays the insurance company.

In order to deduct the policy loan interest, for Federal income tax purposes, the owner of the policy must pay, in full, four out of the first seven premiums. It makes no difference which four are paid. This is a requirement that was added to the tax law, to limit the trafficking in tax deductions in connection with the sale of life insurance. Policies have been designed with substantial cash surrender values in the early years, thereby permitting very large policies to be funded primarily with interest payments right from the start. At the end of seven years, and thereafter, the entire cash surrender value can be borrowed, without jeopardizing the deductibility of the interest.

Suppose A. J. Samuels decides that the $1,000,000 policy should not be for the benefit of his corporation, but instead, the proceeds should be used to provide income and security for his family after his death. His lawyer suggests that A. J. consider having the policy owned by an irrevocable insurance trust, so that his wife, Bernice, can enjoy the policy proceeds during her lifetime, although they will not be subject to estate tax at the death of either A.J. or Bernice. This idea appeals to A. J., but he wants to use the minimum deposit method for paying the premiums, and get the tax benefit of the deduction for interest on the policy loans. How can this be accomplished, when the trust will have no income, while A. J. is living, against which to offset the deductible interest?

In our office, we have coped with this situation by splitting the ownership of the policy. The insured's wife, Bernice, is the owner and beneficiary of the cash surrender value portion of the policy. She does the borrowing against the cash surrender value, to pay that part of each premium which is equal to the increase in the cash surrender value, that year, produced by the payment of the premium, and pays the policy loan interest. A. J. gets the use of the tax deduction for the interest against his taxable income, simply by filing a joint income tax return with his spouse. The trust is the owner and beneficiary of the insurance proceeds in excess of the cash surrender value, and pays the portion of the premium that exceeds the cash surrender value increase.

Some technicians handle this problem by deliberately having the trust agreement violate certain rules which result in the trust being characterized as a "grantor trust." Under the statute, this makes the grantor, the close corporation principal who is the insured, treat the income and deductions of the trust as though they were his. Thus, when the trust pays the policy loan interest, the entrepreneur gets the deduction, reportable on his own tax return. This is an easier technique to use. It also eliminates the problem, which can exist in the case of split ownership, of finding a substitute if the wife predeceases her husband. There are a goodly number of tax people, however, who question its propriety in the circumstance of an unfunded life insurance trust.

SALE OF THE BUSINESS

Let us assume that A. J. Samuels can sell the assets of his company, Samuels-Ritter, for a healthy price like $3,000,000, to Creative Enterprises. What he wants is to have that sum come to him taxable at favorable capital gain rates. Then, after paying his taxes on the proceeds, he will pocket about $2,500,000. To reach this result, A. J. must avoid having Samuels-Ritter, which actually will be the seller, pay a tax on the gain it will realize on the sale of the assets. If the corporation pays a tax on the $3,000,000, and so too does A. J. Samuels, a lot less than $2,500,000 will be in his hands, after-tax.

How is this double tax avoided? Samuels-Ritter adopts a plan to go out of business and liquidate within one year. It then consummates the sale to Creative Enterprises, and before the end of the one year period, liquidates the corporation—which involves paying off all creditors and then distributing the net assets, including the proceeds of sale, to the shareholders, in proportion to their stockholdings. When this is done the corporation, with a few possible exceptions, will not be taxed on its gain. This is true, even in the case of inventory of the business, which may be sold at a price greatly in excess of what it is valued on the books of Samuels-Ritter, so long as the inventory is sold to one purchaser in one transaction. Now A.J. Samuels will get the $3,000,000 subject to only one tax bite, his capital gain tax.

In the case of some special assets, Samuels-Ritter will be taxed on the sale to Creative Enterprises:

● A sale of machinery, equipment and other tangible personal property, for more than the cost less depreciation, produces what is known as "depreciation recapture." That is, the excess of the price over the book value of this kind of property is taxed as ordinary income to the corporation.

● The same tax result occurs in the case of buildings and similar improvements, but only where the selling corporation has used accelerated depreciation. If a factory has been depreciated ratably each year, using the so-called straight line depreciation, there is no recapture.

● The Internal Revenue Service has urged with success that the purchase price of certain assets which have been expensed, in prior years, is taxable to the corporation when they are sold. For example, if Samuels-Ritter has some valuable dies used in the manufacturing process, the cost of which the corporation had deducted in computing its taxable income, the amount the purchaser pays for them is ordinary income to the corporation.

When the time comes to negotiate the allocation of the purchase price of $3,000,000 among the various assets, Creative Enterprises will be happy to inflate the value of the inventory, because it will get the tax benefit right away, a lower gross profit, when the inventory is sold. Fixing a higher price than cost less depreciation for the plant will be acceptable, because Creative Enterprises can depreciate the add-on to the price of this real estate. What Creative Enterprises will resist strenuously is a substantial payment for the Samuels-Ritter good will. What is allocated to good will cannot be deducted, at all, by the purchaser for income tax purposes.

The tax battle lines are now drawn. The representative of Creative Enterprises will urge a much higher number for the "extensive, excellently maintained, wonderfully efficient" machinery and equipment of Samuels-Ritter. That increment can be deducted ratably over a short period, five years. But that means taxable income to Samuels-Ritter that could be avoided by a sale of good will. It is A.J.'s machines vs. A.J.'s good will.

Golden parachutes

Employment contracts and non-competition agreements are often used to create deductions for payments that otherwise would provide no current tax benefits to the purchaser. For example, Creative Enterprises might agree to employ A.J. as a consultant, for five years, at a very substantial annual salary. This would be a "consult at convenience" arrangement, under which A. J. would not have to work regular hours, could enjoy whatever vacations he wanted to take, and would not be required to travel on behalf of the company. Should A. J. die during the five year term of his consultation contract, the payments for the balance of the term would go to his estate or designated beneficiary. This is to make sure that the portion of the purchase price, now converted to a consultation agreement, is paid no matter what.

As an alternative or addition to the consultation agreement, a sizeable sum could be paid by Creative Enterprises to A. J. for his agreement not to compete with the purchaser for a period of years. The amount attributed to this non-competition would be deductible, ratably, over the period of years that A.J. could not compete, irrespective of how it was paid. For instance, if A. J. was barred from competition for three years, in exchange for Creative Enterprises' obligation to pay him $300,000 over five years, at the rate of $60,000 a year, Creative Enterprises would get a tax deduction of $100,000 for each of the three years that the covenant was in effect—whereas A. J. would report the $60,000 only as received.

The Tax Reform Act of 1984 put a serious crimp in the ability to convert a substantial segment of the purchase price for a close corporation business into consulting compensation. A section was added to the tax law, ostensibly aimed at "golden parachutes."

A golden parachute is the term used to describe an agreement calling for the payment of very generous sums, to the top officers of a large publicly held corporation, if control of the corporation is acquired by another. The management of a corporation realizes their company is a likely target for a raid. In the hopes of making the take-over less attractive, and providing some financial amelioration to the management in the event a suitor seeking control is successful, the golden parachutes are put in place. Everyone believed the new tax provision was aimed only at that kind of an arrangement. Here we are talking about a voluntary sale of the assets of a close corporation. The consulting agreement is between the acquiring corporation and a principal of the seller. The close corporation making the sale is not a party to the contract. Nonetheless, the language of the new law seems broad enough to embrace every employment agreement that comes about in the course of a sale of a business. It covers compensation payments that are contingent either on a change in ownership or control of the corporation (a sale of stock)—or in the ownership of a substantial portion of the corporation's assets (a sale of assets).

The golden parachute provisions do not eliminate the right to take deductions for consultation arrangements worked out as part of the sale of the family business or incorporated partnership. They limit those deductions. A safe harbor is established, which is too complicated to explain in detail, but which essentially avoids the application of the golden parachute rules, if the present value of the consultation payments is less than three times the average compensation of the selling owner-employee, during the five years prior to the sale.

What about non-competition payments? Are they golden parachute payments? The answer is not clear. They could fit the definition in the statute. And we were told by one of the staff, who was involved in drafting the section, that it was intended to have very broad application. We will have to await the Commissioner's regulations for the Government's definitive position. My opinion is that payments for a selling owner's agreement not to compete are not within the golden parachute limitations—but I could be wrong!

BASIC GIFT AND ESTATE TAX STRATEGIES

6

Recently, in response to a friend's suggestion that many successful, very bright entrepreneurs really didn't understand the important concepts affecting their own estate planning, I conducted a survey of some of my clients. The idea that income tax matters were not grasped fully by the experienced businessman was tolerable to me, since they are more abstract and are expressed in statutorily defined terms. But certainly the head of a close corporation was knowledgeable about the things that were crucial to his estate planning—for instance, something as well known and significant as the marital deduction. The results of my inquiries showed how wrong I was. Every one of the individuals I questioned acknowledged that there were a number of areas about which he or she was confused, even though planning decisions had been made and implemented.

"Why didn't you say something?" I asked each of the people I talked to. While the responses varied, there was a central theme. The client felt that to get a real handle on what I was talking about would require many interruptions, and that my explanation would probably involve a glossary of estate planning terminology. Some acknowledged that they were concerned that they would look foolish, if the inquiry did not befit persons of their standing and experience. Another businessman said, kiddingly, "At your billing rate, Milt, I couldn't afford to seek an explanation." All of them really accepted the estate planning recommendations, because they put their trust in my competence. As the patriarch of a large family business put it: "Every successful chief executive learns how to evaluate the wisdom of proposals in areas where he truly is incapable of testing their technical propriety. I guess, in large measure, it's the confidence you have in the person who is making the suggestion."

In this chapter I am going to try to clarify some of the key tax concepts that figure into estate planning for the owner of a close corporation. Avoiding estate taxes is a crucial goal because of the devastating effects that such taxes can have on the continued success of the enterprise. A major challenge that the head of a growing close corporation business faces is having enough working capital to meet the needs of the company. These enterprises can't sell securities to the public to raise money. Capital must be generated internally, and even when a bank or other institution lends funds to the company, the repayment of these loans must come from profits of the entity. Tapping the resources of a family business, in order to pay the deceased father's death taxes, may seriously impair the corporation's ability to finance its operations. I have seen a number of cases where the failure to cope with this problem forced a sale of the business. As we will see later in this book, life insurance is a very important source of the wherewithal to pay death taxes. But the close corporation doesn't get the insurance for nothing. Substantial premiums may have to be paid. To the extent that the senior stockholder is successful in holding down the estate tax liabilities, less life insurance is needed, and the out-of-pocket premium cost is reduced.

My focus will be on federal gift and estate taxes. Some states also have a gift tax. Almost all states used to have death taxes, but the modern trend is to eliminate or greatly reduce state death tax burdens. All of the taxes imposed by the states are far less than the federal tax. For these reasons, and because of the variety of taxing formats that are used by the states, I will not explore state gift and estate tax impositions, in any depth.

COMBINED GIFT AND ESTATE TAX CREDIT

A starting point for any discussion of the taxes affecting estate planning, is a recognition of the major change that has been made in the federal gift and estate taxes. During most of my years of practice, there were two separate taxes, a gift tax and an estate tax. They had different rates—the gift tax rates at the same level were about three-quarters of the estate tax rates—and some of the deductions and exemptions varied. For example, $30,000 of gifts during a lifetime were tax exempt, and at death there was an additional $60,000 exemption for the estate tax.

This has now changed. The two taxes are unified, in something like a "cradle to the grave" approach. There is a single set of rates. What is given away while alive, and what is taxable at death, are aggregated in computing the tax liability; and there is one credit which a taxpayer is given, to be applied first against lifetime gifts, and any remaining balance is then offset against the estate tax that is payable at death.

This combination of the gift and estate tax makes sense. Nevertheless, it is confusing to some of the older entrepreneurs. After years of struggling with the differences between the gift tax and estate tax and finally getting a handle on the rules, they must now reorient their thinking. Just as it is harder to correct bad habits in an old golf swing or tennis stroke, these close corporation owners of more advanced age are often frustrated by the difficulties in forgetting the old concepts and learning the new. But there is no choice.

What we now have is a credit, in connection with the integrated gift tax-estate tax structure, rather than the exemptions we had before. What is the difference? A credit is an actual offset against the tax that is calculated. An exemption is like a deduction that is taken in determining how much the tax will be. A dollar credit is much more advantageous than a dollar exemption.

Why a credit is more valuable than an exemption

To illustrate the tax benefit of a credit versus an exemption, let us assume that A.J. Samuels decided to give his children, Sarah and David, some of his stock of Samuels-Ritter Company. The gifts, after subtracting the annual exclusions—which we will discuss next—amount to $100,000, and they fall into a 20% tax bracket. Before reflecting either the exemption or the credit, A.J. would face a tax of $20,000 (20% of $100,000). With an available exemption of $30,000, which is subtracted from the $100,000, the taxable gifts are reduced to $70,000, and a gift tax of $14,000 is payable in cash (20% of $70,000). The exemption has saved A.J. $6,000 in taxes, 20% of the $30,000 exemption. In the case of the $30,000 credit, it would be applied in reduction of the initial tax of $20,000 that had been computed. A.J. would have no gift tax to pay, in cash, and he would have $10,000 of the credit left over to apply against his future federal gift tax and/or estate tax liabilities.

This credit is not fixed in amount until January 1, 1987. It goes up, in steps, calendar year by year until that date. Why Congress decided to do this, I frankly don't understand. One might think, from an equity standpoint, that the opposite philosophy should apply—that is, the earlier one died, the greater would be his tax advantage. As I often say to clients, "If you have no other compelling reason for wanting to live, Congress has certainly given you a tax motivation to stay alive until January 1, 1987."

The "credit equivalent"

Nobody uses the amount of the credit in doing estate planning. It means nothing. What is commonly utilized is the "credit equivalent amount." This is the amount of property, in a given year, that can pass by gift or at death, free of any cash payment of tax, because the tax will be absorbed by the credit. Here is a simple chart that shows the credit equivalent amounts:

If Transfer Occurs	The Credit Equivalent Amount Is:
In 1985	$400,000
In 1986	$500,000
On January 1, 1987 and thereafter	$600,000

In explaining the credit equivalent amount, what somebody will tell A.J. Samuels and his wife, Bernice, is something like this: "What this table means is that if you live until January 1, 1987, and we certainly are going to assume that, each of you can give away, or leave at death, a total of $600,000 to anyone, without having to pay Uncle Sam any taxes at all. Between the two of you, you can dispose of $1,200,000, free of federal taxes.

The existence of the credit against gift and estate taxes has a profound effect on estate planning. Since the $600,000 can pass to anyone, tax free, it does *not* make sense to have that amount qualify for the marital deduction (which is discussed, in depth, later in this chapter). What falls within the marital deduction, when the first spouse dies, automatically becomes subject to estate tax when the surviving spouse dies. Consequently, it is a mistake to take this substantial amount of property, the $600,000 which can escape tax, and do the one thing that will subject it to tax at the survivor's death. If the surviving spouse needs the use of the income from the $600,000, and the protection of the principal, this can be done through a trust, which does not qualify for the marital deduction. The credit also permits the very wealthy close corporation proprietor, who can afford to have some property by-pass his or her surviving spouse, to leave a meaningful amount of stock or other assets to his offspring, at his death, without the payment of death taxes.

Even though the unused credit is available, at the close corporation owner's death, a number of sagacious entrepreneurs have concluded there is a decided advantage to using it up during lifetime, with gifts of stock of the enterprise. A.J. Samuels wants his son, David, to have most, if not all, of the stock of Samuels-Ritter Company after A.J.'s death. The company is growing, and so is the value of its outstanding stock. It makes sense for A.J. to make substantial gifts of shares of the company to David, now, even if he has to use up all of his credit. A much greater percentage of the stock can be given away at this time, simply because the stock is worth less than it will be when A.J. dies. While this technique results in a reduction or loss of the tax credit that can be used at death, it does not require any outlay of cash for taxes. And all of the subsequent growth in the value of the stock given away will not be subject to estate taxes at A.J.'s death, or at his wife's death.

Offset for payment of state death taxes

There is one other aspect of the credit equivalent that must be understood by individuals doing their estate planning. The portion of the credit equivalent amount that one can take advantage of, by transfer to family members, is diminished to the extent of state death tax liabilities. For example, let us assume A.J.'s estate will have to pay a Pennsylvania inheritance tax of $100,000 more than is permitted as a credit against the federal estate tax. If that $100,000 is paid out of the portion of his property that is earmarked for Bernice, and is intended to qualify for the marital deduction, it reduces the marital deduction. You can only get a marital deduction for what actually passes to the surviving spouse, free of any obligation on her part to use some of what she gets to satisfy her husband's liabilities, tax or otherwise. To obtain the full benefit of the marital deduction, and avoid federal estate tax, this state death tax obligation is imposed on the beneficiaries who receive the credit equivalent amount at death. In the case of A.J. Samuels, even after January 1, 1987, the $100,000 of state taxes payable by those beneficiaries would reduce what they will inherit from $600,000 to $500,000.

The federal government gives a decedent's estate a credit for the death taxes paid to the states. This is done on the basis of a formula. If the actual state taxes are in excess of this credit—and this is very common—the offset against the federal estate tax is limited to the formula amount. In this chapter, when an amount of an estate or inheritance tax imposed by a state is given, in any example, I am referring to the excess over the federal credit.

THE ANNUAL GIFT TAX EXCLUSION

Virtually every living close corporation owner is aware of the gift tax exclusion and its recent increase from $3,000 to $10,000. They all understand that they can give away $10,000 per person, in any year, to any number of recipients, with no limitation on how much can be given away in the aggregate. With the other spouse merely consenting to splitting gifts, on a gift tax return, the ante can be doubled. $20,000 can be given in any year to each donee. Here, there is some confusion. Some clients believe that each spouse must give $10,000 to the selected individual, in order to get the $20,000 of exclusions. That is not the case. All of it can come from one spouse, so long as the other consents to split the gift.

Annual gifts, within the limits of the annual exclusion, are a helpful estate tax reduction tool. Why is the tax collector so generous? The exclusion has been in the law for many decades, to free the Government from the administrative headache of policing small gifts, particularly intra-family ones, which are difficult to probe. I recall vividly two partners in an unincorporated partnership, Joe and

Lionel, who invited me to their office with their idea of how to exploit this exemption for limited gifts. Each of them was married, and had three children, which added symmetry to the plan. The idea was simple. Each year, Joe would give $20,000 of stock to each of his three kids and to each of Lionel's children. Lionel would do the same with his three children and Joe's offspring. In this way, the three siblings of each partner would receive twice as much, $40,000 of stock, every year. Unfortunately, as I told them, someone else had already thought of that idea, and it had been challenged successfully by the Internal Revenue Service. Only $20,000 per child would be covered by the exclusion.

Owner's reluctance to give sizeable gifts

Gifts of stock or other assets, taking advantage of the annual exclusions, have not proved to be a truly effective death tax reduction mechanism for principals of family businesses and incorporated partnerships. The owner of the close corporation is generally unwilling to part with sizeable chunks of his cash, marketable securities or favorable real estate investments. This is usually the case because, as with A.J. Samuels, the proprietor has only a limited amount of non-business assets. But I have seen other instances where the amount of cash and marketable securities was very substantial, and still no large sums were given to children. What it amounts to is an expression of the patriarch's insecurity. As a client with more than a $1,000,000 of cash once said to me: "The world is too full of surprises for me to take any financial risks. If this means the children get a little bit less when Tema and I are gone, they won't miss it."

There is a somewhat amusing aspect to the reluctance of the head of a large business to make gifts during lifetime. When it comes to discussing the death taxes that his surviving spouse will pay, at her subsequent death, he has a simple rationale: "Look, Milt, she'll give a lot to the kids and reduce her death taxes." I have never understood this logic. The entrepreneur, who is so much more able to dispose of property, won't do it, and yet he sincerely believes that his wife, alone, frightened and much more dependent, will do so casually.

The problem with gifts of stock

What about stock of the close corporation? At first blush, annual gifts of equity in the enterprise would seem to be an excellent vehicle for death tax reduction, so long as the senior family member retains enough stock to keep control of the company. Here again, in my experience, only a very limited use has been made of this opportunity to transfer shares, free of gift tax, to descendants. Putting stock in the hands of those who are not active in the business creates serious potential conflicts for the family and the business, which are discussed in Chapter 10. However, it would be very difficult for A.J. Samuels, year after year, to give stock to his son, David, who works in the business, and nothing to daughter, Sarah. This offends a parent's need to maintain equality among his offspring. Furthermore, it is difficult to determine with assurance how many shares can be given away within the annual exclusion limitations. And, in any event, an individual who directs a continually threatened business, subject to many risks, may be reluctant to part with any of his property.

Adverse consequences for incorporated partnerships

Annual gifts may have adverse tax consequences where incorporated partnerships are concerned. In the last chapter, I noted that when a gift of stock is made, resulting in the payment of no gift tax, the person receiving the stock keeps the same basis for the shares that the donor had. That is typically a very modest amount. I also pointed out that the situation is different for the recipient of stock who inherits it from a deceased owner. The beneficiary, after death, has a new "stepped-up" basis for the stock, equal to its date-of-death value.

In most incorporated partnerships, the stockholdings of the first partner to die are purchased by the corporation, including any shares the deceased partner may have transferred to any members of his family during his lifetime. The shares purchased from the legatees of the deceased partner, will produce no income tax, since the new basis for the shares and the purchase price payable for them are the same. But the children of the decedent, holding shares with the lower basis that they received as a gift from their deceased parent, can realize a hefty taxable gain—the excess of the price for the shares over their nominal basis. This adverse income tax result, coupled with the reality that no federal estate tax may be due when the entrepreneur dies because of the availability of the unlimited marital deduction, is a big deterrent to giving shares of stock which are bought back when the owner dies.

"Present interest" requirement

There is another important reason why businessmen like A.J. Samuels shy away from using the gift tax exclusions, now up to $20,000 per child per year, to move stock of a family business to the next generation. To qualify fully for this exclusion, the gift must be outright. It cannot be made in trust (except for a trust for minors which ends at 21). This limitation of the gift tax exclusion to gifts of what is known as a "present interest" is not appreciated by many outside of the tax practice.

To illustrate what the restriction means, and its consequences, let us assume that A.J. wants to give stock to his daughter, Sarah, but he won't risk putting the shares in her name at this time. What he wants to do is have a trust of the shares of stock, for the benefit of his daughter, held by a trustee of his choice, with the trust to last for ten years. At the end of the trust term of ten years, the shares will pass to Sarah. At that juncture, Sarah will be 45 years of age, and A.J. feels she will have the maturity to withstand any outside pressures, particularly from her doctor-husband. The "present interest" under this trust, which qualifies for the gift tax annual exclusion, is only Sarah's right to receive the income of the trust for ten years. The value of this present interest is computed by applying a percentage, obtained from a Government table to the value of the stock that is contributed to the trust by A.J. Samuels. In essence, this represents the right of the beneficiary to receive the income of the trust for the stated period. The so-called "future interest," which does not qualify for the exclusion, is Sarah's right to get the stock at the end of ten years. If A.J. went ahead with this gift of stock in trust, the larger segment of the gift, the future interest, would have to be offset by some of A.J.'s combined gift and estate tax credit, which means there will be less tax-free credit equivalent available for future gifts or at the death of A.J. If the credit had already been exhausted, A.J. Samuels would have to pay a gift tax, in cash, on the portion that was not covered by the annual exclusion.

Paradoxically, the shorter the period before the beneficiary of the trust gets the property placed in trust, outright, the smaller the amount that comes within the annual exclusion. Suppose A.J. cut back, and decided to let Sarah have ownership of the stock after five years, when she reached age 40, rather than extending the term for ten years. The qualifying present interest, her right to get the income for five years, would now be a smaller percentage. The disqualified future interest would be greater.

Getting the benefit of the annual exclusions is particularly difficult when the owner of an insurance policy, on the life of the close corporation owner, is a trust established to keep the proceeds from being subject to estate tax, at the deaths of the entrepreneur and his spouse. This kind of trust, having no money of its own, obtains the premiums to keep the policy in force from the businessman. Every one of those transfers of premiums dollars to the trust is a gift. Because of the nature of an insurance trust—all interests are future interests—no part of any contribution is covered by the gift tax exclusions. The same is true of the original transfer of an ordinary or whole life policy to the trust, which involves a gift of the cash surrender value of the policy, plus that portion of the last paid premium which has not been used up.

The solution to this gift tax dilemma, when gifts are made to a trust, was provided by the Tax Court's decision in the *Crummey* case. It works this way. Certain named individuals, children, for example, even if they are minors, are given the right to withdraw stated sums each year that contributions are made to the trust. The amounts subject to this right of withdrawal do qualify for the gift tax exclusions. Certain notification procedures, which are not onerous, must be followed for this to work. Obviously, the arrangement contemplates that no one will exercise the right to take cash out of the trust. One head of a family put it very succinctly: "I'll disinherit any of my kids who withdraws a nickel."

THE OLD 50% MARITAL DEDUCTION

The marital deduction is the most significant tax tool in estate planning. In its original version, the marital deduction was intended to create parity between citizens of community property states and the greater number of Americans who lived in jurisdictions which did not recognize community property. A man with a $1,000,000 died in Texas. Because one-half of his property, $500,000, was deemed to be owned by his wife, his estate only paid tax on $500,000. His brother, living in New York City, died with the same size estate, leaving everything by his will to his wife. The brother's federal estate tax was based on a $1,000,000 taxable estate. Such a different result in the imposition of a federal tax, attributable solely to different state law property concepts, was clearly unfair. To create equality, and mirror to a great degree the community concept, a deduction was granted for those of us who lived in non-community property states. The deduction was limited to 50% of what we would call the net assets of the decedent—his gross estate less the total of his funeral and estate administration expenses and debts. The surviving spouse had to get the property outright, or in a trust which gave him or her all the income and exclusive benefits, and the right to dispose of the property, at least at death, to anyone the surviving spouse chose—including a new mate. Now, when the New York brother died, up to 50% of what I have described as his net estate, could qualify as a deduction, and be subtracted in computing what would be subject to estate tax.

The essence of the marital deduction, since its inception, has been tax postponement, not tax avoidance. When the New York brother died, because of the old 50% marital deduction, his estate only paid a tax on $500,000. But the other $500,000 immediately became potentially taxable to the brother's wife, when she died. That $500,000 didn't escape the estate tax. The time of payment was delayed until the death of the surviving spouse, which could be many years later. There was some tax reduction, since two estate taxes on $500,000 come out to less than one tax on $1,000,000 (by reason of two credits and lower brackets). While this was valuable, the real impact of the marital deduction, in doing a married couple's estate planning, was the improved economic position of the surviving spouse. The survivor had available, for support and maintenance during his or her entire lifetime, the tax dollars, and the income they produced, which were saved by the 50% marital deduction.

THE NEW UNLIMITED MARITAL DEDUCTION

A few years ago, there were some significant changes in the marital deduction. The 50% limitation was removed. Any amount of property can now be left to or for the exclusive benefit of the surviving spouse, and will be subtracted in calculating what is subject to estate tax when the first spouse dies. What this means is that the federal estate tax can be completely eliminated at the death of the first spouse to die. A.J. Samuel's total property holdings might be worth $5,000,000 at his death, and still no federal estate tax will be payable. The tax collector will have to wait until Bernice's subsequent death to collect anything. This tax postponement, coming as it did in a climate when politicians were trying to figure out how to reduce the Federal Government's substantial budget deficit, was a very big surprise. A number of clients, being advised of the consequences of the unlimited marital deduction, have suggested that the 50% limitation will soon be reinstated. My guess is that there will be no repeal, because the amount of revenue raised by the estate and gift taxes is "peanuts" in the scheme of things.

While the emphasis in discussions of the unlimited marital deduction, has been on the tax-free shift of property from one spouse to the other, at death, spouses can also move an unlimited amount of property from one to the other, gift tax free, during lifetime. This permits the transfer of property to the less well-heeled spouse, to make sure, should he or she predecease the other, that there is $600,000 of property that can pass estate tax free because of the tax credit. It also is a boon to the spouse who wants the feeling of independence that having one's own money can produce. We are already witnessing some greater pressures in that direction.

A good case might be made for not taking full advantage of the unlimited marital deduction, in doing estate planning for the owner of a close corporation business. What I am saying, is that it may be advantageous to pay estate tax when the proprietor dies, rather than delaying the payment until the later death of the surviving spouse. To some this may seem like tax heresy. It will mean giving up the income and possible appreciation on the tax dollars paid up front, during the entire lifetime of the surviving spouse. This strategy can result in a substantial loss of money when the first spouse dies. Indeed, there may even be favorable changes in the estate tax law or rates, before the surviving spouse dies. For all of these reasons, I have had only one situation where an entrepreneur decided to pay some substantial estate taxes. Still, I think there is merit to the position, particularly where the business is prospering.

Let us go back to A.J. Samuels and the Samuels-Ritter Company. It is growing at the rate of about 10% a year. In order to take advantage of the unlimited marital deduction, a very large percentage of A.J.'s stock of Samuel's-Ritter will pass to Bernice at his death. Should Bernice survive A.J. for ten years or so, those stockholdings in the family business will appreciate in value very substantially. So too will the estate tax that will have to be paid when Bernice dies. Would it be better to pay the estate tax on some of those holdings, when A.J. dies, in order to avoid a greater death tax at Bernice's subsequent death? Think about it.

Effect on children's inheritance

The change from a 50% to an unlimited marital deduction is delaying children's receipt of their inheritance. They now have to wait until the death of both parents to get a truly significant amount of property. The impact of this change is felt most in the case of larger estates. Assume, for example, that A.J. Samuels dies after January 1, 1987, when the amount of property that can pass, free of federal estate tax, has reached the maximum of $600,000. His estate, after all debts and funeral and administration expenses, is $3,000,000. The state inheritance tax amounts to $100,000. Prior to the change in the law, all that A.J. could qualify for the marital deduction was one-half, or $1,500,000. He could easily conclude that this was sufficient to take care of his wife, Bernice. The balance, after a federal estate tax of approximately $400,000 and the state death tax of $100,000, was $1,000,000 ($1,500,000 less $500,000). This would pass to the two children, Sarah and David, about $500,000 each.

Now, by claiming the unlimited marital deduction, the entire federal estate tax can be eliminated at A.J.'s death. To accomplish this, the amount passing to both children has to be reduced to $500,000. This is the maximum credit equivalent of $600,000 reduced by the state inheritance tax of $100,000. Each of them will only receive about $250,000 when dad dies. The situation becomes even worse for the children when the father's estate is greater and results in a higher state death tax. The children are essentially limited to $600,000 less state tax, no matter how large the estate may be.

The "Q-Tip" trust

As I mentioned earlier, under the old marital deduction law, the surviving spouse had to be given the right to dispose of the property qualifying for the marital deduction to anyone. This right of disposition could be restricted to take effect only at death, so that the surviving spouse couldn't give it away during lifetime. But there was no way of protecting the fund for ultimate distribution to descendants, when the survivor died. Many proprietors of businesses, usually the males, worried a lot about the wives remarrying and leaving a good deal of inherited wealth to a second husband, or making substantial bequests to one or more sisters or brothers. There is an amusing side to this concern on the part of husbands. In my experience, I have not seen any widow who remarried disinherit her children by leaving property over which she had a power to a second husband, or pass on any very large percentage of the property to her collaterals. Widowers, on the other hand, despite the much lesser number of them that I have had contact with, have frequently left sizeable amounts to a second wife.

Under the new marital deduction rules, this risk can be eliminated. A special kind of trust, nicknamed a "Q-Tip" (Qualified Terminable Interest Property), can be set up to qualify for the marital deduction. During lifetime, the surviving spouse must receive all the income of the trust; he or she can be given rights of demand with respect to the principal; and the trustee may be empowered to invade principal for the benefit of the surviving spouse. No one else can have the right to receive anything out of the trust fund. At the death of the surviving spouse, the remaining trust fund devolves as directed in the instrument which established the trust. For example, it may provide for division into equal parts for the children. The surviving spouse can be denied any right whatsoever to change those dispositions, or his or her right to alter the distribution pattern, at death, may be limited. A typical limited power is one to change the amounts going to offspring, or the ages at which a child will receive his share.

With a Q-Tip trust, the marital deduction is elective. The deceased spouse's executor decides whether or not to claim a marital deduction with respect to all, or part, of the property passing into the trust. Once the election is made, the amount that qualifies for the marital deduction is subtracted in computing the federal estate tax liability of the deceased spouse, and that portion or all of the Q-Tip trust fund becomes subject to estate tax, when the surviving spouse dies. Where does the estate of a surviving spouse, who has limited funds, get the money to pay the estate tax on the value of what is in the Q-Tip trust when the survivor dies? Those tax dollars come from the trust itself.

The Q-Tip trust has provided a very helpful vehicle for widow and widowers who have remarried. Picture A.J. Samuels, his wife Bernice having died some years before, remarried to a widow, Doris, who has two children from her former marriage. After the marriage has continued for some years, A.J. decides he would like to make some provision for Doris' support, if she survives him, because she has very little money of her own. But he doesn't want any property to pass to the children of Doris. All of A.J.'s assets are earmarked for his own children, Sarah and David. Before the Q-Tip, he could not get a marital deduction if he eliminated Doris' right to dispose of the trust fund, at her death, as she saw fit—which meant to her family. Now, A.J. can leave some portion of his estate in a trust, to pay the income to Doris until her death, at which time the trust property will pass to his offspring. By exercising the election to qualify this trust for the marital deduction, there will be no estate tax on the trust fund when A.J. dies. At the subsequent death of Doris, there can be a lesser estate tax on the trust fund, or even no tax, because her own assets are very modest, and there is the available credit which can offset $600,000 of her taxable estate.

VALUATION OF COMMON STOCK

The entrepreneur's stock of his business corporation is his most serious estate tax liability. It keeps growing in value, year after year. The close corporation owner, striving to build the profits of the company, has a special partner—the Internal Revenue Service. The Service waits until death—now really the death of the owner and his wife—to claim its share of the profits. But so long as the worth of the business keeps going up, the government's equity keeps increasing. The federal estate tax is very significant as the stock value mounts. The rate when a taxable estate exceeds $500,000 is 37%. It moves up to 45% at $1,500,000, to 53% at $2,500,000 and it reaches the top bracket of 55% at $3,000,000. In 1988, the top tax rate is scheduled to go down to 50%, on amounts in excess of $2,500,000.

To figure out the estate tax exposure, one has to determine what the stock is worth. That is one of the toughest valuation tasks that someone can take on. The standard to be used is ridiculous: what a willing buyer, possessed of knowledge of all the pertinent facts, would pay to a willing seller, under no compulsion to sell. There are no two such persons. The regulations that the Government has promulgated, as an amplification and explanation of the standard, add very little. All they do is list a host of factors to be considered, so numerous and general in nature, that they provide no real guidance. The best measure of value, sales of stock between unrelated parties, are generally not available. Even in the case of A.J. Samuel's stock of Samuels-Ritter Company, the redemption of Ritter's shares has no real significance in the valuation process. The amount paid to Ritter by the corporation did qualify as an arms-length price, involving, as it did, adversary negotiations. However, the deal closed almost ten years ago, which is much too far in the past, for that price to be meaningful in ascertaining the value of A.J.'s stock today.

Valuation experts can come up with and justify widely divergent values for close corporation stock. Some years ago I read all the then reported decisions of the Tax Court of the United States dealing with the issue of the proper value of stock of a close corporation. The government's experts were high. The taxpayer's were low. And the court generally made a finding somewhere in the middle.

Book value

Since there is no public market for the stock of a close corporation, the starting point that is generally used in the valuation process is the book value, per share, of the common stock. With only common stock outstanding, this is the excess of the assets of the corporation over its liabilities, as reflected on the company's balance sheet, divided by the number of shares of stock outstanding. If the close corporation has preferred stock outstanding, the value of the preferred stock has to be subtracted from the excess of the assets over liabilities, to arrive at the overall value for the common stock.

All that book value provides is a "ball park" figure. There is really no correlation between book value and market value. Inventory is generally reflected at cost, rather than market value, and where the inventory figures are submitted by management (i.e. without a certified financial statement) there is often a significant amount of inventory that is not shown. Fixed assets, such as the plant and equipment, are shown at original cost, less depreciation, whereas the real value may be much greater. Nothing is reflected for intangibles, such as consumer acceptance of well-known products, trademarks, patents, a franchise, unique know-how or manufacturing competence, all of which can have very significant worth. On the other hand, the book value of a corporation's stock may exceed its market value. There are many companies, whose stock is listed on the New York Stock Exchange, with stock selling at less than the book value.

Multiple of earnings

When book value is rejected as a valuation measure, businessmen and many of their advisors shift to a multiple of earnings. For example, an entrepreneur, whose close corporation made $150,000 after taxes last year, declares with an air of certainty: "My company is worth at least ten times earnings, which means $1,500,000." The multiple is generally picked out of the air. Unfortunately, the selection of the appropriate multiple is crucial, since a modest difference in the multiplier can produce very varied amounts. For instance, applying a multiple of 8, to the $150,000 of earnings, yields a value of only $1,200,000, or $300,000 less. On the other hand, if the correct multiplier is 12, the value jumps up to $1,800,000. The variance between 8 times and 12 times earnings is $600,000.

Comparison with publicly traded companies

A more sophisticated valuation method, one that is preferred by the Internal Revenue Service, is a comparison with companies that have traded stock. The theory is that by comparing the financial data of the privately held enterprise with comparable companies, where there are frequent sales of stock by willing sellers and buyers, you can better determine the real value of the stock of the closely held company. This is done by a stock valuation expert, and it is a very extensive and costly procedure. Here is a condensed description of how an expert might value A.J.'s stock, using this method:

1. He would select a number of public companies, with a business similar to Samuels-Ritter. Their stock must be regularly traded on a stock exchange or over-the-counter. This is the hardest part of the job, and it involves a lot of judgment calls. As you might guess, finding public companies that are truly "comparable" to Samuels-Ritter is not easy. Invariably there are substantial differences, and both A. J. and his advisors will have to accept the expert's professional opinion that they are, in fact, comparable. Many close corporation owners, reviewing a stock valuation report, which uses the comparative public corporation approach, will say something like this: "Truly, Milt, I don't think one of those damn companies is anything like mine!"

2. Three ratios are used: price to book value; price to net-after-tax earnings; and price to cash flow. That is, the price at which a share of each comparable public company is selling on the valuation date, or the average price over some period prior to that date, is compared to the net worth per share, the net earnings per share and the cash flow per share of that company. Then all of the price-net worth ratios are added up and divided by the number of public companies used in the study, to arrive at an average price-net worth ratio. The same thing is done for the relationships of price to net earnings and price to cash flow of the comparable entities. Many years ago, cash flow was not a financial factor that was generally used in these studies. But the investment bankers have convinced the appraisers that cash flow is as important, if not more important, than net profit. For example, Samuels-Ritter could show very large earnings in a given year, but if a large part of those earnings is in inventory, the financial picture may not be so rosy.

Let us assume that the averages for the comparable corporation used to measure the value of the Samuels-Ritter common stock are as follows:

Price-net worth—1.1
Price-net earnings—12.5
Price-cash flow—14.0.

3. When compiling the data, more than one year's figures are used. There is too much of a risk that the results of a single year are a fluke. Some valuation experts use an average of the last five years, others use the average of the most recent three years.

4. The three ratios are not given equal weight. The price-net worth relationship is invariably given lesser standing, because it is not considered to be as meaningful a barometer of value. Typically, 20% is assigned to price-net worth, and 40% each to price-net earnings and price-cash flow. We will use those weightings in our example.

5. The average net worth, net-after-tax profits and cash flow figures are then compiled for Samuels-Ritter, covering the same period of years. Each of the trio of averages is then divided by the number of shares of common stock outstanding, in this case, 100, to provide a per share amount. We will assume that this produced the following results, in the case of A.J.'s stock of the corporation:- net worth - $20,000 a share; net earnings - $2,000 per share; and cash flow - $2,250 per share.

6. The net worth per share, net earnings per share and cash flow per share figures for Samuels-Ritter Company are then multiplied by the average ratio, in each category of the comparable companies. The resulting figure is then multiplied by the weighting factor, 20% for book value and 40% each for net earnings and cash flow. In our example this would mean:

Net worth
1.1 X $20,000 = $22,000 X 20% = $ 4,400

Net earnings
12.5 X $2,500 = $31,250 X 40% = $12,500

Cash flow
14.0 X $2,750 = $38,500 X 40% = $15,400
                              TOTAL $32,300

7. The valuation expert would now reduce this $32,300 per share figure for Samuels-Ritter Company, to reflect the fact that the stock of this corporation does not have a public market. A purchaser would pay less for stock, if he did not have the ability to sell it, at a fair price, whenever he chose to do so. A 25% discount, sometimes even more, is commonplace to reflect this locked-in aspect of holding stock of a corporation such as Samuels-Ritter. Applying an offset of 25%, brings the per share number down to $24,225. This makes A.J.'s 100 shares worth $2,422,500.

USE OF PREFERRED STOCK TO FREEZE
OWNER'S EQUITY

Preferred stock is a class of stock that is senior in rank to the close corporation's common stock. The holders of the preferred stock are entitled to receive a stated dividend, for example, 12% of the $1,000 par value per share, or $120 a share, before any dividends can be paid to common stockholders. The dividend preference can be cumulative or non-cumulative. With a cumulative preferred stock, if the corporation pays the preferred stockholders less than the 12% per share in one fiscal year, the 12% preference for a succeeding year is increased by the deficiency. Also, in case of the corporation's liquidation, the preferred shareholders get these cumulated amounts before any distributions are made to the owners of the common stock. In the case of non-cumulative preferred stock, the failure to pay dividends has no consequence. There is no carry-over of the deficiency to a subsequent year, or any add-on of omitted dividends in the case of a liquidation of the company. Because of the uses of preferred stock, in tax and estate planning, some of which will be discussed later on in the book, non-cumulative preferred stock is the rule. A cumulative preferred stock is a rarity in a close corporation.

If the corporation issuing the preferred stock is liquidated, there is another preference for the holders of this class of stock. They get the par value, or stated value, of the stock, before any assets are distributed to the common stockholders. In addition, the corporation usually has the right to redeem shares of its preferred stock for an amount set forth in the corporate charter. The company generally can select the shares of preferred stock it wants to buy back, without any requirement of purchasing shares from all stockholders pro rata. This provides flexibility for someone like A.J. to bequeath shares of preferred stock to a surviving spouse, or a child who is not active in the business, and only those shares will subsequently be purchased by the corporation.

A major estate planning use of preferred stock is to help the close corporation owner "freeze" the value of his equity in the enterprise. This is accomplished by converting almost all (sometimes all) of the entrepreneur's equity into non-cumulative preferred stock. This stock does not grow in value. The maximum value of each share is its liquidation preference and redemption price—which are the same.

The future growth in the equity of the corporation is vested almost entirely in the common stock, which is given to members of the next generation. Because the preferred stock absorbs much of the existing value of the entity, the common stock can be distributed with greatly reduced gift tax exposure.

Impact of future growth on owner's stockholdings

The failure to cope with the future growth in value of the owner's stockholdings is the reason why annual gifts, within the limits of the annual exclusions, don't work. Let's go back to A.J.'s 100% owner-ship of the stock of Samuels-Ritter Company. He now wants to make gifts of $20,000 worth of stock, each year, to his daughter, Sarah, and his son, David. A.J.'s stockholdings are increased to 10,000 shares to accommodate this gifting program. The first problem A.J. faces is the need to determine the value of the corporation. His advisors tell him to use $2,500,000. The value of Samuels-Ritter increases at the rate of $200,000 a year.

In the first year $40,000, or 1.6% of the stock can be given to the two children, which means that Sarah and David will receive a total of 160 shares, 80 shares each. In the next four years, if A.J. con-tinues to give away $20,000 of stock to each child, the approximate percentages of the outstanding stock of Samuels-Ritter that will pass to the two children, and the number of whole shares they receive will be as follows:

Year	Percentage of Stock Passing	No. of Shares Gifted
2	1.48%	148
3	1.38%	138
4	1.29%	129
5	1.21%	121

The reason for the annual reduction in the percentage and number of shares that can be given away by A.J. to his two children, is the $200,000 per year increase in value of Samuels-Ritter Company. At the end of five years what does the score card show? A.J. has given away 696 of his 10,000 shares of stock, about 7% of his holdings.

He is left with 9,304 shares, or about 93% of the equity of the corporation. His 9,304 shares, or 93% of the stock of Samuels-Ritter Company, is now worth $3,690,000 (93% of $3,300,000), almost $570,000 more than when he began the gifting program.

This is a familiar pattern. A close corporation owner may give away an even more significant portion of his stockholdings and find that the value of the shares he has left, is more than the worth of his stockholdings when he started transferring shares. Let me reduce the value of Samuels-Ritter Company to $1,000,000, and have the value of the company go up only $100,000 per year. With a five year program of giving away $40,000 each year, nearly 17% of the stock would pass to A.J.'s children. His holdings would be cut to about 83%. But that 83% would be worth approximately $1,160,000. A.J.'s stockholdings would have appreciated $160,000.

Valuing preferred stock

A few years ago, when a close corporation issued preferred stock, as a step in the freeze technique, Internal Revenue Service agents, charged with valuing the common stock, assumed that the par or stated value of the preferred was its market value. Suppose, for example, that A.J. Samuels decided to reduce the value of his common stock, so that he could give shares to his son, David, at a reduced gift tax cost. He has the corporation issue, as a stock dividend, 2,400 shares of $100 par value preferred stock, making the aggregate par value $2,400,000. The liquidation preference is $100 a share; the non-cumulative dividend preference is 12%; and the stock can be bought back by the corporation for $100 per share. In the good old days, the $2,400,000 was subtracted from the corporation's $2,422,500 overall value, reducing the common stock value to $22,500. A.J. could shift shares to David with confidence, believing that the only valuation issue concerned the total value of the corporation, and further, that he had resolved the issue by paying a valuation expert, who came up with the $2,422,500 figure.

This was a remarkable give-away by the Internal Revenue Service. A preferred stock, with a par value of $1,000 a share, calling for a dividend preference of even 15% a year, and a liquidation preference equal to its par value, is not worth $1,000 a share, especially where the preferred is non-cumulative, the corporation has no history of paying dividends and most of the equity of the enterprise has been allocated to the preferred stock. But the bonanza has now ended. In 1983, the Internal Revenue Service published a ruling which highlights the reasons why a non-cumulative preferred stock may be worth much less than its par or stated value.

The effect of reducing the value of the preferred stock of a close corporation is to increase its common stock. Let me explain why. You will recall that we reduced the value of A.J.'s common stock of Samuels-Ritter, $2,400,000, by issuing shares of preferred stock having a total par value and liquidation preference of that amount. Then we subtracted $2,400,000 from the total value of the company, $2,422,500, and came up with the difference, $22,500, as the value of all the common stock. If the Internal Revenue Service is able to turn the tables, and successfully urge that the fair market value of the preferred is only two-thirds of its par value, $1,600,000, rather than $2,400,000, will be subtracted from the $2,422,500 total value, making A.J.'s gift of common stock $822,500, instead of only $22,500. This is quite a difference.

Premium for voting control

What can be done to beef up the value of non-cumulative preferred stock? One way is to make the preferred stock a voting stock, and issue enough shares to give it control of the close corporation. A stock that represents a controlling interest in a business enterprise is entitled to a premium. This premium can reduce, or perhaps even offset, the discount attributable to the lesser investment value of the close corporation's preferred stock.

Of course, there may be objections to having the preferred stock continue as voting stock, after the patriarch's death. Shares may be earmarked for the surviving spouse, or children who are not connected with the business. Preferred stock may be redeemed, after death, to provide liquidity for the owner's estate. A simple solution to this problem is to have the preferred stock cease to have voting power when the owner dies. The Internal Revenue Service has given notice that it will reflect the premium of the voting control in valuing the owner's preferred stock in case of a gift by him or at his death—notwithstanding that the voting right of the preferred ends at his death. This means a greater gross estate at the owner's death. But with the unlimited marital deduction, this should not produce any federal estate tax. Thereafter, when the surviving spouse dies and the preferred stock is subject to federal estate tax, the premium will be gone—since the voting power ended at the owner's death.

The greater value of the non-cumulative preferred stock with voting control may have income tax advantages as well. Often the plan is to have the close corporation redeem the stock of the family head, after his death, as a way of getting money out of the corporation. The estate tax value of the preferred becomes its income tax basis in the hands of the beneficiary. When the shares are redeemed by the corporation, this means a lesser capital gains tax or even no tax at all.

Another idea, sometimes used in conjunction with the voting power is to have a preferred stock—sometimes tagged as preference common—participate to a limited extent in the future growth of the corporation. If the annual earnings of the corporation go above a stated sum, the holders of the preferred stock share in the excess with the common stockholders. The manner of the preferred's participation in these profits, is to increase the liquidation preference of the preferred—what the preferred stockholders will receive, in liquidation, before anything is paid to the holders of the common stock. However, there is a ceiling on the increase in this liquidation preference. No matter what the earnings of the company may be, the holder of this kind of preferred stock cannot receive more than a stated dollar amount, per share, on liquidation. The potential for enhancement of the liquidation position of the preferred stockholders, existing at the time of its issuance, helps to upgrade its value.

Avoidance of gift tax as incentive

The biggest estate planning incentive to make a gift of the future growth in the value of the corporation is the very wide margin of error before any gift tax will have to be paid in cash. We start with the benefit of gift-splitting between spouses. A. J. will actually give the common stock to his daughter, Sarah, and his son, David. His wife, Bernice, will consent to being treated as an equal donor for tax purposes. This means that the father and mother are each making one-half of the gift from a tax standpoint. With two donees, the two children, each of the parents first gets an offset of $20,000 of annual exclusions, or a total of $40,000. Since these exclusions are available on a calendar year basis, a gift in December, 1985 and a few days or weeks later in January, 1986, can result in $80,000 worth of exclusions.

The more important protection against outlaying cash for gift taxes is the combined gift and estate tax credit. As noted earlier in the chapter, the credit permits transfers, without gift tax being payable, of $400,000 per individual in 1985, $500,000 in 1986, and $600,000 in 1987 and thereafter. If the gifts of stock are timed for December, 1985 and January, 1986, the Internal Revenue Service would have to jack up the value of the gifts of common stock beyond $1,080,000 before A. J. would have to part with money. This is the sum of the four exclusions of $20,000 each (or $80,000) plus the amounts that will be absorbed by the spouses' credits, $500,000 for each of them. Of course, to the extent that the credit is taken against the gift tax liability, it is not available for estate tax reduction when A.J. and Bernice die. This is really not a loss, but a pre-application of the credit. Certainly, it is "credit well spent," since it is employed to cut off the escalating death taxes on the appreciation in value of the corporation.

Furthermore, there is a very practical audit advantage of the gift of watered down common stock. In the example just given, an Internal Revenue Service agent has to push the value up beyond $1,080,000 before $1 of tax revenue is collected by him. It is true that by increasing the values, he will be reducing the credit that can be used at the death of the donors. But that is hardly the same incentive for the agent, as setting up a meaningful tax deficiency payable in cash now.

How the freezing technique works

After considering the various ways of handling the escalating value of his stock of Samuels-Ritter Company, A.J. agrees to go along with the freeze format. However, he doesn't want to give any stock to his daughter, Sarah, only to his son, David. He feels that Sarah's having an equity in a family business, where she has no involvement, will lead to strife and problems. He would rather give up the $40,000 of annual exclusions, that including her would give him ($20,000 in 1985 and $20,000 in 1986). A.J. understands that there are ways to equalize Sarah's position with other property, which we will discuss in Chapter 10. The other thing that A.J.

wants, with no "and, if or buts," is absolute control of the corporation as long as he is alive and competent. This assures him that he
can take whatever compensation and benefits from Samuels-Ritter
that he wants.

The starting point in the process is a determination of the corporation's worth. Everyone agrees to use the value fixed by the valuation
expert, based on his study of comparable public companies. This
was $2,422,500, which is rounded out to $2,500,000. The decision
is made to reduce the common stock value from $2,500,000 to an
approximate value of $50,000, before A.J. makes his gift to David.
To accomplish this, $2,450,000 of preferred stock will have to be
issued. This is $450,000 more than the $2,000,000 net worth of
Samuels-Ritter Company. The corporation's attorney says that can be
handled by using a preferred stock with no par value, but giving it a
liquidation and dividend preference, and a redemption price, as
though it had a par value of $1,000 a share.

A recapitalization of Samuels-Ritter Company is then effectuated
by amending the corporation's certificate of incorporation. Three
classes of stock are authorized: non-cumulative preferred, class A
common ("voting common"), and class B common ("non-voting
common"), all without par value. They have the following rights and
privileges:

1. The preferred has a dividend preference of $120 a year.
What that means is that no dividends can be paid in any year to
the common stockholders, until all the holders of preferred stock
receive a dividend of $120 a share.

2. In case of the liquidation of Samuels-Ritter, the holders of
the preferred stock will receive $1,000 a share before anything is
paid out to the common stockholders.

3. The corporation has the right to redeem all or any number of
the shares of preferred stock, at a price of $1,000 per share.

4. Each share of preferred stock has a right to one vote on all
issues that pertain to stockholders, including the election of directors. This voting power ends at the death of A. J. Samuels.

5. The two classes of common stock are identical except that
only the holders of the voting common have the right to vote.
Each share of voting common has one vote.

In exchange for his existing stock of Samuels-Ritter Company, A. J. receives:

1. 2,450 shares of preferred stock. These preferred stockholdings have an aggregate liquidation preference of $2,450,000 (2,450 shares at $1,000 a share) and a total dividend preference of $294,000 a year (2,450 shares, each having a preference of $120). They represent more than 99% of the voting power of the corporation while A. J. is living.

2. 100 shares of voting common. After A. J.'s death, when the preferred shares no longer have the right to vote, the 100 shares of voting common will have the exclusive voting power.

3. 10,000 shares of non-voting common.

A. J. now gives away all of the non-voting common stock to his son, David. This means that David Samuels will hold 10,000 shares of Samuels-Ritter common stock. After the recapitalization and gift of the 10,000 shares of non-voting common to his son, A. J.'s equity in Samuels-Ritter Company is essentially frozen. The preferred stock cannot claim any more than $2,450,000 of corporate assets. While the 100 shares of voting common, still held by the father, can continue to grow in value, they represent a little less than 1% of the total outstanding common stock (100/10,100). Virtually all of the appreciation in value will pass to David, the holder of the 10,000 shares of non-voting common. To translate this into dollars, if the value of Samuels-Ritter goes up $1,000,000, $10,000 will be attributable to A.J., and $990,000 to his son. Assuming combined federal and state death taxes of 55%, at the death of the survivor of A.J. and his wife, Bernice, the resulting ultimate tax saving on the elimination of $990,000 from A.J.'s estate is almost $545,000. There is another significant advantage of the freeze. Reliable can now carry a large policy of insurance on A.J.'s life, to purchase some or all of his preferred stock at his death, for example, or for any other purpose, without the proceeds meaningfully enlarging his taxable estate.

Personal considerations

Does it make sense for A.J. Samuels to give away to his son, David, all the future growth of Samuels-Ritter Company, or should he hang on to some meaningful part of the non-voting common? There is no doubt that by parting with all the non-voting common, the best death tax result will be obtained. So long as A.J. has the voting control and the business is not sold—which is his decision to make—he will not suffer economically because he no longer has those shares of stock. He alone will have control over the business and will determine the quantum of his compensation and what perquisites and benefits he will enjoy. If dividends are paid, they will all come to A.J. because of the very substantial dividend preference of his preferred stock. There are, however, psychological concerns that many entrepreneurs have expressed to me about giving up all the growth. "I don't want my children to be richer than I am." "Will I have the same incentive in the business, if my interest is frozen?" Then there is the unexpressed possibility that the father does not want his children to feel independent of him, because they now hold a very valuable interest in the company.

The most serious worry that A.J. Samuels has is what happens if it makes sense for the business to be sold while he is living. All he sees himself getting is about $2,450,000. "Suppose," he says, "that the business is sold for $6,000,000. I get $2,450,000 and David gets more than $3,500,000. That's not right!" The crucial factor, in considering this concern, is that no sale can be made unless A.J., who has voting control, agrees. Because he is in this driver's seat, and he will fashion the terms of the deal, there are a number of ways he can increase his share of the pot. A.J. can allocate a very substantial premium to his stock, because it represents voting control. A meaningful portion of the purchase amount can be allocated to a consulting contract or non-competition agreement for him. This is something that the purchaser will like, because it is tax advantageous. If these techniques do not produce enough for A.J., he again falls back on his control position. Unless his sons give him a larger share of the proceeds, in one way or another, he will not agree to sell.

Our firm has used this freeze procedure in a great number of situations. In only two instances did the father insist on holding on to a meaningful amount of the growth stock. In one case, he kept 50%, and in the other, one-third. In both instances the fathers regretted their decision. The one who retained 50% finally gave it away— after issuing more preferred stock to reduce the value of the gifted common. Because the corporation has grown significantly in the interim, this delay greatly increased the father's estate.

Close corporation with publicly traded stock

I include within the definition of a close corporation, an entity which has public stockholders, but continues to be controlled by one or more individuals, or a family, who head up the management of the business. While major stockholders of these entities enjoy advantages, because there is a market for their stock, the death tax problem is worse. Here, unlike the typical close corporation, there is a simple standard for the Internal Revenue Service to use in determining the value of the stock. That is the mean between the bid and asked prices of the stock, in the case of shares traded over-the-counter, or the trading prices, if they are listed on a stock exchange. The Government will try to apply that measure to all of the deceased stockholder's holdings. This is unfair. The market for shares of the public close corporation is generally very thin. The bid and ask quotations relate to trades of stock up to perhaps a thousand shares. The price would be substantially lower if the controlling stockholder tried to sell a large part of his stock. In fact, there may be no market for all of the shares owned by the major stockholder. We have seen instances where there was an offering of a substantial number of shares of a company traded over-the-counter, being underwritten by a prestigious investment banking firm, where a large chunk of shares had to be withdrawn from the offering, because no buyers were available at a figure close to the offering price.

The Internal Revenue Service will not readily grant a discount in these circumstances. The agent clings to the bid and asked mean. We have been successful, nonetheless, at higher levels of the Service, in obtaining recognition of the reality that a "willing buyer" would not pay the same price for 20,000 shares that he might pay for 200.

How can the owner of a major interest in a close corporation, with public stockholders, freeze the value of his equity? A recapitalization of the corporation, of the type that was done in Samuels-Ritter, is usually not feasible. What the father can do is create a family holding corporation. He transfers to this holding company his stock of the public corporation. Dad gets back from the holding company the same classes of stock that were issued in the Samuels-Ritter Company recapitalization that was described. This exchange of stock is income tax free. Then he gives away the holding company non-voting common stock.

If the public company pays dividends, this procedure will result in a modest double income tax. The corporation holding the stock of the public company receives the dividends and is taxable on them. Since it is a holding company, it must disgorge these dividends to its stockholders, who will also have to include them in taxable income. The amelioration comes from the fact that 85% of the dividends from the corporation to the holding company are not subject to corporate tax.

Discount for non-marketable minority interest

It is customary for a valuation expert to take a sizeable discount, when the stock interest being appraised represents a non-marketable, minority interest in a close corporation. I had a major valuation battle with the Internal Revenue Service, where a very highly re-garded expert used a 50% discount for this kind of interest. That is high, but a 25% to 35% write-down is common. This is realistic. A minority stockholder in a company, which has not gone public, is locked-in. Generally, there is little or no dividend yield on the stock. The only one who will pay anything meaningful for the stock is the controlling stockholder or the corporation itself. In essence, the mi-nority holder must go to the person who has control, hat in hand, when he or she wants to sell out. The only alternative is to make trouble, such as bringing a suit to force the person, in control, to pay back all the monies he took from the corporation, for what are alleged to be personal needs—rather than real business expenses.

This minority discount has been applied by the courts even where the recipient of a gift of a minority interest is a member of the same immediate family of the donor. For example, there are many deci-sions which would uphold a substantial reduction in value, if A.J. Samuels were to give 10 of his 100 shares of Samuels-Ritter Com-pany to his son. In one case, a judge discounted three gifts to children in trust, made to the same trustee, each of which was 20% of the outstanding stock of the company, or a 60% controlling inter-est, in the aggregate.

For a long time, the Internal Revenue Service recognized this minority stock discount, although its acquiescence was somewhat reluctant. In some court cases, the Government used experts who applied it. But this has now changed. The Service has announced a new policy when a father, the controlling stockholder, gives a minority number of shares of stock to his children. So long as the family member receiving the shares (in our illustration, A.J.'s son, David), has a close enough relationship to the majority stockholder (A.J., his father), that it can be assumed they will vote their stock as a unit, no discount is permitted. Thus, a parent who wants to give less than a majority of the stock of his or her close corporation to a child, and claim a discount, must be prepared to do battle with the Internal Revenue Service.

DOLLARS TO PAY DEATH TAXES

The special death tax problem of the owner of a growing close corporation is not just a matter of paying more money to the Government. The really troublesome issue is where does he get the dollars with which to pay those taxes? Generally, most of the owner's wealth is usually represented by the interest in the corporation. Rarely are there enough cash assets, held by the proprietor and spouse, to meet the tax obligations at death. Thus, the deceased entrepreneur's executors often have to look to the corporate coffers for help in satisfying the tax demands. Life insurance, financed by the corporation, can be a big help in this area. This is discussed, in detail, in Chapter 13, "The Importance of Life Insurance." In other instances, the continuing profits of the company can provide the needed money, if the estate tax payments can be spread over a period of years.

The first tax problem in using the corporation's liquidity to pay the death tax costs of the deceased major stockholder, even if it is sufficient in amount, is how does the estate get the money out of the business. Let us assume that A.J. Samuels has died, his wife, Bernice, having predeceased him, and his son, David, the executor of his father's estate, needs $250,000 for taxes. Fortunately, the corporation is in a very good cash position, having accumulated $150,000 which is not needed for the operations of Samuels-Ritter, and also collected on a $100,000 policy of insurance on the life of A.J. Wonderful! The corporation will pay a dividend of $250,000 to

A.J.'s estate, and David, his executor, can satisfy the tax obligations. Alas, it won't work. The dividends of $250,000 will be taxed as ordinary income, in the 50% bracket, leaving David only half, $125,000, to meet the $250,000 tax liability. The estate will be far short of satisfying its needs.

David consults with counsel, who smiling, says: "Don't worry, David, the estate will sell to Samuels-Ritter Company $250,000 worth of your dad's stock, and there will be little or no income tax to pay on the sale." Remembering the discussions while his father was alive, that a sale of part of a controlling stockholder's shares of stock to the close corporation results in ordinary income, David replies: "But, Milton, when dad wanted to sell some stock back to Samuels-Ritter, some years ago, to get $50,000 out of the corporation as capital gain, you told us that wouldn't work—that the distribution would be taxed just like a dividend. Now his estate holds all the outstanding stock. Why can I, as executor of the estate, holding the same 100 shares of stock, do what he couldn't do?"

The answer is that the tax law gives relief to the owner of a close corporation, whose interest in the business is a meaningful part of his property holdings. Congress, a long time ago, recognized the confiscatory consequences if ordinary income treatment—taxed sometimes at rates even higher than the present 50% maximum— was attributed to distributions from a corporation for the payment of the individual stockholder's death tax. Frankly, without this special tax provision, many family businesses would have gone out of existence or been sold at the death of the senior family member. Here is how this ameliorative section works:

1. The owner's stock of his close corporation must represent more than 35% of what is generally described as his "adjusted gross estate." This is all of his property subject to tax, reduced by the total of his debts and funeral and estate administration expenses. As I noted earlier, most clients think of this as their net estate. The important thing to keep in mind is that the base, against which the 35% is applied, is computed without the marital deduction. Meeting this requirement will be very easy for A.J.'s estate, because his stockholdings of Samuels-Ritter Company represent much more than 35% of his total property holdings. Sometimes, when it is touch and go as to the satisfaction of this 35%

amount, one observes the unusual scene of the representive of the estate urging a higher estate tax value of the stock, and the Government contending that the stock value was overstated.

2. If the 35% condition is met, a sale of stock by A.J.'s estate to Samuels-Ritter, subject to the limitation described in the next numbered paragraph, will produce capital gain, rather than having the proceeds treated as the equivalent of a dividend, and taxed like other ordinary income. Actually, the sale of stock by the estate to the corporation usually produces little or no tax. As was noted in the last chapter, this is so because the deceased owner's stockholdings get a new basis, or tax cost, equal to their estate tax value. If A.J.'s 100 shares of Samuels-Ritter stock are valued, for federal estate tax purposes, at $2,500,000, or $25,000 a share, a sale of 10 shares by David, as executor, to the company for the $250,000 of available cash, should produce no taxable gain at all.

There are advantages, in a situation like A.J.'s, to sell back shares of preferred stock, rather than common stock, as a means of getting dollars for the payment of death taxes. This avoids a conflict for the executor of the entrepreneur's estate. To keep A.J.'s estate tax down, David wants to urge that his father's 100 shares of Samuels-Ritter stock are worth less. But when it comes to selling shares back to the company, David would like to get the maximum amount per share. Obviously, if the same common stock is involved in the estate stock valuation and the disposition to Samuels-Ritter, both happening within a short time span, there is no way to go low on the valuation and high on the sale. You can get around this obstacle by issuing preferred stock, even after death, and having the corporation buy back the preferred stock, instead of the common.

3. There is a maximum amount that can be taken out of the corporation through these favorably taxed post-death redemptions of stock. The limit is the total of the decedent's federal and state death taxes, plus his funeral expenses and estate settlement costs. With the unlimited marital deduction, if the close corporation owner is survived by a spouse, the entire federal estate tax liability may be eliminated, substantially reducing what can move out of the entity with little or no tax. The greater use of the relief provision may occur at the death of the surviving spouse.

There is no mandate that the proceeds of the sale of stock to the business entity must be used for the payment of taxes and funeral and administration expenses. This is merely the measure of the statutory maximum. If David had the $250,000 from some other source, like personal life insurance proceeds, he could still sell shares of stock back to Samuels-Ritter Company. The relief provision then becomes a one time tax advantageous way of getting money out of the close corporation and into the hands of the family.

4. Any number of sales of stock can be made by the estate to the close corporation, so long as they are completed prior to the end of a period measured from the death of the deceased stockholder. The time given is more than sufficient to cover the final determination of all death taxes. The usual procedure is to make periodic sales. For example, David might sell some shares at the time that the federal and state estate tax returns are filed, to cover the tax liabilities shown on those returns, plus the funeral expenses and some part of the estimated administration expenses. If an audit of a tax return produces a deficiency, he can sell additional shares to raise money to satisfy the additional taxes. Near the end of his job as executor, he can take down from the corporation what he requires to pay in full the administration expenses.

EXTENSION OF PERIOD TO PAY
FEDERAL ESTATE TAX

When there are insufficient liquid funds available at death, either inside or outside the close corporation, the only path open for the funding of the federal estate tax may be to use the profits of the business. But the tax is normally due nine months after the owner's death, which does not leave much time to accumulate corporate earnings. Fortunately, in that situation, there are several statutory provisions that permit the federal estate tax on the decedent's stock of the close corporation to be paid over a period of years. Keep in mind that it is only the tax on the business interest that can be deferred, not the entire tax. The most liberal of these tax postponements, the use of which does not require the Internal Revenue Service's prior approval, also requires that the deceased owner's stock must represent more than 35% of his adjusted gross estate. It operates in the following fashion: When the estate tax return is due, which is nine months after the owner's death, no tax is paid on the value of the business interest. On the fifth anniversary of the return due date, the first installment of 10% must be paid; and on each of the next nine anniversaries of that due date, another 10% of the tax is due. Interest must be paid annually on the unpaid portion of the tax. But here again there is a special break. Only 4% interest has to be paid on that portion of the estate tax that is attributable to the first million dollars of value of the stock.

LIFE INSURANCE

A major advantage of all life insurance, as a mechanism for the build up of capital, is the ability to avoid federal estate tax. The insurance proceeds can easily be excluded from the taxable estates of both husband and wife. And this can be accomplished without interfering with the desired utilization of the money. How is the estate tax avoidance achieved? If A.J. Samuels had personal life insurance that he wanted to keep from being subjected to federal estate tax when he died, he would have to do three things:

1. A.J. would transfer the "incidents of ownership" to someone else. What are they? The ability to designate the beneficiary and change that designation; the right to draw down or borrow against the cash surrender value; rights of conversion; and the power over such things as how policy dividends are to be handled, and the manner in which the proceeds are to be paid at his death.

A.J. doesn't have to concern himself about the method of shifting those rights and powers to another person. Insurance companies have printed forms available for that purpose. All that needs to be done is to fill in the blanks, execute the form properly and send it back to the insurance company. The assignment of the incidents of ownership has to be absolute and irrevocable, to be effective for estate tax purposes. That is why this kind of transfer should not be made without careful consideration.

2. The estate of A.J. cannot be the beneficiary of the policy. This requirement will present no problem.

3. A.J. has to live for at least three years after the incidents of ownership are given away. If he dies within the three year period, the proceeds will be included in his taxable estate as a transfer in contemplation of death. The continued estate taxability of gifts made within three years prior to death used to apply to transfers of all kinds of property, including stock of a family business. That concept has been eliminated from the tax law in connection with gifts of almost all kinds of property, although many close corporation entrepreneurs are still unaware of this fact. But it persists for life insurance assignments.

Following these steps will result in the elimination of the estate tax on the insurance proceeds when the insured dies. Where the policy is transferred to a child or grandchild, this means a generation of estate tax has been avoided. But if A.J. were to shift the ownership of the insurance on his life to his wife, Bernice, nothing is really accomplished. By simply making Bernice the beneficiary, and taking advantage of the unlimited marital deduction, the same estate tax result is achieved.

How is the estate tax on the life insurance bypassed completely at the parents' level, while the proceeds still provide income and security for the surviving spouse? Here is where the trust vehicle comes into play. An irrevocable trust is created. Under the trust agreement, Bernice is given rights to income from the proceeds during her lifetime. She can be given some rights of invasion of the principal. The trustee, or her co-trustee if she is a trustee too, can have the discretion to use all or any part of the trust fund for Bernice's benefit. At the death of Bernice, the property in the trust passes on to the descendants of A.J. and Bernice. The incidents of ownership of the policy are transferred to the trust. This eliminates the proceeds from A.J.'s taxable estate. There is no federal estate tax when Bernice dies after him—or perhaps a very modest tax on her right to withdraw principal, if it is operative when she dies—because her lifetime interest as a beneficiary of the trust is not taxable.

ESTATE PLANNING FOR CLOSE CORPORATION OWNERS

7

Estate planning for a close corporation entrepreneur is a complex matter. Most of the owner's wealth consists of a non-marketable, generally non-income producing interest in a business enterprise. The great bulk of his income comes from the company in the form of compensation and fringe benefits, which will terminate when he dies. The patriarch, when confronted with the facts, admits that his death will produce significant practical and tax problems. Nonetheless, most businessmen are not easily moved to tackle the issues that death will occasion. Usually it is the need to draw or revise a will that finally propels the close corporation proprietor into his lawyer's office to consider estate planning. A forthcoming long trip is often a catalyst in that regard.

People often ask why is it important to have a will? The best answer to this query is to explain what happens if you die without one. The phrase for this is "dying intestate." A person who dies intestate has a will prepared by the legislature of the state in which he was a resident. That is, the laws of that state dictate how property passes when somebody dies without a will.

In most jurisdictions, the pattern is all to the surviving spouse, if there are no children—and vice versa, all to the surviving children if there is no surviving spouse. When the person who dies intestate leaves both a surviving spouse and children, the property is divided between them. Absent a surviving wife or child, ancestors (father and mother) and collaterals (brothers and sisters) usually split the property.

The most difficult situation, I feel, is where an intestate leaves a wife and minor children. In New Jersey under those circumstances the wife gets one-third and the children get two-thirds outright. This is costly estate tax-wise, since only one-third qualifies for the marital deduction.

The administration of an intestate estate is expensive and burdensome. A bond, with a large premium, may have to be posted to assure the faithful performance of the widow, as administratrix. When there is a lot of money involved, the bonding company may insist on co-signing checks, in excess of some amount. One has to look at statutes to decide whether a power to do this or that exists. A will avoids all of these difficulties.

In this chapter, which deals with the reasons why business owners keep putting off very much needed estate planning, I will use males as my examples almost exclusively. There is a very justifiable basis for this. Men are invariably the culprits when delay is the problem. Rarely do women procrastinate when it comes to the well-being of the family. In fact, in many instances in my practice, it was only because of the wife's insistence, that we were able to move ahead with an estate planning project that had been put off by her husband for much too long.

PROCRASTINATION—THE BASIC PROBLEM

Consider this situation: a business-owning father, 60 years old, is meticulous about doing everything thoughtfully and promptly. Subordinates in the business are both admiring and envious of his sense of organization. There is an agenda for every day's activities and a commitment to looking ahead and anticipating new developments and change. It carries over to his personal life. Vacation trips are planned many months before. No detail is overlooked. Tennis games are arranged weeks ahead. Reservations at restaurants are made well in advance. No one would ever describe him as cavalier, spontaneous or impulsive. Yet, despite all the pressures exerted on him by his advisors, he has done nothing about his estate planning.

There are plenty of reasons why he should be concerned about what happens after his death. He has a wife who must be taken care of. Two sons who work in the business of the close corporation, which is very dependent on dad's leadership. Then there is his daughter, the apple of his eye, the mother of three, who is married to a brilliant mathematician who earns very little money. Is this an unusual contradiction? Not at all. Many commentators and a substantial number of life insurance companies have identified procrastination as the major reason why people do not get around to planning their estates. I would agree. The challenging inquiry is why do competent and trained businessmen, normally conscientious and decisive, change their spots when it comes to facing up to the issues that death will present? I would like to share with you some observations on that subject.

A shocking explanation

At the outset, I should report one answer that is perhaps the most shocking that I ever heard. It was given by a psychologist who participated in programs dealing with the family business that I conducted. One of the participants in this seminar mentioned this reluctance on the part of so many businessmen to get involved in estate planning. Others echoed those sentiments. The psychologist was pressed for an explanation. He paused and thought for a moment and then responded: "I believe that subconsciously many entrepreneurs do not want to provide for an orderly and effective transition after they die. Quite the opposite. They really hope the business will not operate well. The fact that the business cannot be successful without him is the best proof of the patriarch's uniqueness."

This seemed bizarre to all of us who heard it. Several of us laughed out loud. During the week between sessions, we thought about the psychologist's observation and tried to decide if it provided any explanation for procrastination problems that we were contending with. During the following get-together, at which the psychologist was present, many of us had changed our attitude. We could see its application in a number of situations.

Now we sought from the psychologist the methodology to cope with this attitude. His suggestion was that we substitute a different standard of being unique. "Convince the businessman that if he—because of his thoughtfulness and executive talent—is able to design a plan for the continuing growth and development of the business, one that will contribute to the financial well-being and cohesiveness of his family, he will be doing the unusual."

I have no research findings on the propriety of the psychologist's theory. I must say that when I have discussed it with other estate planning professionals, they often confirmed that the theory probably held true for a number of cases they were handling.

Other reasons for procastination

There are a number of more easily understood reasons why people do not look forward to estate planning. The first, and perhaps the foremost, is that it deals with a subject that is not pleasant—death. The thrust of the whole process is what is going to happen after the individual dies. It brings into focus clearly the inevitability of death. "What will happen to me after I die? Is there really a life hereafter? Is it possible that reincarnation really exists, and I may come back to earth in a different form?" These and many other personal concerns are stimulated by the process of planning one's estate.

Moreover, many issues of self-worth are triggered by estate planning. The starting point is a listing of the assets that have been accumulated. Many individuals are upset by how little they have to show for the activities of a lifetime. Others are unhappy because they have spent money too freely and as a result they feel that they are not in a position to make adequate provision for the family after death. There are even a few cynics who recognize how little enjoyment they have realized from the wealth they have accumulated— and who are bitter at the realization that it will be their children who will have the fun spending the money.

There is also the realization of our insignificance. This may well be the hardest pill for a businessman to swallow. Whatever his achievements may be, he recognizes that the world will go on very well without him. During my lifetime, whenever I started to get carried away by a sense of self-importance, my mother would remind me of the fact that even though Franklin Delano Roosevelt had been President of the United States for so many years—the country got along very well after his death.

The truth is, with very few exceptions, that the death of the owner of a close corporation will have a significant impact only on his business and immediate family. In the case of the older head of the business, who has clung to control too long, his children in the business may be glad to be rid of him and the business will do better without him. Tragically, the father may sense this response. I have had the sad experience of a business head telling me, with great emotion, that he was sure the family would rejoice at his death. However accurate it may be, it serves no useful purpose at this point in the businessman's life, to point out to him that it was his conduct that produced their attitudes.

Another cause of procrastination can be the every day demands on the businessman's time. These include many things beyond the substantial pressures of overseeing the business and affairs of the close corporation. The car has to be fixed. The doctor or dentist has to be seen—and there are more of these visits as we get older. There is a need for new socks, underwear, shirts or what have you. The tennis or golf game, jogging, or the workout at the gym has to be fitted into the schedule—and so on and so on. For most of us there are not enough hours in the day to handle all the things we are committed to do. We are constantly straining to get to our appointments on time.

In the face of these daily pressures, someone suggests that we give some attention to planning what happens after our death. Death is what we choose to believe is an event in the far distant future. Sure we have to do it. But there's plenty of time.

A HARD LOOK AT SPOUSES AND CHILDREN

Some entrepreneurs get nervous about estate planning because they sense they will have to face certain truths that are difficult to deal with. The first one in the minds of many is an appraisal of how good is the relationship with their spouse, normally the primary beneficiary. Do I really care—down deep—about making sure he or she is well taken care of after my death? Professionals can make a very big mistake if they assume that every marital relationship is great, with each spouse devoted and deeply in love with the other. We all know that just isn't so. I am long past that level of perception. I recognize that many marital relationships exist where there's a great deal of hostility. Two people sticking it out, with limited emotional involvement and poor communication with each other.

On the other hand, in my experience, it has been rare for one spouse to take a punitive position toward the other when doing estate planning. I have not had the situation where a client exclaims: "Why should I leave him well off after my death? All he does is aggravate me and try to make my life miserable!" The close corporation owner seems to have a sense of responsibility to the man or woman he or she has vowed to love and honor. Perhaps it is a feeling of guilt if no adequate provision is made for the person with whom you have lived for many years. Whatever the causation, this is a healthy attitude. It is the spouse who needs the financial support in the later years of life. To punish a spouse by leaving him or her little money—and passing it on to the children—can be cruel. The kids are possessed of the vigor and energy that are the attributes of youth. The surviving spouse faces the reality of diminishing vitality and a greater difficulty in going it alone.

Most estate planners accept the spouse as the major beneficiary. They do not probe into how good a marriage it is. No client has to fear that the planning process will require him to explain or justify his relationship with his spouse. But when it comes to the rest of the family, especially the children, the estate planning encounter can be more heart-rending for the client. The concerns and the disappointments over children are spotlighted.

Right at the start, the estate planner gets a family profile. When it comes to the kids, he usually gets their names and ages. If the child is over the age of 17 or 18, the next query is: "What is he doing?" This simple question can bring to the surface a lot of heartache for the parents. There is the bright child who will not accept the discipline of the classroom, and despite his capabilities, will never be a student. Then, there is the dropout who is happier doing work with his hands than coming into the family business or pursuing a high level white-collar or professional career. Sometimes the children are with cults or gurus. Other children may have learning disabilities. Some might be addicted to drugs. Still others might be trying their luck as writers, actors, dancers or musicians.

In addition, of course, there are also children who are physically handicapped, retarded or emotionally disturbed. Oddly enough, while these disabilities pose special planning problems, they are often easier for the father and mother to accept. A parent seems to suffer more with a perfectly normal, or even superior child, who follows an unproductive or "way-out" path.

Unfortunately, parents do compete with one another through their children. Those who have kids who are not achievers, feel a sense of failure or defeat. I am afraid that there are too many sayings—such as "Apples do not fall far from the trees;" or "Like father like son"—that emphasize the tie between what the child does and the worth of the parent.

Other skeletons in the family closet come out in the estate planning interview. A relationship with a brother in the business or with sisters may be bad. A father may have remarried and his children can't stand his new wife.

Sometimes I feel that this estate planning fact-finding takes on the character of a systematic cataloging of the disappointments of family life. In day-to-day living, while there are instances and reminders of these problems, they come one at a time. This allows people to deal with the one or two that have been brought into sharp focus and ignore the others. Suddenly, at the hands of the estate planner, who is simply doing a thorough information gathering, all of the problems are spotlighted at the same time. This can have a severe impact.

HANDLING PAINFUL ISSUES: SOME GUIDELINES FOR ESTATE PLANNERS

The estate planner can do a lot to minimize these upsets. Let me offer a few tips:

1. *Never make judgments about family problems.* People who come to us for planning are worried that because of mistakes they made, or things that they didn't do, they are responsible for the lack of achievement or the nonconforming behavior of their children. They are concerned that they brought about the bad feeling in the family. Don't give your opinions on these issues. That is not what the clients have come to see you about.

2. *Be sensitive.* Don't pry unless the information is essential to your doing a good job. You may be curious to know more about the client's son who has become a member of a cult. How did it happen? What does he do there? What attempts have they made to get him out? With these kinds of inquiries, you may be opening up deep and painful wounds.

When you learn that the son is a cultist, that is sufficient information for your planning. Leaving him money outright or giving him an interest in the corporation may mean seeing it passed on to the cult. This is a predictably undesirable result from the parents' standpoint.

3. *Be empathetic and offer reassurance.* Most of us who have a fairly extensive estate planning practice—or who have friends with children from the ages of 17 to 28—have been exposed to many, many instances of young people who have adopted life-styles, pursued careers, or manifested behavior that upset their parents. It is a commonplace occurrence. Simply making an observation to that effect will reduce the pain of the individuals to whom you are relating.

Besides, problem children often go through a maturation process. There is an initial frustrating period of aggravating behavior. Then, with the passage of time and some greater experience, the child becomes a meaningful person and a very valuable addition to the business. Reporting that to a parent living with these anxieties can help a lot.

4. *Be objective.* Avoid identifying with the clients' problems. We estate planners are usually parents too, worried and concerned about the future of our own children. There can be a temptation to convert the estate planning interview process into a seminar on young adult behavior. The interrogator starts probing for information and answers that will help him in dealing with his own children more effectively. I must admit that I have been tempted at times to delve into some areas in greater depth because of my own anxieties. But I have learned to limit those discussions to friends and acquaintances. It is unfair for the professional to heap his problems on the client.

FAILURE TO COMPLETE AN ESTATE PLAN

Some clients will start the estate planning process but not complete it. This is the most exasperating and costly expression of procrastination. Interviews are held. Memoranda and instruments are drafted. All kinds of illustrations may be prepared. Substantial professional time is put in. Things percolate and significant progress is being made. Then the planning starts to drag. The momentum slows. Repeated communications and follow-ups to the client go unanswered, or are acknowledged with apology. The job never gets finished. Why does this happen? It can be the delayed entry of those factors that prevent a businessman from getting started on his estate planning. But there are two other possibilities that deserve special attention.

Superstition

The first one is superstition. There are individuals who believe that if they sign a will, they will die. I know it sounds preposterous, but a lot of people feel this way. I had perhaps my most disappointing experience in estate planning with one of these people. Let me call him Sam. He was a man in his fifties, a successful and prosperous businessman, married with three children, ages 17, 20 and 24. Sam's accountant, with whom I had done a lot of work, set up the appointment for me to meet with him. The accountant gave me the rather startling history of Sam's estate planning attempts. He had dealt with three different attorneys, the last of whom was a well-known specialist in the field. Each time there were meetings and a will was prepared. Sam avoided executing any of these wills, even though he paid each lawyer in full for the time expended. The reasons and excuses that Sam gave for not finishing the job varied somewhat in each of the three instances. But the end result was the same. The accountant hoped I could think of some approach that would move Sam finally to get a will executed.

The night before my appointment with Sam, I spent almost an hour debating what I should use as my approach to him. The next day, after he was ushered into the conference room with his accountant, and the amenities and coffee were out of the way, I let him have it. "Sam, I'm a very busy lawyer and I don't like to waste my time doing useless work. I know of your history of getting to the moment of signing the will and then backing away. The fact is that you're afraid that if you sign a will you're going to die. That's just plain nonsense. Before we get started on your planning, I want your commitment that you are prepared to execute the will that is ultimately prepared. If you aren't willing to make that pledge, you go home and I'll do something more productive."

I hasten to tell you that this is far from my normal greeting to a new client. But I felt that it made no sense to pussyfoot around Sam's obvious fear—which had to be significant for him to turn his back on three lawyers' instruments.

Sam was very much taken aback by my opening. There was that moment when he debated between making the pledge or picking up his things and leaving. Finally he said: "You're a pretty direct guy. But I do realize that I'm being foolish and unfair to my family. So, okay, I promise that this time I'll sign the will." I wish I could tell you that after the innovative beginning all went well. I did get the will done promptly. But then I goofed. Instead of sitting Sam down, going over the document with him, and pressing him to sign it, I mailed it to him for his review. Thereafter my calls and letters to him, urging him to act, and reminding him of his promise, produced no effective response. Finally, as a means of hopefully getting his attention, I sent him a stiff bill for services. His payment came by return mail. About six months later I learned from the accountant that Sam died of a heart attack on the golf course. He died without a will.

I now use a somewhat different approach when I suspect that a client is hesitant about completing his estate planning because he feels that if he does so he will die. It grew out of a casual remark that was made to me at a meeting of the Tax Study Group. For a long period of time I belonged to this group, which was made up of lawyers and accountants who specialized in taxation. At the monthly meeting, then held at the Faculty Club of New York University, there were discussions on various subjects followed by a summary of current tax events and some presentation to the entire body.

One night while sitting at a table discussion, I mentioned an interesting facet of our estate planning practice. We had done planning for some of the oldest people in our community. They seemed to live on forever. One of the men at the table said: "You're a fool. You should have a neon sign outside your office, shouting with blinking lights, 'Draw a will with Stern and live'." I now relate this story to the nervous individual, and assure him that he is in good hands.

Having nothing more to live for

There is another deterrent to the completion of an estate plan that is somewhat esoteric. I have seen instances where the businessman feels that if he puts all of his affairs in order, he will have nothing to live for. So long as there are some loose ends that require resolution, he has a raison d'etre.

My first awareness of this syndrome grew out of a case where an elderly gentleman was the sole surviving trustee of an orphan home. Because children without parents were now being placed in foster homes, the orphanage became empty. The real estate was sold and

Charlie was sitting on a large sum of money that the sale had produced. Charlie recognized that what he should do with the money was to give it to an institution that was involved with children. He had the legal authority to do that. But if he died before the funds were turned over to another charity, many legal problems would have to be resolved.

Pressure to make a decision was brought to bear on Charlie by the leaders of the community. He kept procrastinating. Charlie always needed a little more information about the prospective recipient. There was always another institution to investigate. While this was going on, the executive director of a child care agency that was the most logical beneficiary of the money in Charlie's hands—and which eventually got it—startled me one day with his explanation for the delay. "Charlie won't make up his mind because he believes that as long as the issue is unresolved, he will stay alive. It is as though the continued existence of the problem guarantees the continuation of his life."

This sounded strange to me. But out of respect for the expertise of the executive director, I urged some of the interested parties to take a different approach with Charlie—and it worked. Those communicating with Charlie convinced him that the choice of the entity to which the money would be paid over, was only the first of a lot of steps that Charlie had to be involved in. They enumerated the problems that required resolution, and in which he would participate, after the allocation of the funds to the child care agency. For instance, to what uses should the dollars be, applied? In what manner? Should the funds be used for regular programs or for new special projects? Did it make sense to utilize some of the dollars for capital improvements?

In essence, there were created a new series of concerns for Charlie. He had new reasons for staying alive. Charlie willingly turned over the money. I now believe that this "nothing more to live for" issue can be a barrier to getting some older people to finish putting the house in order. When I sense that this is happening, I take an approach that parallels what was done with Charlie. My plan is to resolve the major and significant matters. However, a few items are identified and deferred for future in-depth consideration.

In a situation I'm involved in, the pot has been boiling over one unresolved matter for almost three years. The client has recognized a problem that could develop after his death, with respect to his wife's continued participation in the corporate medical expense reimbursement plan. The question is when is the best time to raise it and how best to handle it. Each time that the problem surfaces, I offer a suggestion to deal with it. He counters with the opinion that for a variety of reasons the time is not ripe to resolve the matter. "We'll get back to it in a few months." This particular concern may not be taken care of during the client's lifetime. But by keeping something for future resolution, we have been able to complete the major aspects of his planning.

DELAYS CAUSED BY THE ESTATE PLANNER

The estate planning counsellor must make sure that he doesn't contribute to the client's failure to complete the much needed post-death planning. While many professionals are unwilling to acknowledge it, we may be at fault. First of all, lawyers may not be as prompt as they should be in getting the work out. I once served as a consultant to a very large life insurance agency. My role was to assist the insured's general attorney in tax and insurance matters. I must admit that I was shocked by the length of time it took a practitioner to get a crucial instrument—which we had gone over several times—into the hands of his very good client. As a result of this experience, our firm puts promptness very high on the list of important qualities that we must demonstrate.

Obviously, if the business owner has some reluctance about pursuing estate planning, delay by the professional is very counter-productive. It gives him more time to change his mind about going forward. The close corporation owner has a justifiable basis for ending the relationship with the planner, and avoiding the planning as well. Furthermore, the advisor has to make sure he does not over-complicate the process. This too will turn the businessman away. He is used to being in control, dominating the situation. A process that confuses him and makes him feel inadequate, will not be readily accepted.

LIFE EXPECTANCY AND REASONABLE PLANNING

A hard-nosed head of a business is used to fixing time tables for things. In the case of estate planning, he is faced with the complete opposite. The date on which the plan becomes operative is generally unknown. Rarely is the lawyer relating to someone on the verge of death. We are generally dealing with healthy people who have life expectancies of many years.

There is a great misconception on the part of most people about life expectancy. Most older people have no appreciation of the length of expected life that the current tables estimate for them. Also, there is good reason to believe that even the most current tables fail to reflect the much increased life span that may be anticipated, because of better health care and nutritional awareness, and improved physical fitness.

Let me depict a typical reaction. The interview is with a businessman who is 75 years old. I am making the point that many things can happen in the remaining years of his life. To make my point more forcefully, I tell him that he has an actuarial probability of about 10 more years of life. He is very surprised. "Are you telling me that when I was born, people were expected to live to age 85?" This is the sum of his age, 75, plus the life expectancy number that I gave him.

What he failed to see is that life expectancy is an averaging concept. When he was born, no actuary would have said that all of his "class" would live to 85. The average duration of life would then have been pegged at considerably less. But, over the 75 years, a substantial number of the members of his class died early. Therefore, a goodly percentage of the survivors, people like him, must live much longer to average it out.

The anticipated passage of many years between the time the plan is delineated and its becoming effective means that many things are going to change. Consequently, people must recognize that the program they develop today really should be effective only if death occurs in the next few years—three to five at the maximum. Any expectation of being able to set up a program that will be good for a lifetime is foolhardy.

It is also, in my opinion, a waste of money for a client to pay an estate planner for his time and effort in trying to devise a plan, with complex alternatives, that tries to deal with the various eventualities that may arise. This attempt simply will not work in the great majority of cases. Furthermore, it will make an already complicated procedure so convoluted that the client will undoubtedly be completely confused. This is the kind of "overkill" that experienced professionals avoid.

I set this 3-5 year goal up at the beginning of the planning process. I sometimes kid the client that "There has to be grist for our mill too." But I do take the time to explain why there can't be a plan that will last forever. I do this by relating the potential for substantial change to his personal situation. Without exception, the businessman is relieved by this simplification.

ECONOMIC SECURITY AND HAPPINESS

Another important restraint in fixing estate planning goals is the lack of relationship between economic security and happiness. We have to recognize that simply by providing plenty of money for our family to live on, we do not assure them happiness. Many people unconsciously believe that achieving happiness in life is merely a matter of getting to a point where you have enough wealth to live comfortably. Conversely, they may blame their anxieties and dissatisfactions with their way of life totally on the unremitting financial demands. For these individuals, the simple answer to the problems of the family after death is to make sure they are free of money worries.

I can well understand this attitude, even though I now appreciate how wrong it is. Shortly after I left law school, I worked for the very well known tax authority, J.K. Lasser. I became involved in dealing with the very wealthy. Having gotten through law school on the GI Bill of Rights, and used the last of my savings amassed during my Second World War infantry service to buy an engagement ring for my wife, I was a great admirer of money. While I intellectualized that money wasn't everything, down deep I really believed it made all the difference.

However, I kept observing in my work that individuals who had more personal wealth than I ever imagined existed weren't so happy. While they had different kinds of problems, their impact was just as severe. This was brought home to me particularly by the "plight" of a young woman, the daughter of a man whose family was perhaps the richest client of the office. Her father had recently died, resulting in the termination of several trusts and the distribution to her of a vast amount of income producing property. My assignment was to calculate what quarterly federal estimated income tax payments she would now have to pay—assuming the filing of a joint return with her husband. The year was 1949 and my figure came to $18,500 a quarter. I met with the daughter who panicked when I disclosed the number. She burst into tears. I was dumbstruck.

Compared to her income, this $18,500 per quarter was a modest sum. I knew she was recently married and childless, so I could not understand why the tax payment was so demoralizing to her. Nonetheless, it was obvious that she was terribly upset. Sensing my concern—and perhaps trying to reassure me that I had done nothing wrong—she collected herself and explained her dilemma. Her husband was an engineer. His annual compensation was considerably less than what they would be paying each quarter for the tax on her income. Under this state of affairs, how could her husband maintain his male role?

I now believe, without reservation, that you don't buy happiness with money. If it can't be done during lifetime, then certainly you won't accomplish it after death.

SETTING THE RIGHT GOALS

The aim of an estate plan for the close corporation owner is not to provide happiness. He has the same goals as the head of any family: to leave enough so that his wife and family won't suffer a meaningful change in their style of living; to make sure that their security will not be further impaired by a lack of funds; and to guarantee that the children will get an education and otherwise be prepared to take on the challenges of life. In addition, if his interest in the close corporation is to continue after his death, he has special concerns about the business. It is an important part of his life; his chief legacy. The planning process should be aimed at meeting those needs. They are difficult enough to satisfy. No one should try to assure him of an idyllic world for his beneficiaries.

WHEN SHOULD CHILDREN RECEIVE THEIR INHERITANCE?

Another impediment to the consummation of an estate plan for the entrepreneur is his becoming immersed in broad issues that are not susceptible of prompt resolution. Pursuing these esoteric subjects detracts greatly from the resolution of basic matters. A typical example is the parents' inquiry and concern regarding the right age at which their children, now 14 and 12, should receive their inheritance. There are no guidelines to make a sensible judgment now as to the level of financial maturity and responsibility that these children will reach at various ages. I say this notwithstanding that parents may try to read financial maturity into a young child's taking very good care of his toys and other possessions. There are just too many factors and future experiences and influences involved, for somebody to try and predict whether a child will be a saver or spender, or careful or careless with money.

Some key concepts

All we can do is employ generalized concepts:

1. *Kids are spending more years in a sheltered educational environment.* I have been told that the new definition of a dropout is someone who only has a bachelor's degree. The fact is that young people today are facing tougher career decisions. There are too many lawyers and even doctors. Industry is not waiting for college graduates with open arms.

2. *A distribution of property to a 21 year old is probably a mistake.* In all likelihood he will then be a junior in college or working in a low paying job. A young adult is used to spending $150 a month. Now somebody hands him $25,000. There is certainly a great probability that the money will either burn a hole in his pocket or he will do something foolish with it. He has no experience in dealing with this kind of money.

This was brought home to me forcefully many years ago. A client called me up and said he wanted me to investigate a young man, who was about to marry the client's daughter. After initially resisting, because investigation is not my business, I asked what was bothering him about Harry, whom I had met several times. The client said that he was afraid that Harry might be a compulsive gambler.

This was a surprising announcement. "What reason do you have for suspecting that?" I asked. The client explained that Harry's father had died a very wealthy man, which I knew, and that Harry received a bequest of $85,000 of cash when he was 21. Now four years later, in a discussion about living arrangements with his future son-in-law, Harry told the client that he had lost all of that money. To the client's way of thinking, that could only have happened if Harry had gambled the money away.

I met with Harry and what I learned provided me with a valuable planning lesson. When the $85,000 was handed over to Harry, he did not know what to do with it. Since one of his father's closest friends was a highly regarded investment counselor, everyone assumed that Harry would go to him for advice. So nobody else gave him any suggestions. Harry did seek the guidance of his father's good friend. But the advisor was always too busy to take the time to deal with this amount of money, which by his standard was piddling. So Harry made his own decision.

He decided to go into the television service business in New York City—Manhattan actually—with a friend who had experience in that field. Harry put up all the money to start, $75,000, and the friend put up his know-how. They each owned 50% of the stock of the company. Harry's remaining $10,000 went for expenses. A good part of the initial capital was used to buy three trucks with telephone communications equipment. The idea was that when a customer called to say that his television was not working, a truck in that area could be dispatched forthwith to the customer's residence. The whole concept was impractical and it was not very well thought out. The result was bankruptcy and Harry's loss of the entire $85,000. What I learned was that there are great risks in putting a lot of money in the sole control of a financially inexperienced 21 year old.

3. *It is better to distribute the money in installments.* The reasoning for this is simple. If the beneficiary does something foolish with the first distribution, he will not have blown his entire inheritance. Hopefully, he will have learned from this mistake and will be more careful with the balance of the funds. Beyond 35 or 40, at the outside, delaying a distribution to a later age is pointless, except for tax reasons. For instance, to withhold ownership until someone reaches 50 doesn't serve any purpose. Any individual who is not capable of handling money by 35 or 40, will not suddenly learn how to do so during the next decade.

4. *I encourage clients to use one of two distribution patterns when they are dealing with children who are young. They are either one-half at 30 and the balance at 35; or one-third at 25, one-half the balance (or another one-third) at 30 and the entire balance at 35.* They are reminded that the trustee has the power, at any time before the selected ages, to use the principal for a child's support, education and maintenance. Also, they can always change the ages when the children are older and their fiscal competency can be realistically evaluated.

Spoiling the children

A second perplexing area of concern that is often raised in the planning process is this: "I wonder if it is a mistake to leave children a lot of money. I'm afraid it will spoil them—reduce their drive to make something of themselves." What we have here is an expression of parental guilt. It is based on the premise that by providing too much for a child, he will be ruined.

Many years ago in the course of doing some planning work for an exceptionally wealthy individual, I suggested that he make a tax advantageous gift to his son, who was then 16. The father was very concerned that this action would result in the son, at age 21, realizing that he was wealthy, and this might impede his development as a useful member of society. I told the client that if his son—who lived in a 12 room apartment on Park Avenue, drove around in a chauffered car, spent his summers at a fashionable vacation spot where his family had a large home, was waited on hand and foot by a butler-maid combination and took "pot luck" at some of New York's finest restaurants—didn't know he was wealthy by the time he reached age 21, then his father really would have something to worry about.

A young person measures his family's wherewithal by the way

they live and their material possessions. Rarely does he seek an itemization of the family's assets. My daughter, Tricia, at age 8, went around telling everybody that my sister and brother-in-law were millionaires, because they had a home in Florida with a swimming pool which was part of the house. The reality is that many very rich children become highly motivated successful adults. I am sure the reader can think of some in his or her locale. Some of the best known are the Rockefellers, Kennedys, and Fords.

These productive people from very wealthy backgrounds may have different motivations for the pursuit of success. Their drives may be based on the need for ego gratification, a quest for power or just pride, rather than for the accumulation of more money. Some of them may have a desire to give something back to the society that made them rich. Whatever the causation, many descendants of wealthy parents lead very purposeful lives.

PROVIDING FOR A SURVIVING SPOUSE

8

Sam Cumming is sitting in a conference room, discussing his estate planning with his lawyer. He is 65, married to Emily, who is four years younger, and has two sons, who are 32 and 30. Sam is a successful businessman. His corporation, Cumming Shops, has fifteen stores selling ladies footwear, all of them located in shopping malls. The business was started by Sam, a very astute and organized executive, after he had worked for a large retail shoe chain for a number of years. Sam owns all the stock of the company. Both of the Cumming sons are active in the business.

Sam receives a salary of $250,000 a year from Cumming Shops. He drives a large company car and he has extensive fringe benefits, including a generous expense allowance. Sam and Emily live in a very beautiful and stately home, and they have a summer house near the ocean. They live well, enjoy country club activities, dine out and attend the theatre and opera regularly, travel extensively, and are very generous with their family. Sam's Cumming Shops stockholdings are by far his most valuable asset. The other holdings of him and his wife consist of a limited amount of securities and cash investments, their homes, lovely and expensive household furnishings and a few fairly valuable pieces of art.

After the fact-finding is completed, it is very probable that the lawyer will ask Sam two questions that will confound him. They are simple and crucial inquiries, going to the heart of the estate planning. Sometime later, when Sam describes his meeting with the attorney, he will be very complimentary about the lawyer's competence, using these basic queries as an illustration of the counsellor's "brilliance." This has happened to me many times. Judge for yourself how profound the inquiries are. One seeks to know how much

161

the surviving spouse will need for her support and maintenance. The other, where the money to provide that income will come from.

DETERMINING THE LEVEL OF SUPPORT

The lawyer asks: "Sam, how much do you think Emily will need to live on after your death?" The quest here is for an estimate of how much must be provided for Sam's principal beneficiary, to make sure that she is able to continue to live comfortably and securely after his death. Making sure that Emily is properly taken care of when he dies, is the primary reason why Sam is in the lawyer's office to do his estate planning. Once that figure is established, it becomes the goal of the planning process. Proposals are evaluated to make sure that they will provide Emily with this amount, and if there is a deficiency, the planner starts to suggest ways and means of closing the gap.

The problem is that in many, if not most, instances the husband has no idea of what the living costs are. Ask him what Cumming Shops pays for any number of styles of shoes, and Sam can probably rattle those numbers off, without hesitation. But what he and Emily are spending for food, what she needs for her clothing, what the expenses of maintaining the house and summer home are, what it costs for travel and entertainment, domestic help—and on and on—is unknown to him. By reason of his affluence, an annual budget is no longer prepared. In truth, it is Emily who runs the household, who has a much better idea of what things cost. I certainly don't intend this as a criticism of the Sam Cummings of the world. My wife would be far more qualified than I to provide accurate information about where our money goes. I could only make wild guesses.

Notwithstanding this reality, the probability is that Sam Cumming will not admit his inability to give an accurate answer to this inquiry. Somehow he will feel that to utter that reality will reduce his stature as a responsible businessman and husband. Instead, he will stab at a number, a much lower one than what is realistic. Sam Cumming easily might answer: "Oh, I think Emily could live well on $50,000 a year." Why the number is invariably on the low side, I am not sure, but it is.

In the early stages of my practice, I used to attack these "low-ball" estimates by a client of what a spouse would need to live on when she was widowed. As a technician I realized—and I still do—that planning based on providing a grossly inadequate income for a widow or widower, has to be faulty. It is truly the equivalent of erecting a structure on a bad foundation. Nonetheless, I gave up the confrontation method, because it frequently created serious antagonisms between the client and me.

For the last decade or so, I use a much more effective technique. I would not respond to the figure of $50,000 a year picked by Sam Cumming out of the air, just note it. Then, at the end of the conference with Sam, I would suggest that Emily be present at our next get-together. It is now commonplace, and very sensible, for both spouses to participate in the estate planning process, and the decision-making that is so significant for both of them. When Sam and Emily thereafter are in the office together, at some point early in our discussion, I would mention the $50,000 per year figure that Sam had estimated as the amount of income that would enable Emily, following his death, to live comfortably.

What then happens is predictable. It is a special form of levitation. Emily, flabbergasted, will seemingly rise from her chair. With eyes focused directly at Sam, sometimes angrily, often in a very controlled but penetrating way, she will ask Sam how he arrived at that amount. Now, there is no way for Sam to hide from the facts. In the ensuing dialogue, with Emily probably operating from memory, like Sam does about his business, a much more meaningful appraisal of dollar needs will be made.

Impact of surviving spouse's earning power

An important factor pertaining to the question of how much income Sam must provide to take care of Emily, after his death, is what Emily has or can earn herself. For example, if Emily had inherited or received by gift income-producing property from her parents, the yield on those assets would first be credited against the amount she needs. For this purpose, an anticipated inheritance cannot be taken into account. Emily's family may be very well heeled. But if Emily must wait until the death of one or both parents, to receive anything substantial, that can happen many years after Sam's death.

How to reflect Emily's earning capacity is a much more complex matter. In order to try to cover the various possibilities, I am going to cast Emily in four different roles:

1. She was a very competent designer of lady's shoes and handbags, working for a large shoe manufacturer. In fact, Sam met her, for the first time, at the manufacturer's showroom. Emily continued to work for a few years after she and Sam were married, but stopped when their first son was born. In this role, we will refer to her as *Emily, the housewife*.

2. Emily recently went back to doing some handbag designing, part-time. She needed something more challenging to do to occupy her time. Her income from this activity is not very substantial, but she very much enjoys what she does. Here we have *Emily, the part-timer*.

3. When Emily decided to go to work 15 years ago, she concluded it would be a mistake to be employed by Cumming Shops. Sam agreed that the presence of the boss' wife in the executive suite would cause problems. So Emily went back to working full-time as a designer for a shoe manufacturer. It is a demanding, pressure-filled job. Although Emily is very good at what she does, and earns $45,000, lately she has questioned whether she should keep up the pace. This is *Emily, the career woman.*

4. Emily handles all the buying for Cumming Shops. Because she was restless and bored, staying home taking care of the children while they were infants, she hired a full-time housekeeper and joined Sam's business. Emily is very competent at what she does and works hard, doing the purchasing of inventory for the fifteen stores. Her salary is $65,000 a year. While Sam talks to Emily about other aspects of the business, her involvement is limited to buying merchandise. This is *Emily, the businesswoman.*

Emily the housewife will clearly be in the most dependent position when Sam dies. She really has no potential to earn any "real" money at this point in her life. It is very upsetting to me when a client, trying to explain why his wife can subsist on a very limited amount of income, says: "Well, she can always go back to work. You know, Milt, she was a very capable (whatever)." Look at Emily. Like so many other women who are strictly homemakers, she has been out of the labor market for many years. Whatever her capabilities were years ago, it would be harsh and thoughtless to expect her, at an advanced age, depressed because of her husband's death, to go out and start building a career.

Emily the part-timer is not much better off. Her job produces very limited revenue and its continuity may be precarious, because the management may decide, at any time, that they want a full-time employee for her slot. Even more important, Emily's working is motivated more by her desire for gratification and pleasure than to earn money. If at any time, the position becomes onerous or unpleasant, so that her needs for working are not met, she should be free to walk away.

The situation of *Emily the career woman*, as a widow, will be different. Her income of $45,000 a year is meaningful, and she has a very responsible and challenging position. Nevertheless, she may retire from her job in a few years, when she reaches age 65. Or, she may decide that the demands of the job are too rigorous and leave.

At first blush, *Emily the businesswoman* seems to be in the best economic position, with respect to assured income after Sam's death. She is earning $65,000 a year currently, and after Sam's death, she could take over some of his duties and substantially increase her income. By giving her control of Cumming Shops, or at least a veto power, Sam could enable Emily to protect her position and her income. But Emily's life in the family business, after Sam's death, may be full of travail. Her sons were willing to take orders from Sam, because he was the founder and builder of the organization. Chances are that they will not have the same willingness to accept the dictates of their mother. Other executives, such as the managers of the various stores, may resent Emily's involvement in the overall management of the company, since during Sam's lifetime, Emily's role was limited to purchasing.

A recommended approach

I have developed a simple rationale about reflecting the surviving spouse's income potential, when I am doing estate planning. I urge clients not to take it into account, whenever possible. If the business owner has the wherewithal to provide adequately for his wife when he dies, without counting on her earned income at all, that is how he should do his planning. Ignore her job. This will spare Emily, whether she is housewife, part-timer, career person or business-

woman, from being obliged to keep working, if she later choses not
to do so. This allows her the greatest freedom of choice.

In most instances, an entrepreneur of a close corporation, with
proper planning, can make financial provision for his spouse so that
she will not *have* to work, when she is a widow. To accomplish that
may mean setting aside dollars during lifetime, to build up the funds
required to provide the wife with sufficient income. That is easier to
do, with far less pressure, when the husband and wife are both alive
and producing income.

UNREALISTIC IDEAS ABOUT A SOURCE OF INCOME

What will be the source of Emily's income when Sam dies? Sam
will not even have identified this issue as a concern. Why is the
counsellor worried? After all, look how much Sam is taking out of
the company: an annual salary of $250,000 plus perquisites, includ-
ing an automobile and an expense allowance. Surely, Emily will
have no trouble existing comfortably on that kind of money. The
question remains, however, whether it will be available to her after
Sam's death. Without Sam's leadership, will the business continue to
enjoy the same prosperity? Must someone who will command a large
part of Sam's salary be brought in from the outside to replace him?
Will the sons expect to absorb their father's salary and perquisites, as
an add-on to their compensation and benefits from the company?

Even if there will be a continuing stream of dollars available in
the business for Emily's support when she is widowed, there are
serious obstacles to her getting her hands on the money. Cumming
Shops will not want to pay dividends. The great bulk of the corporation's after-tax profits are needed by the enterprise for working capital and expansion. To compete effectively with the big retail shoe
chains, the management of Cumming Shops must be able to have
large amounts of money to make good buys of merchandise, and to
keep opening desirable outlets. Going to the banks for these funds
will impose a sizeable debt service cost, which Cumming Shops
wants to avoid. In addition, as noted in Chapter 5, corporate earnings which are distributed as dividends may be eroded by income
taxes.

Some of Sam's Cumming Shops stock cannot be sold to create cash, to be held for Emily's benefit. There is no market for the stock of the typical close corporation, other than the company itself. The use of corporate funds to buy stock is often inconsistent with the business needs. In the case of Cumming Shops, it would fly in the face of the policy of accumulating dollars for operations and expansion. Here too, the tax consequences would be unfavorable. Any sale by a family member of some of her stock will not be taxed, for Federal income tax purposes, at the favorable 20% maximum capital gain rate. The proceeds will probably be treated as ordinary income and taxed at a 50% rate.

Why doesn't Emily take over Sam's title as president of Cumming Shops, and draw down his salary? Unfortunately, in order for a corporation to get a tax deduction for compensation paid to a stockholder, the amount of compensation must be reasonable. This can be a problem even for the patriarch who built the business. However, because of his role, capabilities, and experience, most entities can convince the Internal Revenue Service that the compensation paid to the top man, even one of advanced years, is justifiable. This means that it costs Cumming Shops only about $125,000, after reflecting the income tax deduction it receives each year, to pay Sam $250,000. If Emily really did nothing substantial to justify her compensation, the government would deny the tax deduction for what she received as compensation. Consequently, the effective cost to the company would double.

Having the surviving spouse play a significant part in the management of the business, as a means of justifying her salary, is a bad idea. Emily does not want to work in the business, and her sons don't want her near the place. Indeed, the involvement of an inexperienced parent in the family business can greatly exacerbate the personal problems which were discussed in Chapter 1.

In the face of these difficulties in getting money out of the close corporation, to take care of the surviving spouse following the death of the owner, why does the principal, doing estate planning, simply assume that the spouse has nothing to worry about? This attitude has truly puzzled me. If it were merely an abberation, manifested only by a handful of close corporation proprietors, it would not be so troublesome. But it is a widespread conviction, far removed from reality, one that, if not corrected, can lead to horrendous estate planning results.

"The business will take care of things"

I now feel it is an expression of the owner's belief that somehow, someway, in a fashion not really clearly outlined, the business will take care of all things. It will continue, following the death of the controlling stockholder-chief executive, to provide for spouse and children as it has for so many years. There is an aura of the business itself being the person that nurtures and supports the family. Listen carefully to some of the typical responses to the query, "What is your wife going to live on after your death?" One client will say to me: "Milt, you know how successful the business is." Another explains: "I draw a lot of money from the company." A third will ask with some annoyance: "Are you suggesting, Milt, that the corporation can't afford to take care of Mary?" These are really not solutions to the problem.

"The children will take care of their mother"

Hard pressed to try and detail the sources of his wife's income when she is widowed, a husband who owns a family business will often blurt out with pride and satisfaction: "What's the matter with you, Milt. The boys will take care of her." Of course, it has to be gratifying for a father to believe that his family is extremely close knit and that the commitment of the children to their mother is significant. However content the father may be with this prospect, it is repugnant to most mothers. It has been my experience that when an estate plan is presented to a husband and wife, the wife will say something like this: "I am afraid that I don't understand a lot of what you said. What I want to know, with certainty, is that under the proposal you have made, I will never have to ask my children for anything."

A paradox? Yes. On one side we have a husband who glories in the idea that his children will take care of his wife after his death. On the other, we have a wife who demands assurance that she will be independent of her children. I am not entirely sure why mothers usually feel this way. I suspect that it has to do with the nature of a mother's basic relationships with her children. She was the one who provided for them. To be dependent on her children is a reversal of roles. As the saying goes, "One mother can take care of ten children, but ten children cannot take care of one mother."

Another explanation might be called the "in-law syndrome." Mothers will often tell me: "If my son were single, I would have no trouble dealing with him about my support. But I fear that his wife will cause trouble by saying something like 'why does mother have to live in such a fancy house or take such expensive trips?' " This fear may be too harsh on in-laws. But right or wrong, it demonstrates how threatened a mother can be by the thought of becoming dependent on her children.

Whatever the reasons, the fact remains that mothers generally want to be independent of their children. An estate plan that contradicts this principle will most probably lead to an unhappy widow. It may also bring about serious conflicts between her and her children.

LIFE INSURANCE

How can the close corporation provide support for the owner's spouse after his death? The most effective way is the use of corporate dollars to provide funds that are completely free of any tie to the business, i.e. life insurance. The close corporation can obtain a substantial amount of group life insurance coverage for the head of the business. The premiums are paid by the corporation. At the owner's death, the insurance company pays the proceeds of the policy to the spouse or a trust for her benefit.

Split-dollar insurance is another method of creating sizeable sums for the support of the businessman's spouse when he dies. This is an arrangement under which the corporation helps to finance what is really a policy of personal insurance on the life of the stockholder-employee. It does this by becoming the owner of the cash surrender value portion of the policy, and contributing that portion of each premium that is equal to the increase in the cash surrender value that is produced by paying that premium. The proportion of each premium payable by the company keeps going up as the years go by. The spouse, or his or her trust, is the beneficiary of the proceeds in excess of the amount of the cash surrender value of the policy at the insured's death. Here again, the dollars pass at death free of any further relationship with the close corporation. A more detailed explanation of the mechanics of split-dollar insurance can be found in Chapter 13.

PENSION AND PROFIT SHARING PLANS

Pension and profit sharing plans provide another important and tax advantageous means of using funds of the close corporation to build up sizeable death benefits for the entrepreneur's spouse. While these are retirement plans, the owners of family businesses and incorporated partnerships usually do not take down any appreciable part of the benefits while they are still alive, even though they may live far beyond the specified retirement age. The reason for this phenomenon is that many owners continue to run their businesses long past the age of 65.

The controlling stockholder "retires" by working less, but continuing to receive substantial compensation from the company. He or she moves into a role which is akin to that of a consultant. There is limited participation in day-to-day activities of the firm, but the owner still has the major voice in the decision and policy making. So long as the individual does not become disabled, the Internal Revenue Service generally does not question the deductability of his salary. Contributions for the post-retirement executive may cease when he reaches the retirement age fixed in the plan, but his fund keeps earning interest and growing. The compounding is more significant because no income tax is payable until the benefits are distributed to the participant or his beneficiary.

The stockholder-employees who are covered by these pension and profit sharing plans start off with a big advantage. Plans are designed to make sure that the corporate owners involved in management receive the lion's share of the company's contributions. The professionals and organizations who do plan formulations realize that the proprietors are most pleased with a plan proposal that results in a large portion of the company dollars being credited to the owners' accounts, and somehow, someway, that result is accomplished. There are a variety of acceptable methods of beefing up the owners' share of what goes into the plan.

The recipient of a pension or profit sharing plan death benefit is not involved with the close corporation or dependent on its successful operation. The assets of the plan are held in a separate trust fund, and cannot be used to support the business. The trustees of this trust may be corporate executives, but they are legally responsible for the safekeeping of the monies and their proper investment. The plan document spells out the manner in which the proceeds are to be distributed to a participant's designated beneficiary, at his death. While there may be alternatives, which the trustee or the committee administering the plan may pick, each alternative is specifically defined. In the case of the close corporation owner who remains a participant after retirement age, his account is often segregated, and in some instances he can have the right to decide how his separated fund should be invested.

POST-DEATH COMPENSATION

We now come to the first of the two programs, aimed at providing dollars for the spouse of the entrepreneur after his death, which do create a continuing dependence of the beneficiary on the corporation's ability to pay. Post-death compensation is a deferred compensation arrangement between the close corporation and the owner-executive. As additional consideration for his services, the corporation agrees to pay the stockholder-employee's widow money, in installments, for a period of years or for her lifetime. The arrangements can be memorialized in a separate contract or as part of the owner's employment agreement. It is important for all concerned to understand that the surviving spouse will not perform any services for the close corporation. She will have no involvement with the business. All the widow will do is collect what the company has agreed to pay for the work done by her husband.

To the extent that the payments after death are deemed to be reasonable, they can be deducted by the corporation. A rule of thumb, for estimating the maximum justifiable amount is 2-1/2 times the husband's annual compensation at the time of his death. Thus, with Sam Cumming, who is earning $250,000 a year, $625,000 would appear to be deductible. Sometimes the installments are to be paid to the widow for life. The total value of that post-death compensation arrangement is determined from the Internal Revenue Service's life expectancy tables. The factor taken from the table, based on the surviving spouse's age when her husband dies, is multiplied by the annual amount payable to her. There are many instances where lifetime support for the surviving spouse is provided, even though the amount will be in excess of what is properly deductible. The motivation for doing this is simple. The surviving spouse will need this money throughout her lifetime, in order to live comfortably. The worst that can happen from an income tax standpoint, is that the payments in excess of what are deemed to be reasonable, will be treated as the equivalent as dividends—non-deductible by the corporation. There is always the chance that a government auditor will not even give the matter any attention at the point in time, perhaps ten years after the stockholder-employee's death, when the total payments will exceed the deductible limit.

PREFERRED STOCK REDEMPTION

The preferred stock redemption method of getting dollars out of the close corporation and into the hands of the deceased stockholder's family has a different emphasis. Not only income, but principal as well, is moved out of the company into the hands of the family. The format is simple. A class of preferred stock is created, income tax free. This preferred stock is bequeathed by the entrepreneur to his surviving spouse, or in trust for her benefit. The corporation purchases the preferred stock from the widow or her trust, at its par or liquidation value. Even though no Federal estate tax may be payable, by reason of the unlimited marital deduction, the widow or trust gets a new tax basis for the preferred stock equal to its fair market value at death. Thus, there should be little or no income tax on the redemption proceeds.

If the close corporation carries insurance on the life of the principal, then those proceeds, which are received by the company free of income tax, can be used to meet the purchase price obligation. The unfunded portion of the price is paid by the corporation over a period of years (not more than fifteen), together with interest. The interest should be set at a rate that does not result in part of the purchase price being treated as interest. Currently, the minimum annual interest is 9% on purchases where the indebtedness is less than $2,000,000.

Let me illustrate how this redemption works. Cumming Shops issues $400,000 par value of preferred stock to Sam Cumming, the present holder of 100% of the common stock. There is $200,000 of insurance on Sam's life payable to the corporation. Cumming Shops enters into an agreement to purchase Sam's preferred stock from his legatee, at par, 90 days after the death of Sam. $200,000 will be paid at closing. The balance of $200,000 will be paid in quarterly installments of $5,000 each, or $20,000 per year, over a period of ten years. With each installment, Cumming Shops will also pay interest on the unpaid balance at the annual rate of 10%. Sam draws a will bequeathing his Cumming Shops preferred stock to his wife, Emily.

The corporation finances $200,000 of its obligation with the life insurance proceeds. The $20,000 per year, payable quarterly over the next 10 years, must come from accumulated or future profits. These installments are not deductible by the corporation. The interest payments are deductible by Cumming Shops and they are taxable to the recipient as ordinary income. Sometimes a large part of the wherewithal for these preferred stock redemption payments comes from the savings that the corporation realizes, by no longer paying the deceased family head's compensation and benefits.

Emily gets her income from two sources. She receives the interest on the unpaid portion of the price of the preferred stock. This diminishes as the quarterly installments are paid by Cumming Shops. She also receives the income from the reinvestment of the payments that are made to her. This should keep increasing over the payment period.

Until TEFRA was enacted in 1982, the purchase of the preferred stock had to be made from the widow, individually. This meant that very sizeable amounts of money would pass into the hands of the individual spouse. Now a trust for the widow produces the same income tax result. This will enable the surviving spouse to obtain the advantages of a trust, discussed in the next chapter, with respect to these often very sizeable redemption proceeds.

GRANT OF STOCK INTEREST

The income tax advantages of the close corporation electing to be taxed as a Subchapter S corporation were discussed in Chapter 5. With this greater utilization of Subchapter S tax status by close corporations, there may be a temptation to use that income tax concept as an estate planning tool as well. It can be viewed as a simple way to provide income from the corporation for the surviving spouse. For example, why shouldn't Sam Cumming simply give some of his stock to Emily after his death? The double tax risk, first to the corporation on the profits and then to Emily on the dividends, will be eliminated by electing Subchapter S. Cumming Shops will not pay any Federal income tax on its net profits. They will be taxed to the stockholders individually. Emily can only be given non-voting stock thereby avoiding any interference with the desired method of transferring control of the corporation at Sam's death.

I think that making the widow a stockholder can be shortsighted. Emily's insecurities will be heightened, if the income she will have available to spend is directly related to how Cumming Shops does after Sam's death—keeping in mind that the company is now operating without the presence of the person in whom she had the most confidence. Business problems and adverse developments discussed at family gatherings are bound to upset her. Since the sons will then be directing the business, and in control of what is distributed to Emily by the company, she becomes dependent upon them, the very thing she wanted to avoid.

Furthermore, having a mother and her children owning interests in the family business can lead to antagonisms between them. In our example, as the Cumming sons increase their compensation and fatten their fringe benefits, this will have an adverse effect on their mother. The net income of the corporation, in which Emily shares, will be reduced. Also, the surviving spouse will not be happy about the corporation's spending, and possibly borrowing, substantial sums for growth, since this can threaten the current financial stability of the company, in order to achieve enhanced profits, which the widow cares little about. When it becomes important for Cumming Shops to retain a goodly portion of net profits to maintain the company's competitive position—a practice that was started by the father, Sam Cumming—mother may nonetheless resist because of her belief that she needs greater distributions for her well-being. Her sons can be resentful that their mother's needs, rather than the needs of the business, will become the standard for deciding many issues.

Giving mother an equity interest in the family business leads to most of the same problems that ensue when a child who is not active in the business becomes a stockholder. Those are described in considerable depth in Chapter 10. The fact that the non-participating stockholder is the mother of the owner-managers, rather than a sibling, does not make the situation easier to handle. Quite the contrary. It is much tougher for the children working in the enterprise to take a hard-nosed position with a parent.

MANAGING A SURVIVING SPOUSE'S PROPERTY — ADVANTAGES OF A TRUST	9

Spouses doing estate planning have to recognize the actuarial possibilities. The businessman in his fifties must understand that if he dies in the next few years, his somewhat younger wife will live for many, many years. Why is the appreciation of this likelihood so important? The answer is that what must be provided for the surviving spouse, to assure his or her protection and sustenance, will be needed most when the spouse is older. If, in our example, the wife is left a widow at 56, she will usually be possessed of her vitality and health for many years. Her problems in coping will become much more acute in later years—in her 70's, 80's and perhaps 90's.

WIDOWS AND WIDOWERS: GETTING USED TO A NEW LIFE

Today's planning for the spouse who becomes a widow or widower in mid-life must take all of this into account. The estate plan has to extend beyond that point where the surviving spouse has completed raising the children. It must continue to take care of a mate who will probably live to a ripe old age. It is very hard for middle-aged people to appreciate this. They find it difficult to understand that a surviving partner may suffer insecurities attributable to ailments or deterioration. A wife looks at her strong-willed, capable, self-assured spouse, the head of a demanding business enterprise. She finds it hard to believe that there may come a time when he will become worrisome and frightened.

Men are particularly insensitive to the possibility of this change in attitudes by a spouse. Often when I am trying to portray the fears that may beset his wife when she becomes a widow, the husband will say something like this: "You don't know my wife. She makes the major decisions in our household. She runs me, the children and the PTA."

Sure she does. She is now full of verve, possessed of all her faculties, mature and living in a secure environment. She has the comfort and reassurance that partnership with her husband provides. Each has a friend with whom to share the pressures of life. They are sounding boards for one another. The husband can tell his wife his conerns about the business and other problems. When his wife dies, the husband-widower is alone. Gone is the person with whom he could talk about his anxieties. He bottles them up and his stress level keeps rising. He may also recall some horror stories about dependence on children who resented the burden or about moving into a nursing home.

Social readjustment

These feelings of loneliness and grave concern about what lies ahead are accompanied by what I will call the difficult social readjustment. For some period after the death of a spouse, family and friends heap affection and company on the widower. He is included in weekend plans and social gatherings. Couples dine with him. Children call and drop over regularly. Great effort is made by all to make sure that dad is not alone on holidays or important occasions. This involvement helps. But inevitably its beneficial effects are greatly reduced. In some instances the diminution results from a considerably lessened concern of others. The commitment of friends and children wanes. Other deaths, tragedies and personal problems capture their attention.

In fairness, however, in great measure the change in relationships is the result of the dissatisfaction of the surviving spouse. Many widows and widowers have confided in me their unhappiness in constantly being the extra person, the "fifth wheel." I remember the observation one of them made to me: "My friends have been very good to me. They continually ask me to join them for dinner at a restaurant, or to go to the movies. But these get-togethers with my friends make me more conscious of Jill's being gone. We spent a lot of good times together with these people when she was alive. Now when I am there without her, I feel sad."

By contrast, there are some reactions of friends that are not so thoughtful. A goodly number of widows have told me about the propositions from male friends. A "noble" individual makes his pitch on the basis that the widow and her late husband must have had good sexual relations. Now that he is gone, the widow must miss the sexual satisfactions, and the friend will be happy to fill that void. Sounds bizarre? Apparently it is not even unusual.

Widowers often have to contend with a different form of proposition. Because of the dirth of widowers, as compared to widows, the male surviving spouse is besieged by people—mostly female friends—who are trying to fix him up with this or that woman. It is not unusual for an unmarried woman to do her own prospecting. I recall one incident in that regard that a widower-client told me about. An attractive divorcee dropped in on him, at the widower's home, carrying some apple pies. She gained entry and explained to the widower that she had learned of his fancy for homemade apple pie. With his wife having died, there was no one around to bake for him; and so, she had decided to fill the void. Quite a technique for getting to know an eligible man.

The dating game

The surviving spouse who gets back into the dating game, after a long period of marriage, often feels inadequate and unsure of himself or herself. This includes the ostensibly confident, self-assured, sometimes hardbitten close corporation proprietor. He wonders about his judgment, fears involvement, but often wants sexual gratification, which produces ties, and can't stand the artificial small talk that goes with encounters without depth. It is a scene full of turmoil.

I recall vividly a conversation about that subject with a client, a remarkably successful, aggressive, relatively young head of a family business, whose wife had died of cancer after a long period of suffering. He was describing to me his initial reactions when he decided to start going out with single women.

First there was the guilt that he told me he had to contend with. "Will people feel that I am dating too soon after Phyllis' death?" "What will the children think about my romantic involvement with someone other than their mother?" "How will the kids react if I get serious with a divorced woman who has children?" "Should I let the

family meet the ladies I go out with, or keep these contacts secret?"
Although he was the dominant force in the family business, where
his two sons were employed, he was genuinely concerned about
getting the approval of his children.

He acknowledged to me his anxieties about courting techniques.
"You won't believe this, Milt. I went to a singles club dance with a
divorced friend of mine and I didn't know what to do. For a while I
held up a wall. Finally I spotted a gal I thought was very attractive,
took a deep breath and moved toward her. Before I could get there,
another guy asked her for a dance and I turned back. The second
time I started to approach her, she went off to the ladies' room. I
was ready to stop trying, until my friend, to whom I recounted the
experience, pushed me to make one more attempt. It took all my
courage, but I finally got her to dance. Can you imagine me, one of
the most effective marketers around, who never easily accepts no for
an answer, being afraid to risk a turn-down from a woman at a
singles club dance!

"And then, when we started to dance, I felt like a fish out of
water. I wasn't sure how to hold her, or what I should say. I realized
I was very nervous, because I was perspiring far more than the
exertion should have produced. Fortunately, the young lady carried
the ·conversation."

He also feared being taken advantage of. Although he had never
manifested any paranoia before, he admitted to me: "I never let the
women I'm dating know how successful my business is. For a long
time, Milt, I told them all that I was a manufacturer's representative.
If they got wind of my wealth, they could become interested in me
only for my money." I found this to be a shocking attitude, since he
is an extremely good looking, trim, personable and warm person,
with a great sense of humor.

Although my client's problems are probably typical of those faced
by widowers, I believe that widows have an even tougher time than
their male counterparts, when it comes to finding and relating to a
man. There are many more widows than widowers. An eligible
widower becomes a real catch, even if he is not a very attractive
person. I can recall one widow, who belonged to a country club,
telling me: "It's terrible. When that weasel, Joe, walks into the
room, every widow sitting there preens. Just because he is the only
unmarried older man around." Because of this "numbers game"

there is a certain sense of competitiveness that develops among those widows who want to remarry. They are competing for a very limited number of eligible men.

Women are also more sensitive and find many aspects of the "singles" routines offensive. They also have to deal with the real or imagined criticisms of their being forward or aggressive—when the woman's behavior is much less assertive than that which is accepted without comment when done by her male counterpart. Still many women do remarry and their later years of life can be much fuller as a result. I saw that in my own family. My mother was widowed at the age of 44. She was then and has remained a very attractive woman, extremely personable and the role model of the perfect wife. She remarried about four years later. Looking back, I am not sure how this happened. Certainly my mother, with all her charms, was reserved when it came to seeking the company of men. My mother had a wonderful life with her second husband. Unfortunately, she was widowed a second time about twenty years later. She married a third time at the age of 74. This marriage lasted only eight years. It ended in the same manner, with the death of her husband. This third marriage also provided my mother with warm companionship and someone with whom she could share the events of each day.

Mother was very reluctant to marry the third time. She was concerned about what people would say. That included particularly my sisters and me and the family of her second husband—with whom she had developed a close relationship. My sisters and I urged mother to stop fretting about the reactions of others to her marriage. We made her understand that she was not a gay divorcee, flitting from husband to husband. In her case, people would only be sympathetic to someone whose two previous marriages had ended with the death of her spouse. The fact that she was bothered at all shows how sensitive a widow or widower can be to family and public opinion.

WHY A TRUST?

What it boils down to is that the life of a surviving spouse is difficult. Widows and widowers must face new demands and deal with being alone. They are beset by many adjustments and anxieties. All of this adds up to feelings of fear and insecurity. It is my contention that in the face of this changed environment and the severe apprehensions, a trust can take better care of the widow or widower. What I am talking about is a properly drafted instrument which:

> **1.** provides the spouse with assured income; certain rights to demand the distribution of principal without any involvement of the trustee; and
>
> **2.** empowers the trustee to use any part or all of the trust fund to take care of the beneficiary, if, for any reason, he or she is seriously ill or incapacitated.

How do I come to this conclusion, which at first blush seems at odds with the instinct of self-preservation? It is an outgrowth of my experiences and observations in relating to these people. I have observed that the surviving spouse lives better when his or her property is held in trust rather than being owned individually. The serious economic problems produced by serious illness or disability can be dealt with more effectively. In case of remarriage, the spouse's funds can be more easily segregated and protected from erosion, so that they will descend to the close corporation owner's issue—without creating frictions in the second marriage. Finally, the trust protects the surviving spouse from the demands of the people he or she can't easily say "no" to, the children.

TRUSTS EXPLAINED

Before I plunge into a discussion of these advantages of a trust let me offer a short explanation of what a trust is. This is not going to be a complex exposition. My emphasis will be on those facets of a trust which give it the flexibility to help meet whatever circumstances the surviving spouse of a close corporation owner may encounter during his or her remaining lifespan.

A trust is an arrangement in which one or more persons—individuals, a bank or a trust company—hold and manage property for the benefit of others. For example, I can set up a trust in which the XYZ bank holds property as trustee, to take care of my wife during her lifetime, and after her death, to support and educate my children. A surviving spouse can also be one of the trustees. This permits a widow or widower to participate in all investment and other decisions of the trustees. In a situation where there is more than one trustee serving with the spouse, there can be a requirement that no action may be taken unless he or she concurs. This protects the spouse from being put in a minority position. For the surviving spouse's own best interests, he or she should not be the sole trustee. If he or she is acting alone, and an incapacitating event occurs, there will be no one who can promptly use the trust funds to meet the beneficiary's needs.

Testamentary and lifetime trusts

There are two kinds of trusts: testamentary trusts and lifetime trusts. Testamentary trusts are those which are set up by a deceased individual in a will. Lifetime trusts are those which are established during the lifetime of an individual, usually called the "grantor" (sometimes the "settlor"). A commonly used term for a trust created by a living person is an "inter-vivos trust." These lifetime trusts are set forth in trust agreements entered into between the grantor and the trustees. Once in a while, for reasons that I do not understand, these living trust instruments are identified as "indentures."

Revocable and irrevocable trusts

A trust made by a living person can be revocable or irrevocable. Revocable means the grantor can end the trust and get back his property. Revocable trusts do not provide tax benefits, but they can serve other useful purposes. All trusts set forth in a will are revocable until the death of the individual whose will it is. That is so, because until death, that individual can change his will at any time.

Tax savings can be obtained through the use of irrevocable trusts, those which the grantor cannot terminate. A very common irrevocable trust is one that holds a policy of insurance on the life of father, for instance. The goal is to provide sizeable amounts of dollars at the father's death, first for the support of mother and then on to the family, which will not be subject to estate tax at his death—or thereafter when the mother dies. Another common type of irrevocable trust is one that holds stock of the family business. The idea is to shift the future growth in value of the enterprise to the next generation.

There are some changes that the close corporation owner, who created the irrevocable trust, can make without jeopardizing the tax goal, which is to keep the trust fund from being subject to estate tax when the entrepreneur dies. This death tax exclusion is generally forfeited if the grantor has the power to alter the terms of the trust during his lifetime, such as the right to modify the interests of beneficiaries in the income or principal of the trust. But the grantor can have the limited right (once in a lifetime) to remove a trustee and appoint a replacement. He or she can also be authorized to revise the identity of successors, in case one or more of the acting trustees ceases to serve. These rights help the surviving spouse avoid having to live with a trustee, when the relationship with the individual or bank has changed. Sometimes the trustees of an irrevocable trust, rather than the grantor, can undo the trust arrangements. This is accomplished by giving the trustee the ability to pay out all of the trust fund and end the trust.

Principal and income

The assets in a trust fund can be almost anything. Typical holdings are stocks, bonds, mutual funds, bank accounts, certificates of deposit and interests in money market funds or life insurance policies. Real estate can be owned outright or in common with others. Moreover, the trust can consist of stock of a business corporation or own an interest in a non-incorporated business or a partnership.

The property that initially comes into the trust, and all additions and reinvestments, constitute the principal of the trust. Some lawyers call it corpus, but it means exactly the same thing. The yield on the principal, interest, dividends, rents, royalties, etc., is referred to as the income. Sometimes the trustees have the discretion to pay out income or to accumulate it. Any income that is accumulated—which simply is income that is not distributed—is added to the trust fund and becomes principal.

There are a host of complicated issues that relate to the classification of items as income or principal. For instance: how do you treat stock dividends or capital gain dividends from mutal funds? What about the yield from so-called "wasting assets" such as an oil well which will become dry and unproductive in a period of years? Do you charge rental income and compensate principal for the depreciation on a building being held for investment? The resolution of these allocation issues is a matter for experienced professionals. Fortunately, there are many precedents. In any event, most wills and trusts give the trustees the power to decide these questions, thereby avoiding expensive court proceedings.

Powers of trustees

The trustees are actually the legal owners of the property that is held in the trust. They manage it, invest and reinvest it, and keep records of what goes on with the trust fund. The trustees generally can deal with any of the property on terms that they think are appropriate. The "boiler plate" in the will or trust usually confers on the trustees very broad management and investment powers. In essence, they may be empowered to do everything that the individual who formerly held the property could do.

Restrictions on actions by trustees

Despite the extensive control that the trustees have over the trust property, they are subject to important limitations. First and foremost, the trustees cannot pocket the assets; and unless expressly given the discretion to do otherwise, they must distribute the income and principal of the trust in accordance with the will or trust agreement. If the instrument says "pay all the income to my husband, Michael," they must pay it to him. The trustees can't distribute it to Michael's second wife, children or siblings, even if Michael turns out to be a miserable, undeserving person.

Often, the trustee is given discretion "to pay or apply the income (or principal) to or for the benefit of my husband, Michael." Payment to Michael is easy to understand. To apply for the benefit of Michael means to make payment on his behalf directly to the person who provides a service or who sells something to him. This wording gives the trustee the ability to move in and take care of a beneficiary who cannot fend for himself. This protection can be very important for a widow or widower. But the trustee must be able to demonstrate that each such expenditure was for the exclusive benefit of the surviving spouse.

There is one other major restraint on arbitrary action by a trustee, no matter how broad the powers that are given to him. A trustee is held to a standard of performance. He must do what a reasonable, prudent person, handling money for others, would normally do. Thus, a trustee runs the risk of being surcharged if he puts trust money in a very speculative investment or makes any other foolhardy or arbitrary move. To be surcharged means that the trustee is required to make up the loss that the trust suffers because of what he did, from his own pocket.

Because of the personal risk involved, and the ever present hindsight evaluation of their actions, trustees are generally conservative in what they do. In fairness, they are faced with a very difficult balancing act. The trust investments must produce enough yield to provide adequately for the surviving spouse. On the other hand, the principal must be preserved and protected against the effects of inflation for those who will receive it when the income beneficiary dies. There are many complaints about the unwillingness of trustees to invest in things which have a greater potential for meaningful appreciation. A typical comment is: "They won't take risks!"

I disagree with this attitude. Trusts are not intended by most people who create them to be speculators in the market. An intelligent conservatism is far better for a widow or widower. The surviving spouse already suffers from feelings of insecurity. It would be cruel to impose on him or her the terrible fear of seeing a large part of the trust lost as a result of risky investments. I recall vividly the cynical observation of one widow: "If we suffer losses, my income goes down. If the value of the securities goes up, it means nothing to me. The kids will just get more."

Sprinkle trusts

The trustees sometimes are given broad discretion regarding the manner of distributing the income and principal of the trust among a group of beneficiaries. For example, they may be authorized to pay income to or for the benefit of the surviving spouse or children, equally or unequally, with the right to exclude any one or more of the beneficiaries from any distribution. This is commonly referred to as a "sprinkle trust." The name comes from the parallel to a sprinkler casting water here and there over the lawn. A sprinkle trust permits the income to go each year to those beneficiaries who need it that year. That is a plus. It also usually provides that income for which there is no demand in any year can be accumulated and reinvested.

Sprinkle trusts are popular because they offer certain tax advantages. They are commonly used in situations involving widows and children. Consider, for example, the widow of a close corporation owner who is left with three young children. If all the income of the trust is mandatorily distributed to the widow, the top $9,000 per year might be taxed at a 30% rate. After deducting the $2,700 of income tax, the widow would have $6,300 to spend on the children's camp or college or whatever. On the other hand, if the trustee of a sprinkle trust applied $3,000 of income for each child directly, the total income taxes would be about $700. There would be $8,300, or $2,000 more, available for the support, maintenance, and education of the children in that year.

Nevertheless, a sprinkle trust puts the trustee in a position of considerable control over the beneficiaries. Many people forego the admitted tax advantages for that reason. They simply will not accept the idea of having members of their family dependent on anyone. There are some safeguards that may be employed with this form of trust. The trustee is often a person who is amenable to direction, such as the family accountant. He can be trusted to carry out the purposes of the plan and is possessed of all the personal, financial and tax data to make intelligent distribution decisions. In addition, the surviving spouse can be given the right to demand and receive some part of the principal. In this way, if the spouse requires more money, in her opinion, and the trustee won't give it to her, she can make up the deficiency out of principal.

The sprinkling can end when all the children have been emancipated. At that time the surviving spouse no longer gets the benefit of having more dollars, after taxes, to discharge her responsibility of raising the children. The trust then converts into one where the income must be distributed in a designated manner. For example, all the income will now be payable to the widow until her death.

Right to withdraw principal

The proprietor of a close corporation can easily be convinced that an unlimited right to withdraw principal is a mistake. However, he does not want his wife, after his death, to be restricted to living on the income of the trust fund, unless she can satisfy the trustee that her reason for wanting a distribution of principal is a good one. The independent head of a business, used to telling others what to do, understands and appreciates his spouse's reluctance to have to justify to the trustee the propriety of any invasion of the principal of the trust. A typical comment is: "Damn it, Milt, I don't want Kate to have to convince some flunkey at the bank to give her some money, if she wants to take a trip around the world, help the kids out, or make gifts to our grandchildren."

The solution to this problem lies in giving the surviving spouse the right to demand a payment from the principal of the trust, in any year, up to a stated maximum, what we call the "5 and 5 rule." Unfortunately, because of some technical gift and estate tax problems, there is a statutorily defined limit on this annual right to take principal. It is the greater of 5% of the value of the trust fund or $5,000. Obviously, so long as the principal exceeds $100,000, the 5% right of invasion produces the larger amount. Sometimes, there is a cap on how much of the trust fund the surviving spouse can withdraw, using this mechanism. It can be expressed in the form of a maximum number of times that the beneficiary can exercise the withdrawal right. Or, the instrument can provide that the total withdrawals cannot exceed a stated sum, like $150,000, during the lifetime of the surviving spouse. We have even used a fixed maximum annual amount, $25,000 (but never in excess of 5% of the value of the fund), adjusted to reflect any increase in the cost-of-living index.

An alternative right to invade principal sets forth the needs which the beneficiary can satisfy by taking principal out of the trust. Sometimes this is coupled with a dollar limit, but generally it is not. A common one in use in our office provides for the right to demand principal "for the support of my wife in her accustomed manner of living at the time of my death, for her health, and to defray medical, dental, hospital and nursing expenses and the expenses of invalidism."

These are rights given to the beneficiary herself to ask for principal. This situation should not be confused with that in which an additional power is given to the trustees, in their discretion, to pay or apply principal to or for the benefit of the individual. That discretionary power is invariably unlimited in amount, since it covers a myriad of possible misfortunes and problems that may arise. The sums that may be needed simply cannot be predicted. Also, in the case of this discretionary right, the guidelines for using principal for the surviving spouse are usually broad and liberal. The surviving spouse's comfort and security are the primary concern. Bearing in mind that this invasion of principal requires the approval of the trustees, it is common to see an expansive list of reasons for using principal for the beneficiary. Here is a typical one, relating to the invasion of principal for a widower:

> To provide for the care, maintenance and support of my husband, Evan, as well as for any expenses incurred by or for him because of any illness, operation, infirmity, emergency or disability, or for such other purposes, irrespective of cause or need, as my trustees, in their sole and nonreviewable discretion, shall deem to be in the best interests of my said husband.

This broad discretionary right of invasion is the key reason why the trust is a better method of protecting the surviving spouse than his or her absolute ownership—in case of severe illness, disability or emergency. When circumstances prevent the spouse from acting for himself or herself, the trustees can use trust funds for the individual's care and support.

Power of appointment

The trust, of course, states what happens on the death of the principal beneficiary. The property can pass outright at that time to the children, if they are adults. It can continue to be held in trust until the offspring reach stated ages. Sometimes a child's portion of the fund continues to be held in trust for his lifetime—and the ultimate distribution of principal is to grandchildren.

As we noted earlier, an estate plan should be reviewed every three to five years. This permits the plan to be altered to reflect changes that have occurred. But what can be done to make revisions after the client's death? The trust for the surviving spouse will probably be in effect for a long time. The usual expectation is that he or she will survive for many years after the death of the other spouse. Many family and economic circumstances can change during that period. Guesses about the children's future have now been replaced by the actuality. These developments may cause the provisions for the children in the will of the deceased parent to be a great mistake.

One way to build in flexibility is to permit the surviving spouse to change the pattern of distribution for the children at his or her death. The survivor can be given the right, by will, to do any or all of the following things:

1. Make a different division of property among the descendants, including the right to cut a child out completely.
2. Continue a child's share in trust for a longer period, or for life.
3. Give some or all of a child's share to his children (the grandchildren).

This right to make changes is called a power of appointment. It can be shaped in any manner that the person who grants the power chooses. A holder of the power of appointment must conform to the limitations. For example, the surviving spouse can be restricted to leaving the trust property only to descendants.

Conversely, the power of appointment can be very broad. A beneficiary can have the right to distribute the trust property at his or her death to anyone the beneficiary sees fit. This general power of appointment is more "dangerous," since the trust fund may pass outside of the blood line. It was more commonly used before the estate tax law was changed. Under the prior law, to qualify a trust for the marital deduction, the surviving spouse had to be given a general power of appointment.

The preceding cram course on trusts demonstrates their multi-faceted nature and versatility. The lawyer's role in planning a trust is akin to that of the custom tailor. He can design the suit in many different styles. The task is to give the customer what that individual really wants.

HIGHER STANDARD OF LIVING UNDER A TRUST

I am now going to examine how a surviving spouse can better be served through the use of trusts instead of having complete ownership and control of all the assets. It is important to keep in mind that no one is talking about putting all of the property of the spouse in a trust. Mother or father should have a meaningful amount of money in her or his own name, free to do with as the survivor sees fit. This individually owned property, plus the rights given to withdraw principal without the involvement of the trustees, provides the surviving spouse with a lot of dollars to call on whenever he or she wants them. This arrangement should provide significant financial independence. But it still doesn't get to the heart of the client's anticipated question. "Why is it better for me to have property held in trust instead of my having it in my name?"

This query, usually propounded by the wife of the business owner, reflects the belief that a trust is primarily intended to be a restrictive device. The innuendo is that the lawyer has been hired by the businessman-husband to come up with some technique that will prevent the wife, after his death, from irresponsibly depleting the wealth that he worked so hard to build, and the trust is the answer. Admittedly, when I started practicing law, the attitudes that were communicated to me by my mentors on the subject of estate planning were quite chauvinistic. The thrust was that a widow's money had to be tied up to prevent her from squandering it. I was given the clear impression that women whose husbands had died and left them comfortable, devoted a great deal of their time looking for ways and means of spending money. There was no consideration of the emotional upheaval that the death of a spouse would cause. This was an exploration that nobody wanted to pursue.

As the years went by, and my dealings with widows and widowers increased, I kept running into the opposite problem. I found most such people to be penurious. They *thought* poor. They usually cut back on conveniences, clothes and comforts because they were sure that they could not afford them. In fact, I now tell many people that if the banks were to close, and I had to find some place to deposit my cash, I would give it to one of the widows with whom I was dealing for safekeeping.

I recall one experience with a very wealthy widow, Laura. Shortly after her husband's death, Laura became obsessed with the need to establish a sizeable cash fund promptly. To accomplish this, she sold her home. I questioned her about it. Her response startled me: "Now that Jim is dead, if I become seriously ill, I'll have to go into a home. The kids won't want to take care of me. Those nursing homes cost a lot of money, so I have to keep a big cash reserve." I tried to convince Laura that her fears were unfounded. But I sensed I was "talking to the wall."

What I soon discovered was that Laura was typical. No amount of logical persuasion on my part seemed to have any effect on other widows like her. At first, I thought that my being younger and less experienced was the problem. I decided that I was not able to gain their confidence, to reassure them that they had the wherewithal to take that trip, or to rent that apartment in a sunny climate. Then came the happening that made me realize that I was dealing with something a lot more deep-seated than my personal inadequacy. It was my real introduction to the strength of the emotions that are involved.

Mildred's penuriousness

On a cold winter day, passing through the waiting room of our law firm, I saw sitting there a lady whom I will call Mildred. She was then 82 years of age, suffering from a malady which caused her to bend over, progressively more each year. The combination of her fraility and the stoop made her a somewhat pathetic figure to behold. Mildred had been widowed for many years. She never had any children. Her only living collateral relatives were wealthy. She had no one who looked to her for financial support.

As I walked near her, I asked perfunctorily, "What are you doing here?" She responded that she was there to see Herb, our senior partner. I said that I realized that, but I asked the question: "Why aren't you in Florida so that you can be warm and avoid this awful weather?" Her answer was simple: "I can't afford it."

Later that day when I had a chance to think about this exchange with Mildred, I was very troubled. I had just concluded some tax planning work for her. I had firsthand knowledge of how extensive her income producing assets were. In addition, as I noted earlier, she had no descendants for whom she had to conserve property. By all rational standards, Mildred had money to burn.

I took her file home that night. Carefully, I joined together two pieces of cardboard that the laundry sent back with my shirts, and made a visual aid. This graphically demonstrated that if Mildred used up $20,000 of principal each year, and lived to the age of 110, she would still have a meaningful amount of dollars left. (I selected the figure of $20,000 because it then far exceeded the cost of her vacationing in Florida for the entire winter.)

I was very pleased with myself. The next day I called Mildred and arranged a date at her home. I arrived carrying my visual aid. After we exchanged pleasantries, I asked Mildred to sit down at the kitchen table. I placed the visual aid directly across from her on the table, propped up with the back of a chair. Standing next to the cardboard, I first gave Mildred a detailed breakdown and valuation of her assets. Carefully, I explained what the numbers meant. The figures conclusively demonstrated that Mildred could spend each winter in the sun without any concern whatsoever about cost.

Mildred heard me out, smiled and thanked me for my concern. She asked no questions. Although she lived for many years thereafter, she never took a winter vacation. Why? Because in her mind, she could not afford it.

The empty well and other fears

Bothered by this phenomenon of penuriousness in so many well-to-do widows and widowers, I decided to seek the advice and guidance of some psychiatrists and psychologists who were clients or close friends. I raised the issue with them and asked for their explanation, fully expecting a substantial difference of opinion. But the explanations they gave me were virtually identical. They pointed out that what was involved were strong emotions—fears so extensive that they blocked out the intellectual explanations. Two of these counsellors called my attention to the recurring situation where an aged individual is found living in a hovel, with bank books on the premises revealing substantial cash holdings. It is the fear, they said, of outliving your money—waking up one day, destitute and dependent.

One psychiatrist gave me an analogy that has stuck with me. He suggested that an older widower looks at his wealth something like a well that provides needed water. He believes that because of his circumstances, no additional water will ever be added to the well. In other words, the level of the well can only go down, and he has no certainty as to how long the water in that well is going to be needed. The widower decides that the thing he must do is to keep the level of the well as high as possible for as long as he can. In this way there will be no risk of the well going dry in his lifetime.

Having reached this decision that the water must be preserved, any action on the spouse's part which involves taking water from the well—lowering that level—is self-destructive and frightening. Simply stated, so long as the widow or widower is the individual who must make the expenditure, to draw and sign the check, for example, the urging of family and friends that he or she can well afford the particular item falls on deaf ears.

These fears can be fostered through close association with an aged family member or good friend who constantly exhibits anxiety about life's problems—particularly money. Typical is the situation of the children dealing with their father, who was a vital, independent and dynamic head of a sizeable family business, and who now is weakened, worrisome and obviously insecure about the sufficiency of his financial resources. Day after day, they observe firsthand what changes the aging process has produced. Those contrasts are etched in the children's minds. Is it not reasonable to expect that these memories will stay with the sons and daughters when they become old?

Perhaps the most upsetting encounter, from the standpoint of financial fears, is arranging for custodial care of an aged relative who can no longer live alone. The available nursing home facilities, or at home companions and nursing care, are limited, and the costs can be staggering. The savings of a lifetime of an entire family can be wiped out. Unquestionably, this kind of trauma leaves a mark on the younger family members who are involved.

Why does a trust enable the surviving spouse to overcome these fears of spending money and thereby running out of dollars that may be needed, in large sums, to meet these potential crises? The answer is very simple. Someone other than she, in this case a substantial individual trustee or trust officer, knowledgable and responsible, like the deceased business owner to whom she was married, makes the payment. To understand my point, let us examine the position of Dorothy, a widow, who is faced with a large expenditure for a cruise, a trip to Europe or what-have-you, from two perspectives. She will have to pay the bill herself; or it can be paid by a trust for her benefit.

Payment out of her own funds means that Dorothy must take the "water out of the well" herself. This act of lowering the level of her financial security creates anxieties and fear. Her psyche screams: "Hold on to the money. You cannot be sure you won't need it." The urging of family and friends that she can well afford the expense falls on deaf ears. It is easier for Dorothy to convince herself that the safer course is to defer the outlay.

The trustee's reassurance to Dorothy that she doesn't have to worry about the expenditure carries much more weight. He is a professional, charged with the obligation to oversee her well-being. Any assertions made by the trustee to Dorothy are based on complete familiarity with her financial situation. But even more important, he can draw the check. This is the crucial advantage. The trustee thereby relieves Dorothy of the great anxiety that goes with the act of withdrawal. He "takes the water out of the well."

I have verified this phenomenon with many trustees and younger family members. They have witnessed many instances where the parent is not only willing, but even happy to be emotionally blind to this invasion of trust principal. When the trustee says there is plenty of money to take care of mom or dad, and pays for the trip to Hawaii—or to stay with the children in San Francisco—there is acceptance, rather than resistance. It may seem strange. But it works. The ultimate result is that mother or father lives better. Things are enjoyed and purchased that would not be if the beneficiary had to make the outlay.

This trustee can also help the spouse live better by taking over the burdens that accompany the management of money and property. He can keep the income and expense records; clip the coupons; make the deposits; keep the inventory of assets; make income projections—and perform a multitude of other tasks that take time and attention. To the person who has training and facilities, these responsibilities are easily handled. On the other hand, an aged person charged with managing funds can find the task to be onerous and very time consuming. The widow or widower whose assets are in a trust, managed by a competent and accountable co-trustee, is able to travel or vacation, free of these worries, because of the comforting knowledge that a capable person is attending to these details.

PROTECTION IN CASES OF DISABILITY

A trust also provides much better protection for a widow or widower in case of disability. The term "disability" has many different meanings. It is defined along lines relating to the ability to practice your profession—or to do your job—in insurance policies that provide weekly support payments. It is used in another context for Social Security purposes. The Internal Revenue Service has its own interpretation. I define disability very simply. It constitutes the inability to handle your own affairs because of physical, mental or emotional reasons.

A disability can be short lived. For example, an individual has a severe heart attack, a minor stroke, contracts pneumonia or suffers another serious illness. The patient may be out of action for a period of weeks or months. He is unable to function effectively or to manage his finances. The problem is particularly acute for the surviving spouse. There is no partner to step in and take over. The individual can be sedated, "out of it" for one reason or another. Much of the time he or she is struggling to cope with the serious ailment. Mother or father may have lapses of memory and fuzzy periods, and certainly cannot write checks. No one even wants to bother the parent about money matters.

What must the family do? Initially, because the long range effects of the stroke, major operation or serious illness cannot be measured with certainty, and mother or father is incapable of dealing with monetary concerns, they dig into their own pockets and pay the expenses. They are actually loaning money to the parent. But this arrangement can create serious financial pressures for the family and cause frictions because one family member is better able to contribute than another. If some of the children live far away, as is often the case, the mechanics of handling the situation through a family committee are further complicated.

There are permanent disabilities that strike people who the day before were possessed of all their faculties. These may be the hardest to adjust to. The change can be sudden and dramatic. It is upsetting to family and friends to behold.

Let me tell you about Bernard. He was a widower who had a daughter living, a deceased son and several grown grandchildren. Bernard had been a very successful businessman. He sold the family company some years ago, after his son, who was running the operations, was killed in an automobile accident. Bernard lived by himself, an alert, very kind man, with a whimsical sense of humor. He maintained a very warm and close relationship with his descendants.

Bernard was hit with a severe stroke. The impairment was substantial. He had to be moved into a nursing home. I went to see Bernard at the home, taking with me a paralegal who had done a lot of work for him. She and Bernard had become friends. During this visit, Bernard talked coherently to me some of the time. Then he would lapse into unintelligible comments. At one point he turned to me and asked: "How is that very nice young man at your firm who works so hard?" Without hesitation I replied: "Oh, he is fine." Walking out to the car after we left Bernard, the paralegal inquired as to the identity of the young lawyer he was talking about. I told her it was me. Only, Bernard was thinking of the me of 20 years ago.

Many disabilities do not come on so suddenly. Senility caused by hardening of the arteries is a slow progression. The same is true of psychoses that bring about extreme depression or peculiar behavioral patterns. The end result is the loss of contact with reality for extended periods. The newest frightening ailment is Alzheimer's Disease which destroys mental acuity slowly but inexorably. It is terribly upsetting to me to watch long-standing clients, the developers of major close corporation enterprises, towers of strength, become confused and debilitated, dependent on others for care and feeding.

Appointment of a guardian or conservator

When an individual is incompetent for significant periods of time, it is simply not feasible for the person to manage his or her own financial matters. At the moment that the family recognizes there must be a shift in the control of the funds, a bitter pill may have to be swallowed. Widows and widowers strive to have complete control over money so that they can deal with emergencies and financial crises more effectively. They believe that when the dollars are in pocket, they can tap them when the need arises without having to consult others. When disability occurs—which is the very kind of event where they want to have funds at their unfettered control—what is the situation? The spouse can do nothing for himself or herself. The parent's funds can't be touched.

The family has no choice. They must seek to have a guardian or conservator appointed for the incompetent. In some states this is referred to as a committee to manage the affairs of the disabled individual. To get a guardian or conservator appointed legally, there has to be a court proceeding. Proof must be offered of the incompetency. This is not as "cut and dry" as it used to be. Many courts are now recognizing the right of the affected individual to be represented in this proceeding; and they are demanding greater proof than a couple of affidavits from psychiatrists.

An attorney who represents the family may find himself in a very tenuous position when considering an incompetency action. Who is his client? Is it the disabled person, those family members who want the declaration of incompetency or the individual that is being suggested to serve as the guardian? Representing all sides in a proceeding that seeks to deprive a person of the right to manage his own affairs, and to vest the control in another, presents some real conflicts for counsel. How can one lawyer protect the rights of the alleged incompetent, press for the appointment of a guardian and also urge that a particular individual is the best choice as the guardian? The simple fact is that he can't do justice to all these conflicting positions. Courts are becoming increasingly hesitant to accept one lawyer acting for all interested parties in incompetency matters. In those instances where courts require several lawyers, each one representing a faction, this practice greatly escalates the costs—and it extends the time it takes to get the guardian or conservator appointed.

However expensive and time consuming the procedure may be, I have found that the worst aspect of a guardianship action is its effects on the children. They feel somewhat like an executioner. The decision to label a parent "incompetent" in a public proceeding is theirs. I remember sitting with two daughters who were considering a proceeding to have their father, an aged widower, declared incompetent, and to have themselves appointed as his guardians. They were absolutely demoralized. There was no question of the need to take over the father's affairs. He had done many foolish things with his money, including giving away meaningful amounts to virtual strangers. This, however, was a rational reaction to the situation.

On the emotional side, the resolution of the issue was not so simple. This was a man whom the daughters loved and greatly admired. He had been an outstanding and successful businessman as well as father, who throughout their lives had "spoiled" his two daughters. While they were married to productive husbands, dad was always there with that special present, or help with the down payment for a house, and annual cash gifts to enable them to have a measure of financial independence. Guilt filled the apartment in which we were conferring. Were they seeking their appointment as guardians to protect their father? Or, was the real motivation to make sure he didn't fritter away more of their inheritance?

In most states there are disadvantages to a guardianship beyond the anguish and cost of bringing the action. Annual bond premiums may have to be paid. Periodic accountings may be required. The guardian may have only limited statutory powers.

The two major alternatives to a legal guardianship are a power of attorney or a trust. Let us first take a look at the power of attorney.

Power of attorney

A power of attorney is a device whereby an individual, while still healthy, executes an instrument giving another—or perhaps two people jointly—control over property. To illustrate, the aging widow grants to her son a power of attorney. This entitles the son to sell any of the parent's property, withdraw unlimited amounts from her bank accounts, and generally to do anything that she could do herself. The concept is that if anything happens to mother, the son can step in and use her money to take care of her.

Years ago, a power of attorney was generally voided if the principal—the person who granted the power—became disabled. This meant that just when you really needed the power of attorney, it became useless. Then came the durable power of attorney which is now permitted in almost all states. This kind of power gives the attorney-in-fact the right to act even after the principal becomes incompetent.

The main problem with a broad power of attorney is that the principal is at the mercy of the attorney from the time the instrument is executed. The intention is to have it operative only if the principal is prevented from handling her finances because of a disability. But legally there is no such limitation. On the face of it, the holder of the power can do anything he wants with the principal's property at any time.

I have found that one spouse is generally willing to give the other a power of attorney. Trust and confidence in one another have been established. Many assets have been held in joint names for some time, with either spouse having the power to withdraw the funds or sell the stock. Nothing upsetting has resulted from this power to deal with property unilaterally. But our concern in this chapter is with the widow or widower. In the case of this surviving spouse, the most likely choice as the attorney is one of the children. There is an understandable reluctance of a parent to give a child these extremely broad, undefined powers over her property.

A child does not necessarily have to be the attorney. The family lawyer or accountant could be chosen. That does not usually happen, however. It is not an easy task for a professional to act on behalf of an incompetent. I played that role once—including paying bills, medical and nursing expenses, and dealing with a myriad of details—and it was extremely burdensome.

The family advisor also is faced with a serious conflict when someone suggests the establishment of a power of attorney. He recognizes the need for the instrument. He appreciates that its existence will facilitate the care and support of the parent in case of a severe illness, stroke or loss of mental capacity. On the other hand, the advisor realizes the risks that the grant of the power of attorney involves for the principal. He or she is at the mercy of the holder of the power.

Lawyers hesitate to push a widow or widower into executing a power of attorney. They should. However beneficial the concept seems, there will be complete dependence on the integrity and trustworthiness of the child who holds the power. There are too many instances of overreaching by children, in dealing with the property of aged parents, for any counsellor to assume there is nothing to worry about.

Sometimes the widow or widower who is willing to appoint an attorney is beset by bickering among the children as to who should have the power. The selection of one child, as compared to having jointly held powers, is much more efficient. Certainly that is true when the children live far apart. The family appreciates the advantages of having one individual serve as the attorney. But the issue is which member of the family should be placed in that position.

Jealousies and rivalries among siblings and in-laws are triggered by this selection process. For instance, the son who lives thousands of miles away recognizes he is not the right choice. Nonetheless, he hesitates to have his sister appointed because he doesn't trust his brother-in-law. I have had numbers of clients, otherwise willing, who have scrapped the idea of a power of attorney because of the controversy over which child should be that attorney.

Trusts

A trust offers the greatest flexibility in dealing with disability or severe illness. It avoids the disadvantages of guardianship or the use of a power of attorney. The essence of a properly drawn trust is the power of the trustee to use the principal for the beneficiary in accordance with broad and liberal standards. This power permits the trustee to step in and use all or any part of the trust fund to cope with any level of illness or disability. Expenses of a severe illness, or of an incapacity which lasts only a few months, can be handled. So too can the other extreme—the totally disabled individual.

There does not have to be any public declaration of incompetence. The dignity and self esteem of the individual are preserved. The costs, complexities and emotional trauma of a guardianship are avoided. A healthy parent does not have to give a child broad control over his property, as a means of dealing with the possibility that he may become unable to handle his affairs. He is spared the anxieties and feeling of dependence that this produces. With a trust, there is no need for the children to assume even an interim financial burden. This eliminates the squabbles and unpleasantness within the family that differences in financial substance and attitude can cause when the hat is being passed among them.

Moreover, a responsible and trained person, a non-family member, is handling the money. That trustee is accountable for his actions. He operates under an instrument that spells out, with much greater specificity, what may be done for and on behalf of the beneficiary. The outside trustee is totally disinterested financially—except for his commissions for serving as trustee—since he will never personally be a recipient of the funds.

This is a very significant point. When children play the role of dispensing a parent's money, as guardian or attorney, they are really spending their inheritance. There is a conflict, or at least the appearance of one, where the heir to the funds decides whether or not to use the money for mother or dad. I know that there are many instances where children have virtually exhausted the very sizeable holdings of a parent, to assure him or her a comfortable life until death. Their actions demonstrated that they paid no heed to the reality that they were using dollars that otherwise would pass to them. Nonetheless, I repeat, there is the potential for holding back when a child is in this position. Do I select the more expensive, lovely nursing home facility, or will the less expensive and not so attractive one do? After all, mom or dad will probably never know the difference.

In sum, the trust with a qualified non-family trustee is the best vehicle for dealing with disability or severe illness. It is much more desirable than using a guardianship or a power of attorney. The trust is even better than letting a spouse have absolute control, because if he or she becomes incompetent, temporarily or permanently, the spouse will not be able to act. At that time, a desperate need will arise for someone to move in and take over financial matters.

Because of these advantages, there is a growing trend for an aging widow or widower, with most of the surviving spouse's property in individual name, to establish a living trust to deal with this risk of disability or severe illness—or to get help with the management of her property. This is a trust for the individual's benefit, that goes into effect while he or she is still living. The beneficiary receives all the income and can also have the right to demand the distribution of all or any part of the trust assets. A selected trustee serves with the spouse, who is empowered under the instrument, in case of illness or disability, to step in and meet the widow's or widower's needs out of the trust fund.

Since the spouse is a co-trustee, while he is up and around, nothing can be done unless he knows about it. Should he become incapacitated, the existence of the trust gives him the protection that he needs. As further reassurance, the living trust can be terminable at any time the widower so chooses, and all of the property will come back to him.

DEALING WITH REMARRIAGE

A trust is also the best mechanism to deal with the many sensitive issues relating to the survivor's remarriage. I have learned, over the years, that remarriage is probably the number one concern that a wealthy married couple has when they are doing estate planning. For instance, the most difficult problem in drafting a wife's will is the disposition of her jewelry, particularly if her husband survives her. Why not leave the jewelry to husband, if he survives, and then he can give it to the children at appropriate times? That usually is not an acceptable solution. The wife anticipates—quite properly—that her husband will remarry; and the thought of her jewelry adorning his second wife is repugnant.

A story that is enjoyed by women—and often repeated by them— is that of the wife who has a portrait done of herself, showing her wearing many expensive pieces of jewelry that she does not own. When questioned about why this was done, the wife replies, "I want to drive his next wife crazy looking for that jewelry!"

Although women have this fetish about jewelry and even household furnishings being used by a second spouse, men generally tend to be more punitive regarding remarriage. It is commonplace for a young man in his forties to suggest that his wife cease to be the beneficiary under the will if she remarries. When questioned, he acknowledges that it will be a very lonely and difficult existence for his young wife to remain a widow. Often he says that he hopes his wife will remarry after his death. He justifies this termination of her benefits in case of remarriage on the ground that the second husband should take care of her.

When this attitude is manifested by men of advanced years, who have been married for decades and whose children are grown, it is even harder to understand. Intellectually these men understand that if their spouse remarries, that marriage will be more an expression of the need for companionship than a wildly romantic relationship. I suspect, however, that this male hard line position on a spouse's remarriage is the result of a deep-seated resentment against "this guy" who will now occupy the deceased spouse's place. Certainly the second husband should not do it with his money.

It can be very hard on a widow to cut off a significant portion of her funds for support and maintenance if she remarries. The man she desires to marry may not be in a financial position to make up any significant portion of the income that she will be forfeiting. Such a situation encourages an extramarital relationship which may be degrading to the widow and embarrassing to her family. There is a legitimate concern that property belonging to the decedent's family should not wind up in the pockets of the second husband or his family. Particularly is this so, when the surviving spouse owns stock in a closely held family business. But eliminating the surviving spouse's income is a harsh way to achieve the goal of conserving the family's holdings.

Candid and uninhibited communication between spouses regarding remarriage, during the estate planning process, is rare. It is a proverbial "one in a million" experience for a lawyer to hear one spouse declare something like this, in the presence of the other: "If I survive, I expect to remarry and if I use some of the children's inheritance to take care of my second husband, so what!" Usually, there is a lot of hedging or silence in this area. Each spouse somehow feels that the less said openly on this subject, the better the continuing marital relationships will be.

Estate planning advisors must be sensitive to the parties' reluctance to be outspoken when remarriage is being given consideration. They should become more active as discussion leaders and use their communication skills to break through the protective wall of silence. When this matter is handled discreetly, I have found couples willing not only to air their feelings regarding remarriage, but to moderate them. Specifically, I have found that after frank discussion and some reflection, most married people are willing to accept the idea that if the surviving spouse remarries, rights to income—and even limited rights to invade principal—should continue unchanged. If some part of that income is used for food, sundries, vacations, etc., that benefit the new spouse to some degree, so be it!

How then do you assure the result that property will not ultimately pass to the new spouse's family? I always tell clients that it is easier to have his and her towels than his and her money over a lengthy second marriage. Let me give you a typical example. A condominium is to be purchased in Florida. The wherewithal is coming entirely from the now remarried widow. An unthinking local lawyer draws the contract and deed in the joint names of the spouses. Should the second husband survive, he will become the owner of that condominium. A widow in these circumstances may not appreciate the implications of this joint ownership. Even if she feels that the title should be in her name alone, avoiding an unpleasant scene with her new husband may seem to her to be the best course of action. After all, she'll survive him anyway!

To make sure that the assets will pass to the issue of the first marriage, a trust is again the answer. A widow is relieved of the unpleasantness of rejecting a second husband's request for this or that to be financed by her. The co-trustee becomes the person who says no; or if he agrees to advance monies to assist the purchase by the beneficiary of the condominium, he will insist that title is vested exclusively in the beneficiary's name.

Pre-marital agreements

What about pre-marital agreements? Can they be used effectively to safeguard the property interests of the children of a prior marriage? From a legal standpoint, in most jurisdictions, ante-nuptial contracts will work. That is, each prospective spouse can relinquish rights to inherit the property of the other. There are disclosure requirements that have to be met; and each spouse should be separately represented.

What is the need for such agreements prior to a marriage? Absent such a waiver of marital rights, the statutes of many states give a surviving spouse certain interests (such as one-third) in the property of a deceased spouse. In other words, he or she must inherit, whether the other spouse likes it or not.

The problem with these agreements is their "cold blooded" nature. On the eve of a marriage, the two loving people have to conduct negotiations over the effects of the death of either of them. One of the two individuals may be giving up alimony from a previous marriage, and feels substantial concern about also contracting away support rights if the spouse-to-be dies. In some instances, a lawyer may introduce the subject of what the financial arrangements should be in the event that the forthcoming marriage ends in divorce or legal separation.

The concerns are the greatest, of course, when one spouse is very wealthy and the other has limited means. The children of the wealthy individual often feel that the idea of marriage has emanated from the poorer person. "She's just marrying him for his money," is a common observation in this kind of situation. One of the children may even contact the family lawyer to make sure that "dad isn't taken advantage of." The truth is that they do not want to be taken advantage of.

Lawyers have to handle these negotiations regarding pre-marital agreements with sensitivity and care. I have been involved in these discussions a great many times, and I find them to be the most difficult to conduct. That may be so because of the somewhat peculiar role the lawyer is expected to play.

The wealthy spouse-to-be wants protection for her family. She may have been told by relatives or friends of the importance of having a settlement before marriage so that her money—often inherited from her deceased first husband—doesn't wind up in the pockets of her new husband's children. On the other hand, she looks to the forthcoming marriage as a very important event. It means affection and warmth, companionship and sharing—the end of the loneliness and artificial existence that often made her feel like a duck out of water. To threaten or tarnish this relationship, a giant step toward her happiness, by demanding property concessions from her prospective husband, is not an inviting proposition. The lawyer is the person who can save the day. He becomes the "bad guy." It is the lawyer who sits down with the couple about to be married, and explains that the motivation for a pre-marital agreement is not to protect the spouse whom the lawyer ostensibly represents. Not at all. The beneficiaries of this agreement are her descendants.

While my experience in these pre-marital negotiations has been uniformly good, I feel it is a mistake to rely on these arrangements when you are doing planning. A trust for the widow or widower does a much better job of protecting the family's wealth. It eliminates the risks that the surviving spouse will fail to enter into an agreement prior to remarriage; and he or she is spared the anxiety of having to press for such a contractual arrangement on the eve of this important rehabilitative event.

The new marital deduction rules make the trust format an even more effective safeguard in case of remarriage. Before, to get an estate tax marital deduction for property put in trust, a surviving spouse had to be given the right, at least by will, to leave the property in the trust to anyone he or she saw fit. Obviously, this enabled the survivor to dispose of the property to the new spouse or his family. Under the new law, the surviving spouse can be denied any right whatsoever to control the disposition of the trust fund when he or she dies. The decedent can direct, by will, how the property will pass at that time. To get the benefit of the marital deduction, the executor of the deceased spouse's estate merely makes an election.

PROTECTION AGAINST CHILDREN

A trust also protects the widow or widower against children. While planners may worry about widows and widowers being done in by confidence men—which certainly does happen on occasion— the greater probability is that they will be parted from their money by family members. This is a somewhat startling accusation. It suggests that I believe that parents are victimized by scheming children. Not at all. The children's motives may well be honorable. But if the test is whether or not a father or mother parts with money, under circumstances where such actions are a disservice to the surviving spouse's own best interests, financial and emotional, then I contend that more dollars are given up by widows and widowers to their family than to confidence men.

To get this in perspective, we must recognize that the ties to one's family take on much greater significance when a spouse dies. There is loneliness and emptiness at that time and one reaches out for children and grandchildren to fill the void. In short, the affection of the children becomes extremely important to the widow or widower. That makes it much harder to say no when a child asks for something, directly or indirectly. I often use this vignette to make my point:

> Mother is having dinner with her daughter and the daughter's three children, her grandchildren. Where is Tom, her son-in-law? He works in the marketing department of a large corporation doing business all over the world. Tom travels extensively, seeing his wife and children only on week-ends; and when he is home, he needs to get out on the golf course to relax. Her daughter is very unhappy. She has what she describes as a rotten marriage. The daughter cries out that she is raising the children like a single parent.
>
> "What can be done about it?" says mother. "Oh," weeps daughter, "if we only had $100,000, Tom could open up his own business and he would be around all the time." No demand for money has been made on mother. But it is clear to all concerned that the only one that

can end this unhappy set of circumstances for daughter and her children is mother—because she has the $100,000. Parting with such a substantial amount of money will create terrible anxieties for mother. On the other hand, the person who is making the pitch is someone very dear and important to her. This is tremendous pressure.

The story can be told with any number of varied fact patterns. However, they all have one common strain. There is a very serious problem of a child (or son-in-law), calling for money as a solution, and the surviving parent has the wherewithal on hand to provide the solution. Incidentally, the widow or widower may believe earnestly that the suggested solution is not sound. I recall one such situation vividly, when a widower, who ran a very large and successful manufacturing corporation, was importuned to finance his son-in-law's harebrained business venture. Nonetheless, it is difficult to find a way to make the impracticality of the idea appear to be the reason for not putting up the money—rather than the unwillingness to part with the funds.

There are greater risks for the surviving spouse if the children are involved in a family business. These enterprises can need money to meet an emergency, or the corporation may be strapped by the very high interest rates that institutional lenders are charging. Let me relate an incident that shows how a widow (I will call her "Irma") got "trapped" into advancing a very large sum to her sons' business.

Irma's sons owned and operated the family manufacturing company. They urgently required $300,000 for the purchase of some very much needed machinery. The corporation's banker would only give them a five year self-amortizing loan with interest at 2% over the prime rate—which was then 18%. This debt service would have been very difficult for the company to handle.

One of the sons was privy to all of Irma's financial information. She had $350,000 in low yielding stocks and savings accounts. From these investments Irma realized about $25,000 a year. She was content with these holdings, because she had inherited the stocks from her husband and the money in the savings accounts was fully insured. In addition, her income from all sources was more than enough for her to live on.

The sons pressed Irma to sell the stocks, withdraw the cash from the banks, and loan the amount realized to their company. The loan would run for ten years. There would be no amortization of principal, since the principal at Irma's death would belong to her sons anyway. Interest would be paid quarterly at the rate of 10% per annum.

The boys told mom that this loan would be great for her. She would increase her income by about $10,000 a year ($35,000 versus the current yield of $25,000). The repayment would be secured by giving her a lien on the machinery that was purchased with the proceeds of the loan. The reality was that mother would take the sons off the hook. Their business would obtain the loan for the purchase of the machinery at a much lower interest cost, and the sons were relieved of the pressure of repaying the loan.

Irma made the loan to the boys' company. She really didn't want to do it. But she didn't know how she could say, "No," without alienating her children. Interest has been paid regularly on Irma's advance. The business is doing well. What will happen when the note becomes due? Who knows. My guess is that it will be extended.

A great defense to this kind of pressure is the existence of the trust for mother. Now she has the perfect out. "I don't personally have that kind of money. You know, dear, daddy put most of my money in a trust. It's tied up. Maybe you can talk to the trustees and see if they would be willing to advance the money." She has the best of both worlds. The funds will remain intact, still earmarked for mother's protection, as they were intended. Mother, however, does not have to risk an impairment of her important relationship with a child by refusing.

There is a final comment I would like to make before we close this chapter on trusts. Children are usually a poor choice as trustees for their parent. Mothers and fathers do not want to be dependent on their children. This feeling of dependence is not changed because the children are acting as trustees, rather than as individuals. The widow or widower still has to come to them for money, and justify the needs to them, as trustees. I think it is easier for a parent to deal with trustees who are unrelated. The children also have a conflict of interest. They may have to decide whether to invade principal for mother's or father's benefit. Since the money is theirs when the parent dies, they cannot be as objective as someone who is not a potential beneficiary of the trust fund.

HOW TO HANDLE THE CHILDREN WHO ARE NOT IN THE BUSINESS?

10

The only exception to this general principle occurs where the daughter-housewife is the owner of the interest in the corporation to those children who don't work in the business. If they own stock, buy them out! I have seen too much family strife, hostility, and bitter litigation result from the combination of active and inactive family members owning stock in a close corporation. I now believe that the issue is not if there will be trouble in the family—but only when it will occur. This is so because we have an oil and water situation. There is just no way you can mix owner-managers and inactive owners together in a close corporation and have peace and contentment.

The only exception to this general principl occurs where the daughter-housewife is the owner of the interest in the corporation and her husband is a full-time employee. If the daughter and her spouse are viewed as a unit, this is really not a contradiction of the principle. Her husband becomes the vehicle for getting money out of the business and into the hands of the daughter and her family.

THE MORGAN FAMILY — AN ILLUSTRATIVE CASE

Let me try to describe the problems that develop when there is a stockholder in the corporation who is not involved in the enterprise and what it leads to. To make the exposition more meaningful, I am going to use an example that is fictitious but very typical.

Steven Morgan, Sr. worked for a company that distributed cigarettes and candy products. He left to start his own business, Reliable

Distributors, Inc. Reliable put cigarette vending machines in restaurants, bars and taverns. Then Steven added jukeboxes, shuffleboards and other games, including more recently, video games. The volume was expanded by buying some locations from competitors who were primarily active in other areas and through some acquisitions.

Steven died a year ago. Shortly before his death, Reliable made a significant acquisition which added another line of business. It purchased the assets of a company that installed vending machines in theatres, factories and institutions such as hospitals and nursing homes. Steven was survived by his wife, Clara, and three children, Steven Jr., age 46 (always referred to as "Steve"), Susan, age 44, and Leonard who will be 40 in a few months. All of the children are married and there is a symmetry in the offspring. Each of them has two children. The grandchildren range in age from 4 to 18.

Steve and Leonard have worked for Reliable since they finished college. They are very capable and they work well together. Steve handles marketing and finance and Leonard is in charge of distribution, service, personnel and purchasing. After the father's death, Steve became president and treasurer of Reliable and Leonard was elected executive vice president and secretary.

Susan was not considered by her father for a role in the family corporation. "It's not a good business for a woman," he used to say. She had a few different administrative jobs after she graduated from college, the last of which was in the human relations department of a large company. Susan stopped working when she had her first child.

Susan's husband, Bill, is a labor lawyer. He is a partner in a large firm which has a broad based corporate practice. His income from the firm is in the neighborhood of $175,000 a year. Just after Bill married Susan, her father suggested that he come to work for Reliable. Bill refused, having been raised in a legal background (both his dad and older brother are lawyers).

During his lifetime, Steven Sr. gave almost half of his stock of Reliable to his three children, equally. Under his will, the rest of his stock was bequeathed to them, again in equal parts. He felt this was a very fair arrangement. He treated all three of his children the same, but the two sons who were active in the business had control of the enterprise.

The wife, Clara, has nothing to do with the business. Reliable carried a very large policy of insurance on the life of Steven Sr. The proceeds of this policy were used to purchase preferred stock which

Clara inherited from her husband. The income from this substantial sum plus Steven Sr.'s other investments is more than enough to support Clara very comfortably for the rest of her life.

Each of the two sons draws $150,000 a year from Reliable. Following their father's practice, they each use a company owned car, currently an expensive foreign model. They are participants in the corporation pension plan and its very generous medical expense reimbursement plan, which covers spouse and children too. There is $150,000 of group life insurance coverage on each brother.

Steve and Leonard attend all industry conventions with their wives, at company expense. They have extensive dining and entertainment charges that are paid for by Reliable. These have been explained to the Internal Revenue Service as reciprocal expenditures at customers' places of business.

The price that Reliable paid for each company that it acquired, including the purchase of the candy and food vending business it bought shortly before the father's death, was very substantially in excess of the seller's net worth. A large amount was added to the net assets figure, to reflect intangible or going concern value. This add-on was based on a formula, which applied to the average weekly volume of sales at the various kinds of customer locations, a well known, industry-wide multiple. The profitability of the location and the performance of the customer affected the size of the multiple. This kind of formula for determining good will value is common in other industries also. For instance, fuel oil and linen and laundry supply businesses are commonly bought and sold on that basis.

Reliable depreciates its machinery and equipment over a short period of years. Many of the corporation's completely written off vending machines and equipment are still in use.

No dividends have ever been paid by the corporation, despite its excellent liquid position. Because of Reliable's expanding business, the acquisitions and the demands for capital expenditures, the company has avoided an unreasonable accumulation of earnings, with the accompanying adverse tax consequences.

Susan's dilemma—conflicts between active and inactive shareholders

The Morgan family situation highlights the dilemma that is caused by the presence of an inactive stockholder. Everyone recognizes that capital and labor are required for a successful enterprise. The children, including Susan, are entitled to share the return on capital equally. However, only Steve and Leonard—the "workers"—should receive compensation and fringe benefits for their services as senior executives of Reliable.

The problem is how to measure accurately what is a fair return on capital and what Steve and Leonard should receive for their efforts. When all the stockholders are engaged in the business, no one cares about what is being received as an owner and what is being paid for working. For income tax reasons, the proprietors take, as compensation, as much as the corporation can afford to pay, as long as that amount is deductible. The same is true of benefits. By keeping the level of compensation and fringes in accordance with the respective percentages of ownership, there are no antagonisms.

There are no statistics or indices that anyone can point to as a measure of what is reasonable compensation for Steve and Leonard. Much of the evaluation is subjective. We have already noted that the determination of reasonable compensation for the close corporation owner-employee is probably the most difficult issue to resolve in the entire income tax area.

Sibling rivalry is a further complication. Undoubtedly, Susan views Reliable's success as a result of the efforts of her father. She feels that her brothers have been handed a gold mine. From Susan's vantage point, her brothers have a soft life—certainly as compared to Bill, her husband, who often works around the clock in labor negotiations. Susan has good reason to feel she is being taken advantage of. She owns a major equity interest in a successful business and she gets no return from it.

If Susan had the same amount in a certificate of deposit, she might be receiving 10% on her money and the funds would be available to her whenever she needed them. Susan should get more income from her investment in Reliable, since it is tied up in a risky entrepreneurial business. A 15% return would seem to be reasonable. But she gets nothing.

Steve and Leonard may rationalize the failure to pay anything to their sister, Susan, on the basis that she doesn't need it. After all Susan's husband, Bill, is a very successful lawyer, who earns a great deal of money and will probably do even better in the years ahead. Of course, this position is indefensible. Need has nothing to do with it. Susan is a "partner" in the close corporation. She is willing to be silent; but nobody can justify her being deprived of income.

Figuring out what would be a fair return to Susan is a very difficult task. There are two elements involved. What is the value of Susan's Reliable stock? What rate of return is she entitled to receive annually on that investment? Susan and her brothers, Steve and Leonard, are sure to have different viewpoints on these issues.

Susan and her brothers, undoubtedly, will clash over the proper method to use in determining the value of Reliable's business. Each side can muster legitimate arguments in support of its position. Someone representing Susan would start the valuation process with Reliable's net worth, which is approximately $1,500,000. He would then add a substantial amount representing the goodwill of the corporation—calculated by using the multiples of volume formula— plus the excess of the fair market value of the machinery and equipment over its value on the books. This might easily raise the total value of Reliable to $2,500,000. One-third of that figure is then rounded out to $835,000. A 15% annual yield is urged as the proper one, in the light of Susan's locked-in speculative investment. This means that Susan should be earning about $125,000 a year on her stock (15% of $835,000).

Her brothers see it quite differently. They would point out that the formula for valuing intangibles based on volume of sales only applies when you buy some locations or make a small acquisition. That amount would never be realized if the entire business of Reliable were sold. Similarly, there is no basis for adding on value for the tangible assets. Sure, a lot of the machinery and equipment that has been written off is still being used by the company. But a purchaser wouldn't pay anything greater than book value for the fixed assets.

The brothers would insist that a non-marketable, minority interest in a closely held corporation must be significantly discounted. Twenty-five percent to 35% is commonplace. They would concede, at the most, a $600,000 add-on to the $1,500,000 net worth, representing the intangible value. This makes Reliable's overall worth, $2,100,000, and Susan's one-third interest, before discount, is $700,000. Applying a 30% discount and rounding out, Susan's stock value is about $500,000.

A throw-off of 15% will be challenged by Steve and Leonard on a number of grounds. The corporation is in no position to pay out that rate of return to the three stockholders. A substantial amount of the net-after-tax income of the corporation has to be plowed back for purchases of new machinery and equipment, acquisitions and financing customers' receivables.

The brothers will call attention to the much less than 15% annual dividends that large public mercantile corporations are paying on their stock. The certificate of deposit analogy will be challenged. With that kind of fixed dollar investment, there will be no appreciation. Here, everything points to a meaningful increase in the value of Susan's stock of Reliable. The brothers will urge that an 8% return is the highest yield that Susan could hope to get. This means a maximum of $40,000 per year (8% of $500,000). This is far less than the $125,000 per year Susan's advocate would opt to receive. There is certainly room for compromise between these two figures. Unfortunately, fixing the figure is the easier obstacle to get over. The hard part is getting that annual amount into Susan's hands.

Solutions that won't work

Putting Susan on the Reliable payroll for non-existent services is an uncomfortable solution. In fact, there are serious tax risks. The deductions for the amounts paid to Susan could be disallowed, resulting in serious income tax deficiencies, plus interest and possibly penalties. The same holds true for a large retainer that might be paid by Reliable to Bill for very little or no legal work. Assuming that everyone is willing to take the risks, this approach usually fails to resolve the problem. One side or the other will soon be unhappy. If Susan's income from Reliable continues to be much less than that received by each of her brothers, she will be disgruntled. Conversely, if Susan and Bill are paid a high annual sum for doing nothing, let us say $100,000, Steve and Leonard will have a legitimate complaint. Each of them is only receiving $50,000 a year more as full-time employees (overlooked will be the value of their perquisites, such as the car, medical insurance, pension plan and travel and entertainment).

Other solutions are equally unsatisfactory. Paying substantial dividends to Susan means that Reliable must distribute very large non-deductible amounts each year. For Susan to get $50,000, the corporation must declare a total of $150,000 of dividends. This still leaves Susan with much less than her brothers.

Would the situation improve if Reliable elects Subchapter S income tax status? It will eliminate the double tax on the amounts distributed to the three children, as stockholders, because only the stockholders will pay tax on Reliable's net profits. But Susan will still receive less; and she will undoubtedly believe that Steve and Leonard are using their control of the corporation to compensate and benefit themselves more than is proper.

Having Susan exchange her common stock for preferred stock of Reliable is another possibility. The double tax on dividends returns. But now only she will receive dividends—which reduces the spread between Susan's yield and what her brothers get from the corporation. This exchange of common for preferred puts the valuation of Susan's common stock directly in issue. How much preferred stock should she receive? We have seen how wide the difference can be between what Susan and her brothers think her equity interest is worth. Even if the valuation issue can be compromised, Susan's exchange of common stock for preferred freezes her equity in the enterprise. No matter how successful the business becomes, Susan's capital will not appreciate. Because of these factors, this approach is usually rejected.

The only answer: a buy-out

The only permanent solution that really works is the purchase of all of the interest of Susan in Reliable. This is done by the corporation, rather than by her brothers, because Steve and Leonard will have trouble taxwise moving the dollars for payment of the purchase price from Reliable to themselves. Unfortunately, buying out an inactive stockholder is difficult to do. A complex valuation problem arises and terms of payment have to be worked out that will protect Reliable's business. If the corporation pays Susan more each year than it can handle, the "goose that lays the golden eggs" may be destroyed. Sometimes, to protect the corporation's borrowing capacity and credit position, the indebtedness to the retiring stockholder is subordinated to all bank loans and trade creditors.

In addition, there is a technical matter that must be dealt with. In many states a corporation can only purchase stock out of surplus. This may be determinable when the stock is bought back. In some jurisdictions, the test is whether there is adequate surplus when an installment of the purchase price is payable. To meet this surplus requirement, the capital of Reliable may have to be reduced, or assets may have to be written up on the balance sheet.

Many other issues must be resolved. These include: security for Susan; personal guarantees of payment by Steve and Leonard; restrictions on what the brothers can take out of the corporation while Reliable owes money to Susan; whether Reliable can make acquisitions or other major capital expenditures while indebted to her; and what happens if the business is sold or Reliable merges with another company.

These points are similar to what principals and lawyers deal with in any sale of stock. The difference in this case is that the parties are family members. Emotions run high. The negotiations become a forum for venting hostile feelings that may have been repressed for decades. Because of this anger, jealousy and the many resentments, rarely is the purchase worked out with calm and objectivity. In a very high percentage of the cases—most, I would say—there will be a bitter controversy between the family members. Litigation is commonplace.

AN UNSEEMLY SPECTACLE:
INTRA-FAMILY WARFARE

As a counsellor committed to the resolution of problems in a manner that serves human relations needs, I have always been upset by this kind of intra-family warfare. My litigation partners keep telling me that there can be no effective settlement until there is considerable ventilation of feelings by the parties. They point out how deeply felt the emotions are, and how wide apart, financially, the inactive stockholder and those in the business invariably are. A spirit of compromise is required. That comes, they say, only after a good deal of costly battling. I now believe my partners are correct. Reason and logic are put on the back burners when siblings start squabbling. There is also the release of tensions and feelings at dad's death that have been bottled up while he was alive.

The fact that the troubles with an inactive stockholder in a family business generally erupt after the father dies, is not coincidental. Unquestionably, as the years went by, Steve and Leonard resented Susan's ownership of stock of Reliable Distributors. "Why does she have an equal interest in the corporation when she never helps the business?" The brothers probably heard the stories of battles with inactive stockholders that have taken place in their community or industry, that in many cases destroyed or seriously impaired successful closely held enterprises. They worried about their future.

If the sons mustered enough courage to raise the subject with Steven Sr., he most probably reassured them that the Morgan situation was different. Because of father's position of power, Steve and Leonard could do nothing. Fathers rarely face up to these intrafamily complications. The quest for equality among their children, and the need to avoid unpleasantness in the later years of life, take precedence.

Litigation among stockholders of a successful close corporation is a juicy plum for lawyers. The stakes are high and there is the wherewithal for the payment of sizeable fees. However, lawyers are not the fomentors of these battles. The clients start these fights and their strong emotions keep enlarging them. Attorneys are the agents that ultimately bring about a settlement of the controversy.

But while the legal scrapping goes on, it is intense. In our Reliable Distributors example, Susan's lawyers would charge Steve and Leonard with having received excessive compensation and "milking" the corporation. In essence this means using corporate dollars for personal expenses. This raises the spectre of serious income tax consequences to the corporation, if these issues are made a matter of record in the courtroom—and consequently become available to the Internal Revenue Service.

Pre-trial discovery of the facts will be pursued by counsel to Susan. Steve and Leonard may be subjected to an examination of the books and records of Reliable by accountants engaged by Susan. The brothers will be deposed—that is, they will be required to answer questions posed by Susan's lawyer, in some office, out of the presence of a judge.

This questioning can take on the character of an inquisition. Let me illustrate what might be raised with Steve, using as a model a similar matter that I participated in many years ago. Steve is given the oath by the stenotypist reporter who will take down every question and answer and all the comments made by lawyers. Next to Steve is his attorney. Susan's lawyer sits at the conference table, with a host of Reliable's petty cash vouchers in front of him. Both Susan and her lawyer-husband, Bill, are present.

Slowly and deliberately, the lawyer for Susan inquires about each item for which Steve has submitted a voucher and has been reimbursed by the corporation.

Question:– "Why did you dine at X restaurant on this date?"

Answer:– "I make it a practice to eat at restaurants of our customers. It is a way of showing them we appreciate their business."

Question:– "Why do you always take your wife with you?"

Answer:– "It is customary for me to dine with my wife. The customer would think it was peculiar if I ate by myself."

Question:– "On the following dates, you were accompanied by another couple. On these dates there were two other couples with you. In each instance, you were reimbursed for the full amount of the check by Reliable. Why did you have the corporation pay for all of these people?"

Answer:– "I guess it was a good customer, so I decided to spend a lot of money at his place."

There then follows a barrage of difficult inquiries:

"How good a customer was X restaurant as compared to others that you never visited?"

"Didn't you eat at the restaurants I asked you about because they were the best places to eat?"

"Weren't you really celebrating your wedding anniversary when you and your wife took three other couples, on July 16, to the Z restaurant, which is perhaps the best eating place in the city?"

"When other couples ate with you, and the corporation paid the entire cost, did the others pay their share of the check to you, in cash?"

This kind of barrage can go on for hours.

The beating at the hands of the lawyers, admittedly only doing their job, escalates the anger of the adversary family members. The character assassination and belittlement done by the other side's attorney is attributed to the principal. The schism between the siblings grows progressively larger—often reaching the point where there can be no reconciliation ever again.

As the litigation heats up, all the parties keep getting bills from their lawyers for all this activity and for the expenses of depositions, photocopies, etc. It can cost each side tens of thousands of dollars every month, highest of course in the early stages of the proceedings. If it is not settled and there is a lengthy trial, the level of monthly legal fees is even higher.

In addition to the legal charges, there is the interference with the business. Steve and Leonard must take the time to prepare for their depositions. They are constantly being asked about some factual matter or requested to produce some information that is needed. It is hard to manage a business effectively under these pressures. For all of these reasons, most of the cases are ultimately settled.

A phyrric victory

I had an experience that taught me the value of reaching a settlement early in the game—for a reason even more important than the savings in legal expenses and wear and tear.

It was a case where my firm represented the family members who were active in the business. The corporation was extremely successful. The buy-out of sister's one-third interest involved millions of dollars. The parties disagreed on how many millions. There was a lot of legal jockeying. For two years our firm beat the pants off the other side. One day, just after our latest victory had been announced, I met on a tax matter with the brother who was the head of the business. In the course of our conference, referring to the pending litigation, he told me that he now understood better the meaning of a "pyrrhic victory." He hastened to tell me that no disparagement of our legal services was intended by this observation. His comments stick with me:

> We're doing our best to make the business more successful. Our profits are growing. This means that the longer we delay in buying out Sally, the more it will cost. The victories we keep winning in the lawsuit are only postponing the inevitable and costing the company money.

He immediately put in motion a proposal for the corporation to purchase his sister's stock at a price significantly higher than what we had offered. Sixty days later the transaction was consummated. This was a brilliant move. Had the litigation gone on for a few more years, the price would have been much higher. His decision, of course, also saved a lot of legal fees and put an end to the increasing bad feeling in the family.

"PUT" ARRANGEMENTS

Some clients have tried to deal with the inactive family stockholders by giving them an option to sell their stock to the corporation, for a price and on terms that are spelled out in an agreement. They can get out without having to battle or sue. This is what we refer to as a "put" arrangement. The program is worked out while dad is running the corporate enterprise. However, none of the children can sell stock back to the corporation until after the death of father. This protects him from any purchase price payment pressures during his lifetime.

None of these arrangements permit an inactive stockholder to make repeated sales to the corporation of a small number of shares. The usual minimum is one-quarter or one-third of an individual's stockholdings. In most instances, the inactive equity owner must sell all of her stockholdings when she exercises the option. If less than all the shares can be sold by the inactive stockholder, she must, after the sale, to assure capital gain treatment of the proceeds, hold less than 80% of what was owned before.

The method of determining the purchase price must be spelled out. Often book value is used. In other instances, the price is based on a multiple of earnings. There can be combinations of valuation approaches. Moreover, the payments to the selling stockholder must be manageable to the corporation. Invariably they are spread over a period of years, ten to fifteen is common. Interest is payable on the unpaid balance of the purchase price.

A serious risk for the close corporation in these put arrangements is that a number of inactive stockholders will exercise the option at or about the same time. To guard against this potentially very serious financial burden, there is usually a cap (a maximum) on how much the corporation will be required to pay as purchase price installments in any one year.

To illustrate, let us assume that the cap is $100,000. Two inactive stockholders exercise their right to put all of their stock. Under the agreement each of them is entitled to receive $600,000 payable quarterly over ten years. Without reflecting the maximum of $100,000, each of the selling stockholders would be entitled to receive $60,000 of principal payments in the first year, or a total of

$120,000. Since the cap is $100,000, each of them will only receive $50,000 of principal payments and the other $10,000 will be deferred.

The put plan is optional. Legally, any inactive stockholder who feels that the format is unfair, can cause trouble, and even bring a suit, in the hope of getting more money or speeding up the payments. The hope is that because father played a major role in structuring the arrangements, the children in and out of the business will more easily accept the price and terms that he formulated.

DEALING FAIRLY WITH CHILDREN NOT ACTIVE IN THE BUSINESS

The better alternative for dealing with the children who are not active in the business is to keep them out. Don't give them stock of the family corporation. Dad can appreciate the advantages of this course of action. His question is: "How can I exclude as stockholders my children who are not active in the business, and still deal fairly with them?"

The first approach is to give them other assets. The stock of the corporation passes to the offspring who are in the business, and a comparable value of other assets goes to those who are not involved. This solution raises some interesting issues. Should the children who are outside the company receive less than the full value of a working child's stock? The justification for the discount is that they are receiving liquid assets, whereas those who are entrepreneurs have their equity tied up in non-marketable, non-dividend paying stock. The children in the business lose the benefit of diversification. All their eggs are in the business basket.

The other factor that dad must take into account is the contribution to the value of his stock that those children working in the company have provided. It is very common for a father to determine the value of the stock going to his sons—which must be matched with other property for his daughters—at its current worth. He ignores the reality that his sons, through their efforts over many years, have imparted a good deal of value to the enterprise. The daughters should share in what dad built, but not in what their brothers did.

Providing the dollars for equality

What can a father do if his other assets are insufficient to provide his inactive children with a meaningful amount? The answer is to create more property for them and to use business dollars to do it. The easiest vehicle is life insurance proceeds earmarked for those children who are not participants in the corporation's activities. Group and split dollar insurance can be used. This can be augmented by personal insurance on dad's life, financed by increasing his salary from the company. The business is really bearing the cost. All of this life insurance can be structured so that the proceeds are not subject to federal estate tax at the death of father. How to do this is discussed in Chapter 13, "The Importance of Life Insurance."

The children outside the business can also receive some post-death compensation or pension plan death benefit proceeds. The problem is that these funds are usually needed to take care of the mother.

Another way of dealing with the shortage of equalizing property at the death of father, is to allocate to the children who are not in the business much more, or all, of the family's other property when mother dies. The various amounts are left in trust to provide for mother during her lifetime. At her death, instead of the funds being divided among all of the children, there is a weighting in favor of those who did not receive stock of the corporation. If a child dies before mother, then her children inherit in her place.

The difficulty here is that the son or daughter who has no interest in the business has to wait until both her parents die to receive the property. This can be ameliorated somewhat by leaving something to these children at father's death and the balance when mother dies.

These suggestions are not alternatives. They can be used in combination. The goal is to maintain equality among the offspring, without giving stock of the close corporation to any child who is not in the business.

Negotiating the buy-out while the family head is living

If the marshalling of other assets cannot produce the desired result, then the head of the family should negotiate the terms of the child's buy-out, which will take place when he dies. Steven Sr. could have done this for Susan. Let's see how it would have been accomplished.

Susan had received some stock of Reliable Distributors during her lifetime. Steven Sr. would continue the bequest of the rest of his stock to his three children, equally. But while Steven Sr. is alive, an agreement is made obligating the corporation, at his death, to purchase, and Susan to sell, all of her stock of the corporation. A price that Steven Sr. believes fair is worked out with the boys. Terms of payment that the company can handle are set out in the agreement. Insurance on the life of Steven Sr. might have been taken out to fund a meaningful part of Reliable's obligation. Everyone knows what is to happen.

Steven Sr. would have had no trouble consummating these arrangements during his lifetime. By virtue of his position in the family and his role in the business, the children would have readily accepted his judgment of what was fair and reasonable.

This foresight on the part of the patriarch can prevent so much controversy and antagonism, the outlay of sizeable legal fees and the eventual destruction of relationships among siblings. All that is required is a recognition of the reality:- there is no place in the close corporation for an inactive stockholder.

THE INCORPORATED PARTNERSHIP—A BUSINESS MARRIAGE

11

When I refer to an incorporated partnership, I usually mean a close corporation in which two unrelated parties, or collaterals, owning equal interests, are in business together. This is the most common variety of incorporated partnership, by far. For the sake of simplicity, in this chapter and the next, I will use incorporated partnership illustrations where there are only two proprietors.

The key to the nature of the relationships between the proprietors is the term they use to describe themselves. Each stockholder invariably refers to the other as his "partner." They have chosen the corporate form to do business, because a lawyer has advised them it gives them limited liability—that is, their assets outside the corporation are protected against creditors of the business—and it is easier to operate with an incorporated entity. But they view the essence of the arrangement as a partnership between them.

Young lawyers and accountants are disturbed by the constant use of the word, "partner," to identify a holder of stock of the close corporation. It has taken them years to understand the important differences between a corporation and a partnership. Say "corporation" and the attorney thinks of a board of directors, officers, minutes and a legal identity completely separate from the owners of the stock. To him, partnership bespeaks an entity that is really an aggregation of individuals, acting with unanimity and devoid of titles such as president, secretary or treasurer. The accountant knows that corporations are income tax-paying organizations, whereas a partnership pays no tax itself. It merely files an information return disclosing what the partners will pick up in their individual tax returns.

Older professionals accept the partnership characterization without blinking an eye. They have heard the close corporation with a few owners described that way so many times, that it has become an idiom to them. I admit that in my early years of practice I was perplexed by this repeated misnomer. How could these very capable businessmen fail to grasp the significance of the distinctions between a corporation and a partnership? Then I came to realize that it was not an intellectual error by the client. "Partner" was the word that best depicted the closeness of the relationship with a co-stockholder in this type of close corporation.

"BUSINESS MARRIAGES"

The proprietors of the incorporated partnership, in fact, have a very close, intimate business arrangement. A client who owned an interest in this kind of close corporation described his relationship with his partner as a "business marriage." This label stuck with me, because there are many similarities between the business union and the standard form of matrimony.

The business marriage starts with a commitment by each partner to the other. Each of them vows to do his utmost to build the enterprise and to bear the burdens and enjoy the benefits equally. The partners grow closer as they contend with the ever present problems, worries and disappointments, and celebrate the increased volume, new customers and greater profits. Sharing these emotional experiences creates strong ties between the stockholders, as evidenced by their nostalgic recollections of past developments, hectic moments, close calls and humorous happenings. I call these the "remember the time" stories. They remind me a lot of a married couple describing incidents that involve their children.

In most situations, these unrelated principals in the close corporation become good friends. They spend a lot of time together in an environment that is conducive to the discussion of personal problems. The partner is available when the need to ventilate arises. An office is a far better place to tell someone your troubles than trying to do it on the golf course, at the country club, in a busy restaurant, or at a party. Moreover, partners have well developed and comfortable lines of communication. Rapport and confidence in each other have been established. There is an aura of mutual trust. Each owner can count on his peer's commitment not to disclose sensitive information. The stockholders' families often are close as well, spending a lot of non-business hours together. It is common for the children of one to refer to the other partner and his wife as "uncle" and "aunt."

Because of the intimate relationship between the co-proprietors of the incorporated partnership, decision-making is streamlined. Both parties are well versed in all aspects of the business operations. They have in-depth familiarity with the corporation's plans, needs and problems. While they may divide up management responsibility, each of them is aware of everything that is going on. In addition, the governance of the entity is solely in their hands. They do not have to consult with committees, or make elaborate presentations to a board of directors. If something makes sense to them, they do it.

I am constantly amazed by the contrasts I have seen between the abbreviated process of making determinations, exhibited by so many of these incorporated partnerships, and what takes place in law firms like ours. Lawyers can spend inordinate amounts of time deciding insignificant matters. My best example is a discussion among my partners some years ago, lasting almost one hour and filled with brilliant dialectic, as to whether the sender and intended recipient of inter-office memos should be identified by initials or full names. In that same period of time, over lunch, I have seen business partners decide on a course of action of great importance for their company, requiring a large expenditure of capital.

Businesses run by more than two partners

It must be recognized that incorporated partnerships among more than two individuals do exist. Our firm has served a number of enterprises which involved a trio of proprietors. Very early in my practice, I did some work for a company that had five equal stockholders. It is much more difficult to divide up operational responsibilities when there are more than two active stockholders, and to have peace and harmony among them. It is worthwhile to examine the reasons why.

Business marriages, like regular marriages, are hard to keep intact when two people, with different emotional make-ups, characters, and personalities, are joined together. Both the number of split-ups of incorporated partnerships and divorces between husbands and wives attest to that. The introduction of a third partner, with his or her different traits and attitudes, makes the risk of serious unpleasantness greater. Having four partners is still worse, and an incorporated partnership with five equal partners is like a human relations caldron. A colleague of mine once observed that any business with more than three co-owners should have a psychologist in residence.

Governance of the entity is much more complicated when there are more than two partners. Parity is an automatic when there are two equal principals. There is no way that either can take complete control of the corporation, or be excluded from an equal voice. A majority vote is required for any action, and that requires concurrence by both partners. When there are three or four partners, a majority can be achieved without one person's agreement. In short, two or three can gang up on one co-owner. Invariably, the most insecure of the group will be sure that the others will exclude him; and he may insist on all votes requiring unanimity. While at first blush that seems fair, it puts any one of the partners in a position to block any action, simply by saying "No," or just stalling, or even demanding some concession for a favorable vote. When there are five partners, three represent a majority, and factionalism can easily develop. I remember that in the case of the five partner client that I did work for, four partners split up, two and two, on any important issue, and the fifth always seemed to be in a position of being wooed by each side. They finally broke this pattern by requiring the concurrence of four of the five partners for any action. That created other problems.

Two partners have to settle their differences in order to get something done. This creates a give and take, a climate of compromise. If there are more than two partners and a majority voice governs, there can be a very disgruntled and unhappy outvoted stockholder, who feels he has been put down by his partners.

Management and status are also easiest to handle when there are two partners in the incorporated partnership. Enough major areas of activity exist, marketing, production, finance, and sufficient significant titles, chairman of the board, president, executive vice president, treasurer, so that each of the two stockholder-executives can play an important role in the management of the company, and hold one or more offices of prominence. A typical division is to have one of them head up marketing and the other, production, with one serving as president and the other as executive vice president and treasurer—or one as chairman of the board, and the other as the president. This easy apportionment of fields of activity in the company between the two owners, protects employees from the very upsetting experience of having their bosses giving them conflicting directions or contradictory policy decisions.

When there are three or more partners, it is much harder to create equivalence of management roles and positions. There may not be a significant divergence of talents among the principals, so that they will fit into different spheres. For example, what can be done if two of three partners are born marketers, but would be terrible overseeing the production or finances of the business? Certainly, creating titles of roughly equivalent rank is much more difficult when there are more chiefs. If one of the three partners is chairman of the board, and the second is the president, what comparable office is available for the third proprietor? Candidly, the greatest possibility of successful interaction in an incorporated partnership with more than two partners, occurs when one partner, the most competent, dominates the others. This person is the force, the leader. It is he (or she) who holds the top office, runs the day-to-day operations of the business somewhat like an autocrat, but is careful not to demean his "peers." For public consumption, the arrangement is an equal partnership. But everyone inside the organization, including the others partners, knows who is in charge.

There are instances where one of the two stockholders holds a minority position. However, because of the insecurities that this produces for the individual holding less than 50%, and the complexities of protecting him without depriving his partner of all the benefits of control, it generally doesn't work.

GETTING "DIVORCED"

There is another very great similarity between the business marriage and the one that exists between husband and wife. A lot of them end in divorce. With the passage of time, things move in that change the nature of the principals' relationship. The warmth, affection and trust change to distaste, suspicion and ultimately outright hostility. The split-up between the partners involves the same kind of battling and very high level of emotional output that is regularly seen when spouses are divorced. The joys and pleasures of the many years of good days are wiped away by the bitterness at the end.

I have been saddened by the rancor that so often accompanies the separation of proprietors in a close corporation. Men and women who have worked together for decades, shared so much, overcame so many obstacles, handled the disagreements that invariably crop up between strong willed individuals, reach an impasse that they cannot resolve and wind up hating each other. The very stong positive feelings that bound the partners together get transformed into equally powerful negative ones. Serious incompatibility is the ground for this business divorce. There is no "other woman," desertion, or extreme cruelty. The partners simply can no longer live together in the business. I stress the word "serious" because some disenchantment between the owners must be expected in every incorporated partnership. Here again it is analogous to the husband-wife relationship, which has its fights, disagreements, and good and bad days— what a psychologist once identified to me as the "summers and winters of a marriage."

In most instances, the partners are able to handle their disagreements and antagonisms. That is, they are somehow resolved short of creating a real schism. The bond between the proprietors and the recognition that they have a good thing going are sufficient to keep them together. They learn to compromise and adjust. Sometimes, however, the owners of the business reach such a level of discord that they are incapable of further association. The easiest instance to understand is where there are two very dissimiliar personalities who should never have gotten together in the first place. This is basic incompatibility. These relationships usually come to an end in the first decade of a close corporation's existence.

Invariably there are a few incidents of consequence that are pointed to by the parties as the basis for the split. But the truth is that the events used to justify the separation are cover-ups for the real cause. A stockholder may have repressed his hostility to his partner for a long time. Now that the enterprise can afford it, he sees his chance to get out. Suddenly there is a happening that provides the opportunity for him to pour out his anger and discontent. It is analogous to the married couple who start bitter, destructive fighting because one of them can no longer tolerate the spouse's habit of squeezing the toothpaste tube from the top.

The break-ups that are harder to understand are those where the individuals involved have been partners for many, many years. They had been close friends and confidantes who built a very successful business. Over a much shorter period, the relationship sours and eventually there is a separation. Often the split is very acrimonious.

Ironically, the separation between owners is more likely to happen when the business is successful. I have seen a number of situations where incompatible principals somehow were able to work together while the enterprise was struggling and then, when the business prospered, one of them found "cohabitation" intolerable. During the period that the corporation was going through tough times, the partners had much less time to dwell on personalities. Married couples often stay together for the good of their children. Later, when the kids are emancipated, they go their separate ways. Business partners who are unhappy with one another frequently do the same thing. They stick it out while the venture is going through its growing pains and then get divorced when it is really on its feet.

There are other practical reasons why the split-up is delayed until the company prospers. Before that development, a good price can't be realized by either stockholder for his interest in the corporation. Even more important, in the growth period, there is generally no available wherewithal to buy out either partner. When the corporation has more liquidity than it needs for operating capital, and there is a solid base of annual profits, it becomes possible to make a deal. There can be a meaningful purchase price, a down payment for the partner who gets out, plus installment payments over a period of years that the company can handle.

SIX WARNINGS SIGNS THAT A BUSINESS MARRIAGE IS ON THE ROCKS

Many of the split-ups of partners who have been together for many years are a surprise to everyone, friends, customers, business associates, and even employees. A common response to the news that one partner has left an incorporated partnership goes something like this: "What could have happened? They worked so well together for so long, and built a really successful business. On top of that, they were good friends. I can't understand it." The reasons for the separation are not easily identified, because the partners rarely broadcast them. It is not considered good taste to disparage publicly your longstanding partner and compatriot. I am going to describe a half dozen warning signs that the relationship between two partners, who have been in business for a long time, is headed for trouble. If one or more of them happen, and the issues are not addressed properly and openly, the discontent festers and grows, and leads to confrontations, bitter exchanges, and often the end of the partnership. I will use the case of Davcon Advertising as an illustration. In part, I will be doing a post-mortem on the split between Ron Davenport and Ken Connors, long term partners and friends.

Davcon Advertising was a full service, good size advertising agency, with two equal stockholders, Ron Davenport and Ken Connors. Ron Davenport was a 63 year old grandfather, married to Carol. He had two married daughters who were housewives. Neither of his sons-in-law has any connection with Davcon. Ron's partner, Ken Connors, was considerably younger. He was 53. Ken married Grace, a serious artist who was gaining recognition for her work, but was unable to hit the "big time." Grace was often depressed about the limited income and recognition her painting was giving her, and started to pressure Ken to join Davcon Advertising and play an important role in the creative activities of the agency. Ken was ready to agree to this idea, although he could foresee problems, because he felt something had to be done to resurrect the relationship between him and Grace. For a few years, Ken and Grace Connors had been on the verge of separating, and Ken had a number of clandestine affairs with other women.

The Connors had two sons, Ralph, 23, and Paul, 20, and a daughter, Barbara, a school girl, who was 15 years old. Ralph majored in communications at college and was working for an advertising agency in another city. His father hoped that he would join Davcon Advertising after a few more years of learning the ropes. Paul was a junior in college, where he was a marketing major.

Ron and Ken met more than twenty years ago, when they worked together in the same advertising company. Ron was an account executive and Ken did copywriting. They were assigned to a very large food market chain account, and grew very close to the management of that company. They were encouraged to leave and set up their own agency by this retail food client. The client was very much impressed with the talents of Ron and Ken, and wanted to make sure that they would be handling the chain's advertising. In fact, the food company helped finance their start-up costs.

For some time Davcon Advertising was dependent on the food chain's advertising for survival. As time passed, the corporation started doing work for many other customers. Ron expanded the business because he was a cracker jack salesman and he hired and trained a number of very capable account executives.

Ron's major role had changed to overseeing the work of the account executives, participating in presentations to prospective customers and watching over the agency's fairly new public relations and market research divisions. Ron had been the president of Davcon Advertising since its organization. This was considered to be important to Ron's role as the "front man."

Ken built the production side of the agency. He did it under the pressure of keeping the quality up despite rapid growth in volume. Davcon Advertising was well known for its very clever copy and its eye-catching graphics and art work. The agency won many awards. The creative people were typically difficult to manage, and despite the presence of a talented art director and a brilliant copy chief, Ken had his hands full in meeting deadlines and refereeing inter-office squabbles.

After a good deal of prodding by his wife, Carol, Ron agreed, about ten years ago, to the idea of taking a regular three weeks winter vacation. This was in addition to the traveling that he and Carol did in the spring and fall, and the long visits in the summer to see their daughters, who lived a good distance away. Subsequently, the Davenports rented a place for the winter on Longboat Key, near Sarasota, Florida. Three years ago, Ron bought a condominium there, large enough for his daughters and family—one at a time—to come visit him.

Ron and Carol, who are both good golfers, joined a nearby country club in Florida which has a fine golf course. They became very friendly with a large group of residents in their complex, regularly dining and golfing with various couples. A number of Ron's Florida buddies, who are about the same age as he, had retired completely. Others were down there from November through April, staying in touch with their family businesses mostly by telephone and through an occasional airplane trip up North.

Ron had been pursuaded by Carol and his friends in Florida that he worked too hard and should spend more time in the sunny south. Last year he announced to Ken Connors that from November through April he would be in Florida about half the week. Specifically, he would fly down Thursday afternoon and would be back in the office early in the afternoon on Monday. He followed that schedule and continued to take time off for trips to the Near East and Africa and to see his children.

Ken's vacations were much more circumscribed. It was harder for him to get away during the school year, because his 15 year old daughter was a freshman at high school. Even more crucial, his wife does not like to be away from her studio for any significant length of time. Working was far more important to Grace Connors than socializing.

For years, clients and people in the advertising field marvelled at the wonderful relationship that existed between Ron and Ken. They epitomized the closeness and affection that can develop in a successful business marriage. Suddenly, without any awareness that trouble was brewing, the ostensibly great partnership came apart at the seams.

1. Bringing children into the business

Perhaps the biggest cause of disharmony between partners in an incorporated partnership is the introduction of children into the business. This was a very serious concern of Ron Davenport. Ron had no members of the next generation who would be involved in Davcon Advertising. He worried a lot about the entry of Ralph and Paul Connors into the company. That day of reckoning was very near. Ken had indicated that as soon as Ralph finished his apprenticeship at the advertising entity where he was then working, Ralph would be joining their corporation.

The problem for Ron was not Ralph Connors's capabilities. There was every indication that he would be a welcome addition to the business. He had an outgoing pleasant personality, coupled with an inherited creative and artistic talent. Ralph was well educated for a career in advertising and he was now getting excellent practical experience.

Ron's anxieties related to the effects on him of Ralph's coming to work at the agency. How was his partner's child to be compensated?

The initial salary was easy. But what happens when Ralph—and later Paul, if he comes too—has a family and needs to earn much more. Is some part of the son's salary to come out of his father's share of the income of the business?

What about Ron's interaction with Ralph? He agreed with Ken that Ken's son had excellent client relating capabilities and that it would be better for Ralph to be under the tutelage of Ron. However, Ron was very concerned about how he and Ralph would get along. Will there be special strains and tensions when he criticizes Ralph's performance? How will his partner, Ken, react if his son complains that Ron is not treating him fairly? These were legitimate apprehensions.

There are other fears that Ron suffered. Even if he maintained his 50% voting position, the presence of two—and ultimately probably three—Connors in the business, would cause him to feel that his voice in policy had been reduced to a minority. Ron pictured himself sitting down with Ken and his two sons to consider some important management issue and the Connors ganging up on him. The individual facing the prospect of his partner's family coming into the business tends to become somewhat paranoid. He conjures up all kinds of potential problems and his level of concern keeps rising.

One of the things that Ron had been spared was the pain and disappointment of comparing his son, who was drifting along, to his partner's boys who were responsible and committed to join the corporation. In this instance, his only descendants were daughters, who were happily married domesticated mothers. Picture Ron's feelings if he had a son in his late twenties or early thirties who was a struggling musician or actor, a cultist, or a non-achiever. Now there would be a comparison between the family business tradition instilled in the Connors sons and his "failure" to have raised his child with sufficient motivation to take his place at his father's side in the company.

Would these difficulties regarding the entry of the next generation be eliminated, if Ron had children working in the business too? At first blush, you would think that it would help, because the circumstances of each partner were now alike. In fact it might even be worse. What gets filtered into the corporate environment, when both partners have children working there, is the competition among parents. Each partner needs to believe that his child is the most competent. To satisfy that ego demand, he overrates his child's talents and performance and is critical of what his partner's kid does. This is very destructive for the offspring and can result in even more bitter conflicts between the partners. Very often it leads to the most antagonistic parting of the ways.

2. A partner's spouse joins the company

In Chapter 1, we looked at the special problems produced when a husband and wife are both active in running a business. A lot of those difficulties are equally applicable when the spouse of a partner in an incorporated partnership comes to work for the firm. There is, however, an additional significant complication when the entity is a partnership, rather than the couple's family business. The delicate human relations balance between the two co-owners, developed through give-and-take and adjustments to each other's personality, can be altered substantially by the presence in the company of the husband or wife of one of them. The concerns about dealing objectively with the children of a partner are mild, when compared with the almost impossible task of figuring out how you direct and demand performance and accountability from a partner's spouse.

Grace Connors didn't come to work for Davcon Advertising before the break-up that resulted in Ron Davenport's stock of the corporation being bought out. But the possibility that that could happen certainly added to the tensions that developed between the partners. The consequences, if Grace Connors had been employed by Davcon Advertising, illustrate the kinds of serious management difficulties that can ensue, when the spouse of one partner joins the company. Grace had no experience in advertising. In truth, she was looking for a career change because her painting had not produced sufficient economic return or gratification for the amount of effort she had expended. It is very probable that Grace pictured herself, because of her artistic talent, vaulting into a prominent role in the firm in a very short time. Either Grace's husband, Ken Connors, or his partner, Ron Davenport, would have had the unpleasant task of bursting Grace's bubble, and making her realize that it takes a lot more than the ability to paint wonderful abstracts to direct the art department of an advertising agency. Since it was his wife who had to be given bad news, Ken would have found it much easier to shift the job to Ron Davenport, believing that Ron could be more objective. So, Ron would have had to communicate a lot of realities to his partner's wife, which she undoubtedly would resent hearing, such as:

"Grace, the art chief of an advertising agency has to know how to come up with a pictorial portrayal that will produce the response the ad is seeking. A beautiful, attractive picture is not enough. It takes a long time to learn how to tie the picture into the theme of the ad."

"Supervising hard-to-manage creative people calls for real know-how, in order to motivate and constructively criticize them, and evaluate their work in a manner that they feel is fair and objective. You have had no personnel practices experience, and you start with a handicap in relation to other employees, because you are married to one of the owners of the company."

Understandably, no partner enjoys being put into this position.

The presence of a partner's wife in the business also shakes up a number of top level unrelated executives. They cannot deal with the spouse as they would with other employees. Suppose Grace Connors had started to work in the art department of Davcon Advertising. Undoubtedly, the art director, and probably the head of the copy department, would be very concerned. What should they do when Grace failed to meet a deadline? Or, what if she was guilty of insubordinate conduct, such as refusing to do a job in the way that they wanted it to be done, because she felt they were wrong? Her superiors would feel constrained to handle her with kid gloves, because they were afraid of the consequences that would follow if she complained about their actions or competence to the owners. The art director might also have been apprehensive that because of Grace's connections, it was only a matter of time until she took his job. Whatever complaints or concerns Grace's superiors had, they would not have gone to Ken Connors to air their grievances or unhappiness. Ron Davenport would have had to deal with all these problems relating to Grace's employment. Undoubtedly, this would have made him very angry with his partner, for having brought his spouse into the company in the first place.

3. Loss of commitment

Another important cause of disharmony in the incorporated partnership is a significant change in one partner's outlook about life in general, and the business in particular. This change comes in several different forms, but the key ingredient in all of them is a loss of commitment to the business because it no longer provides the same level of challenge and gratification. Other interests become important, often as part of the recognition that life is fleeting. A partner may feel that there are many more years behind than ahead, and that too much time has been focused on one thing, the close corporation.

Motivation starts to wane. If it happens to both partners, the situation is easy to handle. The trouble comes, as it did in Davcon Advertising, when one partner's commitment to the enterprise takes a nose-dive, while the other is going full steam ahead, continuing on the path that both partners traveled for so many years together. Usually, there is no announcement by a partner that he is no longer fully absorbed in building up the business, and the change takes place over a period of time. Here are some of the signals that it may be happening:

PURCHASE OF A SECOND HOME

What I am thinking of here is a house or condominium, at a place removed from the principal place of business and the residence, at which the partner spends a good deal of time. Its location is a matter of the tastes of the entrepreneur and his spouse. For some it is a winter vacation place in a warm climate or near a ski slope. Others have a second home for the summer, near the beach or in the mountains. There are individuals, like Ron and Carol Davenport, who want plenty of people around, so they can have golfing partners and enjoy social activities together. Many want an environment which is a distinct contrast to their way of life at home, with a very limited amount of interaction with humans, and the ability to dress informally. A client of mine, a usually dapper businessman, summarized the change very simply: "While I'm at my summer home, I never wear socks or a tie."

Whatever the locale and the environment, and the activities that are pursued, the second home can easily become a very important part of the partner's life. As compared to the often repetitive, now even boring work that he does at the office, the existence at his retreat away from the office is much more enticing. There is much greater pleasure there. Schedules are mapped out to assure that sufficient time is spent at the vacation home. Slowly but surely, the commitment to the business is sapped by the ever growing attachment to life at "my place in Florida."

And what does this all mean to the business and the other partner? Let's look at Davcon Advertising. With the purchase of the condominium in Florida, Ron Davenport opened up a whole new life in the sunny clime. That is where he wanted to be during the cold weather. He shortened his business hours—essentially from Monday afternoon through Thursday noon—during the six months period from November through April. This did not result in a reduced vacation schedule for the other half of the year. Ron still wanted to travel and visit with his daughters, who were far removed geographically. The distance between Ron, while he was in Florida, and Davcon Advertising discouraged hastily scheduled get-togethers to cope with emergent matters, or the ability of Ken to call Ron over the weekend and say:- "There's something bothering me about the XYZ account. Let me drop over and we'll chin about it."

Key personnel in the agency working under Ron's direction often felt they had been abandoned by him. That was particularly true with the top people in the relatively new public relations and market research divisions. During the long Florida season, when Ron was in the office, he was extremely busy. Actually, he often was frenetic. That's because he tried to cram all his activity and decision-making into a very much shortened work week. It was hard to be able to get Ron to sit down and do any planning or consider policy.

Ron's new mode of life was killing Ken. He was forced to step in and take over a number of the duties and responsibilities that Ron formerly handled. Ken resented this. Not only was he putting in much more time and effort, but he had to contend with his feelings of inadequacy, because he had no confidence in his ability to handle Ron's areas.

The reader may understandably question Ron's prerogatives. By what right did he put in much, much less effort in the business than Ken, and still expect to be treated as a peer when it came to status and splitting the profits? I posed this question in a number of similar situations. Some of the responses, which I will state as though Ron Davenport were making them, were mind-boggling:

- "I didn't tell Ken to work so hard. Why doesn't he take more time off?" More often than not, if that recommendation

were followed, the business would suffer terribly. It could even
fold up.

● "I deserve the extra time off now because for a long time I
worked much harder than Ken." Proving that to anybody's satisfaction is a virtual impossibility. When it is offered as a justification to a beleaguered partner, it invariably produces sparks.

● "I'm ten years older than Ken. I need the extra time off."
This explanation implies that every younger partner has a duty to
support his older partner.

And so the incompatibility between the principals continues. For a
while the Ken Connors of the world permit themselves to be taken
advantage of. But as time goes on and they continue to be overbur-
dened with work and responsibilities, they lose their patience and
understanding. We are now primed for a very harmful battle royal,
unless a constructive solution can be found.

PERSONAL DISCONTENT

Another danger signal that motivation regarding the business is
slipping, is the manifestation by a partner of discontent as to the
worth or significance of what his life adds up to. "Look Charlie.
Here I am, 60 years old, and what have I done that I can be proud
of? Have I made any real contributions to society? All I did, with
your help, of course, was build a successful business that manufactures boxes, and make a lot of money. That's a sad commentary for a
guy who graduated from Yale, and saw himself as doing something
that would really have an impact on people."

This "what does my life mean" attitude may be occasioned by
many factors, certainly better understood by psychologists than me.
But once it grabs hold of a partner in an incorporated partnership, it
pushes him to spend meaningful amounts of time doing things outside of the company. This force can propel a partner to become
heavily involved in other pursuits, such as community service. What
I am talking about is devoting substantial amounts of time to a
charitable or educational organization, bringing to bear the talent that
made him or her a successful entrepreneur—a lot more than just
serving as a member of the board of trustees and contributing money.
Some may decide to offer themselves as counsellors to members of
minority groups or the underprivileged, who would like to go into

business. I have seen successful business people who were attracted to part-time social work or teaching. Then there are those, like me, who may decide to write a book.

The loss of a partner's vital interest in the business can be very costly to his company. Enthusiastic involvement in the enterprise, and the belief that its activities are significant, represent forces that propel an owner to build the business and beat the competition. If there is a meaningful decrease in Ron Davenport's adherence to the importance and value of the services that Davcon Advertising is providing to its clients, he will not sell the agency's creativity and talents with the same ardor. The corporation's accounts will sense the downgraded commitment. Many of them may soon start looking for an advertising agency that "really wants to do a job for us."

BURN-OUT

There often comes a time when a partner in an incorporated partnership has "had it." The things that used to be enjoyable to do are now a pain or just plain dull. Ron Davenport was a good illustration of burn-out. He often confessed to his wife, Carol, that he had many days when he hated to go to the office. Keeping clients happy aggravated him a lot. "I'm nothing but a glorified escort. I swear my success in attracting and keeping clients is less attributable to my marketing talents, and more a matter of being able to get them seated at a plush restaurant, without reservations, when there's a line of people waiting, and coming up with tickets for the 'hot' show on Broadway with little advance notice." When Davcon Advertising was growing and the income it produced was more meaningful, Ron's attitudes were quite different. But when he became wealthy, playing this role offended him.

I have been through this burn-out routine with many clients, listening to them explain about how hard it is to continue to listen to the complaints of customers, relate to the demands of employees, entertain customers, cope with all the bureaucrats, etc. Initially, it was hard for me to be sympathetic. Here was this partner in a very successful business, not working that hard by most people's standards, much more favorably situated financially than all but a very small percentile of the people in our country, complaining how hard it was to keep going. I would think to myself, "Hey, what are you beefing about? You're at the top of the heap. You have the kind of

independence and authority that very few people ever enjoy. Someone in your shoes shouldn't have any trouble coping with his business life, since you and your partner run the show. You have the
luxury of telling people off."

But my attitudes have changed. I came to realize that the discontent is genuine and deeply felt. It is important to appreciate that.
There is a real antipathy and impatience regarding the business, and
the partner's psyche can no longer easily contend with the problems
and frustrations. He becomes less willing to devote his energies and
attention to the enterprise, because his involvement in the business
produces many negative feelings. The result is a much reduced
commitment to the company, and his partner's accurate impression
that he is no longer bearing his full share of the burdens and responsibilities of operating the corporation.

INDECISION AND NEGATIVISM

I have noted, in several places in this book, that most business
people accept the maxim: a business either grows or it declines. It
can't stand still. Like it or not, a proprietor of a close corporation
business has to continue to be willing to take risks, in order to keep
the enterprise strong and competitive. Many of these steps directed
toward growth, such as making acquisitions, establishing new products or services, or opening branches, not only take money, they
demand more devotion to the company on the part of its leadership.

A tip-off that a partner's commitment to the corporation is diminishing, is his rejection of any suggestion made by his partner, that
involves more dedication of time and energy to the enterprise. Ron
Davenport did that and it contributed to the termination of his business relationship with Ken Connors. Ken was the one who pushed
for the expansion of the agency into public relations and market
research. He had attended some marketing sessions at an industry
convention, where he learned that most advertising agencies were
going into these fields, as a natural outgrowth of basic advertising.
Ron resisted the idea, but finally relented. The result was that a
major source of Ron's difficulty in handling his duties, during the
six months that he worked a short week, was his inability to give
time to these new divisions.

After that undesirable step, Ron Davenport flatly refused to go
along with the acquisition of an agency that specialized in handling

pharmaceutical drug products, or the opening of a branch in Chicago, which would be headed by the well-known principal of a small local advertising agency. Ken Connors was dismayed by Ron Davenport's obdurate rejection of these proposals, which was ostensibly predicated on the probable lack of success of each venture. Ken sensed that there was much more to it than that, since the points that Ron made in opposition were weak and easily countered. The truth was that Ron could see that both the acquisition and the opening of the Chicago office would mean greater demands on his time. He was unwilling to make that commitment.

4. Limited involvement due to medical reasons

A partner suffers a heart attack. After a recuperation period, during which his business mate visits him regularly, he returns to the office and announces: "My doctor says I can continue in the business, but I can't work so hard. The big thing is to ease up and reduce my pressures." That is the sum and substance of the pronouncement. It is not coupled with any explanation of what the returning partner will or won't do, or any suggestion of any lesser compensation or equity in the business because of the reduced involvement. The sympathetic healthy partner, thanking his lucky stars for his good health, says nothing. The die is cast—at least from the standpoint of the partner who must avoid stress and strain. He maintains his parity of economic benefit, notwithstanding the fact that his co-owner will be taking on much more of the burden of running the company. He feels free, on an *ad hoc* basis, to delineate what duties are stressful and which are not. As time goes by, this may well become an upsetting inequality, with the overworked partner finally erupting, and demanding a termination of the partnership.

There are any number of physical and emotional conditions which are adversely affected by anxiety and pressure. Some physicians feel that all gastroenterological problems are tied to these factors, to some extent. But to use medical reasons as a means of saddling a partner with inordinate responsibilities with no material reward for his added pressures is unfair. An attempt should be made to pinpoint the few kinds of work that the partner with a physical or mental condition should avoid. These should be shifted to the healthy partner, or someone else in the organization. To the extent the other partner picks up substantial additional duties by reason of this reallocation, some of his burdens, which can be handled by the partially disabled partner, should be moved to that partner. The goal should be to maintain something that approximates an equality of effort between the two partners. If the partner who has a physical or mental condition cannot handle roughly 50% of the work load, he should expect some adjustment to his compensation and/or interest in the corporation, or to be bought out.

5. Rivalry between the partners

It is hard to measure which of two partners in an incorporated partnership is the more valuable to the business. In most instances, each of them plays a very significant role, and the elimination of either of them—as I will discuss in detail in the next chapter—can have serious effects on both the enterprise and the remaining partner. The partners generally complement one another, which often results in a greater strength than the sum of their individual talents. That does not mean, however, that the partners totally ignore the issue of who is the more able or dedicated. There is an understandable competitiveness, a rivalry, between two aggressive, strong-willed individuals laboring in the same company. Each of them looks to the success of the business as the expression of his ego. The partner's self-esteem is tied to his role in the close corporation. As a competitive person, he unconsciously may need to believe that he is more valuable and important to the success of the enterprise than the other equal owner.

The person handling sales believes he has to cope with many very difficult people and face rejection every day, in order to provide what is the essential ingredient for the corporation's activities— getting the business. He compares himself with his partner, "sitting comfortably in the plant every day, just making sure that the guys running the machines don't goof off." But the partner in charge of production sees it very differently. He has to live with all the tensions and pressures of getting the merchandise manufactured and out to customers. His fellow stockholder, on the other hand "has it made." All he has to do is entertain customers at lavish restaurants and take them to shows. What a great life!

This feeling of handling greater responsibilities or working harder than his partner, often crops up when one partner is vacationing and the other is left with the job of directing all aspects of the business on his own. Ken Connors justifiably felt this way during the many times that Ron Davenport was in Florida or traveling around. But even in less extreme instances, a partner may be sure he is doing more than his fair share. The working partner's wife may cause him to feel put upon. When he comes home, after a particularly hard day, she can rile him with an observation like this:- "I'm sure Al doesn't come home, night after night, exhausted and tight, the way you do. It's not fair!"

Another favorite theme is this: "You know you are worth much more to the business than Al. All he does is stay in the plant and make sure nothing goes wrong, while you have to travel all over getting the business." These kinds of comments are generally an expression of a wife's concern for her husband's well-being or her belief in his competence. Nonetheless, they can easily get him upset and unhappy with his partner.

If a partner is able to shrug off this attitude of being taken advantage of by his peer, then the animosity will fade away and nothing will happen. Most times that is the result. This "Oh, what the hell" response may be greatly influenced by the disinclination to start a very divisive dialogue and thereby jeopardize the success of the partnership. But should the inequality in involvement become substantial and continuous, as it did in the case of Davcon Advertising, so that one partner really feels put upon and becomes upset, serious conflicts may occur.

6. Break up of a partner's marriage

The divorce of one partner in an incorporated partnership often affects the company and the other partner. Many things happen in the division of property between the spouses who are being divorced, which have an unfavorable impact on the relationship between the partner getting divorced and the partner who is an innocent bystander. It can easily result in the dissolution of the business marriage too. This is such a significant concern that it is explained, with a detailed example, in Chapter 14.

REMEDIES FOR TROUBLE BETWEEN PARTNERS

What, if anything, can be done to deal with the serious trouble that can develop between partners in an incorporated partnership, even those entities where the principals have worked together for many years? Unfortunately, very little attention and thought have been directed to this question. In the case of the marriage between husband and wife, articles abound on every facet of the relationship, and magazines regularly contain features about things that must be done to save the union. By comparison, virtually nothing has been written on the problems that arise in the business marriage, and how to contend with them. Couples can find many counsellors, to whom they can go for help in arresting and modifying behavior that is destroying their marriage. I personally know of no professional that holds himself out as an expert in repairing incorporated partnerships where the partners are having serious interpersonal problems. It could be a very fruitful specialty. With this caveat, I am going to offer some of my ideas regarding things that might be done to contend with these sources of friction between partners.

Air the grievances

The end of the partnership between Ron Davenport and Ken Connors was triggered by Ken's fury at having accepted "the short end of the stick" for so long. "How can I have been such a fool," he exclaimed to his lawyer. "All that time, killing myself, trying to pick up in those areas that Ron should have been handling, while he golfed and cavorted in Florida and traveled all over the world. What a dope I was to have let myself get in that position. Me, an equal partner? Hell, no, I really worked for Ron Davenport!"

When Ken's feelings of being taken advantage of reached the point where his self-image would no longer permit him to turn the other cheek, he took action. But at that point, the intensity of his emotions would not permit a reconciliation. He could no longer tolerate the idea of having as a partner an "S-O-B- that could be so selfish and unfeeling about what he did to his partner, his good friend." Why Ken Connors didn't speak up much earlier is a question that only a psychotherapist could answer, after some extensive interaction with Ken. It may well be an outgrowth of behavior patterns that Ken developed as a child in contending with his parents and his adolescent world. But this syndrome manifested by Ken Connors is very common: grievances are stored up against the other partner; they become magnified the more they are repressed; feelings smolder on the inside; and finally they explode in a bitter indictment that leads to a parting of the ways.

I would urge, as the number one rule in maintaining harmony in the incorporated partnership, frank and open discussion of attitudes and actions of either partner that are upsetting to the other. It is better to face an issue head on than to make believe that it is not bothersome. Obviously, I am not suggesting that every nit and pick has to be aired. But Ken Connors and Ron Davenport had a number of concerns which could have been helped a great deal by talking them out. Certainly, Ken's failure to let Ron know about the adverse effects of Ron's presence in Florida and his resulting shortened work week, allowed Ron to indulge his gradually reducing commitment to Davcon Advertising. Early in the game, perhaps the first time Ron suggested his new schedule, Ken Connors should have said something like this to Ron: "I'm very concerned about your only being here two full days a week for so many months. I don't think the business can afford to have only that limited amount of your time. Let me tell you the problems I see."

Would this have prevented the break-up that took place between Ron Davenport and Ken Connors? No one can be sure. However, it would have pushed Ron Davenport to understand and appreciate the adverse consequences of the schedule change, and brought to the surface the real problem, Ron's diminished commitment to the business. Once that issue came out, the partners could have grappled with it, and perhaps formulated an arrangement that was satisfactory to both of them.

Planning for the introduction of a partner's child or spouse into the business

While the presence of one partner's child or spouse in the business poses serious problems, they are not necessarily insurmountable. In Chapter 1, I covered a number of the concerns created by having a spouse or children working in the family company, and offered some suggestions as to how these family members could be better integrated into the organization. Those points are equally applicable here. But there is a very crucial additional consideration when one talks about the complications created by having a descendant or spouse of one partner working in an incorporated partnership, namely the effect on the other partner. This is the factor that causes the greatest disturbance in the relationship between the co-owners of the enterprise.

Here again the key is putting the matter on the table for forthright discussion between the principals before the child or spouse actually starts working. All items that worry the other partner should be put on the agenda. The goal is to dredge up what is really bothering the partner who has to deal with members of the other partner's immediate family. The legitimacy of any concern is not relevant. If a fear exists, right or wrong, it has to be faced. Let me repeat some of the major apprehensions that Ron Davenport had about Ralph Connors' coming to work for Davcon Advertising, which should have been talked about:

1. *Will the partner's children be paid only for the true value of their services, and how and by whom will that be determined?* Positive reactions can be produced from a discussion about the remuneration of a partner's son or daughter who is coming into the business. The co-owner may be reassured that the father is sensitive to the issue, and does not want his family, through the employment of children by the company, to wind up with more than an equal share of the profits. This might cause a partner like Ron Davenport, making a lot of money from a very prosperous business, to say to himself: "What the hell. If Ralph makes even $50,000 more a year than he really is entitled to, only half of it comes out of my share of the profits, and it's tax deductible. So what are we really talking about."

2. *Who will supervise and direct the partner's child, and how will it be done so that the father and his partner will not be at each other's throat about the child's performance?* Any program must be designed to make sure dad stays out of the child's training, development and evaluation, and the child is not given special privileges or is discriminated against because of who he is. It is entirely possible that with proper planning, Ron Davenport would have gotten a lot of enjoyment and help from being the mentor of his partner's son.

3. *What steps will be taken to make sure the other partner does not feel he will only have a minority say in the management of the corporation's business and affairs, when the offspring of his partner are active in the business?* He doesn't mean a minority voting position, since it is assumed by all that each of the two partners will continue to vote 50% of the outstanding stock. Similarly, there is no difficulty with matters that call for the action of the directors of the corporation because another "given" in this situation, is that the two partners will have equal representation on the board of directors. The issue here is a simple one: will he feel at a disadvantage debating policy and management matters with his partner and the partner's children? A very simple way to handle this situation is the creation of an executive or management committee, made up exclusively of the partners, which meets regularly—and if required, on an emergency basis—to fix policy and make all management decisions of consequence. Other methods of dealing with the problem may suggest themselves to the partners. The wisdom of the solution is not the crucial factor. The real benefit comes from facing and resolving a concern of the other partner.

In the case of a partner's spouse who is about to join the business, his or her role in the company should be delineated carefully and understood by the spouse. The need for regular, competent and timely performance should be communicated at the outset of the employment, so that there are no misunderstandings. The people in the organization who will supervise and direct the spouse should be identified, and they should be assured that the spouse understands their status and position. In short, the spouse has to be made to understand that the corporation cannot tolerate a prima donna, and the spouse has to accept the outlined working conditions. This may dissuade many spouses from becoming involved in the incorporated partnership business. That is a good result from the standpoint of preserving the good relationship between the partners. It may also help the marriage of the parties involved. My guess is that Grace Connors would not have wanted to join Davcon Advertising, if these terms of employment had been explained to her. Her career as a painter, with its freedom and the absence of rules and regulations, would have seemed a lot better to her, when compared to what she would have had to cope with at the agency.

Help in the resolution of the problems presented by the active involvement of a spouse or child in an incorporated partnership can be supplied by management consultants who are experienced in relating to family enterprises. A director, or the corporation's lawyer or accountant, can also be helpful. As a respected advisor, impartial and familiar with the business and the personalities in the corporation, he or she can serve as a discussion leader and moderator on these matters.

How to handle the less involved partner

Earlier in this chapter, I took a look at some of the indications that one partner had lost a lot of his motivation, and was seeking other satisfactions outside the business. This diminished commitment can cause a serious breach between the partners. Not only are their drives different, but it invariably happens that the still dedicated partner finds himself taking on more than his share of the responsibility, and ends up working harder and resenting the reduced workload of his supposed equal. Before any remedy can be considered, there has to be a mutual understanding that a change has taken place, and that it is unfair for one partner to carry so much more of the load without some adjustments being made. Once again, there should be a confrontation as soon as the warning signs appear. Delay in raising the subject only exacerbates the bitter feelings of the hardworking partner.

Let us assume that the Ron Davenport-Ken Connors problem has been raised and clearly defined. It is now admitted that one partner (whom I will sometimes refer to in this segment as the "less committed partner") is much less involved in the business than the other. The less committed partner has started to shirk some of his management responsibilities. What can be done to ameliorate the relationship between the parties and prevent a break-up of their partnership?

CUTTING BACK

The first line of defense that probably will be taken by the less committed partner—which is how Ron Davenport immediately reacted—is to urge his business mate (the "other partner") to cut back too. This is not a constructive response. In fact, in several cases where the ultimate resolution of the disagreement between the partners was disassociation, this proposal was singled out as an indication of how little the less committed partner cared about the company. A typical comment was: "Can you imagine Milt, the first thing out of his mouth was the suggestion that I work less too. Then I wouldn't be upset by how much time he spent away from the office. I explained to him that I didn't work as hard as I did for the fun of it. I put in all the time because a business as large and complex as ours required full-time, hands-on direction by two partners, and since he wasn't carrying his load, I had to pick up some of his duties—which was killing me. His idea really ticked me off."

I can easily understand why the overworked other partner is offended by the truly ridiculous suggestion that the solution to the dilemma is for both partners to reduce their involvement in the business. It borders on irresponsibility.

SELLING THE BUSINESS

The less committed partner recognizes that he is not shouldering his responsibilities, and he is letting his partner down. He can admit the error of his ways, agree to reform, and resume his former role in the business. But that is not what he wants to do at this stage of his life. What then are the less committed partner's alternatives? The *status quo* cannot continue, since his partner has made that much very clear. He could sell his stock of the corporation, but he anticipates a tough negotiation with the other partner, whose concerns about the ability of the company to fund the purchase price, will tend to make him push down the price and want to pay it over a long period of time. Perhaps he could take a lower salary than his co-owner, and even reduce his future equity in the company. But that too will be hard to accomplish, and the less committed partner is not sure he can take second position in the firm, after all these years as an equal owner. Suddenly, he has the answer, a sale of the entire business.

The sale of the company has a lot of plusses for the less committed partner. This should produce the best price for his interest, and the terms of payment will probably be a lot better. If the purchaser wants him to stay on for a few years, in the interest of continuity, that will be fine. It will help the less committed partner make the adjustment to retirement. Obviously, he will not have the same worries or time pressures if he is an employee of the acquiring company.

The trouble with this idea is that the other partner, most likely, has no desire to sell. The enterprise usually represents a very important part of his life. He enjoys the achievements that the corporation has had and looks forward to its attaining even greater success. The other partner may not want to retire; and if the purchaser wants him to stay active in the business after the sale, to end his career working for someone else will probably not be an inviting prospect. Furthermore, the other partner may not want to sell out his children who are active in the business or expect to join the company in the near future.

I have dealt with a number of partners in the shoes of our less committed partner, who become upset when the co-owner would not consent to a sale of the enterprise. In every instance I have told them:- "Your partner owes you many things; for example, loyalty, support and understanding. But he does not have an obligation to sell out because that is the best solution to your problems. This is an accommodation that you have no right to expect."

A COMPREHENSIVE STRATEGY

I am going to offer another possible approach to the settlement of a controversy among partners in an incorporated partnership, arising out of the less committed partner's reduced attention to the business—which he does not want to change. I am going to combine a number of proposals, each of which failed to prevent a break-up of the partnership, hoping to garner the best points of each, and add a few ingredients which I think are necessary to make the plan work. I will use the Davcon Advertising case to illustrate the concept.

1. A qualified person would be hired to assist the less committed partner in the performance of his duties. He would have a job akin to an assistant to the president, performing those tasks that would be assigned to him by the less committed partner. Thus, when Ron Davenport was away from the office, there would be an available employee, fully conversant with the areas that are Ken's responsibility, who could see that things were done, and provide continuity and service. The compensation of the less committed partner would be reduced by the salary paid to this assistant and the cost of his fringe benefits. He would be treated as an adjunct of the less committed partner, having been hired to provide him with important back-up and support.

2. The less committed partner would continue to be responsible for the proper performance of the functions of the business that are under his direction. For example, Ron would continue to supervise the agency's account executives, the presentations and other activities directed to capturing new clients, and the public relations and market research divisions. His assistant would help him do this properly, but Ron would be in charge of all those areas of activity. Taking another executive and making him responsible for important facets of the business that the less committed partner formerly was in charge of won't work. The executive would be supplanting a co-owner who continues to be active in the company. Undoubtedly, this will cause the executive a lot of concern. If he takes over an assignment that had been under Ron Davenport's control for a long time, he will probably find Ron to be somewhat critical of his performance. Even if Ron's evaluation is wrong, how does the new executive contend effectively with someone in Ron's position?

3. People in the company should feel no hesitancy in contacting the less committed partner, during the period he is absent from the office. When an important manager is frequently away for meaningful periods of time, ease of communication with him must be maintained. His time away from the business cannot be sacrosanct. I appreciate this necessity personally, since I take my summer vacation by spending long weekends, Friday through Monday, at a summer home near the ocean. Because of the importance of staying in touch, everyone in our firm, as well as many of the clients I relate to, know that they can reach me whenever the need arises. Some entrepreneurs that our firm represents maintain contact by telephoning the office every workday at a stated time. Everyone stores up items requiring the owner's attention for that telephone call. The less committed partner may find himself on the phone for an hour on a given day, but the limited invasion of his relaxation is easy to handle. It also allays his anxieties. There even can be occasions when the less committed partner has to hop on a plane and go back to the business, in order to deal with a major matter or crisis. For example, if landing an important new client for Davcon Advertising called for Ron's presence, even though it was on one of his days in Florida, he would have to return.

4. The less committed partner must be prepared, when necessary, to stay in touch with customers, suppliers and others. If there is a serious complaint from a key account, the contact must be made promptly. It cannot be put off until the return to the office. Similarly, if the less committed partner has a long-standing relationship with a supplier of an important material to the company, and there is a delivery problem, he should expect to get into the act promptly. The salvation for the less committed partner is that the telephone provides a convenient medium for coping with these demands.

5. Increase the involved partner's interest in the business. Even when the preceding steps have been taken, the other partner will end up with far more than one half of the management burdens, and the demands of the business on him will increase. One method of reflecting the other partner's greater effort and commitment on behalf of the corporation is to increase his compensation. This should definitely be done. But I don't think it is enough. The other partner should also receive a larger portion of the future profits of the enterprise.

How is this accomplished? The present value of the corporation is fixed by the partners, with the assistance of someone who they feel can be helpful in that regard. (The figure arrived at can be useful if the ultimate resolution of the partners' problems is a buy-out of the less committed partner's interest: the purchase price will have been established by the valuation.) Preferred stock is then issued, 50-50 to the two partners in the amount of the worth of the enterprise. Voting and non-voting common stocks are also issued, consisting of a very limited number of voting shares, and perhaps 100 times more non-voting shares. The voting stock is owned equally by both partners, but the less committed partner winds up with less of the non-voting stock. For example, Ron Davenport would hold half of the very small number of shares of voting common, but only one third of the much larger amount of non-voting stock. The result is that the partner who bears much more of the workload and pressures gets two thirds of any increase in value of the company, and the less committed partner's share of the growth is only one third.

Will this arrangement work? I don't know because I have never seen it tried. Candidly, I have my doubts. Will the less committed partner comply faithfully with his management obligations? How will his performance be measured, by whom, and in what manner?

Can he accept the leadership and direction of his partner? For instance, will Ron Davenport, a co-founder of Davcon Advertising, its only president until he shifted to this revised role in the company, play "second banana" to Ken Connors? It is not an adjustment that can be made without tremendous subordination of ego. Many people in Ron's position could not carry it off.

The plan may be worth a try for a fixed period of time. If it doesn't work, the understanding should be that the stock of the corporation owned by the less committed partner will be redeemed, and he will leave the company.

BUY-OUTS

The most common remedy to the problems caused by having a less involved partner is to buy-out his half of the business. The purchaser is invariably the company—rather than the more active co-owner individually—because it is very hard, tax wise, to get the corporate dollars needed to pay the price into the hands of the partner. From Ken's standpoint, when Ron left the corporation, assuming that both he and Ron owned 50 shares of Davcon Advertising stock, it made little difference whether he held 100 of the 100 shares outstanding (he bought Ron's stock), or 50 of the 50 outstanding shares (the corporation redeemed Ron's stock). In each instance he had 100% of the equity.

This purchase of stock of a partner in an incorporated partnership raises many issues. The price and terms have to be settled. Moreover, the departing stockholder-executive often wants to continue as a participant in the corporation's medical expense reimbursement and group insurance plans. This is achieved by continuing him as an employed consultant. On the other side, the remaining partner may want to continue the terminating stockholder's identification with the corporation for the best interests of the business. This calls for a thoughtful and consistent announcement to all concerned. Davcon Advertising might get out a printed notice that says something like this: "Ron Davenport has decided to limit his business activities. He has earned this respite. We are fortunate, however, that Ron will continue to be associated with us as a consultant. We will continue to have the benefit of his guidance and vast experience in the advertising field."

Indeed a common post break-up problem is the "bad-mouthing"

of the company by the bought out partner. He can have many close relationships with customers and important suppliers. If he chooses to sully the reputation of the company or spreads a tale of how he was forced out of the corporation, it can hurt the business. An announcement of the type described, coupled with a large party honoring the partner whose stock has been acquired, can go a long way to neutralize this risk.

If the terms of Ron's sale of stock are not resolved, an interesting development might occur. Ron's counsel might suggest to him that the best way to raise the ante is to shift to a buyer's position. "Ken, your proposal is so inadequate, in my opinion, that I'll buy you out for the price and on the terms you offered me."

We are now in a poker game. But when there are circumstances akin to those that existed in Davcon Advertising, the partner in Ron's shoes usually has his bluff called and loses. It is just too obvious that the last thing in the world that Ron wants to do is to go into debt to buy out Ken, roll up his sleeves, and work even harder than he did before.

What if each partner has come to the conclusion that the other is not pulling his weight, so that the identity of the probable seller and buyer is not predictable? In this kind of situation, the negotiations regarding the separation are often conducted in the fashion of an auction or lottery. Under the auction format, one partner makes a proposal under which the corporation would purchase the other's stock. Partner #2 counteroffers with a more lucrative suggestion. And it goes back and forth until one of the owners decides that he will accept the last bid that has been made, without trying to better it.

Sometimes a lottery approach is used. The partners and their advisors work out what is considered to be a fair and equitable purchase arrangement, with neither partner knowing who will be selling stock. The belief is that the partners will reach an agreed upon buy-out plan more quickly and with many less confrontations, if there is no knowledge of the side of the fence on which a partner ultimately will find himself.

After the format of the deal is worked out, the selection of seller and buyer is made. This can be done by a coin toss, drawing lots or some other similar method. In many instances, after the terms are finally determined, one of the principals will decide that he wants to get out, thereby making the lottery unnecessary.

LITIGATION

Despite the techniques that have been developed to settle disputes between partners amicably, a lot of them wind up in litigation. This probably stems from the highly emotional nature of the split-up of two people who have developed an intimate business relationship. Like husband-wife divorces, the strong feelings of affection that developed during the happier days of the marriage, are replaced by even more powerful antagonistic ones. In fact, a law suit between partners who worked together for many years, and now are separating, has all the conflict, bickering and mutual contempt that is so common in a divorce action.

Invariably, each partner is convinced of the merits of his position, and the arbitrary nature of his co-owner's contentions. Each side cannot understand the other's narrow-minded attitudes and stubborn defensiveness. Accusations fly back and forth. Name-calling is commonplace and so is defamation of character. For example, the charge that a partner "has been stealing from the company for years," is run of the mill. The court becomes the forum in which each of the litigants seeks to have vindicated the justice of his assertions—and, of course, the complete lack of merit of his partner's claims. Once battle is joined in a law suit, the partners' enthusiasm for victory at all costs starts to wane. So too does the strength of the antagonisms. The litigation process is slow and very expensive. The ultimate confrontation in a courtroom may be years down the road. Even then the decision may not be final. There is always the possibility of an appeal, with more time running and continuing substantial outlays for legal fees and costs. Compromise and settlement become more attractive to the parties. And that is what usually happens.

Deadlock statutes

There is also a special litigation remedy if the owners of an incorporated partnership are unable to resolve their incompatibility amicably. Many states have what are called "deadlock" statutes. If there is an even number of directors and equal stockholders who cannot agree on major issues, the corporation can be brought to a standstill. This can be done by design, to bring a situation within the coverage of the statute. It always fascinates me to watch my experienced law partners mastermind a campaign aimed at taking advantage of this statutory provision.

When there is such a deadlock, which prevents the company from operating effectively, either partner can go to court and seek relief. The court can do many things, such as appoint a receiver, a custodial director, cause the corporation to be liquidated or order the sale of a partner's stock. At first blush this seems like a wonderful way to end a stalemate between the discordant partners. On further analysis, however, there are many negatives.

Nobody really wants a receiver or a custodial director to be appointed. This puts an unknown individual, selected by the judge, in the position of supreme power in the corporation. He will become a well compensated referee to settle disputes between the partners regarding the running of the business. But that is not the heart of the matter. What is required is an acceptable program for permanently separating the combatants.

Other risks also attend the appointment of a receiver or custodial director. His appointment, in and of itself, may have an adverse effect on the business. Customers may assume that something is very wrong with the enterprise. To hedge their bets, customers can start placing orders with others. In addition, the receiver or custodial director can become privy to practices that, if revealed, would be very damaging to all concerned, such as large "gifts" to buyers or purchasing agents, payments on behalf of the proprietors masked as business expenses, people on the payroll of the corporation who perform work for the partners, and so on. All of the skeletons in the closet may be exposed.

The idea of a forced liquidation of the corporation is also not a happy prospect. Destroying a profitable business is a bad result. It is a disservice to the partners; and a lot of employees who are not involved in the dispute are put out of work. Judges shy away from this solution.

The alternative that meets the partners' needs most effectively is the court's power to order a sale of stock. That produces the desired separation. Unfortunately, many of the statutes fall to handle a number of important realities of such a purchase. The court may be prevented from ordering the sale of stock of the partner who starts the lawsuit. This puts a premium on an individual's ability to harrass and delay, if he wants to push his partner out—by making him bring the legal action. There are often two other serious drawbacks. The entire purchase price of the stock may have to be paid in cash.

Installment payments are not authorized. And the court may not be able to require the seller to enter into an agreement not to compete with the corporation's business. This is a serious deterrent. To pay a withdrawing stockholder a lot of money, and then have him use the funds to start a competing company, is bad news.

Probably the biggest benefit of deadlock litigation is the presence of others, early in the proceedings, who can make the antagonists understand what is achievable and what is not. Lawyers will hopefully bring objectivity and detachment to the scene. The judge might be a major force for settlement. Once again, there are also the substantial costs and expenses which dampen the adversaries' enthusiasm to keep the battle raging.

INCORPORATED PARTNERSHIPS— PLANNING FOR THE DEATH OR DISABILITY OF A PARTNER

12

The death or disability of a partner in an incorporated partnership has dramatic effects on the enterprise. The very nature of the corporation changes. Prior to the death or disability, there were two individuals, working side by side, running a business that they owned equally, which was an expression of themselves. When death or disability strikes one of the principals, his active involvement in the business and affairs of the company is over. The affected partner or his estate, if he has died, becomes an inactive stockholder. The remaining partner is left to run the show on his own. The close, intimate relationship that existed between the owners and operators of the business is at an end.

In this chapter, I am going to examine the consequences of a partner's death or disability, and offer some suggestions on how best to handle either of these occurrences. I will use Davcon Advertising, with its co-owners, Ron Davenport and Ken Connors, as my model incorporated partnership in giving examples. I will assume that the break-up, which I covered in the last chapter, did not occur. In my discussion, I will try to kill off or disable Ron and Ken alternatively, as I do in my practice. Perhaps I should explain what I mean. Many years ago, at a conference with the owners of an incorporated partnership, called to consider the consequences of a partner's death or disability, I kept referring to the demise or incapacity of only one of them, whom I will call Gregory. When I was deep into the second hour of our get together, I became conscious of Greg's increasing resentment toward me. Finally he blurted out: "Milt, I'm getting upset about your constantly using my death or disability to make a point. You never get rid of Adam (his partner). I can't help but feel that you're on Adam's side." Ever since that experience, I try to balance the two partners' assumed death or disability.

DEATH OF A PARTNER

The first thing that must be faced are the effects on the business of the loss of a key man. Without question, if Ron Davenport suffered a heart attack and died, Davcon Advertising would be hard hit. It has lost a leader and a very valuable cog in the operation of the agency. Ken Connors' death would also have an adverse impact on the company. He oversees the production of the agency, sees that the work gets out on time, in a quality fashion, and motivates and directs the creative people.

Preparing for the time when a most important executive is no longer available to the enterprise is an important management consideration. It is nonetheless one that is very often ignored in a close corporation. A major difficulty in that regard is attracting to the company a person who has the capabilities to replace an owner. Even if that can be accomplished, the chances are that he will not be groomed for that position. Most principals in incorporated partnerships do not contemplate giving up their top executive status at any age.

Developing back-up

There are things that can be done to cope with the consequences of the death of an active owner in the incorporated partnership. Back-up can be developed. Davcon moved in that direction, admittedly without planning, when Ken Connors and others had to step in and assume Ron's duties while he was away in Florida or on trips. The experience of having others fill in for Ron will reduce the adverse impact of his no longer being associated with the company.

This is a very common occurrence in the case of older proprietors of close corporations. They can get fed up with being workaholics and start looking to get more enjoyment out of life. This is what happened to Ken Davenport. Sometimes the change in commitment to the office or plant is precipitated by a health scare—a diagnosed heart condition or a serious operation. Whatever the reasons for the change, it helps in preparing for the time when a partner dies. The partner's reduced involvement means others start doing his tasks. The anxiety over succession at death is somewhat alleviated, because there are people who are familiar with, and have performed, the duties and responsibilities of the decedent.

Bringing in a replacement

I have seen many survivors who have dealt with the management vacancy caused by the death of a partner, by bringing in a top level replacement. If the dollars that used to be paid to the partner who died, including his fringes, are available for this purpose, a very juicy offer can be made to capture a qualified individual, without taxing the corporation's finances. Some farsighted entrepreneurs have the corporation carry insurance on the lives of the stockholder-employees, to provide funds that can be used to get a good successor. The desired senior executive may insist on receiving an equity interest in the corporation. This can take the form of stock, usually non-voting, or units in a phantom stock plan. This equity ownership by an unrelated executive is discussed in detail in Chapter 4.

SURVIVING PARTNER'S LOSS OF A SOUNDING BOARD

In my opinion, it is easier to find someone who can take over the work of the partner who has died, than it is to find another person with whom to share real decision-making responsibility in the incorporated partnership. This is the real deprivation. If either Ron Davenport or Ken Connors died, the surviving partner would now have to make all the important decisions, without the opportunity to brainstorm with a knowledgeable and experienced mate, with whom rapport and ease of communication have been developed.

I recall vividly the deep anguish expressed by a client, whose partner of more than twenty years, had suffered a fatal heart attack at the age of 53: "I feel lost, Milt. So alone! When the time came to design the lines for the new season, I found myself following the old pattern—starting to walk to Sam's office, to sit down with him and get his reactions and guidance. Now it all rests on my shoulders, and I'm scared that I overlooked something—the kind of thing that would come to light and was corrected when Sam and I batted the ideas around. There are other major problems like that, every week, where I have to take on the entire responsibility. Adele says I'm nervous as a cat, and she's right. It's getting to me."

The problems occasioned by the loss of a familiar sounding board have not been given sufficient publicity. Perhaps this results from the disinclination of the owner, left alone in the business, to admit that the partner's absence has hit him or her so hard. Al, the client who poured out his heart to me, also expressed his embarrassment about feeling so inadequate. That was unfortunate. All concerned must recognize that there is an interdependence between the members of an incorporated partnership, a give and take on issues, a compromise on different points of view, that contributes to the success of the enterprise. It is an important synergistic factor in the smooth running of the business, and when one partner is gone, much has been lost.

Interestingly, when a husband and wife are partners in a business, the decease or incapacity of one of them always brings recognition of the terrible sense of loss that the remaining spouse must feel. "It must be hard for John to go to the office everyday, where he and Janice worked together for so many years." While a business relationship between unrelated partners is not as intimate as that between husband and wife, it is still very close. There is a common goal, the growth and development of the company, daily contacts, confidences exchanged that are shared with no one else, and a close friendship. When this business union is ended, there are significant consequences. They should be anticipated and understood.

PROSPECT OF DECEDENT'S FAMILY BECOMING AN INACTIVE PARTNER

The departure of a partner, through death or disability, causes other major changes in the corporate environment. In the case of Ron Davenport's death, Ken Connors can't be sure who his new partner will be. That is controlled by what Ron provides in his will, a confidential instrument, which Ron Davenport can revise whenever he wants to. Under today's estate tax provisions, the likelihood is that all or a major part of Ron's stock of Davcon Advertising will go to Carol Davenport or a trust for her sole benefit. This will happen because Ron wants his estate to get the benefit of the unlimited marital deduction—discussed in Chapter 6—and thereby avoid the payment of any federal estate tax when he dies. To get that marital deduction, when the close corporation stock interest represents so large a part of a deceased stockholder's estate, a significant portion of his stockholdings has to pass to or for the exclusive benefit of the surviving spouse. But whether the person succeeding to the shares held by Ron Davenport, at his death, is Ron's wife, Carol, or his daughters—or trusts for the benefit of wife or children—makes no difference. Since no one in the Ron Davenport family works in the agency, the new partner or partners will be inactive stockholders.

Would the result be different if Ken Connors were the first to die? Conceivably, Ken could leave all his stock of the company to his son, Paul, because he is poised to come to work for the agency. But it won't happen. Such a disposition would produce terrible estate tax consequences, since what passes to Paul will not qualify for the marital deduction. And, more importantly, Ken would be excluding his wife and his two other children from any share of his most valuable asset, his Davcon Advertising stockholdings. That would be terribly discriminatory. If Ken Connors predeceases him, Ron Davenport too will have to deal with some stockholders who will not be employees of Davcon Advertising.

What lies ahead for Ken Connors if his new partner is an inactive owner of stock in the close corporation? The answer is a lot of unpleasantness. He faces all the problems that were discussed in Chapter 10:

1. What is a fair measure of Ken's compensation and perquisites for his efforts on behalf of Davcon Advertising? More precisely, what level of salary and benefits will satisfy both him and the Davenports?

2. How can the 50% of the profits attributable to capital pass to Ron's family, without terrible income tax results?

3. How can Ken discuss important business matters with a bunch of housewives, or even worse, some sons-in-law who will feign know-how to maintain their male egos?

4. What will Ken do if Carol or one of Ron's sons-in-law, or a grandchild, is selected to come into the business as the representative of the Davenport family?

Ron's family will have their serious misgivings too. "Our major asset consists of a 50% stock interest in a complex advertising agency, about which we know nothing. We are completely dependent on Ken Connors. He can do anything he pleases. How can we be sure he doesn't take advantage of us, like charging personal things to the company? Ron got a regular salary, bonuses and benefits. What income are we going to get to live on?"

Bluntly stated, Carol Davenport and her children don't want to be owners of Davcon Advertising. What they seek, in place of their stockholdings in that enterprise, is a fund of money that can be invested in safe, income-producing holdings. Ken shares that goal. He doesn't want them as partners either.

BUY-OUT ARRANGEMENTS

The best solution, and perhaps the only practical one, is a purchase of the deceased partner's interest at a fair price, and on terms that the corporation can handle. If this is negotiated after the event, we run into a host of difficult issues which have been discussed earlier in this book. The major one is the "fair" price. The key to accomplishing a sound, sensible plan for the buy-out of the interest of a deceased partner is to negotiate the agreement while both parties are alive and well. Why? The answer is very simple. Neither party then knows who will be selling and who will be buying. It is like the lottery arrangement that is used to separate incompatible partners which was described in the last chapter.

During the negotiations, each of the stockholders wears two hats. When he sees himself as the first to die, he wants to make sure that his wife and family are left financially in very comfortable fashion. His life's work should produce an economic return that is substantial. These factors push the purchase price up. Then, when he switches to the possibility that he will be the survivor, his outlook changes. He does not want a price and terms that will bring the company to its knees. Certainly he wants to avoid crushing obligations in the latter stages of his life.

This is a healthy ambivalence. It augurs well for the establishment of a plan that will ultimately be very equitable, when viewed either from the perspective of the first to die or the survivor. The fact that the identity of the seller and the buyer is unknown is also the justification for one law firm's representing both parties in the formulation of a stock purchase agreement. This would be unethical if the price and terms were negotiated after the death of a partner.

Ron is ten years older than Ken. Does that change the concept of a partner being unsure as to which side of the transaction he will find himself? Because of the age disparity, will Ron negotiate strictly as a seller and Ken as a buyer? In my experience, even greater differences in ages have not resulted in the elimination of the dual thinking by each partner. The stockholders appreciate a very important reality. An insurance company, dealing with a sample of millions, can bet that a man, age 63, will die sooner than a man who is 53. When the sample is reduced to two, neither party is willing to risk all his stake on the propriety of the life expectancy tables. Along the way, each of us has seen too many instances of the young dying before the old.

Setting the price

In the usual incorporated partnership stock purchase situation, the "how much" question transcends the quest for a fair price. What is paid for the stock interest at death can have the most significant effect on the amount of income and protection that the wife and family of the deceased partner will enjoy. In other words, this is more than a mere valuation of stock problem. The way of life of the decedent's beneficiaries may ride on the amount that is paid. This is a very important thing for advisors to keep in mind. In this non-adversarial environment—since neither partner knows who will sell or buy—it is a mistake to use expertise as a means of pushing the price down. It can even be offensive to the parties themselves.

I believe that the worst example of this short-sightedness is the counsellor who urges the partners to keep the price low to avoid paying large death taxes. This is crazy. With the unlimited marital deduction, all federal estate tax can be avoided, if there is a surviving spouse. Even when taxes are payable, the rate is far less than 100% (the maximum is about half that). A partner who accepts this tax reduction theory, as a justification for fixing a lower price, winds up making a gift to his co-venturer at the expense of his family.

Because of the close relationship that usually exists among the partners and their families, each owner would like to see the other's family comfortable in case of death. The survivor does not want to feel that he has cheated his very good friend's family. However strange it may seem to outsiders, who view the partners as tough, hard-bitten entrepreneurs, a surviving partner may suffer discomfort, regret or even guilt, if he finds the family of his deceased partner in trouble because the purchase price of the stock was pegged too low.

A suggested approach

In the last ten years, recognizing these realities, I have used a rather different approach when introducing the subject of price to proprietors of an incorporated partnership considering a buy-sell agreement. Picture the circumstances. The corporation has a net worth of $600,000, so that using book value, each of the proprietors' interest has a value of $300,000. I say to the two individuals: "If it didn't cost you anything, and you were the surviving partner, wouldn't you be very happy to see the family of your partner get a million dollars for his interest in the corporation, so that they can live more comfortably?" My clients look at me askance. "Are you nuts? Of course, we would like to see our families get as much as possible from the business when we die. But it takes money to do that, a lot more than we can afford."

There is "method to my madness." It is an effective way to introduce what I believe is the essence of this planning. The major concern of each partner is highlighted. When he sees himself as the survivor, a partner is scared of the financial burden the corporation and he will face in funding large purchase price installments. This is the issue. No one is trying to be hard on the family of the deceased partner or pinpoint the precise value of the stock.

What my question demonstrates is that how much the corporation should pay for the deceased partner's interest and how to pay for it go hand-in-hand. Intellectually, these are different inquiries. Practically, in working out a stock redemption program, they are one. Until the partners feel that they can readily meet the purchase price obligation, they will resist a generous price.

What this leads to is an approach that has pleased many clients. The price that is fixed is the highest that the corporation can afford to fund with insurance, after taking into account other death benefits that the corporation has financed—for example, pension and profit sharing plan death benefits and group and split-dollar insurance.

This focus eliminates the frustrating search for the "true value" of each partner's stock interest in the corporation. As we noted earlier, the exact valuation of the stock of a close corporation is really an impossible task, involving a meaningless standard, a multiplicity of factors, and great variances even among experts. The line of inquiry has now been honed in the right direction. How can we make sure that the survivor, who may be on in years when the first partner dies, is not saddled with an undertaking that may literally kill the business and him as well?

The cost of the insurance coverage is now the targeted inquiry. Illustrations are presented and poured over, usually with the assistance of the corporation's accountant. The advantages of life insurance, in general, are discussed in detail in the next chapter. But I want to note here the one attribute which is of crucial importance to the determination of what should be paid at the death of a partner. The use of life insurance to cover all, or the great bulk of the purchase price, means that the undertaking is converted into an installment funding arrangement, which is financed when both principals are living. Premiums are paid periodically. The cost is virtually predictable. The burden is being met while both of the partners are active in the business. It does not become the lodestone of the survivor.

In a sense we have a program of mutual insurance. The partners jointly contribute to the creation of a guaranteed fund which can be paid at the death of the first of them to die. Nobody cares that what passes at death to the family of the deceased partner may be considered by others to be more than the value of his stock. The survivor can feel good about that result, because he is left with complete ownership of the entire business, which he has paid for with half of the premiums that he contributed.

Marshalling the assets

Why do I suggest that all the other corporate supported death benefits—pension and profit sharing, group and split-dollar insurance—should be taken into account when fixing the purchase price of the deceased partner's stock? This is responsive to the needs of the parties. Each partner is essentially concerned about how much the corporation will provide for his wife and family when he dies. Except for the differing tax consequences, neither the owners nor their beneficiaries care about what kind of plan produces the money at death. By lumping all these funds together, when the stock purchase is being planned, a more realistic price can be fixed for the stock. The justification for this marshalling of assets is that the corporation is picking up the tab for all of these benefits.

The windfall problem

In those cases where the purchase price of the stock is fully or very substantially funded by insurance, the survivor can have a sizeable windfall. Let us assume that each of two equal partners in Davcon Advertising, Ken Connors and Ron Davenport, is covered by $500,000 of insurance on his life, payable to the corporation. After three annual premiums of $12,000 have been paid on his policy, Ken Connors dies. The proceeds of Ken's $500,000 of insurance are applied in full payment of the purchase price of his stock. The survivor, Ron Davenport, a 50% owner of the company, indirectly paid only one-half of the three premiums, or a total of $18,000. Ron personally benefitted from the entire $500,000 of insurance proceeds which the corporation collected, because they were used to buy out his partner's interest in the corporation, making Ron the sole owner of the company. He has a profit of $482,000.

The longer the policy is in force, the smaller this windfall will be. That is so because the survivor's one-half portion of the premiums keeps enlarging as more of them are paid. Nonetheless, there will always be a profit, since the proceeds of insurance are invariably in excess of the premiums paid. What should be done about this? Most partners, when they are made aware of this result, say "so what!" They are willing to accept the result, because the price is satisfactory and no one knows who will be the beneficiary of the windfall. Others accept this consequence, reluctantly perhaps, since they do not want to get involved in increasing the price to reflect the windfall, then having to carry more insurance to cover the now larger price, thereby creating an even larger windfall—and so on.

An often employed compromise is to leave the stock purchase price alone and pay some post-death compensation to the wife or children of the first partner to die. This reimburses the decedent's family, in part, for the windfall of the survivor. Also, it is easier for the survivor to handle these payments, because they usually add up to an amount that can be fully deducted by the corporation for income tax purposes.

TOTAL DISABILITY OF A PARTNER

Now we turn to the situation of the disability of a partner in an incorporated partnership. Unlike death, which generally is an easily identified event, the determination of when a partner is disabled is much more complex. The clearest case of disability is when one of the co-owners suffers an illness, accident, or episode which renders him incapable of working. We will call this "total disability." Even in this instance, we are not talking about a partner's being unable to work for a few weeks or a month. Generally, in a case of an owner of an interest in this kind of enterprise, there is no change in status for a meaningful period. Six months is a commonly utilized time frame. The idea is that the proprietor is entitled to be carried fully by the company for that long.

When the partner is still unable to resume his duties after the specified number of months, there must be a mechanism to give him income to live on. The best way to do this is with disability insurance. The weekly amount should be substantial. This will enable the disabled individual to continue a reasonable standard of living and meet the special expenses caused by his incapacity. The cost can be kept down by delaying the start of the payments until the disability has existed for some time.

From an income tax standpoint, it is better to have the stockholders own the insurance. The disability payments will then be free of income tax. That is more important than having the corporation be the beneficiary to get a deduction for the much lesser insurance cost. The corporation can assist the partners in paying the disability insurance premiums through increased compensation.

Period of partial disability

Another type of disability is when a stockholder is not completely disabled, but he can no longer give the business the same time and effort. The entrepreneur suffers a serious heart attack and is told by his doctor that he must reduce his stress and strain. Or, the partner suffers a "minor" stroke which enables him to operate at 90 percent of his prior capacity. One can conjure up a goodly number of illustrations of this kind of disability, which I am calling "partial disability". The reduced role, commitment and availability resulting from this partial disability lead to the same problems that we saw in Davcon Advertising, when Ron Davenport cut back. The partner who is forced to assume more than his fair share of the burdens of running the business is equally exploited, whether the reason is his partner's disinclination to work full-time, or his physical inability to do so. Thus, the issues discussed in the last chapter must be faced and resolved. How do you determine the extent of the economic preferences that should be given to the healthy partner? Where and how do you slot in the partially disabled owner who wants or needs to work less hard? Can the less able stockholder, an equal for so long, psychologically adjust to a subordinate status? On balance, the most sensible solution may be the buy-out of the partner who can no longer shoulder his equal share of the duties and responsibilities.

WORKING OUT THE ARRANGEMENTS
BEFORE ONSET OF DISABILITY

Imagine this situation. Ron Davenport has just suffered a severe stroke. He is paralyzed on his left side and he cannot talk. The prognosis is very poor. The doctor advises Ron's family and his partner, Ken Connors, that the most that can be hoped for—and this will only be achieved after a long period of recuperation and therapy—is that Ron will be able to walk, dragging his left leg; there will be limited use of his left arm and hand; and he may be able to utter some words and sentences, which will be very hard to understand.

What a contrast! This gifted and creative advertising agent, salesman par excellence, who could win over new accounts and keep clients happy with his charm and savoir-faire, now relegated to the status of an uncommunicative semi-invalid. There is heartfelt sympathy for Ron Davenport. He has just been dealt a severe blow. His wife, Carol, and his daughters and grandchildren, are in a state of shock, fighting to mask their grief, and somehow help Ron maintain some optimism about his future. There are also the serious financial fears. What will Ron and his spouse live on now that it is clear that Ron will never be able to work in the only business that he knows ever again?

This is the environment in which Ken Connors must raise the question of what should be done, now that it is clear that Ron Davenport cannot play a role in the management of Davcon Advertising. It will be so hard for Ken to take a tough stance on any matter, when he is dealing with a close compatriot and good friend of many years, who is permanently incapacitated and at the low point of his life. Compassion and continuing financial support will be expected from Ken, the lucky one, who has the good fortune to be blessed with good health. His problems and anxieties in running the business on his own will be given very short shrift.

Earlier in this chapter, I pointed out the advantage of fixing the terms of a buy-out of a deceased partner in an incorporated partnership, while both partners are living. Objectivity is much more easily achieved, because neither owner knows who will be selling and who will be buying. That is equally true, of course, when the subject of disability is considered by two healthy partners. But there is another greater benefit of working out the disability plan before either party is incapacitated. However hard it may be to deal with the family of a deceased partner, the stress of working out a fair arrangement with a disabled partner is much greater. It took the partners in our law firm more than eight months before any one of us was able to raise with Herb Hannoch and his family the adjustments in his compensation that should be made because a series of strokes substantially impaired Herb's ability to practice law.

Buy-out of a disabled stockholder

When a partner in an incorporated partnership suffers total disability, his stock in the corporation should definitely be bought out. This removes an inactive stockholder from the close corporation which avoids many problems. A buy-out is often the best answer when a partial disability prevents a partner from continuing a full-time, significant role in the business. Working out ahead of time the details of a stock purchase in the event of a partner's disability involves fixing a fair price and determining how that price will be paid by the corporation, so that the financial well-being of the entity is not adversely affected. All of the other terms that would apply to the purchase of a deceased partner's stockholdings should apply as well. For a long time, a major difference in the development of a plan for the redemption of the disabled partner's stock was the absence of insurance to help the corporation pay the price. Such insurance exists today. Policies are now being sold which provide a lump sum if the insured becomes disabled. This can be a big help.

Partners working out a combination death and disability stock redemption program can face a substantial cost for the various kinds of insurance. First there is life insurance to fund the purchase in case of death. Then there are the two kinds of insurance to cope with disability: (1) the insurance which is to provide income to a disabled partner, to replace some of the compensation he received when he was working; and (2) the lump sum insurance to provide some of the wherewithal to acquire the stock of the partner who is disabled. When an incorporated partnership finds that it cannot afford the premiums for all this insurance, the life insurance is invariably the first priority coverage. Disability income usually comes next; and the least carried kind of insurance is the lump sum disability.

A lower cost disability plan

Some years ago, we developed a disability buy-out plan that omits the lump sum disability coverage. To make this work, all of the life insurance policies carried to provide dollars to fund the stock purchase at a partner's death must have a waiver of premiums in case of disability. This means that premiums no longer have to be paid if the insured becomes disabled. The outlay for this benefit is very modest.

Here is how the plan works:

1. The definition of disability in the stockholders' agreement should be the same as it is in the waiver of premium provision of the life insurance policies. If disability is defined differently in two or more insurance policies that are carried by the corporation on the lives of the proprietors, the agreement should mirror the one that is harder to satisfy—or if one policy has a much larger premium, the one contained in that policy. The goal is to have a partner's disability eliminate completely, or at least reduce substantially, the annual cost of keeping his life insurance in force.

2. The disabled individual's stock in the incorporated partnership is redeemed. He ceases to have an equity interest in the corporation.

3. Nothing is paid by the corporation on account of the purchase price set out in the agreement, until the death of the disabled partner. At that point, the insurance proceeds are collected by the corporation and paid over to the estate of the now deceased stockholder. Any balance of the purchase price is paid in installments that are spelled out in the agreement.

4. Interest is paid by the corporation periodically, usually quarterly, on the unpaid balance of the purchase price. The rate of interest can be fixed or it can be pegged to the prime rate of a named bank. This interest can be substantial. For instance, if the purchase price is $400,000, interest at 12% means the corporation must pay almost $50,000 a year until the death of the disabled stockholder. While his life expectancy may be greatly reduced by the disability, he certainly could live for many years. Where does the corporation find the money to meet this interest charge?

The dollars come from a few sources. First there are the savings on his life insurance cost obtained through the provision for waiver of the premiums in case of disability. The corporation has available the excess of the disabled person's compensation and fringe benefits over what must be provided for his replacement. Then there are the income tax savings produced from the deductibility of the interest payments.

5. For his support and maintenance, the disabled partner receives a combination of benefits. There are the payments from his disability income replacement insurance. These are augmented by the interest on the purchase price of his stock—$48,000 per year in the example. This interest should be taxed at moderate rates because the disability income is non-taxable. In addition, there may be payments from social security and the corporation's pension and profit sharing plans, because of the disability.

THE IMPORTANCE OF LIFE INSURANCE

13

Our firm believes strongly that life insurance plays a very important role in structuring many of the close corporation's affairs. We are so committed to the use of life insurance that a suspicious close corporation entrepreneur, listening to me emphasize its desirability as a solution to a number of his problems, once asked me accusingly: "Does your firm share the commissions on the insurance that you push people to buy?" Our belief in this product is not based on our splitting commissions with the agent. That is something we have never done and cannot do. We are great advocates of life insurance because we have observed, firsthand, the many benefits it produces.

BASIC INSURANCE TERMS MADE SIMPLE

Many clients appreciate the many uses of life insurance in planning for the close corporation, but they are befuddled by the plusses and minuses of the various kinds of products that are thrown at them. There are a veritable "grab-bag" of policies: one year renewable term; term for a fixed period of years; decreasing term; renewable and convertible term; ordinary life; ten or twenty payment life; extraordinary life; and now, universal life. Businessmen are also bothered by the misnomer—"dividends"—that insurance agents stress in their presentations. The fact is that policy dividends are not a return on an investment. They really represent a reduction in cost. The insurance company realizes a better yield on its investments than it projected when rates were fixed, and the overage is distributed to the policyholders.

The life insurance jargon is also confusing to entrepreneurs.

Terms are bandied about by insurance professionals as though they
are household words—which they are not. Typical are "minimum
deposit," "incidents of ownership," "split-dollar," "split ownership," and "fifth dividend option." This confusion discourages the
close corporation owner from purchasing any insurance. By nature,
these proprietors do not like to rely on the judgment of others, no
matter how competent and well-respected the professional advisor
may be. They want to understand, evaluate, and make an intelligent
decision.

I am not a life insurance expert. However, I have participated in
so many placements of insurance during my years of practice, that I
have become fairly adept at acting as a quasi-interpreter on the
subject. My role generally is to try and explain to the puzzled close
corporation owner what is being suggested to him by a usually
competent underwriter, who has made the right recommendation, but
is having trouble communicating it. Let me try to clarify these
different kinds of insurance, and explain the mechanics of some
important premium funding techniques for the close corporation and
its stockholders.

Term insurance

One year term insurance is probably the best example of pure
insurance. The insurance company agrees to pay a stated amount if
the person who is insured dies within a one year period. The premium is based on the nearest age of the insured when the policy is
taken out. When the one year period ends, so does the insurance
coverage. If the same amount of insurance is to be continued for the
next year, a new policy has to be procured. Should the individual's
health have become impaired during the year, the insurance company
can decline to issue a new policy or to do so with a "rating." A
rating is an extra charge that is tacked on, because the insured has a
medical problem that increases the probability of death. The extent
of the add-on to the regular premium depends on the severity of the
health problem.

This is where the "renewable" feature becomes important. When
a policy is renewable, the insured can keep it in force no matter what
changes may occur in his insurability. It is very sensible for an
insured to obtain renewable coverage. In every case with which I

have been associated, where one year term insurance was taken out, it was of the renewable variety.

The economic problem with one year renewable term insurance is the increasing annual cost. The close corporation gets a bargain when it acquires this type of policy on the life of its 40 year old policyholder. At that age, it can handle the premium for many hundreds of thousands of dollars of insurance. But the probability of the insured's death while he is in his forties is slim. That is why the premiums are so low during this period. When he survives into the sixties or seventies, the ever increasing premium can become very burdensome to the company. As the expectancy of death grows nearer, and the need for the funds may be even more intense, the corporation can find itself unable to meet the cost.

A term policy for five, ten or twenty years is an attempt to average the outlay during the selected period. The premium is fixed. It does not increase annually. Should death occur during the term, the choice of policy was a good one. However, if the insured is alive at the end of the policy's duration, there is no more insurance in force.

This points up a crucial factor in the selection of life insurance. Term insurance makes sense if the need for funds exists only for a limited number of years. Here are some examples where a term policy is a good choice:

1. The close corporation has to amortize a loan over fifteen years, and wants to be able to pay it off in case the controlling stockholder dies during that period.

2. A stockholder has been bought out, with the purchase price payable in installments, and all concerned want insurance coverage on the remaining stockholder-chief executive, so that the entire unpaid balance can be discharged if he dies.

3. The company will need to have a sizeable amount of money to beef up the management in the event of the death of a 65 year old head of the business. A group of executives have to be recruited, who should be ready to take over, certainly in ten years. They had better be ready by that time, since the chief executive will then be 75 years old.

4. An unrelated important executive will reach retirement age in fifteen years. At that time his retirement benefits will be very

substantial. He wants the company to help him carry insurance, for the protection of his family, from now until he retires.

In a number of these instances, decreasing term insurance could be used. Each year during the period of coverage, the amount payable in case of death goes down—until it finally disappears. The premiums are less than straight term insurance because of this declining death benefit. The most marketed kind of decreasing term policy is one that is sold to pay off the principal of a residential mortgage at death.

Ordinary or whole life insurance

For most close corporation life insurance requirements, term insurance does not fill the bill. There is no finite number of years at the end of which the need for cash is eliminated. Think of these uses and you will appreciate what I mean: to pay death taxes; to take care of a widow; to provide dollars for the owner's children who are not active in the enterprise; to purchase the stock of a partner when he dies or is permanently disabled; to give offspring more money when the first spouse dies. The need in these situations is permanent.

When the insurance must be provided until death, irrespective of when that event happens, we shift to ordinary or whole life insurance protection. This is a policy that stays in force, with a fixed premium, during the entire lifetime of the insured individual, no matter how long or short his lifespan may be. There are policies that are fully paid up after a certain number of premiums are paid. Ten payment and twenty payment life insurance coverage was often taken out in the early years of my practice. With the need for dollars in the business and the sizeable premiums that have to be outlayed for a meaningful amount of insurance, these limited payment policies have virtually disappeared from the close corporation insurance scene.

How can a policy be issued that has the same premium when a person reaches age 40 or 65? Obviously, his chances of dying are much greater when he is 65. The answer is that the premium paid at 40 is an overcharge, and the one due at age 65 may be too low. In the early years, the overpayment—the amount that exceeds the cost of the insurance risk at that age—is placed in a reserve. The insurance company is able to invest that reserve and accumulate the yield.

At the advanced ages, when the premium is less than the insurance cost, the deficiency is made up from the reserve fund.

The annual premium for whole life insurance is greater than for term issued at the same age. Part of this increase is attributable to the fact that it remains in force throughout the insured's lifetime. In addition, there is an investment element in the permanent insurance. The policy has a cash surrender value. At any time, the policyholder may borrow against the cash surrender value, or he can withdraw it all and terminate the insurance. If the full cash surrender value is taken down, the actual out-of-pocket cost during the period the whole life policy was operative is the total premiums that were paid less the cash that is received.

Sometimes a close corporation proprietor may recognize the desirability of whole life insurance, but the company simply cannot afford to carry the amount required to cover the needs. The probability is that in a few years the corporation's financial picture will improve, to the extent that paying whole life premiums for the needed amount of insurance will be manageable. The solution is to take out convertible term insurance—term insurance that can be changed into whole life, without proof of insurability at the time of conversion.

A major concern with the ordinary or whole life policy is that when the insured dies, the beneficiary only receives the face amount of the policy. The cash surrender value disappears at death. As the years go by, with the cash surrender value growing, the insurance company's risk keeps going down and the policy owner becomes a greater co-insurer.

Let me illustrate this concept. There is a $100,000 ordinary life policy, with an annual premium of $4,000. The present cash surrender value is $40,000. From the insured's standpoint, the $40,000 cash surrender value is his. He can put it in his pocket whenever he chooses. Were he to die "yesterday," his beneficiary would receive his $40,000 plus $60,000 from the insurance company.

The next premium comes due and he pays it. The cash surrender value jumps up to $42,000. Now, if he dies, his beneficiary will receive his $42,000 and the insurance company's contribution will drop to $58,000. The longer he lives and the more premiums he pays, the less the insurance company will be out-of-pocket when he dies. Many years ago, to cope with this co-insurance problem, some insurance companies came out with a policy that paid, at death, the face amount plus the cash surrender value. This was called "extraordinary life." It enjoyed a good deal of success in the life insurance market.

Minimum deposit funding and the fifth dividend option

Another way in which the death benefit can increase is through the use of policy dividends. Many people think only of applying the dividends to reduce the cost of carrying the insurance. But they can be used to acquire additional insurance. Most policies permit the purchase of additional permanent insurance, with cash value. More recently, the so-called "fifth dividend option" was added. This permits the policyholder to buy one year term insurance with the annual dividends, usually at least equal in amount to the policy's then cash surrender value. This fifth dividend option, which produces coverage similar to extraordinary life, plays an important part in the minimum deposit funding and split-dollar insurance plans, which I will discuss next.

The owners of close corporations, increasingly hard pressed for cash to operate their businesses, continued to object to investing corporate funds in life insurance policies. What they wanted was permanent insurance with a cost closer to term. The creative life underwriters in the field came up with a solution that combined a number of factors, including income tax savings. Minimum deposit funding was the method they developed.

To understand minimum deposit, the reader must keep in mind that when a premium is paid on an ordinary or whole life policy, the cash surrender value automatically increases, and this increase can be utilized to pay that premium. In the earlier illustration, a $4,000 premium payment resulted in a $2,000 increase in the cash surrender value. It is not necessary for the insured to pay the $4,000 premium in full and thereafter borrow the $2,000 of additional cash surrender value. The two steps can be joined together. The $4,000 premium can be paid by borrowing $2,000 against the new cash surrender value and paying only the balance, $2,000, in cash.

Here is how minimum deposit funding works. Take the same $100,000 policy with the $4,000 annual premium. Each year, with the exception of four of the first seven years of the policy's existence, the holder of the policy is going to borrow the increase in the cash surrender value, apply that against the premium, and pay the balance of the premium. The income tax rules and benefits, pertaining to this method of funding life insurance premiums, are described in Chapter 5.

These policy loans are not the same as bank loans. They do not have to be repaid. So long as the policyholder pays the premiums, when due, together with interest on the policy loans, the insurance remains in force. When the insured dies, the insurance company first repays the policy loans to itself, and remits the balance of the proceeds to the designated beneficiary. In the earlier example, if the $40,000 cash surrender value had been fully borrowed when the insured died, $40,000 of the proceeds would have been applied to discharge the loans and the balance, $60,000, would have gone to the beneficiary.

This format of borrowing the increase of the cash surrender value greatly reduces the amount that the owner of the insurance pays on account of premiums. In our example, in the year that the $4,000 premium was paid by first borrowing $2,000, the owner of the insurance only outlayed half the premium in cash. Since the cash surrender value increases go up as the policy ages, the borrowing percentage increases and the cash payment towards the premium keeps going down. Of course, the policyholder also has to pay the interest on the loan. The interest increases annually as the policy loans keep enlarging. The benefit here is that the interest is income tax deductible, whereas the steadily declining premium payments are not.

A significant negative consequence of the earlier minimum deposit programs was the conversion of the ordinary life insurance into the equivalent of decreasing term insurance. Each time that the cash surrender value of the policy was borrowed against, the proceeds that would pass to the beneficiary at the insured's death was reduced to the same extent. The death benefit kept declining. Extraordinary life insurance was the first way around this obstacle. Since the death benefit consisted of the sum of the face value and the cash surrender value, borrowing against the cash surrender value still kept the face amount payable at death. This continues to be a solution.

The less expensive, and now much preferred alternative is the fifth dividend option. Each year, the policy dividend is used to purchase one year term insurance equal to the cash surrender value. When the insured dies, the loan is paid off with this extra coverage and the face amount goes to the beneficiary. There is one hitch. After some age, usually in the seventies, the cost of the one year term insurance is more than the annual dividend. The beneficiary's portion of the insurance coverage then starts to go down.

Split-dollar insurance

Some innovative life underwriters have come up with still another procedure under which a close corporation can assist an owner to carry personal life insurance. The proprietor, who is the senior employee of the company, may want to take out a policy of whole life insurance to protect his wife, or to provide money for his children, when he dies. The concept that has been developed is to split the ownership and beneficial enjoyment of the policy between the corporation and the stockholder, and use some of the available corporate liquidity to maintain it. This program is referred to as "split-dollar insurance."

Here is how it works. The ownership and beneficial enjoyment of a whole life policy of insurance on the life of a stockholder are split. The corporation is the owner and beneficiary of the cash surrender value portion of the policy. The close corporation owner's designee, an individual or trust, owns and is the beneficiary of the death benefit in excess of the cash surrender value. The corporation undertakes to pay that part of each premium on the policy which is equal to the increase in the cash surrender value. The beneficiary pays the balance of the premium. Let us go back to the $100,000 policy with a $4,000 annual premium, which, when paid, produces a $2,000 increase in its cash surrender value. Under a split-dollar plan, the corporation would finance $2,000 of that premium and the balance, $2,000, would be paid by the insured.

The owner-executive who is the insured has to pick up some taxable income. It is called the "P.S.58" cost, which is a reference to the government table that is used to measure the benefit that the insured receives from the corporation's participation in the funding. But this is a much lesser cost than what is being financed by the corporation. When death occurs, the corporation receives the then cash surrender value of the insurance policy and the beneficiary gets the balance of the proceeds. The company gets back all of the dollars that it has outlayed. In essence, the enterprise has made an interest free loan to the stockholder-executive, secured at all times by the insurance company's guaranteed cash surrender value.

Very often, to take advantage of the favorable interest rate on policy loans, the corporation borrows against the cash surrender value of the policy to pay its share of the premiums. To qualify the interest on the amounts borrowed from the insurance company for an income tax deduction, certain tax rules (discussed in Chapter 5) must be observed.

Unless something is done about it, the proceeds that will pass to the beneficiary, at the death of the insured under a split dollar program, keep reducing. The corporation's share of the coverage keeps enlarging with each advance that it makes toward the payment of premiums. To prevent that result, an extraordinary life policy, which pays a total of the face value and the cash surrender value, can be used. Or, policy dividends under the "fifth dividend option" can be used to purchase additional one year term insurance equal to the cash surrender value.

Universal life insurance

The newest phenomenon in the life insurance market is "universal life insurance." It has been reported that approximately half of all new premium dollars received today by life insurance companies in the United States are for universal life, or other forms of policies where the premium varies. This kind of policy passes on to the policyholder the benefits of high yield investments that the insurance companies are able to make. No longer is the policyholder stuck with the conservative estimate of earnings on the reserve that insurers use in fixing ordinary life insurance rates. In this inflationary era, with high prime rates of interest, the appeal of universal life is great.

While there are many variations, the essence of universal life is rather easy to grasp. Most of the premium dollars are deposited directly into an income-earning fund. Some companies permit the policy owner to choose the kind of fund he wants. For example, stocks, government bonds or long-term corporate bonds. The amount deposited is credited with the yield of the fund. The cost of the individual's life insurance protection is paid out of what he has on deposit in the fund.

Unlike the typical ordinary life contract, there is no fixed charge when you buy universal life. The cost of carrying universal life depends on how much the yield is on the premium deposits made by the policyholder. If the fund realizes a 10% return on its investments, the insurance charges would be less than they would be if the income realized was only 6%. As a means of providing some downside protection, a minimum rate of income return is generally guaranteed. But it is not substantial. For instance, a 4% rate is often used as a minimum.

The volume of universal life business indicates that people are betting that the level of investment income return will stay up. A 40 year old insured may be making a very long term wager on that probability. Only time will tell whether the purchasers of universal life were very wise or foolish. I have offered only one caution. When deciding on how much universal life insurance the close corporation, or its owners, can afford, they should not assume that the recent 12% return will last throughout the life of the policy.

DRAWBACKS OF LIQUIDITY AND CASH RESERVE METHODS OF PROVIDING FUNDS

Throughout this book, I have addressed the problems occasioned by the death of a close corporation owner and suggested some solutions. In many cases, the best way to handle the difficulty is to have a fund of money available in the corporation when the stockholder dies. The dollars may be used for such things as providing for a surviving spouse, redeeming stock, paying death taxes, or repaying or securing a loan. In the discussion of these topics, the emphasis has been on how the solutions are accomplished in an effective and tax advantageous manner. Actually, however, there is a more basic inquiry that has to be made when a plan is based on the availability of corporate funds to cope with the concerns produced by the entrepreneur's death: Will the corporation have the necessary dollars when he dies?

I find it bewildering, when an experienced head of a business in addressing this issue says pridefully: "Don't be concerned, Milt. Look at this financial statement. Our company has a lot of liquidity, more than it needs to run the business. It's been that way for years. My estate will be able to tap the corporation for whatever it needs."

There can be a long stretch of time between today and the unpredict-able date of the client's death. All kinds of things can happen which will eat into these liquid funds:- substantial plant and equipment purchases; acquisitions; developing new products; research expendi-tures; outlays to cope with environmental protection or OSHA re-quirements; or one or more other unanticipated cash drains. The truth is that no one can be sure that the corporation will have excess liquidity when the proprietor dies.

Other close corporation principals have urged that they will set up a cash reserve to meet the need for corporate dollars. That doesn't work. Over what period of time will the reserve be fully built up? If the corporation decides to fund the required amount over a long period, and the covered individual dies earlier than anticipated, the total accumulations can fall quite short of the mark. That is only one risk. My real objection to the reserve method is that few close corporation proprietors will be willing to maintain the reserve intact, no matter what.

Consider for a moment what is required of the head of a business when he takes on the commitment to build a sizeable fund internally, to meet some needs when he dies. He must be willing to forget about the availability of the money to meet a business crisis which may threaten the continued existence of the company. A desirable acquisi-tion must be passed up, if it would require invasion of the reserve fund. The owner must be willing to borrow substantial amounts of money, at the prevailing interest rates, and personally guarantee re-payment by the corporation, even though this could be avoided by using the accumulated dollars. This is too much to ask of the owner of a business, and when confronted with these realities, virtually all owners will admit it—particularly when the alternative of life insur-ance is available.

MAJOR USES OF LIFE INSURANCE

Life insurance is truly the best answer to any requirement for an assured amount of dollars at the death of an individual. A sound, carefully regulated insurance company is contractually obligated to pay the money when the insured dies. The proceeds of the policy are paid within days after death occurs, with no rigmarole or red tape. The insurance industry is justifiably proud of its long record of meeting its commitments. The corporation or individual that owns the policy, generally pays a known premium, which can be a level amount throughout the lifetime of the insured, and sometimes can be reduced through substantial policy dividends. Even if the insured dies long before the tables say that he or she should, the full amount of the policy is paid. Now the close corporation has only periodic premiums to meet. All the rest of its cash assets are available for its business needs.

Clients have complained to me that life insurance is a poor investment. That is not the issue. For the close corporation and its owners, life insurance is the only way to make regular deposits, called premiums, and be certain of the availability of a fixed number of dollars at the death of the insured. The fund springs into being at the moment that death occurs and it is needed.

In the following sections, I am going to examine some of the major uses of life insurance for close corporations and their stockholders.

Taking care of a surviving spouse

With the death of the head of the family business, the income available to his or her surviving spouse may be substantially reduced. Life insurance can be carried to replace the compensation and fringes the decedent formerly received from the enterprise. This is really personal insurance. The only tie to the company is that the company may provide the dollars to finance the premiums, through an increase in the stockholder-executive's salary.

Life insurance is often employed to help the corporation meet its obligations to the deceased stockholder's spouse. For example, there may be an undertaking to pay a widow a sizeable amount of post-death compensation for a long period of time, or for her lifetime. Preferred stock may have been issued during the lifetime of a business-woman, which is to pass to her husband at her death, and then be purchased by the corporation. This is an excellent way to get dollars out of the company into the widower's hands, with very little income tax cost.

The existence of this insurance on the life of a parent, the proceeds of which are payable to the company, diminishes the dependence of a surviving spouse on the children who take over the business when the parent dies. I learned the importance of this early in my practice. I proposed to Deana Stark and her husband, Bob Stark, my idea of how Deana would be supported after Bob's death. The Stark family, which included two sons, operated a successful business. All the members of the family worked there, including Deana, although she only was in charge of accounting and administration. Her sons handled marketing, production, and finance, with her husband, Bob Stark, serving as the chief executive officer.

It was obvious, after an inventory of the property holdings of Bob and Deana Stark was made, that there were not enough income-producing assets outside of the business to provide adequately for Deana after Bob's death. Elevating Deana to a loftier position in the business, after the death of her husband, as a means of increasing her compensation, would have greatly offended the sons. I supplied the solution—a good one, I thought. Bob and the corporation would enter into a contract obligating the company, after his death, to pay Deana a sizeable amount, quarterly, as long as she lived. In fact, the annual amount that Deana would receive after Bob's demise, under this arrangement, would be sufficient to enable her to live comfortably. This would permit her to work or not, conditioned on the state of her health and her desires.

Admittedly, I was pleased by my recommendation. But Deana Stark was not! "You're asking me to rely on my sons to take care of me. When Bob is no longer alive, they will run the company, and in effect they will be handing me money every quarter. I can almost hear them explaining to their wives, that the reason they can't raise their salaries is because they have to provide support for their mother." Chagrined, I realized that as far as Deana Stark was concerned, I had violated the most important rule in estate planning: never put a surviving spouse in a position where he or she feels dependent on the children for support. My response that the payments would be made to her, not as a voluntary gesture by her sons, but because of a contractual commitment negotiated by her husband had no effect whatsoever.

The day was saved for me when I asked Deana Stark if she would feel differently if the company's undertaking to her was funded while Bob was living. Her answer was simple: "Of course! Under those circumstances, I would not feel I was taking something from my sons." A policy of insurance on Bob Stark's life became the mechanism for providing the funds that would be needed to cover the post-death payments. Actually, there were excess insurance proceeds when he died, because we had calculated the amount required for Deana's lifetime, using her age at the time the policy was taken out, and her husband didn't die until about fifteen years later.

Providing dollars for death taxes

In Chapter 6, I explained how a stockholder's estate can get money out of the close corporation for the payment of death taxes in a tax advantageous manner. While I will not repeat that discussion, I do want to note that when the marital deduction was limited to a maximum of 50%, some estate tax had to be paid when the first spouse died, and an equivalent or perhaps a somewhat greater amount was due at the death of the surviving spouse. Now that the marital deduction is unlimited, no federal estate tax is payable when the first spouse dies. The real need for money to pay taxes comes when the surviving spouse die.

Because women have a longer life expectancy, some professionals feel that the way to handle this cash need for taxes at the death of the surviving spouse is to shift the life insurance coverage from husband to wife. Although there is a greater probability that a male spouse will predecease his mate, you can't bank on it as a certainty. Some life insurance agents recommend the purchase of a policy which becomes payable on the death of the survivor of a married couple. In my opinion, it works just as well if the insurance is carried only on the life of the first spouse to dies.

To illustrate my point, I'll use the case of Tony and Tina, a married couple in their sixties, with children and grandchildren. Many years ago, a life insurance agent convinced Tony, the controlling stockholder in a family business, to take out a $350,000 policy on his life, to pay taxes at his death. After the unlimited marital deduction became law, Tony raised the question of what should be done with the insurance on his life, since if he died before Tina—which Tony was sure would happen—there would be no federal estate tax to pay.

It was decided to keep the $350,000 of insurance on Tony's life, but to transfer it to a trust. If Tony died before Tina, the $350,000 of insurance proceeds would be paid to the trust, to be held and invested until Tina's subsequent death. At that time, the assets of the trust would be converted into cash, and the money could then be used to help defray Tina's substantial death taxes. During Tina's lifetime, she would enjoy the income from the $350,000 held in the trust. How will the cash move from the trust to the executors of Tina's estate, so that it can be applied in payment of her death taxes? The trustees of the trust can purchase non-liquid assets from Tina's estate, such as stock of the family business. Alternately, the money can be loaned by the trust to the estate.

Redeeming a deceased shareholder's stock in a close corporation that has gone public

A close corporation that has gone public, one where ownership and management still go hand-in-hand, may have a "thin" over-the-counter market for its shares. What this means is that there is so little trading activity in the stock, that a sale of perhaps as many as 1,000 shares can be done easily, but the disposition of a much larger number of shares cannot be accomplished without pushing down the stock price significantly. In addition, if the selling stockholder is the estate of an individual whose family is in control of the company, the public may be concerned that the stock is being unloaded by an insider because the prospects of the corporation are not good. This may depress the stock price even more. Consequently, there is no assurance that dollars needed by the controlling family for death taxes can be obtained through a sale of shares to the public without taking a beating on the price at which the shares can be sold. A formal underwriting may not be feasible because of general market conditions; and even if it is a possibility, the costs may be staggering.

To avoid these market risks, the corporation itself may agree to purchase the shares from the estate. Absent life insurance, such an undertaking by the company could be very dangerous. The major stockholder's death could come at a time when the financial condition of the corporation would be seriously impaired by such a stock purchase obligation. The minority public stockholders undoubtedly would be able to block this redemption transaction if it in any way threatened the corporation's well-being. That is why a fully insured plan will work. The death of the senior stockholder-executive brings all the dollars required for the purchase. The "gain," the excess of the life insurance proceeds over the premiums paid by the company, is free of income tax. When the shares are bought, the number of outstanding shares are reduced, resulting in an increase in earnings per share.

As a further "sweetener," the price at which the shares are purchased might be somewhat less than the mean between the bid and asked quotations. The seller may be happy to accept this discount, because there will be an assured market for the shares at that price, and there will be no commissions or other significant expenses of sale.

Taking care of children who are not in the business

In Chapter 10, the problems of having an inactive family member in the business were considered. I repeat here the conclusion that I articulated in that chapter: a child who is not involved in the business should not be made a stockholder in the corporation; and if he (or she) is a stockholder, the child should be bought out. The difficulty that the entrepreneur-parent finds with this mandate is how to deal fairly with those who are not working in the enterprise. Typical is the reaction of Carla Green, who worked with her now deceased husband in the family business, and took it over after his death. Under her direction, the business has grown into a much more successful enterprise, worth several millions of dollars. Carla has two sons, Humphrey and Richard, both of whom are active in the company and a daughter, Maria, who is not. Doing Carla's estate planning, I pointed out to her the problems that would be created if at her death she gave Maria stock of the corporation. While she appreciated these difficulties, she said to me: "Milt, I don't have enough assets outside of the business to give Maria the equivalent of the value of the stock that each of the boys will receive. She is my child, too." Actually, Carla was closer to her daughter, Maria, than either of her sons.

The solution was life insurance. A policy was taken out on Carla Green's life, payable to Maria in the amount required to give her parity with her brothers. The moment the insurance was in force, this result was guaranteed. In one way or another, the premium load for the insurance can be shifted to the corporation.

What if Maria had already been made a stockholder? Life insurance on her mother's life would still play an important part in the mother's estate planning. The usual buy-out format calls for installment payments of the purchase price for the inactive stockholder's interest in the corporation. So long as Carla Green lives, everyone feels secure that the enterprise will meet these payments to Maria.

But the same confidence would disappear if Carla died when a substantial balance of the purchase price was still unpaid. Insurance on Carla's life, declining in amount each year as payments are made but still covering the entire unpaid balance, will resolve these worries. If Carla dies while monies are still owing to Maria, the corporation will be handed the dollars to pay Maria off, in full.

There are times when the corporation cannot handle the payment of a fair purchase price for the stock of the inactive individual. Five hundred thousand dollars may be the amount that Maria should get, but the company can only afford to pay $300,000, in installments of $20,000 a year for fifteen years, plus interest at the rate of 10% on the unpaid purchase price. There may be another difficulty in setting too high a price. It may hurt the estate planning of Carla Green and her sons, or create embarrassment for Carla if recent gifts of stock that she made are audited by the Internal Revenue Service.

The excess of what Maria should have received for her stock, over what she will actually be paid, can be made up by insurance. A policy in the amount of the difference can be taken out on Carla's life, with Maria as the beneficiary. She is also named as the owner in order to keep the proceeds from being included in the taxable estate of Carla. Here again, the wherewithal to maintain this insurance can come from the business.

Buying out a partner's interest at his death

Insurance on the lives of the principals in the incorporated partnership is the key to a sound arrangement for the purchase of the interest of the one who dies first. It enables the partners to provide a very good price for the family of the deceased partner, without adversely affecting the company's stability and the survivor's well-being. The cost of the program—the insurance premiums—is paid in manageable periodic outlays, while both partners are involved in the business. Absent these insurance proceeds that the survivor can count on, a commitment to pay a lot of money for the decedent's stock can be scary. When the agreement is made, no one knows who will be the first to go, at what point in time it will happen, and what the financial condition of the corporation will be when the death occurs.

I learned of the perils of an unfunded stock purchase arrangement early in my practice. An accountant referred to me, for estate planning, two equal partners in an incorporated printing business. Art was then 66 and his co-owner, Bernie, was 63. Their agreement, which had been in force about eighteen years, called for a substantial sum to be paid by the corporation, following the death of the first partner, in installments over a period of ten years, together with interest. There was no insurance in force backing up the corporate undertaking. Art was no longer insurable, because of a serious heart condition. An examination of the company's financial statements revealed a very non-liquid situation. The stockholders had consistently drained the corporation's profits with very large bonuses. The ratio of current assets to current liabilities was bad. All of the new presses were being financed and the annual outlays were substantial.

I was troubled by this state of affairs. In case of the death of either party, the remaining stockholder, now at an advanced age, was going to have a real "nut" to meet. He would have to roll up his sleeves and work harder than he probably had at any time in his life. The pressures and anxiety might very well kill Art, and they could severely shorten Bernie's life expectancy. In as understated a manner as I could muster, I inquired innocently whether the survivor would find it very burdensome to carry on the business on his own and make the large installment payments to the deceased partner's estate. This simple inquiry opened the flood gates. During the next hour, the partners' true feelings came out. "It makes no sense for me, in my 70s or 80s, to be struggling and worried sick in order to make Art's family rich." "Frankly, if Bernie died, I would have to sell the business right away, even if the sale produced less for me than what I owed him. The alternative of keeping the business going and paying his family would put me in my grave."

The final resolution was a sale of the business about six months later. This was the only course of action that freed Art and Bernie from the risk of enslavement in their golden years. Had an insurance plan been put into effect years earlier, this "forced sale" could have been avoided.

Criss-cross purchase agreements

There are instances where the purchase of a deceased stockholder's equity in the close corporation is not made by the corporation itself. Despite the advantages of being able to use the corporate finances for the purchase, in certain instances, a redemption can alter voting and equity relationships in a manner that the parties will not accept. Consider, for example, the case of Johnson Engineering. The company was started by Harvey Johnson. He is now dead. His sons, Mark and Gary, now in their sixties, presently own 50% each of the voting stock and run the business.

The corporation, a very successful enterprise, was recapitalized some years ago, to freeze the sons' equity along the lines outlined in Chapter 6. Mark and Gary also hold the preferred stock that was issued in the recapitalization, but they have given their non-voting common stock to their adult sons. They both have two children who are active in the business, so that each of the four descendants holds 25% of the non-voting common stock, the class that has a hold on virtually all the growth in value of Johnson Engineering.

The group is now considering what should happen on the death of any of the children of Mark and Gary who are stockholders in Johnson Engineering. The first idea was to have the corporation purchase the stock of the deceased child. The trouble with that format is the dislocation it causes in the equity of the two families. If one of Mark's offspring died, for example, and his non-voting common stock was acquired by Johnson Engineering, the Mark Johnson family would now hold only a one-third interest in the corporation's future growth, instead of 50%.

The way to avoid that result, is to set up a criss-cross purchase arrangement. The two sons of Mark Johnson will agree that if either dies or is disabled, his brother will purchase his stock. Gary Johnson's sons will do the same. The only way that this can be accomplished, realistically, is for each brother to carry insurance on the life of the other, covering all, or the greatest part, of the purchase price. Johnson Engineering will help by increasing the compensation of the offspring so that they can pay the life insurance premiums.

Providing for children when one of the parents dies

In Chapter 6, it was pointed out that because of the ability to claim an unlimited marital deduction, rather than the former 50% maximum, children have to wait until the death of both parents to inherit a truly significant amount of property. This is the case even where the amount passing at death for the exclusive benefit of the surviving spouse is far more than he or she needs.

For example, a woman, with a husband and two children, died years ago with an estate worth $3 million after debts and expenses. Under the old law, only one half of the estate, or $1,500,000, could quality for the marital deduction. She decided that that was sufficient to take care of her husband. The balance, after the payment of $500,000 of federal and state estate taxes was $1 million ($1,500,000 less $500,000). This would pass to the two children, $500,000 each.

Now, by taking advantage of the unlimited marital deduction, the entire federal estate tax can be eliminated at mother's death. Assuming her death occurs after January 1, 1987, when the maximum tax credit is in place, the two children will receive only $600,000 reduced by the state death tax. Even if there were no state tax to pay, each child has been cut from $500,000 to $300,000. With a state tax of $100,000, the two offspring split $500,000, which is half of what they would have received when the 50% maximum marital deduction was in the law. The adverse consequence to descendants of this change is even greater in larger estates.

One way for the very rich mother to give her children more is not to take full advantage of the marital deduction. But that means her estate will have to pay taxes at her death that could have been avoided. Few parents are willing to pay more tax when the first of them dies, to speed up the flow of money into the pockets of their children. Insurance can provide a better solution. The mother can take out a life insurance policy and dedicate the proceeds to her children. It can be payable to them outright or in trust. If she lives for three years after the transfer of the ownership of the policies, the proceeds will not be included in her gross estate for federal death tax purposes. This way her descendants receive a greater amount when she dies, and still avoid the payment of a federal estate tax.

Providing dollars when a key
stockholder dies

Many adverse consequences can flow from the death of an owner of a close corporation. The family business may face a loss of bank credit because the decedent's guarantee of the corporation's indebtedness is no longer available. The enterprise may have to go out and "steal" a very exceptional and capable executive to fill the deceased stockholder's shoes. If Ron Davenport dies in the near future, Davcon Advertising could use some cash to attract someone to handle client relations and new business presentations for the agency. Life insurance can provide the dollars for these purposes at the moment in time when they are required—the death of the key man.

One of our clients, whom I will call Dean, added a refinement to this key man life insurance coverage concept. He had his corporation take out a sizeable policy of insurance on his life. Dean is the controlling stockholder, chief executive, and chief operating officer of a large, successful enterprise. There are a number of non-family executives in high positions, but Dean is clearly the boss. What moved Dean to make sure that the company will have this very substantial cash fund when he dies? His thesis is that his successor and the other top executives of the company must be provided with a generous compensation package following his decease. An important part of this plan will be an incentive arrangement for those executives who remain with the company, rewarding them handsomely for keeping the level of profits up after Dean's death. Dean feels that a large influx of income tax free cash, the insurance proceeds, will make it easier for the corporation to handle these commitments to the new leadership.

Providing dollars when the remaining
stockholder dies

Life insurance is also the answer to the problem of the remaining stockholder's death, when the corporation still owes a former partner money for the purchase of his stock. Let us assume that Ron Davenport had agreed to sell his Davcon Advertising stock back to the corporation, with the price to be paid in installments over 15 years, together with interest. Ron might be very concerned about the likelihood of his getting paid in full in the event that Ken Connors dies.

Let me illustrate a format that can be used to handle this situation. The corporation agrees to carry insurance on the life of the partner who remains in the business. Let us call him the "remaining partner." The amount must be sufficient, at all times, to discharge fully the unpaid balance owing to the stockholder who was bought out (the "selling stockholder"). This eases the apprehension of the selling stockholder about the effects on him of the death of the remaining partner.

The family of the remaining partner also benefits from the life insurance, in the event of his death at a time when a goodly amount is still owing to the selling stockholder. The remaining stockholder's interest in the corporation, most likely, is his most valuable asset. His heirs can now decide what to do with the business, without the pressure of having to meet the installment payments of the purchase price.

This technique is often followed when a close corporation takes on a substantial indebtedness to finance capital expenditures. Insurance is procured on the life of the head of the business, at all times equal to the unpaid balance of the obligation to the lender. If the top man dies, the corporation knows that it can make the adjustments occasioned by his death, free of the burden of the debt service on the loan.

FINDING A GOOD UNDERWRITER

This chapter highlights the importance of dealing with a good life insurance man. Considerable reliance has to be placed on his expertise and integrity. There are obvious conflicts of interest when a businessman is dealing with a professional underwriter whose compensation is a percentage of the premium that is paid for the policy that he writes. It suggests that the insurance man will invariably push for the most expensive policy.

However naive it may sound, my experience in dealing with many premier life insurance agents—I have worked with scores of them who are at the top of their field—is that they do not overreach. The good ones recognize that if they are greedy and ignore the client's best interest, it will catch up with them. Even more important, from a practical standpoint, the satisfied customer is the best source of new business opportunities for the underwriter.

How do you find a good life insurance agent? One way is to talk to some business friends and see if they have someone they are happy with. If that doesn't produce a result, look for a C.L.U., a Chartered Life Underwriter. The holders of this designation have been required to study all phases of life insurance and they must pass tough examinations on these different subjects. Their association also sponsors many Institutes, held at different university campuses, where there is continuing education for these C.L.U.s. I have been a lecturer at a number of these Institutes, and I can attest to the high level of the participants' knowledgability and their commitment to staying abreast of all developments that affect their clients.

EFFECTS OF OWNER'S DIVORCE ON THE CLOSE CORPORATION   *14*

The inclusion of a chapter on divorce in a book dealing with close corporations may raise some eyebrows. Is divorce among close corporation owners so prevalent that this subject merits this kind of attention? Are the effects on the entity so significant that they constitute a real concern? The answer to both of these queries is "yes!" The divorce rate in our country is very high and it has been for some time. I am not suggesting that divorce is more common for entrepreneurs than for other groups in our society. However, if the divorce rate is the same as the national average, the number of close corporation stockholders whose marriages will end in divorce is very meaningful.

IMPACT OF EQUITABLE DISTRIBUTION

Twenty years ago, I probably would have responded differently in measuring the consequences of an owner's divorce on the corporation. Except in the case of residents of the limited number of community property states, divorce involved primarily issues concerning the amount of alimony for a wife, the extent, nature and duration of child support, custody and visitation rights. Property division was not a matter of substance. Then came equitable distribution. This is a doctrine which results in a division between the divorcing spouses of all the property acquired during the marriage.

The underlying rationale of equitable distribution is the treatment of a marriage as the equivalent of a partnership between husband and wife. When both spouses work, it is clear that they are jointly contributing to the accumulation of wealth. In those instances where a wife has been at home, in charge of the household, feeding and caring for the family, she nonetheless is a contributing partner. The performance of her role enables her businessman-husband to handle his business duties and responsibilities more effectively, able to concentrate all his attention to developing the enterprise.

How marital property is distributed

Under equitable distribution, the length of the marriage prior to divorce and the existence of offspring are the major factors used to determine how much property will be awarded to the less well-heeled spouse. Generally, the maximum is a 50/50 split of the assets.

Here is how the division of property is accomplished. The property that was acquired during the marriage is placed into three categories: (a) jointly owned; (b) owned by the husband; and (c) owned by the wife. I'll assume for the purpose of illustration that there is a jointly held residence, which has a net value of $200,000 inclusive of furnishings, that the property in the husband's name amounts to $1,000,000, and that the wife only has $50,000 of assets in her name. The value of the jointly owned residence is split evenly, so that each spouse starts with $100,000. This amount, added to the husband's separately owned property of $1,000,000, makes his total $1,100,000. The wife's $50,000 of assets, coupled with her one-half interest in the residence, leaves her with $150,000, $950,000 less than her husband. An even division between the spouses of the $1,250,000 of total property, $625,000 to each, would mean that $475,000 of the husband's holdings would be awarded to his spouse.

Property subject to distribution

A number of issues arise when courts are called on to divide the marital property of spouses who are seeking a divorce. The principal stumbling block often involves the determination of what "property" is subject to equitable distribution. The decisions have concluded that it embraces a broad gamut of items, tangible and intangible, including pension and profit-sharing benefits, deferred compensation, life insurance, and rights to receive commissions in the future.

Gifts and inheritances

Property acquired by gift or inheritance usually does not enter into the equation. This is a sound exclusion, since the partnership between the husband and wife did not produce this property. Moreover, before gifts and inherited property were shielded from the risk of equitable distribution, many parents hesitated to pass property to their married children. In particular, the concern about divorce and an accompanying division of property caused many entrepreneurs to forego lifetime transfers of stock to their children, even those who were active in the business. Some close corporation owners put the stock in a trust that ran for the lifetime of the child. The idea of the trust was that nothing would pass to the child during the marriage.

Property acquired prior to marriage

Another common exclusion concerns property acquired by either spouse before the marriage. This rule leads to some interesting issues. Must the spouse claiming the benefit of this exemption trace the exact property from its pre-marital ownership to the date of the divorce proceeding? For example, if the husband had a portfolio of marketable securities, worth $100,000 when he got married, and he sold most and purchased others during the marriage, what, if anything, is free from equitable distribution? The resolution of this issue depends on the level of the proof that can be offered. If the make-up of the spouse's securities holdings at the time of the marriage can be clearly established, and the sales and reinvestments can be tracked, the entire portfolio as it exists at the time of divorce will probably be excluded from apportionment. However, a failure to maintain adequate records often makes it impossible to establish the claim.

Perhaps the most troublesome application of the exclusion for property owned before marriage involves the case of the close corporation stockholder who owned his shares when he was married. The same tracing issue can arise if the corporation was recapitalized during the marriage, and the husband exchanged those pre-marital stockholdings for other shares of stock. But the really hard-to-swallow situation occurs when the value of the stock has multiplied during the marriage, largely through the efforts of the husband.

Consider this example. Jeffrey gets married at the age of 32. He is an insurance broker, operating through a close corporation. On the date of his wedding, he owned all of the stock of the company, which probably was worth only $50,000—including the value of his rights of renewal.

During his 22 year marriage, blessed with three children, now ending in divorce, Jeff built up his business tremendously. He presently has one of the largest insurance brokerage operations in the state, employing 50 people, including several other producers.   A conservative valuation of the stock, at the time the complaint for divorce is filed, is $1,000,000. This interest in the brokerage corporation is by far the largest property holding that Jeff has.

Will Jeff's wife be denied any right to share in the value of the business because Jeff started the company before they were married? During their "partnership," that value went up twenty times, due almost entirely to Jeff's efforts. In a number of jurisdictions, including New York, appreciation in the value of "separate property" during marriage is considered "marital property" subject to equitable distribution only if, and to the extent that, the appreciation was due in part to the contributions or efforts of the other spouse. Undoubtedly, this modification was motivated by the inequity of depriving a spouse of any participation in the growth of a business interest owned by a mate prior to the marriage. However just the concept may be, it calls for a finding of fact in a very difficult area: how much did the working spouse contribute to the success of the enterprise.

In Jeffrey's case, because he is the only principal, it is easy to attribute the great increase in the value of his stock solely to his efforts. Let me alter the facts of Jeffrey's situation, to show how the issue of measuring his contribution to the corporation's growth in value can become much more complicated. Assume that Jeffrey received a minority stock interest in the insurance brokerage business from his father before he was married. Both Jeffrey's dad and his brother worked in the company for many years. The father was the head of the service enterprise until five years before the divorce, when he retired. Jeffrey succeeded his dad as president of the corporation, and he worked side-by-side with his brother, each of them playing a very important role in the success of the business. To measure the portion of the almost $1,000,000 growth in value of the stock of the corporation that resulted from Jeffrey's contribution, rather than from the efforts and talents of his father and brother, will be extremely difficult.

DISTRIBUTING STOCK IN A CLOSE CORPORATION

Equitable distribution was not designed with the close corporation owner in mind. When a divorced couple's assets are primarily cash, marketable securities, and divisible real estate, the application of the concept is relatively simple. The property can be readily apportioned. If a fixed dollar amount is awarded to the wife, the husband can sell something to provide the cash.

The difficulties are much greater when the major asset subject to equitable distribution is stock of a close corporation. Awarding a part of the husband's stock to his wife doesn't solve anything. There is no market for the stock, except for the corporation itself. Little or no income can be realized from the stock, because of the income tax disadvantages of paying dividends. No one wants the wife in the business, particularly her own children. Even more important, she certainly does not want to work there.

Instead of awarding the stock itself to the spouse, a court may come up with a value for the husband's stock, fix a dollar amount of equitable distribution to be paid to his wife, and give the husband the right to pay that sum to his wife over a period of years. This solution avoids having a former wife as a stockholder of the close corporation. That is a real advantage. The husband's dilemma, however, is how to get the money to pay his former wife what he owes her.

Dividends are a bad way to get dollars out of the corporation to the husband, from an income tax standpoint. Election of Subchapter S for the company will help to avoid the double tax on corporate income. But even in that case it will be hard to satisfy an equitable distribution obligation (involving payments that are not deductible) with 50 cent dollars. The simple fact is that satisfying a wife's equitable distribution share, when the husband's main property holding is stock of a close corporation, is hard to do. Here are two methods that can be used to resolve this problem:

1. The sum attributed to equitable distribution can be reduced deliberately. This method often proves useful where the divorced couple have children in the business, and the wife wants to make sure that under no circumstances will the equity in the close corporation pass to a second wife or to the offspring of the husband's second marriage. In exchange for keeping the non-deductible equitable distribution figure at a manageable level, the husband agrees that he will only give or bequeath the stock, or any proceeds realized from the liquidation of the corporation or the sale of the shares, to the children of the marriage. Under this format, the wife avoids imperiling the well-being of the business by saddling her husband with very burdensome equitable distribution payments. At the same time, she makes sure that her children will receive the benefit of this concession.

There is one other condition to this gesture by the wife. The amount of her alimony is very generous. It will enable her to live very comfortably. Because the alimony is deductible by the husband, and it is payable in installments, this is a plus for him. To make sure that the husband's death doesn't affect her standard of living, substantial amounts of insurance on his life are made payable to her.

2. Another solution is the redemption of stock by the corporation. The husband gives his spouse some shares of stock of the close corporation to settle his equitable distribution undertaking. The corporation then redeems the stock from her at a negotiated price. Her gain is taxed at capital gain rates, with a maximum of 20%. The purchase price for the wife's stock will be made in installments that the corporation can contend with, together with interest.

Under this method, the husband is using locked-in corporate dollars to meet the obligation to his wife. There is no double tax, as there would be if dividends were paid to him. The need to convert to Subchapter S tax status is avoided. His wife ultimately gets cash, which is what she wants. In the interim, the interest on the unpaid balance gives her a good return on the stock value.

I am sure there are other sound ways to contend with equitable distribution when a close corporation owner is divorced. They are often not explored because of the intensity of the feeling that exists in a matrimonial matter. The antagonisms between the parties can run high. The wife may really want to "sock it" to her husband, particularly if he has another woman.

What must be kept in mind is that the negotiations in connection with a divorce are quite different from those that take place between unrelated and objective parties. Emotions run high when a divorcing couple are trying to work out a property settlement. If I may paraphrase a bit: a wife may well cut off her nose to spite her husband's face.

EFFECTS OF DIVORCE ON CHILDREN IN
THE FAMILY BUSINESS

It is commonplace today for couples who have been married for many years to get divorced. When this happens to the head of a family business, the battle between the spouses can have a serious impact on the children who are making that business their career. While they may suffer fewer emotional scars because they are adults, these offspring must still face grave concerns about their financial well-being.

I remember the situation of Mort Freund, who at the age of 62, after 26 years of marriage, decided to divorce his 57 year old wife, Margaret. She was a warm, effervescent, sociable person, who enjoyed the company of friends. Mort's main interests in life were his company, Better Software, Inc., his sculpting, at which he could work for many hours at a clip, and watching all kinds of sporting events on television, which Margaret despised. Mort was an introvert, bored by the conversations at gatherings, which he described either as trite or gossipy.

The break-up of Mort and Margaret's marriage was triggered by Mort's developing an attachment to a female computer consultant who loved to paint and shared Mort's enthusiasm for sports viewing and his penchant for privacy. Margaret Freund had mixed feelings about the idea of being divorced from Mort. She would appreciate being liberated from maintaining a household and cooking for a man who showed her little feeling, talked to her only occasionally and shared very little with her. Margaret recognized that she and Mort had very little in common, particularly now that their two sons, Clyde and Merrill, were grown men, with their own families, working hard at Better Software. On the other hand, she was frightened by the prospect of having to provide for herself in the future, and she told her divorce lawyer that his job was to make sure that she was given money to live comfortably for the rest of her life. After her attorney saw the financial report of Better Software, which was going great guns, he assured Margaret that he would get her a very sizeable equitable distribution payment.

The battle then began. Margaret's counsel obtained a court order, permitting an accountant to go over the books and records of Better

Software, Inc., with a fine tooth comb. When Mort Freund's lawyer tried to head this off, by asking for a settlement proposal from Margaret, her lawyer demanded a ridiculously high sum, which was rejected forthwith. "Don't worry, Margaret," her attorney told her, "their attitude will change as we start to unearth some tax shenanigans your husband pulled—and close corporation owners always play fast and loose with the tax collector." Sure enough, when the probing led to some questionable expense deductions, and a number of trips that Mort took with his paramour, which the corporation paid for, Mort's representative made a counter-proposal. Stock of Better Software would be given to Margaret and redeemed for $400,000, to be paid over a period of years, with a modest rate of interest. "Okay," said the lawyer for Margaret, after conferring with his client, "except the price is $500,000, and its to be all in cash—and that is non-negotiable."

Throughout this period of "negotiation" Margaret paid no attention to the consequences that her actions would have on her two sons. Frankly, she was so concerned about her own well-being, that the boys' plight never entered her mind. Certainly, her lawyer cared nothing about Clyde and Merrill. Even during the frequent get-togethers between Margaret and her sons, and their families, neither Clyde nor Merrill said anything about their worries. Somehow, they could not bring themselves to bother their mother about the things that were causing them anxiety. But here is the picture that their father painted for them, at various stages of the litigation:

1. "Can you imagine, boys, your mother is going to court, to convince the judge to let her accountant go over all of our tax returns and financial records. What they want to find are things that could get us in trouble with the Internal Revenue Service— subject us to big tax deficiencies, plus interest, and even penalties. Then they will blackmail us to pay your mother more than she is entitled to get. I am going to try and head this off by having my lawyer work out a fair settlement."

2. "Just as I told you, when my attorney talked about trying to avoid this invasion of our business privacy, they asked for such an exaggerated amount, that it's clear that they want to hold us up. The only place we can find the money to pay your mother is in

the business. To pay her what her lawyer asked for, would bankrupt us."

3. "My lawyer just called to let us know that Margaret's accountant has come up with some items, that could cause us a lot of serious tax trouble. We agreed that I should make an offer along these lines. I'll give Margaret some shares of stock of Better Software, and then the company will buy them back. I discussed this with our accountant, and he thinks that the company can handle $400,000, payable over ten years, with interest at 9%. So I authorized my attorney to communicate this, but to make it clear that this is a firm offer, the most we can carry."

4. "Sons, we're in a really tough spot. Your mother's lawyer, that S-O-B-, says that he discussed our proposal thoroughly with Margaret, and she insists on $500,000, all cash. I feel as though I have a gun to my head. What this means is that Better Software will have to borrow the money from our bank—if they'll loan us that much—and repay it, more rapidly, with interest probably at 2% over the prime rate. The three of us will have to personally guarantee the repayment of the loans. Clyde and Merrill, we're going to have to tighten our belts to do this. It may mean cutting back on our salaries and fringes. Frankly, I can't understand why your mother wants to do this to you!"

If self-preservation is the first law of man, this scenario had to cause Clyde and Merrill to resent their mother. They are the innocents, standing by and watching the company, that represents their security, being threatened because of their parents' marital dispute. While it was their father's affair with another woman that led to the divorce, and the sons may appreciate how difficult their father was to live with, they have been brainwashed into believing that it is their mother who is trying to destroy the business, through her underhanded tactics and outrageous demands. The boys may even be angry at themselves, for not having intervened with their mother earlier, to try and make her tone down her demands, so that their bread and butter would be protected. What it boils down to is that children, who are active in the family business, invariably wind up, in a divorce between their mother and father, sympathizing with the position of the parent who is the owner of the business interest. They side with the business owner to protect the integrity of the enterprise.

HUSBAND AND WIFE IN SEPARATE BUSINESSES

A divorce proceeding can really be complicated where each of the spouses owns an interest in a close corporation. With two different corporate entities involved, the determination of the respective property holdings of the two parties can become mind boggling. All kinds of permutations and combinations are possible in such a case:

1. The husband may have an equal partner in his incorporated partnership business, while his wife owns 100% of the stock of her enterprise. Should the value of the husband's stock be discounted because he only has a 50% interest, and if so, by how much?

2. There may be publicly traded companies, which are comparable to one spouse's business, that can be used to compute the value of that spouse's stockholdings in the manner described in Chapter 6. The other spouse's corporation may not be comparable to any publicly traded entities, which means the process of fixing value involves much more guess work.

3. The husband's company may have a recognized industry-wide formula for measuring goodwill, such as multiplying the volume of sales by a factor, the parameters of which are well-known. No such standard may apply to the wife's business.

4. The husband may own stock in a business that has been around for a few generations. It has stability and a corps of capable non-family executives, who could run the company without him. The wife's entity may have been started much more recently, and its success may be much more dependent on her talents. Since it is questionable whether the wife's business could continue to operate, as profitably, without her being involved, considerably less goodwill value, or perhaps none at all, can be attributed to her stock.

There will have to be in-depth investigations of the financial data of both spouses' companies. The husband's representatives will want to pour over all the books of the wife's corporation for the last three years. In response, the accountants for the wife will probably broaden the areas they want to look over carefully, and they will go back five years. The determination of stock values will become a means for each spouse to aggravate the other in the divorce proceedings.

The people doing the investigations into the financial history of the respective corporations will be much better prepared, than in the usual case when only one mate is the owner of a business. The skeletons in the closet of each enterprise may be well known to the combatants, having been learned in the happy days of the marriage when confidences were readily exchanged. The wife can tell her lawyer about the husband's consistent practice of understating the value of the inventory of his business, as a means of keeping down the income taxes of the company. He, in turn, can recall some of his wife's loose tax practices in the operation of her business, such as deducting the cost of some furnishings which were purchased for their residence, as though they were to be placed in the company offices, and having the housekeeper treated as an employee of her corporation.

Fixing alimony will be another extremely difficult task. One of the spouses may draw a lot more money from the business than the other. The position of the spouse who regularly takes more money out of his company is predictable: "She could draw a lot more salary out of her business. We didn't need the extra income, so we decided she should take less, in order to plow money back and build up her sales. I shouldn't pay her a nickel of alimony. She can live very nicely on what her business will throw off." The spouse with less compensation undoubtedly will see it otherwise. Particularly will that be the case if the marriage is ending because of one spouse's romantic involvement with another man or woman. "Why should he have all that money to lavish on his girlfriend, while I have to live on peanuts!"

There is also the problem of identifying how much each spouse receives from the business, which is available for support. If the husband earns much more than his wife, for example, she will be the one seeking alimony. To determine how much she should receive, she starts with a budget of her dollar needs for all purposes, including travel and entertainment, clothes—the works. The amount that her business yields her is then subtracted, and the difference is what her lawyer demands that she receive as alimony from her husband. Obviously, the greater the amount her company provides for the wife to live on, the less alimony the husband faces. Conversely, in deciding whether the husband is in a financial position to pay alimony, you start with the husband's income, deduct what he needs for his living expenses, and if there is a meaningful balance, the husband is able to pay alimony.

It must be kept in mind, however, that in assessing the availability of income to husband and wife, the salary that each of them takes from his or her corporation cannot be viewed in isolation. That is only one part of the throw-off from the business. Fringe benefits and travel and entertainment expenses must be factored into the computations as well. This opens the door to some extensive and frequently embarrassing examinations of the books and records of the two corporations. Those in-depth attempts to convert ostensibly deductible business expenses into outlays for the personal benefits of the stockholders, can have very serious tax consequences for the owner of each business.

Divorce involving partner in an incorporated partnership: the story of Alex and Audrey

When the husband in a divorce proceeding is the owner of a close corporation he has an advantage. He can use corporate dollars, as he sees fit, to contend with the demands of his wife. This is not the case when a husband has only a 50% interest in the corporation. Now he must try to convince his partner to assist him in his divorce settlement. Let me illustrate this problem by telling the story of Generics, Inc. This is a very successful business which manufactures and distributes generic drugs. Alex Strong, 47, and Sidney Brant, 53, the "partners," are very competent managers. Alex and his wife, Audrey, who is 45, have had many marital problems during their 21 years of marriage. They have a son, 18, a freshman in college, and a daughter, 16, who attends a private secondary school. Sidney has two sons. One works for Generics, and the other, now finishing graduate school, will also become associated with the company. Alex fell in love with Eleanor, who is the director of personnel of Generics, Inc. He decided to leave his wife, Audrey, and marry Eleanor. He announced his intentions, moved out, and began living with Eleanor. Audrey was shocked, then infuriated. After concluding that the separation was permanent, Audrey commenced an action for divorce.

Alex Strong's major asset is his 50% stock interest in Generics. He and Audrey jointly own a residence, worth $350,000, with a $250,000 mortgage. In addition, Alex has cash and marketable securities of about $50,000. Alex and his partner, Sidney, each currently receive annual compensation of $250,000. The automobiles used by Alex and Audrey are owned by the company, which pays for all gas, maintenance, and repairs. Both partners have substantial interests in a profit-sharing plan. Alex's account is now up to $150,000. A goodly amount of the personal travel and entertainment expenses of the two owners and their families has been charged to the corporation. There are other items of a personal nature that Generics, Inc. has paid for.

In 1984, Generics, Inc. earned $375,000 after taxes. The after-tax profits in the two prior years were $275,000 in 1983 and $250,000 in 1982. The current net worth of the corporation is about $2,000,000.

The opening gambit

Audrey engaged a very experienced lawyer who specializes in matrimonial matters. She got his name from a divorced friend, who kept bragging that her lawyer had brought her businessman husband—who left her for another woman—to his knees. This was just the kind of counsel that Audrey wanted.

After doing some preliminary fact gathering and getting answers to interrogatories, the attorney representing Audrey concludes that the crucial issue is the value of Alex's stock interest in Generics. He explains this to Audrey, and recommends that an expert, an accountant who regularly does valuations of the stock of close corporations in divorce litigation, be retained to make an appraisal. Audrey explains to her counsel that she exhausted all the cash available to her to pay his sizeable retainer. She asks: "How will I pay this accountant?" Her lawyer responds: "Don't worry. We'll get your husband to pay something substantial to get the expert started (and the court did order that), and you'll pay him the balance out of your equitable distribution award."

Meanwhile, Alex is full of guilt. He is struggling to maintain a relationship with his children and to reassure them that he has no intention of leaving them in the lurch.

Alex's first choice to represent him is a partner in the law firm that is the general counsel to Generics, Inc., who is a very competent divorce lawyer. He is told that there may be a conflict of interest. While Alex does not fully understand this, he selects as his lawyer for the divorce proceeding one of the three matrimonial practitioners recommended to him by the firm. Soon he will learn why there will be conflicts among him, Generics, Inc. and his co-stockholder, Sidney Brant.

At the first conference with his lawyer, Alex explains that he wants to make sure Audrey and his children are able to live comfortably. "Don't nickel and dime Audrey's lawyer. I've already told Audrey I want her to have the house, as well as substantial alimony. I'll take care of all the children's education expenses and see that all their medical and dental expenses are paid, either through our company's medical insurance or by me."

Patiently, the attorney explains to Alex that the major concern is Audrey's right to equitable distribution with respect to the business equity. This could be a very big number. He warns Alex that his generosity in the area of alimony and child support will not forestall Audrey's fervor to get a large property settlement. "Hell hath no fury like a woman scorned!"

How the case will proceed

The battle lines have now been drawn. Here is a list of the kinds of things that will most probably happen in the Alex Strong-Audrey Strong divorce proceedings:

1. *Opening the books.* Audrey's lawyer will ask the court to allow their accountant-stock valuation expert to audit the books and records of Generics. Sidney Brant will be furious at the thought of a representative of his partner's embittered spouse pouring over those books and records. The nervous accountant for Generics will agitate Sidney even more, by explaining the embarrassment to all concerned, that will ensue if certain expenses are questioned. Sidney will direct the corporation's law firm to go to court and prevent some outside accountant from putting his nose into the company's private records. Counsel for Generics, Inc., acting under Sidney's orders, with Alex's blessing, of course, will advise the judge that such an audit will seriously interfere with the conduct of Generic's business. The corporation will be happy to give the accountant for Audrey copies of its certified financial statements for as many years as he wants. But Generics, Inc. should not be made to do more than this. After all, neither the company nor Sidney Brant is a party to the divorce controversy.

The judge will grant the request of Audrey's lawyer. He will order Generics, Inc. to make its books and records available for examination by Audrey's accountant. There are legitimate reasons for permitting this examination. Assume, for example, that the accountant is able to show that the annual net income of Generics, Inc. was understated by $50,000, because personal items were treated as business expenses, and fringe benefits were taken by the partners. If the stock of Alex Strong is being valued by applying a multiple of ten times earnings to the net income of the corporation (as explained in Chapter 6), an additional $500,000 of value of the corporation results. Alex's 50% stock interest will be increased by $250,000, since he has a 50% interest in the corporation. This could produce $125,000 more equitable distribution for his wife, Audrey.

2. *Heightening of tension between partners.* Sidney Brant and Alex will become increasingly more anxious about the prospects of an unfriendly accountant poking around, trying to show that inventories have been understated or that improper charges have been made against the income of Generics, Inc. They will realize that while Audrey knows nothing about the business, she may be aware of her husband's use of corporate dollars for personal items. The potential income tax ramifications of the accountant's findings will become clear to the partners. Their own advisors may play an important role in heightening their worries on that score.

3. *Digging for dirt.* Audrey and her attorney may lose sight of the reality that the creation of tax problems for Generics, Inc. and Alex is not in Audrey's best interest. It is surprising to me how the hostility of a spouse in a situation like this can push her to lose the forest for the trees. Triggering sizeable tax deficiencies, interest, and possible penalties as well, diminishes the amount of property that is available to her for equitable distribution. Her counsel may appreciate this intellectually, but the competition and fighting with Alex's lawyer may cloud his perspective as well.

There is a fine tactical line that has to be followed when the specter of improperly reported income or deductions is raised. If it scares a close corporation owner enough to make him raise the equitable distribution ante, the tactic worked. On the other hand, should this approach produce sizeable additional income tax assessments, it can be disastrous for everyone involved.

4. *Upping the ante.* The parties will be wide apart when the jockeying is over and they sit down to work out a settlement for purposes of equitable distribution. Valuing the stock of a close corporation is always a difficult issue and it becomes even more so in this kind of environment. There is a wife, Audrey, seeking revenge for her rejection by Alex. The corporation involved, Generics, Inc., has understated its earnings because the business picked up the tab for some of the stockholders' personal expenses. Furthermore, the salaries and benefits of the partners are so large that Audrey's attorneys, undoubtedly, will urge that a substantial segment of the compensation and perquisites should be treated as additional profits of the company.

Alex will be pressured to keep the figure low. It has now become crystal clear to him, that he will have to use the coffers of Generics to pay off Audrey's equitable distribution claim. It will be difficult enough for Alex to convince Sidney Brant to go along with some stock purchase by Generics at a reasonable price. To have Generics pay a premium to get rid of Audrey, will be intolerable to Sidney.

It is very easy to justify very divergent values, even without restating the earnings of Generics, Inc. Those acting for Alex will use a three year average of net-after-tax earnings—$300,000— and a capitalization rate of eight times earnings. This makes the value of the corporation $2,400,000, and of Alex's one-half interest, $1,200,000. Then they may seek a modest discount because Alex holds a position of equality, but not control. But Audrey's representatives will say: "Bunk! The last year's after-tax-earnings, $375,000, are the better measure particularly since everything points to next year's profits being even higher. And the right multiple is ten times, not eight times." The total value now escalates to $3,750,000; and Alex's 50% interest is up to $1,875,000, or $675,000 more. On top of that, the accountant for Audrey will surely add something substantial for the capitalization at 10% of the understated income of Generics.

5. *Dragging the other partner into the fight.* Sidney Brant and

Generics, Inc., will become more and more embroiled in Alex's equitable distribution problems. Any suggestion that Audrey Strong hold stock in the corporation is absolutely repugnant to Sidney. However, Alex is not in a position to give her a cash settlement, even if the value of his stock is computed on the low side, and he is given the right to pay off the equitable distribution in installments. Half of $1,200,000 is $600,000. There is no way Alex can meet that obligation out of his existing income and resources—particularly when he is going to marry Eleanor, buy a house, etc. The wherewithal has to come from Generics.

Raising Alex's compensation, so that he can pay off Audrey won't work. The extra amount of compensation he would have to take down each year would be very substantial. Sidney, of course, would have to receive the same increase. The probability is that much, if not all, of this augmented compensation would be held to be unreasonable, resulting in a disallowance of the income tax deduction. This means that about 75% of this additional distribution would be eaten up by income tax. Any portion that does pass as compensation would still be taxed at 50%.

What about a Subchapter S election for Generics, Inc.? This would be a better method of getting the company's earnings into the hands of Alex Strong. But Sidney Brant's estate planning will be jeopardized if Generics becomes a Subchapter S corporation. The tax partner in the law firm that represents Generics has recommended to Sidney, that he freeze his interest in the corporation and shift the future growth in value to his two sons, in a manner described, in detail, in Chapter 6. To accomplish this, Generics has to be recapitalized and a lot of preferred stock issued. Unfortunately, Subchapter S tax status is not available to a corporation that has preferred stock outstanding. Delaying the recapitalization until Alex pays Audrey all that he will owe her, can cost Sidney's family a lot of extra estate taxes.

6. *Exploring some alternatives.* Alex's lawyer, or perhaps the accountant for Generics, will suggest that Alex make a gift of half of his Generics stock to Audrey. This will be followed, after the divorce is final, by a redemption of the shares at a negotiated price and agreed upon terms. This will avoid the 50% tax on the dollars, when they go from Generics to Alex to Audrey. This suggestion raises a host of questions. If Alex gives half of his

stock to Audrey, which is then redeemed, his equity in Generics
and his voting power will be reduced from 50% to one-third, or
33 1/3%.

Let us assume that Alex and Sidney now own 100 shares each
of Generics stock. Alex will give 50 of his 100 shares to Audrey.
When those 50 shares are bought from Audrey by the corporation,
the outstanding Generics stock will be reduced to 150 shares, 100
still owned by Sidney, and 50 left in Alex's hands. This is not a
result that Alex wants to accept. The prospect of becoming a
minority stockholder in Generics is upsetting to him. Alex will
ask if there is not a way that this redemption format can be
utilized, without his loss of his equal voting and equity status.

Maintaining Alex's 50% voting power is easy to accomplish.
Generics would first be recapitalized, by issuing a voting common
stock with very limited equity, and a non-voting common that
represents virtually all of the equity. Alex would then transfer only
shares of the Generics non-voting common to Audrey.

Alex will appreciate this protection of his equal power. But he
still will be unhappy about the loss of a good part of his 50%
share of the appreciation in value of Generics. He also recognizes
that if Sidney Brant holds more stock than he, then Sidney will be
drawing down a greater amount of compensation and perquisites.
Alex presses for a mechanism of purchasing stock from Audrey,
which avoids that consequence.

Someone may find the way of doing that too. Again, it involves
a recapitalization of Generics. In this instance, the corporation
will issue shares of preferred stock to the stockholders, in addition
to the two classes of common stock. The value of the preferred
that Generics will issue would be sufficient so that one-half of it
will be somewhat in excess of the purchase price that Audrey will
receive. For example, if Audrey is to get $1,200,000, Generics
might issue shares of preferred stock having an aggregate liquidation preference and redemption value of $3,000,000. One-half, or
$1,500,000, would pass to Alex and a like amount to Sidney
Brant. Then Alex would give Audrey $1,200,000 worth of his
preferred, which later would be acquired by Generics. Alex is left
with 50% of the common stock. His equity in Generics has been
reduced by a fixed figure, $1,200,000. But he continues to have a
50% interest in the profits.

Sidney Brant will now be able to move ahead with his estate tax reduction plan of shifting the non-voting common, the growth stock, to his children. The "arms-length" transaction with Audrey may even help him in the valuation of the gifted stock. That is a plus. But what about the fact that he will now have more capital in the corporation than his partner?

To compensate Sidney, Generics, Inc., might pay dividends on the preferred stock that he will hold. If the non-deductible nature of dividends is objectionable, some part of what would be a fair return on the $1,200,000 used in my example, can be converted into additional compensation or special perquisites and benefits for Sidney.

7. *A falling out between the partners.* The relationship between Alex Strong and Sidney Brant will take a turn for the worse. There was Sidney, the owner of a 50% interest in a very prosperous business, with great prospects to become even more successful. He earned a lot of money and enjoyed the "good life." Suddenly, out of nowhere, Sidney sees his well-being threatened.

He has to contend with a hostile accountant who will pour over the books and records of Generics, hoping to find things that can cause the corporation and him a lot of tax trouble. Generics will have to take on a sizeable commitment to satisfy his partner's wife's equitable distribution rights. Who caused these troubles for Sidney? Alex! Sidney is like the innocent bystander who gets shot by a policeman pursuing a robber.

Then there will be the pressure that Alex exerts on Sidney. "Be a pal, Sidney, have Generics buy stock from Audrey. But let me keep my 50% vote and continuing equity." This is asking a lot of your partner.

How the case will be resolved

How will it all end? This very much depends on the willingness of the actors in this drama to compromise, and how far the close corporation owner in Sidney Brant's position is willing to go to accommodate his partner. The jilted wife may remain arbitrary and bitter to the end of the divorce litigation. Many times the hostility subsides enough to permit the accomplishment of a reasonable settlement.

The proprietor who is not the party to the martrimonial battle may refuse to have the corporation take on a financial burden, solely to accommodate the needs of his partner. Or, he may agree to help on condition that the divorcing partner give up equality. Sometimes an Alex Strong has to sell his entire interest in the corporation. In sum, it is safe to say that the divorce of a partner in an incorporated partnership certainly can produce a lot of discontent and difficulty.

HUSBAND AND WIFE IN THE SAME BUSINESS

The ultimate in partnership problems precipitated by a divorce happends where the spouses are equal partners in the same business. These husband-wife business combinations, as I observed earlier in this book, pose special management problems to begin with. Disputes and misunderstandings that originate in the home carry over into the office, and can greatly exacerbate the already difficult nepotism problems. They become much worse as the marriage deteriorates. Even before the final divorce, the situation can get so bad that the spouses separate, resulting in extremely adverse effects on the business. By then it is impossible for the couple, full of hostility towards one another, to hide their antagonism from employees of the company.

Consider the problems that might ensue if the marriage of Melvin and Shirley Taylor, equal owners and managers of a successful business, came apart. Each spouse, during this period, has a need to strike out at the other. A wonderful way to "sock it to him," is for one spouse to criticize the performance of the other, particularly in the presence of other senior executives. So you get comments like these: "Did you see the way Melvin handled that big customer. At times, he is just plain dumb!" Or, "I've told Shirley a hundred times to make sure we have an up-to-date inventory of replacement parts, so we can respond to a request real fast, but she never gets off her rear end and does it." The employees in the business don't know what to do. They are fully aware of the trouble between the Taylors. But how do they respond? Should they take sides, and if they do, which one of the spouses should they be loyal to? What does this battle between the bosses mean for the future of the company—and more important, for their jobs?

When the relationship between spouses degenerates to the point where they cannot function in the company as a team, one of them should get out, or the business should be sold. It doesn't make sense to destroy the morale and efficiency of the enterprise, which may have taken many years to build. Who gets out? When one spouse is clearly the head of the business, and the other has a minor role, this issue is easy to resolve. The lesser light will leave. However, when both spouses are very involved in the business, contributing significantly to its success, the decision of who stays, and who leaves, is very tough.

It is is not merely a matter of deciding how much the departing spouse should be paid for his or her interest in the corporation. That, of course, is going to be negotiated. It is also a matter of preserving the parties' self-esteem.

The ties between a close corporation owner's being and his business have been noted earlier in this book. His main achievement in life is usually the success of his company. For example, both Melvin and Shirley Taylor take pride in the identification between the business and themselves. Sharing that sense of accomplishment while all was going well in their marriage, did not take anything away from Melvin or Shirley. In fact, their husband-wife business partnership was viewed as adding a special, distinguishing feature to the company. To be the spouse who leaves the corporation means the end of that identification. Shirley might ask: "What will I do to keep busy?" Melvin might exclaim: "I will be a nobody!"

Melvin will probably suffer special ego problems, if he gives up his position in the company. He may have been teased or kidded, even while all was well with his very capable wife, who was a powerhouse in the company. Someone may have said to him: "Boy, I wish I had a wife who could help pay the bills." Melvin laughed at this kind of jibe, but perhaps down deep inside, he worried that his image as a businessman was being tarnished because people recognized his wife's talents. Now, Melvin pictures what he will face, when he is no longer involved in the company, and his wife is running the whole show. Will Shirley's staying on serve as demonstrable proof that she was the more capable, that she was the one who carried him?

Shirley's attitude may be very much affected by her status as a woman. She had to overcome a lot of prejudice to get where she is.

Her own mother, a committed housewife, may have made her feel guilty by questioning her ability to be a full-time businesswoman, and still raise her two children properly. Shirley's dad, a lawyer, questioned whether his daughter could handle a top executive position in a demanding manufacturing business. Even some of her women friends were critical, perhaps out of a need to justify their unwillingness to take on such a challenge. And, of course, there were the snide remarks and kidding that Shirley regularly contended with. Because of this conditioning, when the suggestion is made that Shirley should be bought out, she might very well scream out: "Why should I leave? Just because Melvin is a man, and I'm a woman, he assumes that the business is his domain. The truth is I'm more important to the business than that male chauvinist."

Unfortunately, one of the two has to leave. I did hear of a situation where a married couple, in business together, decided to get divorced, keep their stockholdings and continue to work together. I never heard how that experiment worked out. Frankly, it doesn't seem feasible to me.

The terms of the severence are most easily negotiated, before there is a decision as to the identity of the spouse that is staying, and the one that will be leaving. One way to do this is to fix the price, the terms of payment, and other conditions, and then draw lots to see who sells out. Another possibility is to determine everything except the price, and then let the couple get involved in a bidding contest. The spouse who is willing to cause the corporation to pay the highest amount, remains, and the other spouse leaves.

GOING PUBLIC — WHY, WHEN, AND HOW

15

This chapter examines the first public offering of stock of a close corporation. This is the major step, involving as it does, a major change in the confidentiality that is enjoyed by a privately owned corporation. Before a company goes public, its operations, governance, financial position and even the identity of its owners are private matters. Once the decision is made to sell stock to the public, that changes dramatically. As a condition of obtaining the right to sell shares to outsiders, the entrepreneurs now must disclose a good deal of information about the business enterprise and the corporation. To help the reader understand the motivations that move the proprietors to sell stock to non-family members, the plusses and minuses, the timing and the methods of going public, I'm going to use one close corporation as an example throughout this chapter.

My illustrative company is Bradley Cosmetics, Inc., a successful manufacturer of cosmetics, beauty supplies and toiletries, primarily sold through beauty parlors under the name, "Top Of The Line." Bradley Cosmetics was started by James Bradley, shortly after the end of the Second World War. He was a very hard-working, innovative businessman, who built the company up to a sales level of $5,000,000 a year, with annual profits averaging $150,000, before taxes, before his death about ten years ago. James Bradley's wife died a few years later.

Both sons of James Bradley, James, Jr. ("Jim") and Edward ("Ed"), who are now 59 and 57 years of age, respectively, came into the business after graduating from college. With the advice and guidance of a management consultant the company hired, Jim and Ed Bradley moved, step-by-step, into different management areas in the firm. Jim has been active in marketing and advertising, and after the father's death, he became the president of Bradley Cosmetics. The younger brother, Ed, moved up to become the head of production and administration, and he is the more knowledgeable sibling when it comes to financial matters.

The nature of Bradley Cosmetics has changed since the death of James Bradley from a typical family business to more of an incorporated partnership between Jim and his two children in the business, as one 50% faction, and Ed and his son as the other one-half owner. The two brothers are economic peers, drawing very substantial identical salaries, always having been paid equal bonuses, with essentially equal expense allowances, offices, and both driving company owned Mercedes automobiles.

Jim Bradley has two children, a daughter, Donna, 35 years of age, and a son, Sean, 31. Both children are married and they work in the business. Donna heads up the sizeable sales force that calls on beauty parlor operators, demonstrates and sells Bradley Cosmetics products to them, and sees to it that they have an adequate supply of products on hand, at all times. She is a ball of fire. Sean, who took mostly business courses at college, majoring in accounting, is serving as assistant controller of the corporation. The game plan is for Sean to become principally involved in financial management.

Brother Ed has three children, a son, Pat, age 32, and two daughters, Elizabeth, 30 and Maureen, 27. Pat and Elizabeth are married and Maureen is single. Only Pat is associated with Bradley Cosmetics, overseeing purchasing, packaging and shipping. He is being groomed to be in charge of manufacturing. Elizabeth, the mother of two infants, is married to a young man who is a partner in his father's Chevrolet dealership. She does not work. The youngest child of Ed, Maureen, is a graduate of a well-known law school, with honors, recently admitted to the bar, and presently working as an associate in a local law firm.

Bradley Cosmetics has enjoyed even greater success under the leadership of Jim and Ed Bradley. Annual sales have climbed to $35,000,000, and last year the company made almost $2,000,000, after taxes. At the urging of their accountant, who was worried about the corporation being hit for the penalty tax, because of the failure to pay dividends (discussed in Chapter 5), $200,000 was distributed as a dividend in each of the last four years. Because of the great acceptance of their Top Of The Line cosmetics, the introduction of several new beauty products that really caught on, and the steady increase of the sales of toiletry items, even greater profits in the next few years seem to be assured.

One afternoon, after a round of golf, Jim Bradley sat in the 19th hole of the country club, having a drink with his partner in the foursome, an investment banker named Stu. The young Wall Street executive was telling Jim how tired he was, because he had over-seen, that week, the underwriting of the stock of two corporations that had completed their first sale of shares to the public. Jim Brad-ley posed a lot of questions to Stu, about the amount that the selling stockholders had realized, how the stock was priced for sale, what the process of going public entailed, etc. Finally, he asked directly: "Stu, you know a lot about our business. What would the company be valued at, if our annual net-after-tax earnings were $2,000,000?" Without any hesitation, Stu answered: "It's hard to give an accurate prediction without knowing a lot more about the business, and such things as the company's cash flow, future prospects, and position in the industry. But if you want a ball park, with a net income of $2,000,000, I would guess that your corporation is worth at least $20,000,000."

Jim quickly realized that this meant that his 50% stock interest in Bradley Cosmetics had a value in the neighborhood of $10,000,000, a staggering figure for someone who has only about $75,000 of cash and marketable securities to his name. Even before he showered, Jim called his brother, Ed, and arranged to stop at Ed's house on his way home from the country club. When Jim got to his brother's house, in a very excited tone of voice, he recounted his conversation with Stu. "Do you realize, Ed, that if we sold 30% of our stock, 15% each, with a value of $20,000,000 for the company each of us would get $3,000,000. Even after I paid my tax on the gain, I would have more than $2,000,000 in cash. Isn't that great! I think I'll call Stu and have him come over to the office, and talk to us about how we can sell stock."

Ed, in typical fashion, was cautious in his response. "Hold it, Jim, let's not go so fast. Going public is complicated and expensive, and I'm not so sure we want to have a lot of stockholders poking their noses in our business. We have to think it through carefully, and weigh the pros and cons. I think it's a mistake to get Stu involved at this point. Instead, let's set up a date with Milt (the

company lawyer) and Jack (the corporation's accountant), and talk it
out with them. I'm sure they can give us a lot of background on how
selling shares to the public works, and what the pitfalls may be."
And so, that meeting among Jim, Ed, Milt and Jack was arranged.

TWO KINDS OF OFFERINGS DISTINGUISHED

The first item on the agenda of the conference was an explanation
of the two different ways a privately owned company, like Bradley
Cosmetics, Inc., "goes public." This is a summary of what was
said:- the corporation, Bradley Cosmetics, itself could sell shares to
the public. This puts money into the corporate treasury, which Bradley Cosmetics has no need for. Jim and Ed Bradley will get nothing.
From the investors' standpoint, this sale of stock by the enterprise is
advantageous. The capital of the company is beefed up by the
amounts that are paid for the shares of stock.

"We don't want the corporation to sell shares," exclaimed Jim
Bradley. "The whole purpose for our going public is to put some
cash in our pockets." In a somewhat patronizing manner, Milt, the
lawyer, says: "Of course, you want a secondary offering. However,
we'll have to find out from the underwriter whether Bradley Cosmetics has enough financial substance to support an initial sale of stock
to the public in the form of a secondary offering. Those who purchase shares from the stockholders see their cash enriching only the
owners of the company. They may be concerned about the "bail-out"
implications. For this reason, it is common for an underwriter to
urge that the corporation first market some stock, to be followed in a
few years by a secondary offering."

Ed Bradley is confused. "You keep talking about a secondary
offering, Milt. I thought my brother made it clear to you that we
don't want our sale of stock to be second. We want the first offering
of shares to be made by us." Then comes the explanation. A secondary offering doesn't mean the second public sale. The term is used to
describe a sale of stock to the public by the shareholders rather than
the company. "I guess a sale by the company is the primary offering
and one by the stockholders, themselves, is the secondary." It is
agreed that the only transaction that will be considered is one in
which the individuals sell some of their stock to the public.

ADVANTAGES OF GOING PUBLIC

The motivations for Bradley Cosmetics going public is quite evident. The brothers, Jim in particular, want to sell some of the pieces of paper they hold for cash, taxed at favorable capital gain tax rates. Converting some of the owners' stock into money is the most sought after benefit of going public. Instead of having all paper values, the entrepreneur gets a significant amount of spendable dollars. There are, however, other benefits that the close corporation and its proprietors can realize from going public, dependent, of course, on the company's situation and circumstances.

Building capital for the enterprise

For many close corporations, the opportunity to finance growth with equity, rather than debt, is what pushes them to market stock to the public. This is a direct sale of shares by the company, with the proceeds earmarked for corporate purposes. The Bradley brothers rejected this approach because they had the good fortune of owning a company that had plenty of cash. But many, perhaps most, privately held enterprises are not so lucky. Here are some typical financial problems that call for an influx of capital from the public:

1. The close corporation, perhaps a printing company, is in a capital intensive business. Rapidly improving technology makes existing machinery and equipment obsolete, requiring the company to purchase improved and more expensive models. Financing the purchase of these high cost fixed assets, particularly with higher interest rates, is very burdensome.

2. The "hi-tech" enterprise has staggering research and development costs. The sales forecasts are tremendous if all the bugs can be worked out and the manufacturing process streamlined. Regular money lenders are hesitant to advance large sums, because the company has very limited assets.

3. The business does not have nearly enough working capital to finance its operations. It has to go to the bank every year and borrow more money, to meet the financial demands of the growing enterprise. The bank loans are personally guaranteed by the owners, who are becoming increasingly anxious about how deeply in debt they are at the height of the manufacturing cycle. "If we could only get some money that didn't carry a 14% interest charge, and that we didn't have to pay back."

The sale of stock to the public can give the close corporation debt-free funds to meet these capital needs. New, more efficient machinery and equipment can be acquired, increasing the profitability of the business. Research and development can be stepped up. More working capital can improve the company's ability to capture more of the market with a "hot" product, or to avoid a disaster if a recession sets in. In exchange for giving up some of their interest in the enterprise—but still keeping the major share of the melon and management control—the proprietors bring into the company the needed cash.

Personal satisfaction

Going public provides the owners of close corporations with recognition of their success, in the most desirable manner. They do not have to blow their own horns. The information that must be set out in the prospectus, when the stock of the company is offered for sale, does the bragging for the proprietors.

Jim Bradley, for instance, will have many pleasant daydreams, when he contemplates the idea of Bradley Cosmetics becoming a public company. Imagine the reactions of his friends, when they learn how successful his company is, by seeing the profit figures that will now be public knowledge. And his status as a multimillionaire will be known, without his having to utter one word of self-aggrandizement.

But there is a more personal kind of satisfaction to becoming a public company than the publication of the controlling stockholders' financial success and material wealth. To many proprietors of close corporations, widespread recognition of the company and its accomplishments is an end in itself. It is viewed as the crowning achievement to have "my business" move from its humble beginnings to public corporation status. The owners walk taller. They believe that now "they have made it."

Lawyers can easily understand this. Law firms talk a lot about the change from an association of well-known lawyers in the community to an institution which has existence apart from any individuals. Typical examples are the large so-called Wall Street firms whose well-known names are those of partners who are no longer alive. Achieving institutional status is a goal for most of the partners in the growing legal enterprise. They seek to emulate the standing of these older, respected organizations.

The successful businessman attains some of this kind of prestige when his corporation goes public. It too takes on an institutional character. The owner moves along the same path as the great industrial figures who preceded him. Public recognition is a special status symbol for the Bradleys, whose family name is borne by their widely known company. The importance of this ego kick cannot be measured with exactitude. The decision to go public is always coupled with very practical reasons for taking the step. My gut reaction is that improved identity is a very significant factor in the decision.

Diversification

About 15 years ago I participated in a seminar at which the president of a very large trust company spoke on investment strategy. In the course of his presentation, he confessed that the most successful trust fund his organization ever administered was one where the decedent directed that his holdings in IBM, the only stock that the trust held, were not to be sold. The president said that notwithstanding the tremendous success that this trust realized from keeping all its eggs in one basket, it was a mistake to do this. "The risks" said he, "are simply too great."

But this is the typical situation of the entrepreneur. His interest in the business generally represents the bulk of his wealth, and it is invested in a highly speculative stock. No matter how successful a company may have been, even one with continuing great future prospects, any number of things can happen which can reverse the trend and send the corporation on a fast slide downhill.

Look at Jim and Ed Bradley. They own a business with an estimated value in the neighborhood of $20,000,000. The rest of their assets are minuscule by comparison. Each brother, by selling 15% of his stock to the public, or a total of 30% of the outstanding equity of the company, can realize about $2,400,000, in cash, after taxes. This substantial sum can be used to establish a portfolio of less risky investments. Thereafter, no matter what happens to Bradley Cosmetics, Jim and Ed, and their families, will have enough to live on very comfortably.

This procedure of selling shares to the public reduces the close corporation owner's total dependence on the success of the business. The shift of capital into areas other than the speculative enterprise is the start of diversification for the entrepreneurs. It is akin to cashing in some chips after a successful run at the crap table. Nonetheless, the Bradleys still have plenty at risk even if they dispose of 30% of their stock: a hefty $14,000,000 (70% of $20,000,000). They also continue to have the opportunity of reaping very substantial future appreciation in their Bradley Cosmetics stockholdings, which easily could bring them back to the $20,000,000 investment they had when the corporation went public. But there has been removed from the hazards of a terrible downturn, often attributable to circumstances over which the close corporation proprietor has no control—enough to maintain a good life, no matter what. In addition, further diversification can be achieved, from time to time in the future, by marketing more shares to the public.

Attracting unrelated executives

Attracting capable unrelated executives frequently is cited as a motivation for becoming a public company. The theorem is that talented young executives would prefer to work for a corporation that has stock in the hands of outsiders. In this instance, however, we are talking about a publicly held close corporation where ownership and management are still tied together. The situation is exactly the same as the close corporation which has no stock owned by the public. Why then should the fact that the stock is traded, probably very inactively, make the corporation a much more desirable place to serve as an executive?

I have raised this query with numbers of knowledgeable people, as well as with some unrelated executives working for close corporations. Many of them had accepted the conclusion without really analyzing the premises. Others offered these kinds of answers:

1. "The fact that people saw fit to buy the stock of this company is evidence of its significant growth potential. That is what the investment community expects to happen, when an equity position in an enterprise is marketed. I will have many more opportunities to enlarge my role and increase my compensation in a growing business."

2. The willingness of the controlling stockholders to have stock owned by the public—and to accept the required disclosures and regulations—indicates that they have more forward thinking attitudes. These owners put the well-being of the business ahead of their self-interest. This reflects a more enlightened management, one that will be more accepting of non-family executives at senior levels.

3. The opportunity for an employee to become rich, through stock ownership, is much greater with a corporation that has publicly traded stock. In every community there are the stories of Mr. X or Y, now a multimillionaire, who became, so wealthy because of the stock he got working for a company.

In my opinion, this chance to build capital has the greatest attraction for capable personnel who are charting career paths. The entity has accepted the idea of dealing with outsiders who own an equity interest. Certainly, it would seem to be more tolerable and beneficial to the control group, to have stock in the hands of key employees. The presence of a market for the stock makes employee stock options and stock purchase programs much easier to implement.

Marketing an inactive family member's stock

In Chapter 10, I articulated a deep-seated conviction regarding the ownership of stock of a close corporation by a family member who is not active in the family business. My rule is simple:- don't give stock to children who are not working in the company; and if by chance, the family head has already done so, then arrange for the shares to be bought back.

However desirable this principle may be, a close corporation owner may find it difficult to achieve while still maintaining some modicum of equality among his children. The Bradley family is a good illustration of this difficulty. Jim Bradley has the good fortune of having both of his children, Donna and Sean, working in the business. But Ed Bradley has two daughters, Elizabeth, the housewife-mother, and Maureen, the lawyer, who have no connection with the operations of Bradley Cosmetics. Ed has almost $10,000,000 of personal worth represented by his Bradley Cosmetics stockholdings. His other investments are modest. To provide almost

$7,000,000, which is about two-thirds of the value of his stock—and that number will continue to grow larger—through the medium of life insurance for his two daughters, is not feasible. Creating a class of stock for his daughters, which the corporation can redeem at Ed's death, won't work either. While Bradley Cosmetics is in an excellent cash position, draining the company of this quantum of dollars to buy back some of its stock, could be very detrimental to its financial stability. Moreover, the redemption procedure would probably result in a sizeable reduction in the Ed Bradley family's equity position.

Going public takes away a lot of the strain of giving stock of a family business to a child who is not involved in the management of the company. The stock often becomes income-producing because the corporation starts paying regular dividends as a means of attracting the public to purchase shares. But the real difference is the ability of Ed Bradley's daughters to convert their shares of stock of Bradley Cosmetics into money. After the stock is publicly traded, his daughters can sell shares at a predictable price, from time to time, by calling a broker—or if the number of shares to be sold is very large, through an underwriting handled by an investment banking firm. With prior planning, this ability of children, who are not involved in the business, to sell stock of the now public company, can be accomplished without any adverse effect on the family's voting position. The Bradley brothers, for example, would not want Ed's daughters to be able to sell to outsiders, what could be a significant block of voting stock of Bradley Cosmetics. This voting problem can be handled, as I will explain later on.

The corporation can also assist the family stockholders of the corporation in the marketing of a large number of shares through an underwriting. Is is common to have agreements, under the terms of which the corporation obligates itself to accomplish, and to pay for, all the things that are required for a public offering. This includes such items as filing a registration statement, updating financial material and having all the printing done, the most expensive out-of-pocket costs. All the selling stockholders have to pay for are their legal fees, which are fairly modest since the corporation's lawyer does most of the work, and some other odds and ends.

Getting dollars to pay death taxes

At various places in this book, I have noted the serious liquidity problems of the close corporation, imposed by the need to fund the death taxes of an owner, or the owner's spouse, if full advantage is taken of the unlimited marital deduction when the owner dies. The burden of coming up with the needed tax dollars usually shifts to the corporation, since it is rare that the entrepreneur or his family can accumulate sufficient individual wealth to make any real contribution towards the required amount. Life insurance, financed by the company, is a very important means of providing funds to pay the death tax. But carrying a lot of life insurance can be costly. The crucial reality is that unless steps are taken in advance to prepare for the day of the death tax judgment, the drain on the corporate treasury for these funds may imperil the financial well-being of the entity.

After a corporation goes public, the scene changes dramatically. The estate of a deceased major stockholder has a new avenue for getting money for the payment of death taxes. The estate can sell shares to the public, and use the proceeds of the sale for taxes. It may be that the sale of a large quantity of shares will bring a lower price per share than is reflected by the bid and asked prices for a sale of perhaps maximum of 1,000 shares. But this may not be disadvantageous. Often it is a benefit to have a significant reduction in the price at which the shares are sold to raise the tax money, because the lowered stock valuation will produce a much greater reduction in the amount of the estate taxes that have to be paid.

Other advantages of going public

I have heard suggestions of other advantages of going public. Here are some of them:

1. "Customers prefer to deal with suppliers of substance. A public company has a better image of strength, reliability and continuity."

2. "It's easier to make acquisitions when you have traded stock. You can use shares rather than cash. If you need to raise money to buy another enterprise, you can sell more stock."

3. "Bankers are more comfortable making loans to publicly held corporations. The total financial situation is a matter of record."

I can't evaluate how significant these benefits may be. They seem to me to be add-ons, rather than primary motivations for bringing strangers into the close corporation bailiwick.

There is one additional plus of going public, however, that applies to those entrepreneurs who are significant contributors to charitable causes, and there are lot of them. A great percentage of the business clients that I have dealt with are generous donors to charity. I explained in Chapter 5 that the owner of a privately held company can give shares of stock of the corporation to a pet charity, and get a valuable charitable deduction in computing his income tax liability. However, to make the gift usable by the recipient organization, the business has to redeem the transferred shares. This can hurt the corporation's cash reserves. With a public company, the buy-back doesn't have to occur. The charity can dispose of the stock to the public, through normal market channels.

DISADVANTAGES OF GOING PUBLIC

With the imposing list of benefits of going public, one might think that every close corporation that qualified would break down the doors of the investment bankers to sell shares to the public. But that is not the case. The owners of many eligible entities cling to their private company status. Certain disadvantages of having the public own stock in the enterprise outweigh, for them, the benefits they might otherwise obtain. Let me outline some of these disadvantages.

Disclosure requirements

The first and generally most objectionable aspect of going public is the necessity of disclosing financial and other information about the business and the company. When one or a few individuals, or a family, are the only stockholders, data pertaining to the business is kept totally confidential, except in two instances. First, tax collectors are entitled to receive all information required to evaluate the propriety of the corporation's tax returns. And secondly, institutions that loan the business money, or companies that sell merchandise on credit, have a right to scrutinize financial material and reports.

Many entrepreneurs flatly refuse even to consider the idea of disseminating secrets. For some the attitude may be an expression of their fears about opening up to others. Ed Bradley finds the prospect of giving out detailed material about Bradley Cosmetics much more threatening than his brother, Jim. This may be explained by the difference in personalities. Ed, the more pessimistic in his outlook about life, more secretive, less trustful of people, always sees any change through more frightened eyes than his brother. From his viewpoint, the prospect of disgorging very confidential information that competitors or regulatory bodies, or the tax authorities, may grab hold of, to the disadvantage of Bradley Cosmetics and him, produces genuine anxiety. Jim's reassurance and conviction will probably override Ed's hesitations, as it has done so many times in the history of their association in business. But if Ed were the sole head of the business, with complete control over the choice of whether or not to go public, Bradley Cosmetics would probably remain a private company.

For whatever reasons, the fact remains that most proprietors of successful privately-owned businesses will not run the risk of sharing secrets about their enterprise and themselves with the public. "I'll be damned if the S.E.C. will dictate what I have to disclose to the world. I understand they can make me break down my profitability, product by product. Boy, would my competitors love to have that information." This kind of comment is heard regularly. Advisors cannot allay the concern completely. They can only point to others that have taken the step of becoming a publicly held company, and have prospered. But this kind of counselling is unlikely to overcome the client's convictions against opening up to the general public.

FEAR OF DIMINISHED PREROGATIVES

Early in this book, in describing the nature of the close corporation, I compared the head of the business to a "king." Others, particularly the employees, might change this comparison to "dictator." In any case, one noticeable characteristic of the owner/top manager is his autocratic position. He or she is the boss, calling the shots, occupying the seat of ultimate power. Indeed, most executives believe that taking a strong stand against the entrepreneur, objecting to the manner in which the controlling stockholder exercises his leadership, in short, doing anything to challenge the proprietor's prerogatives is a sure path out the door. This sentiment is shared by most sons and sons-in-law of the head of the family business.

When this "king" or "dictator" contemplates the involvement of public stockholders in his company, and the accompanying supervision of even more bureaucrats, he is not happy. A typical reaction is: "Now, I can run the business as I see fit. I am not answerable to anyone. But if we become a public company, a lot of people will be looking over my shoulder." Some proprietors, contemplating a public offering, have voiced this worry in very concrete terms. They picture a lawyer, acting on behalf of the public stockholders, bringing an action to have the principals account for expense reimbursements and justify fringe benefits they received. Although this is not always a realistic possibility, the level of their concern is very high.

Here is where the advisors' communication ability really pays off. I have found that the key is to encourage the owners of the company to articulate these concerns and to make sure they are faced thoughtfully and in depth. All too often, a knowledgeable corporate lawyer dismisses this issue with a cryptic comment such as: "Don't worry, Ed. I can assure you that you and Jim will be able to do things in the same way after you go public, and nobody will bother you." That is a ridiculous response, the equivalent of telling someone who has anxiety about something, "you have nothing to worry about, because I say so." The job is to take the fears about the consequences of going public, analyze them, and through dialogue demonstrate, in detail, why they will not materialize.

Loss of control

The great notoriety recently achieved by corporate raiders has created a new apprehension about converting to a public company. There is now something like a conditioned reflex: "If our stock is being traded, someone can make a tender offer, snap up the shares held by the public and take over the corporation." The fallacy here is that the amount of stock that a raider might pick up will not be enough to gain control. Invariably, in the first offering of shares less than 50% of the stock of the close corporation is sold to the public. The owners, the family or the incorporated partners, continue to hold the number of shares required to elect directors of their choosing, and to determine all corporate actions. That makes this kind of public company very unattractive to corporate take-over barons.

There is, however, a set of circumstances where voting relationships could be seriously affected by going public. It is illustrated by the Bradley Cosmetics situation. Let us assume that the brothers, Jim and Ed, move ahead with the plan to sell 30% of their stock of the enterprise to the public, 15% each, to get a good hunk of cash in their pockets. Ed, the more worrisome sibling, wakes up to the fact that this public offering may affect the two families' voting equality. He explains to Jim that with 30% of the stock in the hands of the public, each of the two of them, will now hold 35% of the issued shares (one-half of the 70% still in the Bradleys' hands). If one brother is able to acquire 16% of the public's 30%, or join forces with the owners of that amount of stock, he could garner voting control. The prospect of a battle for this control is frightening to both Jim and Ed.

What can be done to prevent this change in the balance of power? The two Bradleys might enter into an agreement assuring the election of an even number of directors, one-half of whom would be selected by Jim Bradley and the other half, by Ed Bradley. Each side would have the right to designate a successor, if either Jim or Ed was unable to serve. In this way, no matter how many shares of stock each family owned, the vote would remain 50-50. This would facilitate subsequent sales of stock by family members, since the dispositions would not imperil their voting position. The enforceability and permitted duration of such an agreement must be checked under the governing laws.

A simpler answer is to market only non-voting common stock. That is, Bradley Cosmetics, before the public offering, would create two classes of common stock, identical in all respects other than one. The Class A stock—and it is always better to have the publicly held stock have the preferred title—would be non-voting. The second class of stock, Class B common, would have the exclusive right to vote. Only the shares without the power to vote would be sold to the public. The existing voting rights would continue unchanged. Many good sized companies have taken this route. To the average investor, who owns a limited number of shares of the "public close corporation," the denial of the right to vote means nothing. He brought his stock knowing full well—and perhaps even desiring—that the insiders would be running and governing the corporation.

The existence of the voting control agreement or the issuance to the public of only non-voting stock, would bar the shares from being traded on the major stock exchanges. They might be ineligible for other reasons, as well. But the chances are that the Bradley brothers would much sooner give up the national exchanges than take a chance of becoming embroiled in a battle for control of Bradley Cosmetics. I believe that it is much wiser to forego listing on a stock exchange, in the interest of preserving the balance of power.

Other disadvantages of going public

There are other disadvantages of being a public company, that are sometimes raised, usually after the fact. Here are some of them:

1. Having stock in the hands of the public calls for greater formalities in governance of the entity. Meetings of stockholders and directors must be held regularly. Gone are the days when major decisions were made at the luncheon table, with no further action. Now the senior executives have to put in many hours preparing for and attending these meetings. All determinations have to be recorded in the corporate minute book. This means more legal fees.

2. Various forms must be prepared and filed with the S.E.C. (the Securities and Exchange Commission). Even with the recent streamlining of the procedures, it takes a good deal of time and effort to meet the requirements. Here again, there will be an increase in the charges of the corporation's lawyer and accountant for preparing these documents.

3. Many arrangements for the use of corporate dollars to serve the controlling stockholders' personal and estate needs will have to be eliminated or curtailed. Travel and entertainment expense allowances and other perquisites are generally reduced. The risk of a disallowance by the Internal Revenue Service now takes on greater consequences in the minds of the principal stockholders. Not only does it produce a tax deficiency, but it could generate a lawsuit by the minority stockholders for misappropriation of corporate funds—which happens very rarely. The use of the corporate treasury for the owners' estate planning is no longer feasible. For example, Jim and Ed Bradley will have to scrap a plan to have Bradley Cosmetics issue preferred stock, which would have been redeemed by the company at death, as a means of putting cash in the hands of their wives.

These complaints are generally aired long after the first public offering, when the benefits that the corporation obtained are downgraded. The money that was raised for use by the business has been spent. Or, if the initial offering of shares was made by the owners themselves, they have conveniently forgotten how much they realized in cash when the company went public. The great complainers about these annoyances, understandably, are the sons and daughters of the selling stockholders, who are now running the company, living with the presence of public stockholders without the consolation of having become rich through the process. The selling stockholders who have dissipated what they got when the stock of the company was originally sold may also be resentful of "what we got into."

PREPARING TO GO PUBLIC

Bradley Cosmetics, Inc. will have to do a number of things to get ready for its first offering of shares to the public. Some of these steps are necessary to comply with the requirements of the S.E.C. But most of them will be taken to make the company stock more attractive to investors.

The underwriter of the stock—the organization that heads up a team of investment banking firms who actually market the stock to the public—plays an important role in delineating the changes that should be made. While these changes are couched as helpful suggestions, most entrepreneurs accept them as gospel. The representative of the underwriter is often treated like a guru who will lead people like the Bradley brothers to fame and fortune, provided that they comply with his teachings. In fairness, most underwriters are very knowledgeable and capable. But hard-bitten entrepreneurs, who are tough on other advisors, no matter how good they are, accept direction from underwriters in a very different fashion. They are meek and submissive. Nobody knows how the investment bankers managed to achieve this aura, but all other professionals dealing with close corporation owners envy them.

Here, then, are some of the more common things that must be done, before a company like Bradley Cosmetics has its initial offering of stock to the public:

The financials

A crucial factor in evaluating a corporation that is going public for the first time is the reliability of its financial information. The investing public wants to be assured that the balance sheet of the enterprise is accurate, and even more important, that the net earnings for the last few years are authentic. Proper presentation of financial data is also the main concern of regulatory bodies such as the S.E.C.

When a corporation has certified financial statements, there's no problem. Fortunately, Ed Bradley listened to the advice of a partner in the firm of accountants engaged by Bradley Cosmetics, and agreed to have certified statements prepared. This will pay off when the company goes public. But if the close corporation does not have certified financial reports, particularly where inventory figures have been submitted by management, the financials have to be reconstituted. As I pointed out earlier in this book, the absence of reliable inventory figures means that the gross profit on annual sales cannot be measured with certainty. Since the cost of goods sold in any fiscal year is the total of the inventory at the beginning of the year, plus purchases made during the year, less the inventory at the end of the year, management's inventory numbers, if they are inaccurate, can distort the final profit figure.

There are methods of adjusting uncertified financial statements, so that they comply with the requirements of the S.E.C. Nevertheless, the knowledgeable investor and the investment banking community are wary of these after-the-fact revisions. Their greatest worry is that a nice trend of enlarging annual net earnings may not be correct. Some of the profits from one year might properly belong to another period.

Combining all related companies

Let us picture that a number of years ago, when Bradley Cosmetics introduced its line of toiletries, someone came up with an income tax idea. A separate corporation, Fashion Toiletries Corp., was organized to market these products, and some of the stock of the new entity was given to the children of Ed and Jim Bradley. Then Fashion Toiletries elected to be taxed as a Subchapter S corporation, which means the corporation paid no federal income tax on its profits. The stockholders paid tax on the earnings of Fashion Toiletries, and then were able to draw the dollars out of the company, tax-free. This was a great way to get some of the net income of the combined enterprise into the hands of the two families, with a single tax on those profits and with the children's shares being taxed at lower rates.

Can shares of Bradley Cosmetics be offered to the public while Fashion Toiletries is maintained as a private company? The answer is no. No responsible underwriter will sell shares of the primary company to the public if that means excluding the public from sharing in the income of related entities, since the opportunities for fleecing the outsiders would be too great. Moreover, the propriety of every transaction between the corporations under common control would be suspect and a number of suits would probably be brought by the minority stockholders of the primary entity.

All of the companies that are part of what is truly one business will have to be amalgamated. In our example, Fashion Toiletries will need to be merged into Bradley Cosmetics. The shareholders of Fashion Toiletries will receive stock of Bradley Cosmetics, in exchange for their Fashion Toiletries stockholdings—probably, nonvoting common.

What about the main manufacturing plant used by Bradley Cosmetics, which is owned by Jim and Ed Bradley, individually? That is not objectionable, provided that the corporation is assured of long term possession at rentals that are not at the whim of the major stockholders. I usually suggest that the reasonableness of the rent be backed by an appraisal done by a recognized expert.

Recomposition of board of directors

Another important step in getting ready for the public offering is the recomposition of the board of directors. Since the organization of Bradley Cosmetics, the Bradley brothers and their wives have been the directors of the company. Some solid citizens should be elected to supplement the owners, spouses and children. Bankers, well respected businessmen, outstanding lawyers, key management people, and the like, lends substance to the company. The addition of these new directors will mean additional formality and the payment of directors' fees. But the improvement in the corporation's image will substantially outweigh those negatives.

Other preparatory steps

Other things may have to be done. A good management team, including successors to the more senior executives of the close corporation, should be in place. If the company's success is dependent on one or two older stockholders, investing in the company becomes less attractive. This is not a problem in the case of Bradley Cosmetics, because there are three younger family members who have significant and varied roles in the business. There is Donna Bradley, who is in charge of beauty parlor sales; her brother, Sean, who is involved in financial management; and their cousin, Pat Bradley, Ed's son, who now supervises purchasing, packing and shipping, and is being groomed for the manufacturing vice-presidency. In addition, there is a corps of very competent unrelated executives.

When there is depth and breadth of talented management personnel, a company's prospects are much brighter. Its stock should command a better price when the corporation goes public. Many investment bankers, when asked what the most important criterion is for deciding whether a company's stock is a good investment, will reply: "The first three criteria are management, management, management!" Having the top executives, particularly non-stockholders, under contract is another plus.

The close corporation may also have to be recapitalized prior to the sale of stock to the public. If Bradley Cosmetics had gone forward with its plan and issued a sizeable amount of preferred stock, the underwriter would probably suggest that the preferred stockholdings be converted back into common stock. Sometimes long-term debt securities, or warrants or options to purchase shares, are issued as part of the offering of common stock. I have participated in some offerings where a long term institutional loan was put in place before the sale of stock.

TIMING THE OFFERING

Having taken the necessary steps in preparation, Bradley Cosmetics is clearly ready to go public. Jim and Ed Bradley can realize $6,000,000 in-pocket (before taxes), $3,000,000 each, by selling only 30% of the stock of the corporation. If they had the offering five years ago, when the value of the company was much less, the only way they could get the same $6,000,000 would have been to sell more than half the outstanding stock, something they would have been unwilling to do.

I learned about the importance of this kind of timing many years ago. A very prominent underwriter was bought in to discuss the feasibility and desirability of having the owners of one of our close corporation clients sell stock to the public. He was a very close personal friend of one of my partners. Frankly, that was the only reason he took the time to meet with us. The underwriter had received and studied the company's financial statements covering the five preceding years. My partner had filled him in about the business. After some discussion, the eminent gentleman gave his opinion:

> There is no question in my mind that you could sell $3,000,000 of stock to the public. But you would have to give up about 40% of your equity to get that.
>
> Your profits are going up. The prospects for considerable expansion of your annual after-tax earnings, in the next few years, are excellent. Also, it is my opinion that the capitalization of earnings rate is going to increase.
>
> My advice is to put off the secondary offering for three or four years. The higher net earnings per share, plus a larger price-earnings ratio, could mean that you would only give up 20% of your equity for the $3,000,000—rather than 40%.
>
> The postponement could make your stockholdings, after the public sale, worth $3,000,000 more. That is a lot of money. You are relatively young men. If you need dollars for a house or a boat, borrow them.

The advice was taken. The underwriter's predictions came true. In fact, the two stockholders were able to market 30% of the stock of the corporation for $5,000,000.

The two stage approach

Some enterprises go public in two stages. First there is a private placement. Venture capitalists take an equity position or a debt convertible into equity. This is often done by corporations that are not yet ready to have a public offering. In other instances, entrepreneurs feel that having a good investment banking firm, as well as some of their customers, become financially involved with the corporation, will be a big plus when the stock is ultimately sold to and traded by the public.

There are many capitalists who are interested in investing in private companies with significant potential for growth. Interestingly, some large corporations with widely diffused stockholdings set aside funds for this purpose. These investors are looking for sizeable appreciation if the business is successful. They rely on the judgment of a new kind of investment advisor, a venture capital expert, or an investment banking firm. Usually the venture capitalist or investment banking organization itself acquires an equity position.

The second step is the "pay off." The stockholders, including the venture capitalists, sell stock to the public. This can be done on a pro rata basis or by giving the outsiders some priority. They can sell whatever number of shares they choose, including all of their stockholdings.

The investment climate

The timing of the close corporation's first offering of stock can sometimes be adversely affected by general market conditions. For example, the owners of the private enterprise may be ready to sell, and the public offering can be accomplished, but the investing public may not be willing to pay a good price for a new issue of equity stock. It might be that shares of giant corporations, those used to compute the Dow-Jones average, are trading at prices that reflect a low multiple of the corporations' earnings. Not too long ago, investors were only willing to pay about ten times earnings for the stock of ostensibly solid companies. That is why Stu, the investment banker, sitting with Jim Bradley in the 19th hole of the country club, estimated that Bradley Cosmetics' $2,000,000 of net-after-tax earnings would produce a value, in the neighborhood of $20,000,000, for its outstanding stock. A return to the markets of the late 60s and early 70s—when prices of thirty times earnings were commonplace—would make going public a lot more attractive. With that kind of pricing, the value of Bradley Cosmetics would be approximately $60,000,000, and the Bradley brothers would realize $18,000,000, rather than $6,000,000, if they sold 30% of their stock to the public.

Another important timing ingredient has to do with the line of business that the close corporation wanting to go public is in. There is a big advantage in marketing the stock of a company that is now in a glamour industry. Unfortunately, hot industries come and go. At various times, electronics, pharmaceuticals, computer related products and systems, health care, medical testing, genetic engineering, satellites and micro-technology have been viewed as probable investment winners. If the first sale of stock to the public takes place at a time when the public is captivated by the potential of the corporation's product or service, the sellers will get a better price for their shares.

A critical issue for the close corporation seeking a public sale of stock is the equity investment attitude of the individual investors. They are the predominant buyers of the stock of an enterprise making its inaugural offering. Large institutional purchasers of stock shy away from over-the-counter securities with a thin market. They feel insecure about the ability to get out of the holding without driving the price down significantly. Institutions with a large block of shares of an over-the-counter company have found that the only real potential purchaser, at a respectable price, is the company itself.

THE PROCESS OF GOING PUBLIC: A TEN STEP SUMMARY

Even in a situation where all factors affecting the close corporation's first public offering are favorable, and the company's financial data is in good shape, it takes four to five months between the owners' decision to move ahead—"Ed," says Jim Bradley, "let's do it"—and the day when the underwriters hand over the proceeds of sale. This time span is attributable to the lengthy process which must be carried out to effect the initial sale of the close corporation's stock to the public. The process can be summarized as follows*:

1. An underwriter must be selected, and the compensation arrangements worked out.

2. The marketing plan has to be developed, including a determination of the probable offering price. This is a key consideration for the sellers of the shares.

3. A registration statement has to be prepared and filed with the S.E.C. This is a major task, and a lot of time, perhaps a

---

* I am indebted to my partner, Ellen Kulka, for this summary and her other contributions to this Chapter.

month or 6 weeks goes into it. The aim of the S.E.C. is to make sure that complete and accurate information about the company is given to the public, so that investors can make an intelligent decision whether or not to purchase shares. A tightrope has to be walked to comply with this objective. There must be full disclosure about the company, its business, its position in the industry, including all negative factors, even contingent ones. But puffing and overstatement must be avoided like a plague.

The close corporation owners are kept busy in connection with the registration of the stock. The Bradley brothers, Jim and Ed, the individuals who have the most complete knowledge about the corporation's business, will have to attend many conferences with lawyers and accountants. Because accuracy is so important, Ed Bradley, the most capable financial and administrative person in the company, will be very much involved, back at the company offices, in garnering and verifying information.

4. The "clean up" of the corporation has to be completed. A recapitalization and merger of related companies may have to be accomplished. Minutes, leases and other documents must be updated. Employment contracts may have to be prepared. Inappropriate arrangements will have to be terminated.

5. Drafts of the registration statement must be circulated and reviewed by underwriter, counsel to the underwriter, the company and its lawyers and accountants. As comments are received, the text is changed.

6. The underwriter, the attorneys and the accountants must examine the various financial data with "due diligence." This means that they have the responsibility of verifying items of information that the corporation's representatives have submitted. Questionnaires calling for formal confirmation by the corporation's officers and directors are delivered. If any troublesome issues arise in connection with this due diligence, there are face-to-face meetings to consider them.

7. State "blue sky registrations" must be completed. Many states, notwithstanding the existence of Federal regulation through the S.E.C., insist on their own registration, before any securities can be sold in the state. Each has a bureau of registration, or some equivalent, with its own rules and regulations. In essence, the state is saying: "We will protect the citizens of our state against deception. The S.E.C. approval is not enough."

8. The S.E.C. has to review the registration statement and issue its comments. This can take another four to six weeks.

9. Right after the S.E.C. comments are received, the final meeting between the selling stockholders and the underwriter is held. An amendment to the registration statement, responding to the points made by the S.E.C., must then be filed by the corporation. This can be done by a competent securities lawyer within a few days after the receipt of the S.E.C. comments.

10. Now the stage is set for the crucial decisions. When will the sale take place? At what price will the shares be offered to the public? When these issues are resolved, a final pricing amendment and a request for acceleration of effectiveness are submitted to the S.E.C. The registration thereafter becomes effective. The shares are purchased by the underwriters, and the offering to the public commences. Jim and Ed Bradley will now get their money.

ROLE OF THE UNDERWRITER

The key figure in the going public story is the underwriter. The role of the underwriter is much more substantial than just acting as the broker of the stock—particularly in the case of the initial offering. The underwriter structures the offer. He prices the deal and directs changes in corporate practices to make the company more attractive. A representative of the underwriter often serves as a director of the corporation.

Frequently the underwriting firm and the corporation develop very close continuing ties. A member of the underwriting firm becomes a special financial advisor to the enterprise. The underwriter's know-how and contacts are used for a variety of needs. The underwriter may also make a market for the company's stock, thereby helping to maintain a representative price for the corporation's shares, and facilitating subsequent sales by the owners and members of their families.

Some of the top underwriters may not be available to the close corporation making its first public offering, since the amount involved may be too small to capture their interest. However, a lot of the smaller and less well-known underwriters are very capable. In any case, the owners should shop around for an underwriter. They should meet with candidates and interview them. Certainly, the Bradley brothers should not choose Stu's firm, just because Stu is a good golfing companion. A good way to get leads about underwriters is by talking to friends or acquaintances whose companies have public stockholdings.

The process of engaging an underwriter is often commenced by the execution of a non-binding letter of intent. Either side can end the relationship with no obligation to the other, except that the letter of intent often requires the corporation to pay certain expenses of the underwriter whether or not a public offering is actually consummated. The letter may also establish certain conditions the underwriter expects the company to meet, if the offering is to go forward. It may grant the underwriter a right of first refusal for any subsequent equity capital offerings by the company. It is, at best, a "moral" commitment by both the company and the underwriter.

There are two basic types of underwriting: a "firm commitment" underwriting and a "best efforts" underwriting.

Firm commitment

A firm commitment means the underwriter agrees to purchase a specified number of shares of stock and resell them to the public. The undertaking is subject to certain customary "outs," which can be exercised just before the effective date of the sale to the public. The underwriter buys the stock at a discount from the price at which the stock is to be offered to the public. This spread is the principal compensation for the underwriter.

An underwriter, in this kind of committed purchase, usually acts on behalf of a syndicate of other broker/dealers. This makes the marketing of the shares easier, since each member of the syndicate can solicit its customers. The identity of the participants in the syndicate is listed in an advertisement—called a "tombstone"— which is published in a major newspaper when the selling starts.

Best efforts

In a "best efforts" underwriting, there is no commitment by the underwriter to purchase the stock. The underwriter merely agrees to do its best to market the shares. In this kind of underwriting, the underwriter serves as the agent for the sellers—the close corporation and/or its stockholders. For these services, the underwriter is paid a specified percentage of the price at which the stock is sold. A best efforts deal indicates some doubt on the part of the underwriter that the shares of the company, going public for the first time, can be sold easily at the offering price. With a business as sound and substantial as Bradley Cosmetics, an underwriter should be willing to make a firm commitment, rather than hedging with a best efforts understanding.

Often in a best efforts arrangement, there is an agreement that the underwriter will sell all the stock being offered, within a stated time period, or none will be sold. This is known as a "best efforts, all or nothing" underwriting. Some advisors believe this arrangement serves to maximize the underwriter's selling efforts. The underwriter only gets paid if the entire issue is sold out.

There are other varieties of best efforts underwritings. They are shaped to meet the then existing circumstances of the close corporation and the public market. One has been tagged a "minimum-maximum" underwriting. Here the underwriter agrees to try to sell not less than a specified amount of stock within a period of time; and no more than a greater number of shares in a longer time period.

THE OFFERING PRICE

How much the shares of stock will be sold for is of primary importance to the close corporation proprietors, when they consider becoming a public company. The Bradleys really got motivated to move ahead with this major step when they realized they could get $6,000,000 by selling only 30% of their stockholdings. After recapitalizing the corporation by increasing the number of outstanding shares to 1,000,000, the offering price for the 300,000 shares to be sold to the public will have to be about $23 per share, in order for the two brothers to receive their $6,000,000 after deducting the underwriter's compensation and all costs. A lower price means getting less dollars or giving up more of their equity in Bradley Cosmetics.

Because of the vital significance of the price determination, Jim and Ed Bradley will be upset when the representative of the underwriter makes it clear he will be happy to discuss the parameters of the probable offering price, but he will not fix it in advance. Entrepreneurs are often befuddled and annoyed by the underwriter's unwillingness to fix the price at which the stock will be sold, even in the case of a firm commitment underwriting. The likelihood is that Jim Bradley, frustrated by the underwriter's position, will say something like this: "When a customer wants to know what I am going to charge him, I can't tell him: 'It depends on what the market is when the goods are delivered.' Why do the underwriters expect to get away with that?"

The answer is that the market for securities is much more volatile than the markets for products. The swings in stock prices can be significant in a short period. Quotations can drop appreciably in one day, if there is bad economic news, threatening world events, or some other kind of development that has a bad portent for the future. The underwriter cannot accept these risks over the long period of time between the start of the going public process, and the moment when the shares may be sold, since it has no control over the price. The investing public determines whether stock prices go up or down. And stock prices can also be moved in one or another direction by brokers, investment advisors, publications, hunches or what-have-you. By being able to delay the price-fixing until just before the stock is marketed, the sellers may benefit. This flexibility enables an underwriter to fix a fair price, without feeling financially imperiled. If there were insistence on a definite selling price, at the start of the process, every underwriter would have to "low ball" to prevent insolvency.

ROLE OF THE ATTORNEY AND THE ACCOUNTANT

The other important players, when a close corporation goes public, are the attorney and accountant. The lawyer serves as the master strategist and the coordinator of efforts. Handling the legal aspects of the initial marketing of stock is not a job for the general practitioner. It demands very special knowledge, expertise, experience and judgment.

The accountant for the close corporation also plays a crucial role. Public acceptance of the company depends, to a large extent, on the company's financial condition and fiscal future. The price at which the stock is sold is measured by the earnings per share. Adjustments may have to be made to past years' numbers, because of deviations from the accounting standards set by the S.E.C. Everyone is relying on the accuracy of the financial information prepared by the accountant.

Years ago, underwriters pushed to displace the close corporation's accountant, if the accounting firm did not have national recognition and prominence. The theory was that "things will go more smoothly with the S.E.C. and the investors will trust their figures." This attitude was troublesome for close corporation proprietors who tend to rely heavily on the company's accountant. Sometimes a partner in the former firm of accountants had to be brought into the business as a financial officer.

Today, medium-sized firms, and even some small ones that have developed the capability, remain in place as the accountant for the corporation. I have seen many of these non-big eight accounting organizations that do this public offering work very well. Their lack of worldwide image has not hampered the public's willingness to trade in the company's stock.

This change in attitude about the identity of the accountant may be attributable, in part, to the notoriety given the litigation involving well-known companies that run into financial difficulties. Invariably, the big accounting firm is joined as a defendant in these lawsuits and charged with the failure to do its auditing job properly. In fairness, this involvement of the major accounting firm may be attributable to its having "deep pockets." There is a much better chance of recovering money from the very substantial accountant than the financially troubled corporation or its officers.

COST OF GOING PUBLIC

What does all this cost? A lot! Fortunately, the corporation can pay the major part of the expenses, even though the stockholders are selling the shares and getting the money. The corporation can make these outlays without any adverse income tax consequences to the individuals. Let me highlight the significant expenditures, starting with the underwriter's compensation. The underwriting cash discount, or cash commission, on a new issue generally ranges from 7%

to 10% of the public offering price. The maximum amount of direct and indirect underwriting compensation is regulated by the NASD (National Association of Securities Dealers).

The three largest additional expenses are legal and accounting fees and printing costs. Legal fees for the first offering generally will be between $55,000 and $115,000, with $75,000 to $100,000 being typical. This amount includes not only the preparation of the registration statement itself, but also all of the corporate work, housecleaning and other detail which is occasioned by the public offering process.

Accounting fees can vary significantly. The crucial factors are: (1) the complexity of the business; (2) whether the financial statements to be included in the registration statements have been audited in the normal course; and (3) the extent to which the independent accountants may be involved in the development of financial and other information to be included in the registration statement. If there have been no prior audits, and new accountants are engaged at the time of the offering, fees of $65,000 and higher would not be out of line.

Printing expenses for registration statements and various underwriting documents typically range up to $100,000. Larger charges are not unusual. Overall printing costs are subject to many variables: How long is the prospectus? What is the extent of the updating required between the original filing and the final printing—because of stale financial statements, S.E.C. comments or other intervening developments? How many copies are required? Are the alterations made by the parties excessive?

There are, of course, many miscellaneous costs. The S.E.C. has a filing fee of .02% of the maximum offering price of all the shares of stock to be sold. There may be original issue and transfer taxes, the fees to a transfer agent and registrar, "Blue Sky expenses," and a host of other out-of-pocket disbursements.

LIFE AFTER THE PUBLIC OFFERING

After the public offering, Jim and Ed Bradley will be in much better financial positions; and neither they nor their children who are active in the company will see any meaningful change in their business lives. The two families will continue to control and direct the operations and affairs of the corporation, without interference from the outside stockholders. The principals may be a little more careful about their perquisites and travel and entertainment expenses—at least for a little while after going public. Because Bradley Cosmetics has outside stockholders and must now do some reporting to the S.E.C., more formalities in the governance of the entity will be observed. But it is unlikely that any of the fears about people sticking their noses in the operations of the company will materialize. The basic character of the enterprise, and its management, control and human relations problems, will continue unchanged after the sale of shares to the public.

SALE OF THE BUSINESS 16

Imagine a close corporation that is conducting a thriving business. After paying the owners substantial salaries and fringe benefits, the company nets $250,000 a year, after taxes. The entrepreneurs take a lot of time off, vacationing and relaxing. They are living "high off the hog." One day, the community learns that the business has been sold. A lot of eyebrows are raised. "If I had a gold mine like that, I'd never sell out!" "Why should Bob, who is coining money and can still play golf three times a week, want to give up the business?"

There is no simple answer to this inquiry. The motivations for such a sale are varied. It often happens that the most significant reason is not readily apparent. The proprietor, himself, may not be able to identify with certainty the forces that are triggering the sale. Indeed, the decision whether or not to give up a profitable business is rarely a black or white issue. Invariably, there are advantages and disadvantages to be weighed and considered. The entrepreneur struggles with the plusses and minuses, until one day, his mental scale tips heavily in favor of a disposition. At that point, the commitment to sell is made.

HAROLD HUNTER'S BOMBSHELL

I remember well Harold Hunter's decision to sell his very successful business. Harold was in his mid 40's, married, with two sons, 12 and 9. He had taken over a small maintenance business, Hunter Maintenance, Inc., which his father started. The corporation did window cleaning and janitorial services for industrial plants and commercial establishments. Harold combined two talents that are not

often found in one person. He was a fabulous salesman and a wizard
at production efficiency and cost control. Through internal growth
and acquisitions, Harold Hunter built Hunter Maintenance into a
large volume, highly profitable company.

Hunter Maintenance's accountant and I were doing some estate
planning work for Harold. We developed what we thought was a
good estate plan and we met with Harold at his office to finalize
certain aspects of it. He complimented us on a job well done and
invited us to lunch. At his favorite restaurant, where a table was
always reserved for him, he delivered the bomb shell. "I have decided to sell the business. My timetable is to get out next year."

The accountant recovered from the shock faster than I did.
"Harold, why do you want to sell? You're a young man and Hunter
Maintenance is growing by leaps and bounds. If you hold off selling
for five more years, the company will be worth much more."

Harold smiled wanly. He then delivered his response, which was
so full of emotion that even he, who usually maintained remarkable
composure, could not suppress it:

"Gentlemen, do you know how I realized that I'm rich? Any man
who can personally guarantee almost $3,000,000 worth of his compa-
ny's debts has to be wealthy. But that's not the way I want to be
affluent.

"My idea is that a man is rich when he has enough money to do
anything he wants, without being concerned about what it costs.
That's not my situation. While I live well, the dollars are in Hunter
Maintenance, not in my pockets.

"I have been worried sick about the business for a long time now. I
find myself losing sleep when a good customer complains about our
work, or tells me he can get the job done cheaper and just as well by
another firm. The loss of an account panics me.

"It has even ruined my golf game. I am irritable with Barbara and
the kids. My patience with people in the office is bad.

"The final straw is the stomach trouble I developed. I thought I
had an ulcer or something. But after a whole batch of tests and seeing
a specialist, that was ruled out. The diagnosis is that it's stress-
related.

"So, I'm calling it quits. My guess is that if I sell I can net, after
taxes, at least $5 million or $6 million. That should take care of us all
very well."

After I digested this obviously heart felt declaration, I asked
Harold what he would do after the business was sold.

"Milt, when I told Barbara my decision, she asked me the same question. The truth is I don't know. Maybe I'll work for the purchaser for a while. I may get more seriously involved in sculpting. Play more golf. It's possible that I'll go back to school.

"The one thing I know, though, is that I can't go on the way I am now. It's not that I'm overworked. I simply can't stand the constant apprehension, because so much of my bread and butter is tied to the success of Hunter Maintenance."

Harold Hunter did what he said he would. The business was sold about 18 months later. He realized even more than he had projected. Harold was employed by the entity that acquired Hunter Maintenance. That didn't work out. He and his family relocated to the west coast. The last time I had contact with him, about ten years ago, he was golfing, sculpting, and trying to write a book. But he seemed a lot happier.

No one relating to Harold Hunter in business would have sensed the depth of his concerns. I certainly did not. That experience was a very valuable one for me. It made me appreciate how highly personalized the attitudes of successful entrepreneurs can be regarding the enterprise they are involved in. One can find his greatest gratification and pleasure at the office. To sell this expression of himself would be unthinkable. To another, the business may be the source of his most serious anxieties and unrest. A sale is viewed by him as an emancipation. In between these poles lies a broad spectrum of attitudes.

FACTORS CONSIDERED IN A DECISION TO SELL

There are a number of factors that can lead to the sale of a close corporation business. Let me describe some of them:

Avoidance of further risk

It should always be kept in mind that the owner of the close corporation risks his entire equity every day. The earnings of the business are plowed back. More capital may be required, which means increased borrowing. The pressure may become unbearable. Our now deceased senior partner, Herbert Hannoch, had a saying about this: "The difference between 0 and $1 million is $1 million.

The difference between $10 million and $11 million is also $1 million. But a man who takes the same risks to go from $10 million to $11 million, as he did to go from 0 to $1 million, is a fool."

However correct this saying may be, the entrepreneur cannot honor it. So many businessmen would like to stay just where they are. But they know in their bones that an enterprise either grows or shrinks. It cannot stand still. Even a very successful close corporation must keep expanding. The owners have to sink more and more money into the enterprise. What is the effect of this constant quest for growth? The concentration of the entrepreneur's wealth in the business keeps increasing. This makes the good life for him and his family dependent on the well-being of the company. If the business bubble bursts, the entrepreneur is in serious trouble.

Every day we read about major enterprises that are in serious financial difficulty. Economists predict recessions, run-away inflation, and escalating interest rates. Competition has become fierce, stimulated by an influx of foreign products. Today's entrepreneur has plenty to worry about. So many risks and so little control! If the entrepreneur is older, he or she may no longer be "lean and hungry." In the early stages of the business there was a lot to gain and very little to lose. Now, the situation is reversed. The owner can lose a great deal, while an increase in value of the business might mean very little.

The sale of the business is viewed as a solution to these gnawing fears. A number of clients have explained it to me like this: "I can get a lot of money for the business, and my family and I will be financially secure. We will have enough income to live well."

Product liability and adulteration

Product liability and adulteration produce special anxieties for the owners of close corporations in certain industries. Here again, the notoriety attending many situations puts fear in the owners' hearts. They are positive that their companies could not survive developments such as the asbestosis claims that put Johns-Manville in bankruptcy, or the Tylenol episode, which Johnson & Johnson with its great resources and marketing brilliance was able to handle.

Insurance can help meet some of the adverse consequences of product liability or adulteration claims. The liability coverage is now very costly and some amount of self-insurance may be required, because of substantial deductibles. But insurance cannot offset the biggest loss—the destruction of product goodwill. That is what brings the close corporation to its knees. Selling the business is seen as a way to escape these perils.

Absence of involved family members

A very common reason for the disposition of a business is the lack of involvement by younger family members. The father has developed a good company. Now he's on in years. None of his children have seen fit to work for the corporation. Because dad can't attract good management—or because he doesn't know how to delegate responsibility—he finds that running the operation has become onerous.

A good illustration of this problem might be Don Rogers' corporation, Speciality Products, a mail-order house. Don was 63 years old. His wife, Anne, had been the bookkeeper and office manager in the early stages of the business. Now she was retired. Their two sons were professional people, one a doctor, and the other, a lawyer. Their daughter was married to an automobile dealer.

Speciality Products conducted a successful mail-order business. It had an extensive customer list and a host of items. Because Don Rogers resisted automation and computerization, most things were done manually. Filling the orders, monitoring the shipping, and keeping the billing records were tedious tasks. Anne had been nagging Don to take more time off from the plant. "Why do you have to spend so much time working? Now that the kids are all grown and on their own we should go away more and spend more time at the club!"

Don Rogers' answer was that he had no one who could "watch the store," while he was gone. Anne's retort was: "Hire somebody good. Pay him a good salary. You could even afford to overpay, so long as you get a person who could take charge during your absence."

Don tried. He went through three very qualified individuals, in succession. His criticism of them was often picayune. I remember one very distinctly: "The guy never turns off the lights when he leaves." If the second in command showed any initiative, or tried to streamline the procedures, Don resented it. In truth, he did not know how to interact with senior employees. And so, the first one was fired. The next two quit. At that point, Don acknowledged to his wife that he did not have the temperment to turn over any real responsibility or authority to "a young turk." "The only way I'll slow down is if the business is sold." And that's what happened.

Being "fed up"

Sometimes a business is sold because the principals have "had it." They are fed up with the repetitiveness and boredom of their vocation. The operations of a lot of close corporations are not stimulating or intellectually challenging. The better organized the company, the less the demands are on the owners. Many of them get bored. They seek fulfillment in other activities like community or philanthropic service.

This phenomenom is seen most often in the second generation of ownership. The founding father has such a strong attachment to the corporation that it is a vital part of his being. He built it from scratch. During this period of growth, there was excitement galore. All kinds of obstacles had to be overcome. It is dad's creation. He has little inclination to part with something that means so much to him.

His children, on the other hand, have very different feelings about the enterprise. They may have been pressured into joining the company. Their subordination to their father is regularly brought home to them. It is his company, not theirs—even if they have been given part of the equity. Dad runs the show and the children do what he tells them to. They have very little sense of accomplishment or real contribution.

Then dad gets old, or retires, or dies. The children seize the opportunity to convert their stockholdings into cash. This will provide them with enough income so that they can pursue a career which has much more appeal, without enduring any economic deprivation.

I have seen the offspring of some entrepreneurs become social workers. Others got advanced degrees in psychology. One son, I recall, became a brilliant physicist and joined the faculty of a well known university. A few practiced law or became teachers. Then there were those who went into very small businesses such as running a travel agency or framing pictures. A number became real estate investors.

This is a powerful attraction: to work in a field that you really enjoy, without worrying about how much income your labors will produce. From time to time during my legal career, usually when the world was kicking me around, I fantasized about being in such circumstances.

Inability of children to manage the business

Perhaps the most unpleasant reason for selling occurs when the head of the family concludes that his offspring can't properly manage the business—and there is not a good enough team of unrelated executives who can do so. A father might simply not have enough confidence in his children's ability to turn over this very valuable asset to their control. Of course, the father is often the person who stunted his children's management development by dominating them, refusing to give them responsibility or authority, and carping more about their performance than that of other employees. Then, having thwarted them, dad delivers the *coup de grace*. He sells the business out from under them.

I have been privy to a few of these situations. In only one did the father try to camouflage the motivation for the sale. In the others the family head let the sons know that their lack of competence was the cause. This was a bitter pill for them to accept. It hurts a lot when you are branded a failure by your father. Unfortunately, a decision to sell in these circumstances usually makes sense. If there is no competent successor management, a sale when the enterprise is doing well is prudent. Delay can mean a drastic reduction in profitability and a substantial reduction in the ultimate sales price.

Whatever the reason for selling the business, the seller must be prepared to explain it. Potential purchasers will be probing for the real reason behind the owner's offer. They want to make sure that the owners are not unloading because of pessimism about future prospects, or because of serious problems.

FINDING A PURCHASER

How does one find a purchaser for the business? A simple way is to put an ad in *The Wall Street Journal* or some other major newspaper. The trouble with this method is that you can be overwhelmed with responses. One of our clients got almost 300 inquiries. He started to screen them, to determine which ones were real possibilities, but finally he threw up his hands, realizing that he would have to spend much more time on it than he could afford.

Business brokers are sometimes engaged to sell a company. The effective broker usually has a relationship with a number of companies looking for acquisitions. In some instances, these entities seeking businesses compensate the broker, rather than the seller. Consequently, it is important that the terms of the broker's engagement are clearly spelled out. Commissions should only be payable if the deal closes. If the purchase price payments are to be made in installments, commissions should be paid at the same rate. If the broker wants an "exclusive," which means he alone can offer the business for sale, there should be an explanation of what efforts he will make to justify this arrangement. The time period for the "exclusive" should be kept within reasonable limits. A wise businessman will realize his inexperience in negotiating an arrangement with a business broker, and will turn to his lawyer for help.

Many times, an entrepreneur who wants to sell his business will communicate his desire to a major company in the industry, or to a well known conglomerate. This contact can be direct or indirect. The indirect approach means planting a seed with an executive, who can see that the idea gets before the right people in the organization. Lawyers, accountants and bankers can be helpful in producing buyers. Many of these professionals have clients or customers who may actively be looking for expansion through acquisitions.

There are other potential purchasers. Some senior executives can get together with venture capitalists and arrange a leveraged buyout, or an ESOP (Employees' Stock Ownership Plan) can become the buyer. Financing for these deals comes from a bank or insurance company.

KEEPING QUIET ABOUT THE SALE

Many owners who want to sell are worried about the broadcast of that information. They don't want the trade to think that the corporation is in trouble and that the business is being peddled. They are afraid that competitors will use the publicity about a sale to hurt the business or that customers may hesitate to place orders for fear that the people they have relied on, for many years, will no longer be in charge. They worry that suppliers may insist on faster payment of their bills or that key employees may become uneasy about the change in top management.

It is very difficult to attract purchasers and keep secret the fact that the business is up for sale. But some things can be done to soft-peddle the intention to sell:

1. The fewer people who know about the owner's intention to sell, the greater the chance of keeping a lid on the contemplated disposition. Friends and relatives, in particular, should not be told. The entrepreneur's best buddy will only tell one person, perhaps a spouse, in confidence of course, who will tell only one other person—and a week later, the close corporation proprietor will scratch his head, trying to figure out how the whole community knows of his plan to sell out.

2. Confidentiality can be helped greatly, if the corporation's lawyer or accountant, a professional who is ethically required to say nothing to any outsider, is informed of the desire to sell, and he or she has the contact with prospects. When the selected lawyer or accountant is part of a firm, the client should request that the proposed sale not be publicized in the office, in any way. Specifically, no reference to the sale should be made in a new matter listing, or on the title of a file.

3. None of the preliminary meetings with possible purchasers, or their representatives, should be held at the company's place of business. The presence of unfamiliar people closeted with the head of the business, on the corporation's premises, always whets the curiosity of the company's employees. On the other hand, the announcement that the boss is going to see his attorney usually creates no suspicion. If there have to be a lot of trips to see the lawyer, within a short time frame, the owner should merely say that he is going on some errand, such as shopping for shirts, searching for a gift for his spouse, or looking at some pieces of art. These are all activities where he understandably will not be reachable.

RISK-TAKING

The seller must be careful in any transaction that he does not take the major financial risks. There is a big difference between a deal where the purchase price is paid in full, and one where it is paid in installments that are to be satisfied out of the profits of the business. In the case of an all cash sale, the principals and money lenders of the purchaser accept the hazards. When there are installments, which are dependent on the continued success of the business, the seller bears the risks.

The fact that the selling close corporation is given a lien on the assets does not eliminate the peril in deals where a sizeable amount is to be paid over a period of time. Machinery, equipment, and inventory often produce only a fraction of their intrinsic value when disposed of in a liquidation sale. Accounts receivable can dwindle and be subject to all kinds of set-offs. Even a plant may bring much less than its worth in a forced sale.

All cash or no cash are not the only alternatives. In many sales, a sizeable portion of the price is delivered at closing. The balance is payable over a few years. Clearly, this is riskier than a sale in which the entire price is paid when the transaction is consummated. However, many owners do accept this kind of arrangement. It may be the best offer that can be obtained and the security for the balance of the purchase price is considered to be sufficient.

DETERMINING THE PRICE

It is not unusual for a beleaguered entrepreneur, fed up with his business, to declare: "I don't care what I get for the company. I just want to get rid of it!" Don't believe it. When the time comes to get serious about disposing of what represents a lifetime's hard work— or in some instances, what was built by two or more generations— the seller wants to get a top price for the business. As a result, the amount that the business will be sold for is the most important issue that must be settled in negotiations between seller and buyer, right up front. This price determination involves the parties in one of the most complex valuation tasks that someone can take on. It involves a lot of advocacy and horse trading.

The balance sheet

Generally, the starting point in fixing the price for the business is the corporation's balance sheet. The excess of the assets of the company, over its liabilities, constitutes the book value of the enterprise. This book value is not a true measure of the corporation's net worth. The actual value of certain assets, particularly the inventory and fixed assets like plant, machinery and equipment, can be much greater than what the books show. And nothing is reflected on the balance sheet for intangible assets, such as goodwill, valuable tradenames, trademarks, secret processes and the like.

Inventory

The close corporation owner will urge that he is entitled to receive market value for the inventory, no matter what the accounting records of the company show for this asset. "You should pay what the inventory is really worth to you. That's the correct approach." He is right, and that is what generally happens. The parties arrange for a physical inventory—a count—to be made shortly before the sale is closed, and agree on a procedure for pricing that inventory. This should produce a price for the goods on hand that is acceptable to both buyer and seller.

Fixing an increased value for the inventory often makes the seller whose company has an "inventory reserve" very nervous. What concerns the proprietor is this: inventory figures have been deliberately understated. Since the cost of goods sold in any taxable year is reduced by the amount of inventory on hand at year end, the entrepreneur simply tells his accountant that the inventory at the close of the fiscal year is less than what it really is, in order to minimize the corporation's income tax liability and thereby help the liquidity position of the company. Of course, for this to happen, there must have been no physical inventory supervised by the accounting firm. The company's financial statements would need to be uncertified and the accountant's report would simply state that "inventory has been submitted by management."

This inventory reserve can be a very sizeable figure. Since the closing inventory figure in one year becomes the starting amount for calculating the cost of sales in the next year, one might wonder why any reserve would be kept at all. Indeed, the formula for computing cost of goods sold is inventory at the start of the year, plus purchases during the year, less the inventory at the end of the year. The answer has to do with the increasing volume of sales. As the corporation's gross income goes up, so too does the inventory, thereby permitting the inventory reserve to grow.

What the selling owner fears are the possible adverse tax consequences that could ensue, when the corporation receives far more for the inventory than the reported figure. Will this prove that the inventories shown on previously filed tax returns were deliberately reduced to avoid taxes? Usually there is no need to fret. When a business is disposed of, the purchaser pays the market value for the inventory. The seller, however, has consistently used the much lower cost of the inventory for accounting and tax purposes. Thus, a price for the inventory substantially in excess of what is shown on the corporation's books is understandable.

Fixed assets

The selling company is also entitled to receive the true worth of its plant, machinery and equipment. Those are shown on the financial statements at original cost less depreciation. With the inflation and rapid depreciation write-offs, there is often a tremendous disparity between the market and book values of these fixed assets. It is, however, more difficult to determine the appreciation over book value, since value judgments are involved. An important issue in that regard is whether the plant, machinery and equipment are to be valued as parts of a going concern, or at what they would bring in a liquidation sale. Each side makes its own appraisals, and the disparities are somehow compromised.

Intangibles

When it comes to intangible assets, the situation is very different. Except for a handful of industries, where there is a formula for calculating goodwill—for example, linen supply, maintenance, fuel oil, and vending machine businesses—there is no simple method of computing what one should fairly pay for intangibles. When the seller starts demanding a significant add-on to the price, to reflect things like going concern value, manufacturing know-how, patents or tradenames, a shift in the entire approach to valuation invariably occurs. The selling price is now based on a multiple of earnings. That is, the annual net-after-tax earnings of the company are multiplied by a factor, for example, ten times. The seller will urge the use of the profits of the last completed fiscal year, if they are the highest earnings the company had. The purchaser will push for an average of several years' earnings. The multiple that is used is greatly influenced by the ratio of the price per share to earnings per share of comparable publicly held companies. There is a lot of room for compromise in the resolution of these issues. Through give and take, the price is arrived at.

BEEFING UP THE EARNINGS

Once the price is to be calculated by applying a multiple to after-tax profits, there is a considerable incentive for the stockholders of the corporation being sold, to demonstrate that the "real earnings" of the company are substantially higher than what the financial statements and tax returns show. Let us assume that the seller can convince the purchaser that the reported net income has been understated by $50,000. If the multiple being used is ten times earnings, the price goes up $500,000. That's significant!

What kind of upward adjustments to earnings can the proprietors of the selling corporation convince the buyers to accept? Unreported income is not one of them. That kind of disclosure would probably kill the deal, and could subject the sellers to serious income tax troubles. Failure to report income is a crime. What follows are examples of the kinds of items that are most commonly urged as reasons for augmenting the reported profits.

Excessive compensation

Throughout this book, I have noted that, for tax purposes, compensation is an advantageous way of getting business profits into the hands of the close corporation owners. This incentive pushs the proprietors to maximize their compensation. In essence, the stockholder-executives are being paid for two things: (1) their services and (2) some return on the capital they have invested as owners. Until the entity is sold, the principals never worry about apportioning their compensation between these two elements. So long as what they take is enough and so long as it is deductible by the corporation for income tax purposes, the entrepreneurs are happy.

But when the business is about to be sold and it is clear that the owners will get much more if their salary figures are reduced, the owners' attitude changes. Let's go back to Bradley Cosmetics, Inc., which we met in the last chapter, and assume that instead of going public, the business is going to be sold. Jim and Ed Bradley are each receiving $350,000 a year, as compensation, consisting of a base salary of $200,000 and an incentive compensation bonus of another $150,000 a year, making their total annual compensation $700,000. The purchaser is a large public company, with widely diversified stockholdings and the executive who will head up its Bradley Cosmetics division after the purchase is consummated presently earns $175,000 a year. A production chief will have to be installed by the buyer, to take over Ed Bradley's duties. His salary will be about $90,000 a year. Under these circumstances, the person negotiating on behalf of Bradley Cosmetics will undoubtedly urge an upward revision of the corporation's earnings, along these lines: "Look, the Bradley brothers are taking $700,000 a year as compensation. A lot of that is really a return on their equity. A fair measure of what they are actually being paid for their services, is what you will pay the people who will take over their duties and responsibilities. A good guess is that that will run around $300,000 a year. This means that our earnings should be increased by $200,000 a year, which is one-half of the difference between $700,000 and $300,000. I took off 50% because the corporation got an income tax deduction for the compensation that Jim and Ed Bradley received."

The increase of $200,000 in the after-tax earnings of the company, after being multiplied by the agreed upon ten times earnings formula, can produce an extra $2 million for the Bradley brothers (10 times $200,000), $1 million each. Will the purchaser agree to this? After all, the negotiator for the Bradley company estimated the annual cost of replacing the services of Ed and Jim to be $300,000, whereas it will actually be only $265,000. The chances are that there will be a substantial concession by the purchaser on this point, but how far their representatives will go is difficult to predict.

Miscellaneous income adjustments

There are several other items that are frequently eliminated as offsets in calculating the net income of the selling company that is to be capitalized to determine the sales price. One is that part of the annual contribution to a pension and/or profit sharing plan that has been greatly inflated because so much of it is allocated to the owners. Purchasers appreciate that these plans have been designed to give the stockholders of the close corporation the lion's share of the benefits. Another elimination covers the premiums for life insurance policies carried by the company, the proceeds of which are earmarked for use for the principals' estate planning. Moreover, the cost of cars, in addition to those provided for the working members of the family, can often be identified and eliminated from a computation of the corporation's earnings.

Personal expenses

Personal expenses usually turn out to be a very sensitive area in discussions regarding revisions of the corporation's profit and loss figures. I am talking about such things as trips, dining out, theatre and sports tickets, household supplies, and other items attributable to the proprietors, all of which have been treated as expenses of the business and deducted by the corporation in computing its income tax liability, despite the fact that the value of what was received has never been reported as taxable income by the stockholders. This tax treatment, of course, is illegal. Personal charges should not have been deducted by the company, since the payments were really the equivalent of dividends. And the stockholders should have picked up the value of the benefits they received in their individual tax returns. If the non-business character of these expenses can be demonstrated, both the company and the owners will face serious income tax problems. Not only will there be tax deficiencies and interest, but substantial penalties will probably be imposed as well. Where the improprieties are substantial in number and amount, criminal prosecution can result.

Nevertheless, these disguised expenditures are frequently very substantial. The temptation is great for the sellers of the business to try and get the purchaser to recognize that expenses, such as travel and entertainment, have been padded, by the inclusion of items that were really for the personal benefit of the owners. Once again, the effect of eliminating certain of these ostensibly legitimate expenses is to increase the "real" profits of the enterprise, and produce an even greater enlargement of the purchase price, since every dollar of extra after-tax earnings enlarges that price by a sizeable multiple. The stockholders of the close corporation would like to achieve this favorable enhancement of income without being too specific about where they have converted personal expenditures into business expenses. They are fearful about confessing their income tax sins to strangers. On the other hand, the purchaser is unwilling to take the owners' word for it. "Show me what these items are," is the usual response to this type of claim.

I strongly recommend to clients who are selling a business that they forget about the expenses which have been improperly charged to their corporation. Describing to strangers, in depth, the instances where tax fraud may have occurred is too big a gamble to take, no matter how much is at stake. If the purchaser is willing to accept a generalized reference to the existence of a greatly exaggerated amount for "T & E" (travel and entertainment expenses), and add something back to income for the overstatement, on the theory that the business will now be operated with more effective cost control, that's fine. Sometimes raising this issue, and giving up on it, leads to a concession by the buyer on another point. But the sellers must not record the particulars of their indiscretions in writing.

GENE'S DUMB STUNT

Some years ago, I was involved in a sale where one of the principals of the company being sold, a very talented son whom I will call Gene, was unable to accept my advice. I had been brought in to represent a company that was working out a sale of its business to a nationally known Fortune 500 company listed on the New York Stock Exchange. The prospective purchaser's negotiating team consisted of its vice-president for acquisitions, a very able and experienced partner in a midwestern law firm, and two partners from its big eight accounting firm.

Our people were hard at work trying to beef up the earnings that were going to be used to compute the price. The parties were slightly apart in the earnings multiple that should be utilized, but it was obvious that this issue could be readily compromised. We hit an impasse, however, on the matter of identifying specifically the personal items that had been charged to the company as expenses.

Gene was dismayed by the potential loss of purchase price dollars that would occur if the stockholder costs were not added back as income. In truth, the difference was negligible, when one considered the size of the transaction. He went to work and prepared an elaborate restatement of the net profits of the corporation for the last three fiscal years. It was titled "The Actual Earnings of X Company." Salaries and perquisites of the stockholder-employees were limited to what were described as "Reasonable Compensation and Benefits of the Stockholders." Then there was an item identified as "Travel and Entertainment Expenses That the Purchaser Would Have To Pay." It was the amount of the travel and entertainment expenses that had been taken, reduced by those that were eliminated as personal expenditures. There were detailed back-up sheets for these revised figures.

Unknown to me, Gene submitted the restated earnings and worksheets to the vice-president for acquisitions of the prospective buyer. The two of them then hammered out a price. The new earnings statement was turned over to counsel for the purchaser, to be appended as a schedule to a letter of intent. The purchaser wanted this document signed so that it could issue a release to the public regarding the acquisition.

I received a frantic telephone call from the close corporation's accountant. He had seen Gene's handy work and learned that it was going to be a public record. There was shock and disbelief in his voice: "Our people are handing out a written document proving that their compensation and benefits were unreasonable and they have charged personal expenses to the company. I had no idea they were stealing from the company. The Internal Revenue Service will cream them. They may even find themselves facing fraud charges. How can they do this?"

Because I was unaware of what Gene had done, I slowed down the accountant and had him explain to me what had happened. When the ramifications of Gene's blunder finally hit me, countermeasures were instituted immediately. On short notice, I held a brief meeting with all the stockholders of the corporation, and the accountant. After a discussion about the implications of Gene's worksheets, everyone agreed that Gene's document could not be part of the letter of intent or any other instrument. In addition, there would be no declaration by the sellers that the "proper earnings"—or "the earnings, if the purchaser were operating the company"—would be the greater number that Gene had come up with. All of this was communicated forthwith to the purchaser's acquisitions vice-president and counsel. As a result, the restated profit summary that Gene had prepared was eliminated, and the purchase price was reduced.

NEGOTIATIONS AND PAPERWORK

The extent of the negotiations and the number of complications that arise in connection with a sale of the business are generally upsetting to the close corporation owners. They are used to making major decisions rapidly and with little formality. The delineation of the terms of a disposition of a good sized enterprise is a slow, deliberate process. The paperwork is elaborate and complex.

I remember an extremely big deal which I worked on early in my practice. It involved the sale of a chain of stores, each of which was a separate corporation. There were so many documents that the day before the closing, everyone got together to sign the papers—to be delivered the next day when the money would be paid. The president and sole stockholder of the selling corporations was divorced. So he had made his mother the secretary of each company. This meant that she had to sign a truckload of papers. After she was at it for an hour, she called a halt. At her request, her son, the senior partner handling the transaction, and I, who was assisting him, joined her in an adjoining room. She turned to her son and declared: "Joseph, all these papers to sign. It's ridiculous. Look, they'll give you the money and you'll give them the keys!"

It would be nice if it could be done as easily as that. Some deals are unnecessarily complicated. But it is the responsibility of counsel to make sure that the purchaser gets what he bargained for. This can only be accomplished with extensive documentation. The entrepreneur who is selling his business has to be educated about this reality.

The most explosive reaction, during the formulation of the sale arrangements, generally occurs when the purchaser's draft of the sales contract is received by the close corporation owner. "What are their lawyers trying to do, kill the deal!" This outburst is provoked primarily by the long list of representations in the contract about the corporation's business and affairs. They "cover the waterfront." Financial statements are declared to have been prepared in accordance with generally accepted accounting practices. The non-existence of contingent liabilities is promised. Compliance with all applicable rules and regulations is affirmed. The absence of binding commitments, which hamper the purchaser's flexibility, is attested. And so it goes, for pages and pages.

The principals of the close corporation have to understand the chief purpose of these proposed representations is not to entrap them or enable the purchaser to sue them in later years. Instead, the aim is to push the owners, who have been running the business for a long time, to disclose information and problems that the purchaser needs to know about. This concern is emphasized by the format of the draft contract, which generally says something like: "Except as stated in Schedule A," there are no this and that. In short, the purchaser wants to learn about any possible problems during the negotiations, rather than after the transaction is closed.

Representation by counsel

I am a firm believer that close corporation principals should use a representative in the negotiations, usually an attorney with know-how. The proprietors tend to make decisions too quickly. Since they are the owners, any commitment they make is binding. They can't use the "out" that an executive negotiating for a public company has: "Of course, the board of directors has to approve the terms."

It is better for a lawyer to make the tough demands and take the hard lines. This technique enables the selling entrepreneurs to get a better reading of the purchaser's attitudes and reactions on significant points. They can then think through and brainstorm the responsive position that should be taken, rather than having to react on the spur of the moment.

Under this negotiating format, the owner's image of being a nice guy is maintained. "Milt, I agree with X. What you have asked for is clearly unreasonable." The seller utters this criticism, even though it was he who directed the lawyer to assert the concept.

Preserving good relations is particularly important when one or more of the entrepreneurs who are selling, will work for the purchaser. That transition is difficult enough, without having the top executives of the purchaser anxious to get back at the former entrepreneur, now an employee, for his offensive attitude during the negotiations.

SELLING ASSETS AS OPPOSED TO STOCK

It is much easier to sell the assets of the corporation than its stock. The purchaser of the assets decides which ones it needs for the operation of the business. It can decline to purchase marketable securities or other investment type properties. Cash and sometimes accounts receivable can be retained by the seller. The purchaser acquires only the assets needed to operate the business. But the biggest advantage of an asset purchase is that the purchaser does not take over all of the corporation's liabilities, existing and contingent. The liabilities that will be assumed in an asset acquisition are spelled out. The rest continue to be only the seller's worry.

Taking on all the close corporation's liabilities, known and unknown, is the greatest deterrent to the purchase of stock. All the skeletons in the closet can appear and haunt the company that buys the stock. A major concern is usually income tax liabilities for the tax years not barred by the statute of limitations.

Coping with these liabilities when stock is sold is burdensome. The already elongated sales agreement is expanded further by provisions identifying: (1) the liabilities that shall continue to be the responsibility of the seller; (2) who will defend claims that may be made in the future; and (3) how the costs of defending any claims will be apportioned. A significant part of the purchase price is usually held in escrow, to assure the buyer that it will be reimbursed if it has to pay some contingent liabilities that the seller is responsible for. This requires the selection and compensation of an escrow agent and the preparation of an escrow agreement.

ALLOCATING THE PURCHASE PRICE OF ASSETS

In Chapter 5, I discussed the tax considerations involved in the sale of a business. A major topic covered in that treatment was the allocation of the purchase price among the various assets that are transferred from seller to buyer. What I was talking about, specifically, is how to handle that portion of the price that exceeds the book value of the assets. This apportionment can be a bone of contention between the selling close corporation and the buyer, because of their differing tax positions. I am now going to summarize how the average purchaser wants to apportion the price for the assets, and how the seller will react to the purchaser's desires.

What the purchaser wants

The purchaser wants the excess purchase price over the book value of assets attributed to: (1) inventory; (2) depreciable assets, primarily machinery and equipment that can be written off over a short period of years, and then to plant and other buildings; and (3) consultation and non-compete payments to the individual stockholder-executives of the selling corporation. The inflated inventory value reduces the gross profit when the product is sold, which confers an immediate income tax benefit. Depreciation on the fixed assets can be deducted. The consulting payments are deductible against the purchaser's ordinary income. Finally, the non-competition amount is amortized and deducted over the term of the restriction, even though the payments run over a longer period.

How the seller reacts

The purchaser's allocation suggestions get mixed reviews from the seller. The increase in inventory value is fine, if the corporation is going to be liquidated within one year. There is no corporate tax on that inventory profit. Likewise, the amount fixed for buildings is usually okay, because here again no corporate tax is recognized and the proceeds come into the hands of the owners, on liquidation of the close corporation, as capital gain. But the tax treatment of the excess value attributed to the machinery and the equipment is very different. The close corporation has to pick up as ordinary income all of the increase over book value, to the extent of the depreciation taken on these assets.

The consulting and non-competition payments are all ordinary income to the recipient stockholders. This usually means that they will be taxed at the top income tax rate rather than at more favorable capital gain rates. Today the difference is between keeping only 50%—rather than 80%—of what is cast as consultation or restrictive covenant payments.

Of course, the seller would prefer that a large part of the purchase amount in excess of the book value of the assets be treated as goodwill. This approach results in no corporate tax and a capital gain tax to the individuals whose business is being sold. The buyer will resist, because goodwill cannot be deducted for income tax purposes—notwithstanding the fact that a publicly held corporation, for financial reporting, must write off the goodwill against its earnings reported to the public, over not more than 40 years. The conflicting positions of seller and buyer have to be compromised. They usually are. But a good deal of the negotiating time goes into these issues.

EMPLOYEE SAFETY AND HEALTH, AND ENVIRONMENTAL PROTECTION

There are now extensive rules and regulations governing employees' safety and health, and environmental protection, that affect close corporation businesses. Failure to have complied with these requirements has become a substantial impediment to the sale of a business. The seller will be asked to make a representation that it has faithfully adhered to these rules and regulations, and, for certain, the company disposing of its assets will have to warrant that there are no existing violations.

All kinds of problems may have to be faced when the employees' safety and health, and environmental protection issues are raised by the buyer. There can be OSHA violations and sometimes outstanding citations. Warnings to employees about safety hazards or the presence of toxic materials may not have been properly given. The corporation may be faced with substantial expenditures to eliminate the pollution of water, atmosphere or surrounding land. Chemicals and other toxic materials which were dumped on the company's premises, may require clean-up. It may take many months, or even years, to correct these conditions. The costs can be large. Money may have to be escrowed to handle the work, if the parties do not want to delay the consummation of the sale. There have even been cases where the environmental problems killed the deal.

WORKING FOR THE NEW OWNERS

How do the stockholder-managers of the close corporation keep busy after the business is sold? A lot of them continue to work for the new owners. This is usually a relationship of short duration. I have observed a number of these new job opportunities for the proprietor of the successful business who is selling out. Rarely do they work.

Edward Kinney's experience was typical. Ed was a very bright, capable person. He was a beneficent despot. Everyone in his very good-sized organization knew that Ed was the boss. The critical operational decisions were made by him. Fortunately, most of them were sound. When Ed reached the age of 58, he decided to sell the business. No member of the family was involved in the business. In case of his death, there was nobody who could step into his shoes and run things. It made sense to Ed to sell now, since he could participate in an orderly transition to the new ownership, thereby enhancing the price that a buyer would be willing to pay. In any case, he was tired of worrying about competition and motivating and directing subordinates.

The best offer for the business—and it was a big one—came from a large, publicly held company that sold office equipment. They felt that integrating office supplies into their product line was a natural. With pride, Ed Kinney told me that the purchaser wanted to give him a five year contract to be in charge of the Office Supplies Division that would be established. "You know, Milt, I think it will be very challenging and enjoyable to run that operation." Ed was shocked and upset by my reaction. "Ed, I really doubt that you will be happy. I don't think you'll last for two years."

Ed pressed me for an explanation. I told him how I felt. "I don't think you realize how independent you are. You are accustomed to doing what you want and when you choose to do it. You are accountable to no one except yourself. Everybody in your company bows and scrapes in your presence. When you walk through the front door of your plant, there is a sense of: This is my kingdom.

"That is going to change. You will be asked to make projections and give reports. Conform to procedures. Present yourself before management committees, and perhaps the Board of Directors, and give your five year plan. How are you going to feel when you receive a communication from some Harvard M.B.A., pointing out that your division's net income is off and demanding your explanation of the reasons for the downturn?

"You're going to be one of a number of peers and you will have superiors. You have never been part of a large organized management team. Except in your early days with the company, when your dad was the head of the corporation, you have never been subject to anyone's authority in business."

Edward Kinney paid no heed to my pessimistic outlook. Gung-ho he jumped into the role of head of the Office Supplies Division. Eighteen months later, he and the purchaser agreed that it was in everybody's best interest for his employment to end.

This experience is so common that one of our reminders, when a close corporation is sold, is to explain to the owners that working for the acquirer will not be easy for them to do. There are just too many adjustments for most entrepreneurs to make.

Two aspects of the problems have been repeatedly highlighted by close corporation owners whose employment by the purchasing entity didn't work out. The first is resentment due to the different economic position of the former proprietor. Having just sold his business for a lot of money—the details of which are known to some and exaggerated in amount by others—he is rich. Snide comments are made by the professional top managers, who are constantly looking for another $5,000 a year after-tax, to fulfill some desire. "You don't have to worry any more about the size of your salary."

The other surprising revelation is the extent of the office politics. Executives seeking to move up the management ladder in large corporations are constantly searching, among the handful of top bananas, for the one who will emerge as the chief executive officer, or at least the head of operations. The idea is to get close to him and demonstrate your loyalty and commitment to his advancement to the top. Hopefully, this will pay off in promotions.

The former business owner does not get involved in this intrigue. He has no similar aspirations and this kind of maneuvering is foreign to him. One would think that fellow executives would appreciate the neutrality of the new employee. Quite often, they are annoyed with him, because the entrepreneur has sufficient wealth so that he can be independent of these wiles.

There is an important bit of lawyering that must be done, when the close corporation owner is going to be employed by the buyer of the business. His principal place of employment has to be kept close to home. The last thing the owner wants is to relocate. The extent of his obligations to travel should also be considered and defined.

THE RETIRING ENTREPRENEUR

What about the entrepreneur who sells his business and doesn't go to work for the purchaser? Or, whose employment has come to an end. How does he fill the hours of the day? These hard-driving individuals find it hard to be unemployed. They have most of the same problems that are experienced by anyone who has worked hard all his life, and then, one day, is completely retired. The advantage of the business seller is that he has enough money to travel extensively and vacation where he wants.

A lot of these former business proprietors do something part-time. They may serve on the Board of Directors of another close corporation. Many of them get very involved in charitable activities or with a hospital in their community. Some pursue things they have wanted to do for a long time, studies, painting, sculpture, or writing. One owner I knew, who had a very successful chemical company, became a chemistry professor at a junior college.

Another handful of very thoughtful businessmen I once worked with did a very clever thing, in anticipation of the sale of their company. They acquired a small unrelated enterprise. When the major business was sold, they continued to operate the new one. As one of these gentlemen said to me: "It keeps me occupied, without being a burden. And I don't have to worry about building it up, because I don't need the money any more."

A common mistake is the decision of the bought-out entrepreneur to cure his boredom by putting a lot of capital into a new venture, in which he has no experience. We have seen a number of them lose a lot of money this way. The latter stages of one's life is not the time to plunge into unfamiliar waters.

The younger owner-managers, children and sons-in-law, have the toughest situation when the business is sold. There is the same lack of probability of a long career with the buyer. They are too young to be retired or engaged only in limited part-time activities. Frequently, the bulk of the purchase price has gone to dad, so they are not even independently wealthy. A very frequent motivation for the development of a second business, which is not sold, is to provide a career path for the next generation. I admire those businessmen who had the foresight to do this. They did a great service to their offspring.

Absent that refuge, the younger family members have to look for some other occupation to keep busy. Many of them seek employment in a service business. Selling stocks and bonds is a common choice.

The long and short of it is that many owners, old and young, are not as happy after the business is sold. Patterns of existence that have been followed for many decades are hard to change. But for the individual who built the enterprise, much more has happened. The business that is gone is an important part of him. It was the major source of his ego gratification and sense of self-esteem. That is a big loss. For many, the dollars that are received—however substantial—cannot fill the void.

TECHNIQUES OF COUNSELLING THE CLOSE CORPORATION

17

Clients want lawyers who care, who know how to deal with them, and who pay attention to their matters. If an attorney meets these needs, hᵉ can lose a case and still be appreciated. If he ignores them, winning will not overcome the bad taste in the client's mouth. Good lawyers understand that having the answers is not enough. To be effective in our dealings with people, we must know how to relate to them.

COUNSELLING ENTREPRENEURS GENERALLY

The typical successful close corporation owner has a strong personality.

1. He is a very effective, hard driving individual. Every facet of the business is intimately known by him. His involvement and commitment to the enterprise are deeply felt.

2. He relies primarily on his own decisions. To accept your recommendations, he needs to understand your ideas thoroughly, to mull them over, ask questions about them and then decide what to do.

3. He is aggressive. He had to overcome substantial obstacles to reach the top in the highly competitive American business world.

4. He is decisive. The pressures of heading an organization, require him to reach his conclusions and move on.

5. He reads a good deal, attends meetings and shares ideas with others. He uses information he garners from hither and yon to test his advisors. "Today is my country club day!" an accountant once exclaimed to me on a Monday morning. "Every Monday morning during the golf season my phone keeps ringing off the hook with calls from my clients, telling about something they learned over the weekend at the country club—and asking why their company isn't doing it. I spend all morning explaining why the concept doesn't make sense in the client's circumstances."

HANDLING ISSUES VERSUS WORKING WITH PEOPLE

Many lawyers have confided to me that they very much enjoy the intriguing corporate and tax issues that are found in dealing with close corporations, but they don't like the client relationships. That is a mistake, for the very essence of successful counselling of the enterprises is developing close ties with the proprietors so they will communicate their goals, feelings, desires, and fears.

The crucial starting point is to develop a sound relationship with the stockholders—and in the case of large organizations, the other key executives, as well. Eggheads and introverts will generally strike out with the leaders of close corporations.

Lawyers best demonstrate their involvement by becoming confidantes and good listeners.

Awareness of the entrepreneur's feelings is necessary for the counsellor to do a good job. In my experience, close corporation owners are moved as much by what they feel in their gut as by what is filtered through their brain.

What Owen really wanted

Here is an example of what I mean. I once had a client named Owen who was the oldest of three brothers who ran a successful second generation retail business. The most senior child of the trio was Owen's son, Andy, who was 15 years old. A life insurance agent, who knew the brothers, urged them to put in place a buy-sell arrangement which would become effective if one of them died. This recommendation was unquestionably sound. The other alternative-,having the family of a deceased brother own an interest in the enterprise, was clearly unacceptable, for the reasons explained in Chapter 10. I was called in to try to implement the plan.

In my early meetings with the brothers and the insurance man, I sensed resistance from Owen. He kept nit-picking over details. He frightened his partners about the possible adverse effects on the liquidity of the business that might result from paying the life insurance premiums. It was obvious to me that he was straining to find reasons to kill the idea.

I decided to meet with Owen alone. After some amenities and generalizations, I got to the point. "I'm a newcomer to your situation. It is clear to me that you have some objections to this buy-sell format. Since you're the head of the business, it is important for me, if I am to do a good job, to know what they are. I decided to meet with you alone, because I felt it might be easier for you to discuss your reservations out of the presence of the insurance agent and your brothers."

After some hesitation, Owen disclosed his real feeling about the purchase of his stock at death. "I have a son, Andy, who is interested in the business and will probably want to come to work here. My father gave me and my brothers the opportunity to do that. If I die and my stock is bought out, I have really sold my son's birthright."

Since Andy was only 15 years of age, there was no assurance that Andy would ever decide to join the company. In any event, Andy would not be able to take a significant role in the company for many years. It really made no sense for Owen to jeopardize the financial security of his wife and other children, following his death, solely to make sure that Andy, if he so desired, could be the owner of a one-third interest in the corporation.

All of these were accurate rational observations. But Owen was racked by an overwhelming emotion, guilt, which was harder for him to cope with. Unless and until that was addressed and dealt with, there would be no agreement. In our dialogue, I got Owen to agree that it would not be in anybody's interest, including his son's, to insist that Andy be an equal owner of the business before he reached at least age 25. By that time, the question of Andy's career path would also be settled. In addition, if the decision were made to have Andy succeed to the equity interest of Owen, some financial provision would have to be made for the post-death support and maintenance of Owen's wife and other children. The only workable plan, if Owen died before his son, Andy, was 25, was a purchase of his stock by the corporation.

A compromise was made that Owen could accept. The buy-sell arrangement would run for ten years, at which time Andy would reach age 25. Then the parties would reconsider the matter, and do what then seemed sensible. The papers were promptly drawn and executed; and the life insurance was put in force.

Reading between the lines

I can remember many other times in my practice when an entrepreneur's belated and, perhaps, unintended disclosure of vital information was the key to a successful legal strategy. Here are a half dozen snippets from actual conversations I had with clients who were owners of close corporations, followed by brief accounts of the actions I then took on each speaker's behalf. Test your reaction to each disclosure against mine and consider whether you would have formulated a different strategy.

1. *Client's disclosure:-* "Hard as it is for me to acknowledge it, my son, Kevin, is just not as capable or mature as his brother, Roy."

Resulting strategy: The corporation was recapitalized in order to create a class of voting stock with a nominal book value. Dad gave Roy one more share of voting stock then Kevin was given, so that he would be in control of the corporation.

2. *Client's disclosure:-* "My son-in-law, Woody, is a very competent executive. He has probably done more for the business than my son. But I don't trust him. I have the feeling that one week after I'm dead, he'll start pushing around my son and cheating on my daughter, his wife."

Resulting strategy: The daughter's stock in the corporation was put in a trust for her benefit that ran for her lifetime. At her death, the money went to her children. The trustee of the trust was a person whom the father felt sure would protect his daughter and her children from the son-in-law's overreaching.

3. *Client's disclosure:-* "I realize that shifting the future growth in value of the company to my kids will save a lot of death taxes. However, I don't want to feel that I'm working for my kids. I need some continuing incentive."

Resulting strategy: In this instance, the father was advised to give away only 50% of the growth common stock. He held on to the other half, until much later in his life, in his 70's. Psychologically, he was not ready to take such an ultimate step until active participation in the business no longer appealed to him.

4. *Client's disclosure:-* "The other night, when we had a house full of company, my son, Walter, outspokenly disagreed with my evaluation of the Governor's performance in office. He refused to back down, even when I took a strong contrary stand. This has been happening a lot recently. Frankly, I think he's getting too big for his britches."

Resulting strategy: The father's gift of stock to Walter was put off for a long time. It would have been repugnant to the father for Walter to be financially independent.

5. *Client's disclosure:-* "I know it makes sense to accept the offer for the business. It's a great deal. But when I gave the boys their stock ten years ago, I never expected that they would get as much as they will, if I go ahead with the sale."

Resulting strategy: I advised the sons that no disposition of the business would be made by their father, who held the voting control, unless his share of the pie was increased substantially. I explained to them that this was the message he had given me to tell them. Reluctantly, but wisely, the sons agreed to let him convert his preferred stock into a substantial chunk of the non-voting common stock—thereby increasing his portion of the sales price for the assets of the corporation.

6. *Client's disclosure:-* "My wife, Gail, and my daughter-in-law, Bill's wife, don't get along. Gail is sure that after my death, our daughter-in-law will push Bill to stop making the payments to Gail from the corporation."

Resulting strategy: Insurance was taken out on my client's life to cover the corporation's post-death undertaking to his wife. I was designated as the escrowee-agent of the corporation to make sure that the premiums were paid, and, at my client's death, to receive, hold and invest the life insurance proceeds to make sure that the contractual obligation to his wife was met.

Regardless of the strategy you may have taken, the basic point is this: lawyers who fail to probe for the entrepreneur's most strongly felt and private convictions on matters connected with the running of his or her business, are bound to be ineffective.

THE TEN COMMANDMENTS OF GOOD COUNSELLING

My partners and I often exchange ideas about counselling close corporations. We try to examine why we failed to establish desired relationships in some cases and what helped us to succeed in others. Let me share with you some of the "do's and dont's" we have developed. These are our 10 commandments for good counselling.

1. *Never sit in judgment of a client or be God-like.*

When a client seeks the help of an attorney, he is not looking for an evaluation of his personality or attitudes. Whether or not he is a good person—judged by the subjective standards of the lawyer—is totally immaterial to the job at hand. We need to know this side of the close corporation owner's make-up so that we can serve him more effectively, not to rate him as a human being. In other words, the true feelings of a client may be callous, unreasonable, selfish, even paranoid, but it is not the province of the advisor to criticize or be shocked.

I tell associates in our firm whom I am training: "The estate planning client, an obstensibly happy family man, tells you that he has a mistress in the Far West, whose child he has fathered. He wants to provide for both woman and child after his death, without embarrassing his family about their existence. Your job is to figure out how to accomplish this. That is what you are being paid for. You are not to react negatively to his disclosure, or in any way emanate an attitude that bespeaks criticism of his conduct."

This is an extreme example, perhaps, but it accurately reflects my point of view. The only time lawyers have a right to make judgments is when we are asked to do something that offends our ethical standards. In that circumstance, we say "No" even if it means losing the client.

2. *Listen and observe carefully. Hear what the entrepreneur actually says. Spot the emotionally charged issues by the client's choice of words and his body language.*

There are many synonyms that can be used to express a thought. Some convey much more feeling and impact than others. A worldly-wise businessman, in response to a question about his wife, tightens the muscles in his face, tenses his body, and exclaims, "I can't stand to be in the same room with her." His marriage is in more imminent danger of collapse than if he had said, "She's O.K. But we don't spend much time together." When the response is full of intensity, that is a tip-off to the counsellor that he has touched a nerve, an area of concern that is deeply felt by the client.

A drama involving an incorporated partnership once reached a climax right in my office. Sam was in business with his brother-in-law Dave, a very difficult person. Things had never been great between the two of them. But Sam, who was a fairly placid person, somehow managed to keep turning the other cheek. Sam's son, Harry, came to work for the corporation in his mid-twenties. He was talented and he worked hard. But Dave made Harry's life in the company miserable. In the interest of keeping peace, Sam kept urging his son to ignore Dave's comments. "That's just the way he is. He really doesn't mean the things he says."

Harry had complained to me a number of times about his problems with both his uncle and his father. He felt like poking his uncle in the nose on a number of occasions. And he was annoyed at his father's continued passivity in the face of his uncle's mistreatment—which had gone on now for almost ten years.

It so happened that Dave wanted to retire. It would be hard for the corporation to buy him out, because the capital of the enterprise was tied up in a very valuable plant and some expensive machinery and equipment. Recognizing this, Dave was pressing for a sale of the entire business. He produced a very interested prospective purchaser. Sam had no desire to stop working. His son, whose business career had just gotten started, was devastated by the idea of the sale. They came to the office to discuss what to do.

I asked father and son for their reactions to the proposed disposition of the business. Sam started out in typical fashion, very understanding of his brother-in-law's desires, and intellectually appraising the pros and cons of selling out. Harry, his son, was quiet until I inquired about the possibility of buying out Dave, instead of getting rid of the entire enterprise. Harry then said that this alternative made a lot more sense to him. He emphasized that the company had developed a new product—which I later learned was Harry's creation—that had great promise. "It would be a shame to sell out now and give up the potential of this product. My uncle doesn't care that the company has very good prospects. All he wants is to get his hands on cash."

Easy-going Sam suddenly changed. He moved forward on his chair. His body stiffened. His teeth clenched and he made fists with both his hands. "I don't give a damn what it takes. That bastard is not going to dictate to me and my son. We won't sell, no matter what, and if he wants to sue us, let him!" I knew it was the beginning of the end of the business relationship. The emotional level of Sam's declaration made that clear. The lid he had placed on his feelings toward Dave, for so many years, had finally blown off.

There was no sale, and Dave didn't sue. The corporation purchased Dave's stock, borrowing against the real estate for a down payment, and paying the balance over a period of years. The business prospered. The tip-off that this arrangement could be accomplished was Sam's change in attitude. He manifested that by the words he selected to express his feelings and by the intensity of his body language.

3. Don't overcomplicate things or use technical language.

Young lawyers, untrained and inexperienced in dealing with clients, are understandably worried about being face-to-face with a busy, hard-bitten entrepreneur. "I've got to impress him," they say to themselves. So they use words and phrases that they feel demonstrate erudition, and make references to sections of the law to show their grasp of the subject matter. But this approach is a real "turn-off" to the average close corporation owner, who resents the unfamiliar jargon.

Good lawyers make themselves understood by using words that are simple, and by using examples, summaries, charts and other aids to understanding if the occasion warrants.

4. Don't overwhelm the close corporation owner with a host of recommendations at one time.

A common mistake is to "cover the waterfront" with your suggestions. For example, an interview with the proprietor of a good size close corporation might reveal all kinds of problems. Anxious to do a thorough job, the proprietor's lawyer than submits a lengthy written report pointing out a dozen areas where substantial changes should be made. After examining the lawyer's list of recommendations, the entrepreneur will probable decide to do nothing. Why? Because people resist change. This is particularly true of the operators of successful close corporation enterprises. A limited number of well-explained and highly advantageous proposals, which represent a tolerable amount of readjustments in the owner's way of life, have a good chance of being accepted. On the other hand, if the principal feels that he will be altering his world too much, the whole program can get stalled.

I now restrict the number of recommendations I put before close corporation clients to three or four. That number can be absorbed without making the client anxious. He can accept that much revision without feeling that everything that is familiar to him is going out the window. Furthermore, by restricting the number of recommendations, I can keep the cost of implementation within an acceptable range.

5. *Learn how to communicate ideas.*

Many years ago I was reading the advertising column in *The New York Times*. The reporter stated that the following notice had been posted on the bulletin board of a leading advertising agency. "An idea, no matter how brilliantly conceived, artfully presented and well-articulated, that does not sell the product, stinks!" That thought has stuck with me because it has equal applicability to client counselling. You can do everything right. Garner all the relevant information. Identify the problems. Come up with solutions that are effective and tax advantageous. But if you can't motivate the client to carry out your ideas, you have failed.

This may be a harsh evaluation. It is true, nevertheless. The measure of success in counselling a close corporation is whether your proposed courses of action become actualities. In my judgment, the biggest obstacle to getting the job done is the weakness in the counsellor's method of communicating those recommendations to the client. The first mistake that lawyers make is giving top preference to written communications. This may be a carry-over from our law school training. Possibly, attorneys like letters and memos because it puts them in control, working in their own comfortable environment, rather than facing the powerful client on his turf.

Whatever the reason for the invariable resort to written communications, it is a mistake to operate that way. Face-to-face discussions are much more effective. The counsellor can absorb the principal's reactions. When he spots confusion, he can amplify. He is able to answer questions. But even more importantly, the proposals receive the owner's undivided attention.

Just think about what happens when your lengthy, complex missive arrives in the entrepreneur's office. It is combined with all the other pieces of mail that are placed on his desk. No one can anticipate what his mood or state of mind may be when he starts to pour over the contents. A crisis in the plant may demand his attention. All kinds of interruptions may occur. This is the environment in which the client, on his own, and undirected, may try to digest a set of critically important recommendations.

Most experienced professionals recognize the advantages of being in front of the close corporation proprietor, when significant ideas are being considered. They worry, however, that an unstructured conference can turn into a rambling, confusing discourse, in which alternatives are juggled and few decisions are arrived at. Furthermore, they worry about wasting too much time in meetings that drag on and on. There is merit to this criticism. The first way to combat the "bull session" problem is to prepare an agenda and a summary of the proposals, which includes illustrations with numbers. These are distributed at the start of the meeting. The lawyer acts as a discussion leader and resource person, moving the businessman and other advisors through the agenda. The summary is used as an aid to better understanding of the proposals.

We used that technique in our firm for some time, with pretty good success. About five years ago, I started to experiment with a variation, which my partners and I believe has a number of other advantages. Here is how it works:

1. After the fact-finding and initial discussions, a letter is sent out outlining our recommendations. A copy is given to all of the people who are involved in the decision making process. The proposals are expressed and explained in concise, uncomplicated terms. No alternatives are offered.

2. The client is advised, at the outset of the communication, that these ideas are being submitted to him solely for his evaluation. He has agreed to nothing.

3. The preface further explains why the proposals are set forth definitively, rather than as alternatives. We have found that entrepreneurs find it easier to review, evaluate, revise and yes, even reject concepts, when they are expressed in a direct and untechnical form.

This approach serves another valuable purpose. The changes in the plan that are made at the meeting where it is reviewed, can be noted in a simple written communication. Everyone will then have an understandable blueprint of what is to be done.

6. Develop workable fee arrangements.

New clients want the lawyer's compensation to be discussed up front. Close corporation owners, who are invariably cost conscious, want to know what they are getting into. Having a clearly defined fee arrangement is sensible from the standpoint of the professional as well. The hard part is learning how to handle the demand for a specific amount, a range or a maximum.

In the early stages of my practice, I had a lot of trouble handling the fee-fixing pressures. I got help from a wonderful man, Al Mannheimer, now deceased, who was an outstanding estate planning lawyer.

He told me a little story to relate to my clients:

> "Sir, let us suppose that you called up a carpenter, told him you wanted some work done in your house, and asked him what it would cost. If on the basis of that sketchy information, the carpenter quoted you a charge, you would know that you were dealing with a thief. How could an honest carpenter possibly estimate his charges, if he really has no idea what he is going to be doing?
>
> "I am in exactly the same position as the carpenter. Until I get a picture of your situation and your needs, there is no way I can reasonably predict how much time it will take to do a job that will satisfy you.
>
> "Let me suggest this procedure. We will go forward with this interview. At the conclusion, I will tell you the areas I feel require primary attention; what, in general terms, is involved in dealing with them; and the minimum and maximum legal costs for the work. I use this range, rather than a flat fee, because we bill on the basis of time expended, and it is impossible to forecast exactly the time that will have to be put in. In that regard, should something develop that could not have been anticipated—which rarely happens—I may have to notify you and adjust the fee levels. If you are unhappy about my estimate or these arrangements, you will pay nothing and we will part as friends."

This approach has worked remarkably well for me. It is honest and fair. The successful entrepreneur does not get hit with a large charge, just because he is rich. The attorney does not get stuck with a grossly inadequate fee, by reason of his literally picking a number out of the air. There is really no bargain for the businessman who out-negotiates his lawyer and pushes him to do work for much less than what is reasonable. As the saying goes, "You get what you pay for." If the attorney feels that he is taking a financial beating in a matter, he may unconsciously start cutting corners and fail to give it the attention that it really requires.

The fee arrangements should be reduced to writing and sent to the client at the outset. This eliminates substantial misunderstanding. If unanticipated difficulties do arise, which will escalate the time and the cost, that must be communicated to the client promptly.

Do retainers make sense when handling close corporation clients? We don't think so. There is not enough predictability or regularity with respect to the services that are required for this kind of entity. The blending of corporate and stockholder issues is a very significant complicating factor. Invariably, in any fiscal year, either the law firm finds itself with time charges greatly in excess of the retainer amount, or the corporation owners feel that they are overpaying substantially for the attention they are receiving.

The most common procedure for the regular client is periodic billing, based on the hourly rate and the time of each person in the firm who did work for the company. The longer the period covered by the bill, the greater will be the potential problems with the recipient of the invoice. Nobody likes large bills. It is easier to get acceptance of three monthly bills for $4,000 each, than one for $12,000. In addition, when the charge closely follows on the heels of the services, the corporation can verify and evaluate the work much more easily. The speed-up also helps the lawyer's cash flow problems. For these reasons, we now submit bills monthly, although we formerly billed quarterly.

The main problem with charging close corporations on a time basis is the consciousness of some proprietors that the "meter is always running." You get comments like these: "I hate to call you on the phone and realize that every extra word is costing me money. Do you charge portal-to-portal? Does your time clock run while we're having lunch together?" These attitudes have to be met. Our firm has let our continuing corporate clients know that we don't charge for the typically short telephone conversation. When a luncheon is a working session, talking about the corporation's problems, the time is recorded. A purely social lunch is not. Travel time of any consequence is logged, since the entrepreneurs have concluded, for their convenience and time-saving, that the meeting should be held at their place of business rather than at our office.

7. *Make sure the production of your legal work is cost effective.*

Successful businessmen are committed to operational efficiency and cost control. They invest large sums in machinery and equipment to achieve those goals. Competition forces them to keep at it, without letting up. The close corporation owner doesn't want to pay larger fees to his professional advisors because they are disorganized and poorly staffed. The cost of each item of work must be justifiable. An experienced specialist can justify a charge of $200 an hour for creative advice, but he can't expect to be paid at that rate for doing tasks that much lower paid people can do, such as revising a corporate charter, doing routine minutes, drafting boilerplate provisions, calculating tax costs or doing research.

As a rule, legal work done for a close corporation should be pushed down to the lowest level within the firm at which the work can be done effectively. Paralegals in our office, at $55 an hour, can do most repetitive tasks better than lawyers. Properly trained and supervised associates can do many things for the company just as well as a partner, but at a fraction of the cost. In our firm, we have associates with varying degrees of know-how and experience. Consequently, the more sophisticated work goes to the more senior people, while other items, such as research or simple drafting, can be assigned to the newer people, whose hourly rates are lower.

Specialists have to be developed along a broad spectrum to reduce the "learning time" which businessmen hate to pay for. In certain areas, for instance environmental problems, creditors rights, and real estate matters, we have put together a team of specialists so that the client can be serviced more efficiently. Furthermore, there has to be a considerable investment in technology. The days of starting to draft an agreement from scratch are over. The entrepreneurs of close corporations will not pay for reinventing the wheel.

Various kinds of instruments should be prepared, approved by lawyers and then stored on word processing disks or tapes. In the case of often used documents, almost the entire text can be prepared by simply running it off. Extensive segments of other agreements and wills, particularly the lengthy boilerplate, can also be reproduced with a minumum of professional time.

Finally, the counsellor must appreciate the reality that close corporation owners are more willing to pay for constructive suggestions than for negative advice. Rightly or wrongly, they are much more impressed by what you tell them they can do—than by what they can't. Spending pages and pages of brilliant prose to justify your conclusion that something is not "doable" is not smart. The client who respects your judgment generally accepts that determination, without expecting you to prove that you are right.

8. Have reasonable expectations about the entrepeneur's reactions to your advice.

It can hurt when you do a good job of finding sound solutions to a principal's serious problems, communicate your ideas to him, and get no feedback at all. A total void. Weeks and months go by without any word. At last, you are forced to rekindle the matter. Of course, delays should be anticipated in many situations. There are number of reasons for this, including the following:

1. There are multiple demands on the owner's valuable time and attention.

2. The severity of the client's position may be much more bothersome to the lawyer than to the client.

3. There may be resistance to a recommendation because you are pushing the individual to do something that is unpleasant, or about which he has ambivalence.

When, at last, the proprietor does get back to the lawyer, his response often is far less than what the professional hoped for. The fault, in this instance, rests with the lawyer. There is no reason to believe that the businessman will be full of praise. From his standpoint, top-notch performance is what he is paying for. To look for compliments about your ideas is an unrealistic expectation.

9. Make sure you work with the client's other advisors.

The lawyer who represents a close corporation is usually not the only advisor on the scene. An accountant, a life insurance agent, and a consulting firm are often serving the client as well. For this reason, our firm has stressed the importance of coordination among all of the advisors to the close corporation. Otherwise, the principal owner's of the corporation will get caught between the conflicting and antagonistic points of view of their many advisors, particularly, their accountants and lawyers.

In this kind of counselling, too many cooks do not spoil the broth. Quite the opposite. Each of the disciplines can impart know-how and the benefit of prior experiences, resulting in a much better plan. Certain of the close corporation owner's points of view and feelings may be known to one advisor and others, to the second. When an attorney is called on to do substantial counselling for the close corporation, he should work with the accountant in every instance. When another expert is involved, he too should be consulted.

These professionals should meet and design a unified plan for presentation to the owners of the company. Disagreements should be aired and resolved among them, out of the presence of the client. Should a difference of opinion remain, the alternatives can be put before the entrepeneur in a concise, unemotional way, free from any advisor's defensiveness.

This format works. We know, because we have followed it for years. It gets the job done and it saves a lot of wear and tear for all concerned, particularly the client.

10. *Have the right match-ups with your clients.*

One of the key ways to break down a cohesive defense in basketball is to create a mismatch. By a series of maneuvers, a 6' guard winds up trying to cover a 6' 10" forward. Teams work hard to learn the techniques of preventing bad match-ups. The same problem can develop in counselling a close corporation client whom you have represented for many years. I might have started with the client when the children were very young. The years roll by. Two sons come into the business. Then, slowly but surely, they take over more important roles, duties and responsibilities in the company.

In the eyes of the sons I am their father's lawyer. When conflicts develop between the father and his sons, the younger men find it hard to confide their problems about their father to a lawyer whom they see as his champion. They need someone of their generation, who will better understand their needs.

To combat this problem, our firm introduces younger partners into these two generation family companies. The offspring find it more comfortable to relate to an attorney who is closer in age to them. Although my younger partner and I are members of the same law firm, we try hard to respect each other's sphere of interest. The younger partner does not come running to me to report every comment about the father that the sons have made to him. Nor do I share with them what the father may have told me about the son's behavior. We honor the importance of each generation's being able to ventilate their hostilities without leading to confrontations.

* * *

These are our firm's counselling tips. They are offered with an important *caveat*. No matter what steps a lawyer takes to interact effectively with the heads of close corporations, some of them will seek other representation. You can't keep them all. Relationships may sour. Oil and water personality situations may develop. Difficulties over fees may ensue. A child or an in-law may become a lawyer, join a law firm, and the client may take his legal work to another organization. All you can do is the best that you can.

EPILOGUE

I have put in many, many hours designing and writing this book. It was very hard work, since this is my inaugural effort.

The project occasioned nostalgic recollections of my experiences with a host of very unusual, exciting people, entrepreneurs who risked, struggled, worried, and made things happen. They are courageous people with dedication and commitment, who refused to play it safe, venturing all they had in pursuit of success, defying the competition and the odds. It has been my good fortune to have followed a career path that led me to close association with these close corporation owners.

This book is aimed at creating much greater awareness of the very significant impact of family and partner relationships, on the continued viability and operational effectiveness of the close corporation. I am convinced that once those in control of these enterprises move human relations higher up the ladder of priorities, and are willing to contend with the sensitive issues that are involved, there will be a marked improvement in attitudes. These entrepreneurs have the resourcefulness to meet this challenge, in the same way that they handle all kinds of other tough problems. Unfortunately, the head of the family business all too often pays little attention to the complex psychological factors that affect the family members who work in the company. Partners close their eyes to escalating causes of friction, instead of contending with them, head-on, in the early stage of their development.

I have tried in this book to report accurately the serious consequences that can ensue if these important emotional problems are ignored. Resentment between parent and child, and among siblings, replaces warmth and affection. The climate among principals, ostensibly striving to build a business through cohesive effort, may get so bad that continued compatability is no longer feasible. The health of both the corporation and its stockholder may be seriously impaired. One or more participants may be forced to leave the company. In other instances, a sale of the entire business may be the only solution. These events are sad. I have been upset both by their frequency and their destructive effects.

The close corporation—where the owners manage the business— is a truly distinctive American institution, our country's most common form of doing business. It provides an important vehicle for self-expression and individuality, a sharp contrast to the impersonality and dependence that so frequently accompany a career with the widely held company managed by non-owner professionals. I hope these family business and incorporated partnerships continue to flourish.

INDEX

A

B

H

I

M